To Amy, Jon, Kirsten and Lyn

Four people in whose favour I readily admit to being more than a little prejudiced

Prejudice

Its Social Psychology

Rupert Brown

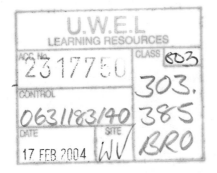

BLACKWELL

Oxford UK & Cambridge USA

350 Main Street, Malden, MA 02148-5018, USA
108 Cowley Road, Oxford OX4 1JF, UK
550 Swanston Street, Carlton, Victoria 3053, Australia

First published 1995 by Blackwell Publishing Ltd
Reprinted 1996, 1997, 1998, 2000, 2001, 2002, 2003

Library of Congress Cataloging-in-Publication Data

Brown, Rupert, 1950–
    Prejudice: its social psychology/Rupert Brown
        p.   cm.
    Includes bibliographical references and index.
    ISBN 0–631–18314–0 (hbk)—ISBN 0–631–18315–9 (pbk)
    1. Prejudices. 2. Prejudices in children. 3. Stereotype (Psychology)
4. Social psychology. I. Title.
    BF575.P9B74   1995   95–5920
    303.3'85—dc20   CIP

A catalogue record for this title is available from the British Library.

Set in 10.5 on 12.5 pt Bembo
Printed and bound in the United Kingdom
by MPG Books Ltd, Bodmin, Cornwall

For further information on
Blackwell Publishing, visit our website:
http://www.blackwellpublishing.com

Contents

Plates

Figures

Tables

Acknowledgements

This books has many creditors. Two – and intellectually perhaps the two most important – are sadly no longer alive: Gordon Allport and Henri Tajfel. I first read Allport as an undergraduate and then, as now, I was profoundly impressed by the depth of his thinking and the lucidity of his writing about prejudice. I studied with Tajfel as a postgraduate and he more than anyone was responsible for my abiding interest in problems of intergroup relations. His life-long (and personally experienced) concerns with questions of identity coupled with his passionate intellectual ambitions for social psychology provided me with an irresistible academic role model.

Others, too, have made a significant contribution to this book. Lorella Lepore, whose arrival at Kent was largely instrumental in rekindling my interest in prejudice, read every page in draft. Her incisive criticisms and perceptive comments were a much-needed antidote to my tendency to sloppy and prolix writing. Steve Hinkle, my collaborator this past decade, has contributed both personally and professionally to sustaining my interest in intergroup behaviour. Tom Pettigrew reviewed the entire manuscript and made several helpful comments. Although he and I have our intellectual disagreements, I feel very privileged to have received the critical attention of someone who has been for so long at the forefront of world research on prejudice. Other colleagues played their part as well, either in their enthusiastic collaboration in joint research or by providing helpful feedback on various chapters. Amongst these Pete Grant, Miles Hewstone, Sue Leekam, Pam Maras, Francine Tougas, and Jim Vivian deserve particular mention. I would also like to thank Katy Greenland for compiling the indices with her usual care and precision, despite having to do so under personally distressing circumstances. Finally, for the production of the manuscript itself special thanks are due to the staff of the Keynes Secretarial Office. If my colleagues regard me as something of a Luddite for my obstinate persistence with such unfashionable technologies as fountain-pen and paper, it is the superb typographic skills and unending patience of Elizabeth Dorling, Lisa Rigden, and Emma Robinson which permit me (happily) to remain so.

The author and publisher wish to thank the following for permission to copyright material:

Academic Press, Inc., for adapted table 7.1 from J.F. Dovidio and S.L. Gaertner (eds), *Prejudice, Discrimination and Racism* (1986); figure 3.3 from J.J. Skowronski *et al.*, 'Implicit versus explicit impression formation: the differing effects of overt labelling and covert priming on memory and impressions', *Journal of Experimental Social Psychology, 29* (1993) 17–41; table 7.2 from J.B. McConahay, 'Modern racism, ambivalence and the modern racism scale', from Dovidio and Gaertner (eds), *Prejudice, Discrimination and Racism* (1986); table 4.1 from D.L. Hamilton and R.K. Gifford, 'Illusory correlation in interpersonal perception: a cognitive basis of stereotypic judgements', *Journal of Experimental Social Psychology, 12* (1976) 392–407;

Academic Press Ltd, for figure 6.1 from G.M. Breakwell, 'Some effects of marginal social identity', in H. Tajfel (ed.), *Differentiation Between Social Groups* (1978);

American Psychological Association, for figure 8.5 from R.E. Slavin, 'Effects of biracial learning teams on cross-racial friendships', *Journal of Educational Psychology, 71* (1979) 381–7, copyright © 1979 by the APA; figure 5.1 from J.H. Langlois *et al.*, 'Facial diversity and infant preference for attractive faces', *Developmental Psychology, 27* (1991) 79–84, copyright © 1991 by the APA; the following material from *Journal of Personality and Social Psychology*, figure 7.3 from S.L. Gaertner and J.F. Dovidio, 'The subtlety of white racism, arousal and helping behaviour', *35* (1977) 691–707, copyright © 1977 by the APA; figure 6.6 from S.C. Wright *et al.*, 'Responding to membership in a disadvantaged group: from acceptance to collective protest', *58* (1990) 994–1003, copyright © 1990 by the APA; figure 6.3 from N. Ellemers *et al.*, 'Effects of the legitimacy of low group or individual status as individual and collective status-enhancement strategies', *64* (1993) 766–78, copyright © 1993 by the APA; figure 4.5 from R. Weber and J. Crocker, 'Cognitive processes in the revision of stereotypic beliefs', *45* (1983) 961–77, copyright © 1983 by the APA; figure 4.3 from C.W. Perdue *et al.*, ' "Us" and "Them": social categorization and the process of intergroup bias', *59* (1990) 475–86, copyright © 1990 by the APA; figure 4.2 from J.W. Howard and M. Rothbart, 'Social categorization and memory for ingroup and outgroup behaviour', *38* (1980) 301–10, copyright © 1980 by the APA; figure 4.1 from J.M. Darley and P. H. Gross, 'A hypothesis-confirming bias in labeling effects', *44* (1983) 20–33, copyright © 1983 by the APA; figure 3.2 from B. Simon and R.J. Brown, 'Perceived intergroup homogeneity in minority–majority contexts', *53* (1987) 703–11, copyright © 1987 by the APA; table 3.4 from S.L. Gaertner *et al.*, 'Reducing intergroup bias: the benefits of recategorization', *57* (1989) 239–49, copyright © 1989 by the APA; figure 7.1 adapted from H. Sigall and R. Page, 'Current stereotypes: a little fading, a little faking', 18 (1971) 247-55, copyright © 1971 by the APA; figure 5.3 for J. Hraba and G. Grant, 'Black is beautiful: a re-examination of racial preference and identification', *Journal of Personality and Social Psychology*, 16 (1970) 398-402, copyright © 1970 by the APA; table 3.5 from M. Quanty, S. Harkins *et al.*, 'Prejudice and criteria for identification of ethnic photographs', *Journal of Personality and Social Psychology*, 32 (1975) 449-54; figure 8.2 for Fletcher Blanchard *et al.*, 'The effect of relative competence of group members upon interpersonal attraction in co-operating inter-racial groups', *Journal of Personality and Social Psychology*, 32 (1975) 519-30. Copyright © 1975 by the APA;

Edward Arnold, for tables 2.2 and 5.1 from A. Davey, *Learning to be Prejudiced* (1983);

the British Psychological Society, for adapted table 6.1 from C. Kelly, 'Intergroup differentiation in a political context', *British Journal of Social Psychology*, 27 (1988) 314–22;

Guildford Publications Inc., for table 6.2 from T.J. Crawford and M. Naditch, 'Relative deprivation, powerlessness and militancy: the psychology of social protest', *Psychiatry*, 33 (1970) 208–23;

Harcourt, Rinehart and Winston Inc., for figure 4.4 from R. Rosenthal and L. Jacobson, *Pygmalion in the Classroom: Teacher expectations and student intellectual development*, copyright © 1968 by Holt, Rinehart and Winston Inc.;

the Institute for Fiscal Studies, for figure 6.4 from A. Goodman and S. Webb, *For Richer, For Poorer: The changing distribution of income in the United Kingdom, 1961–91* (1994);

Institute of Race Relations, for table 6.3 from R.D. Vanneman and T.F. Pettigrew, 'Race and relative deprivation in the urban United States', *Race*, *13* (1972) 461–86;

Russell Sage Foundation, for adapted table 7.1 from J.F. Dovidio and R.H. Fazio, 'New technologies for the direct and indirect assessment of attitudes', in J.M. Tanur (ed.), *Questions about Questions: Inquiries into the cognitive bases of surveys* (1992);

Sage Publications Inc., for adapted figure 8.3 from M.R. Islam and M. Hewstone, 'Dimensions of contact as predictors of intergroup anxiety, perceived outgroup variability and outgroup attitude: an integrative model', *Personality and Social Psychology Bulletin*, *19* (1993) 700–10; table 3.2 from M.B. Brewer *et al.*, 'Social identity and social distance among Hong Kong schoolchildren', *Personality and Social Psychology Bulletin*, *13* (1987) 156–65; and figure 7.2 from F. Tougas *et al.*, 'Neo-sexism: plus ça change, plus c'est pareil', *Personality and Social Psychology Bulletin*, in press;

the Society for the Psychological Study of Social Issues, for figure 8.1 from D.L. Hamilton and G.D. Bishop, 'Attitudinal and behavioral effects of initial integration of white suburban neighborhoods', *Journal of Social Issues*, *32* (1976) 47–67; and figure 5.2 from S.R. Asher and V.L. Allen, 'Racial preference and social comparison processes', *Journal of Social Issues*, *25* (1969) 157–66;

the Society for Research in Child Development, for figure 5.4 from P. La Freniere *et al.*, 'The emergence of same-sex affiliative preferences among pre-school peers: a developmental/ethological perspective', *Child Development*, *55* (1984) 1958–65; and adapted figures 5.5, 5.6 and 5.7 from M.D. Yee and R.J. Brown, 'Self evaluations and intergroup attitudes in children aged three to nine', *Child Development*, *63* (1994) 619–29;

John Wiley & Sons Ltd, for figure 6.5 from R.C. Tripathi and R. Srivastava, 'Relative deprivation and intergroup attitudes', *European Journal of Social Psychology*, *11* (1981) 313–18; table 3.6 from M.G. Billig and H. Tajfel, 'Social categorization and similarity in intergroup behaviour', *European Journal of Social Psychology*, *3* (1973) 27–52; table 3.1 from H. Tajfel *et al.*, 'Social categorization and intergroup behaviour', *European Journal of Social Psychology*, *1* (1971) 149–78; figure

6.2 from I. Sachdev and R. Bourhis, 'Status differentials and intergroup behaviour', *European Journal of Social Psychology*, 17 (1987) 277–93;

Every effort has been made to trace all the copyright-holders but if any have been inadvertently overlooked the publisher will be pleased to make the necessary arrangement at the first opportunity.

'The Nature of Prejudice'

1   Still from the BBC documentary *Black and White* (1987)

In England in the mid 1980s these two men went in search of the same accommodation, jobs and leisure entertainment, each carrying a hidden camera and microphone. On several occasions the man on the left was refused while the man on the right was accepted. The resulting television documentary was a powerful demonstration of the reality of discrimination faced by many ethnic minorities in Britain today.

In 1954 a Harvard social psychologist called Gordon Allport published a book from which this chapter takes its title (Allport, 1954). Brilliantly written and encyclopedic in its scope, the book has rightly come to be regarded as point of departure for modern investigations into the nature of prejudice and methods for its reduction. Allport provided not only an incisive analysis of the origins of intergroup discrimination, anticipating some discoveries in social cognition and group behaviour which have only recently been made (see chapters 3–6), but also a series of influential policy recommendations for its elimination (see chapter 8). Indeed, it is no exaggeration to say that most practical attempts to improve interethnic relationships in American schools over the last 40 years have had their basis in Allport's theorizing.

It is thus entirely appropriate that in this first chapter we should take another look at some of the definitions and assumptions which guided Allport's scholarship. After presenting a few contemporary illustrations of prejudice in action, I examine how the term 'prejudice' has traditionally been defined. Though finding much to agree with in these conventional accounts, I propose a simpler and more inclusive definition which eschews any reference to the putative 'falsity' of a prejudiced thought, word or deed. After this terminological discussion I outline in broad terms the perspective to be adopted in the remainder of the book, a perspective which simultaneously seeks to treat prejudice as a *group process*, and as a phenomenon which nevertheless can be analysed at the level of *individual* perception, emotion, and action. Finally, I relate this social psychological approach to the analyses offered by other disciplines – history, politics, economics, sociology and so on. Endorsing the position held by LeVine and Campbell (1972), I conclude that each of these various perspectives can independently offer valuable insights into the nature of prejudice without being subservient or reducible to some more fundamental level of analysis. At the same time, I recognize that ultimately – in some future social scientific Utopia – each level of analysis will need to be consistent with the others and may well impose conceptual and empirical constraints on theorizing in those other domains.

What is Prejudice?

It is 5 o'clock in the afternoon somewhere in Bristol in the west of England in the mid-1980s. Geoff Small, a Black man in his twenties, has just been shown round a flat which is being offered to let by a White landlord.

SMALL: Am I the first one to see it?
LANDLORD: . . . Yes, you are actually but there are several other people coming round, you know. Well, another one in a moment – ten past – and some more at six.
SMALL: Ah, right. Then what's your criterion for allotting the place?
LANDLORD: Well, I'm going to see the people who come along. Then, you know, give them a call and let them know . . .

Ten minutes later a second man, also in his twenties, calls round to the same flat. His name is Tim Marshall. He happens to be White. After being shown round, he asks how the landlord will decide on who will be the tenant.

MARSHALL: Is it on a first come first served . . . that is, if I wanted it . . . ?
LANDLORD: (hesitating) . . . er . . . yeah . . . well . . . yes . . . someone sort of suitable I would say yes, I would. But . . . otherwise I might say 'I'll let you know' (embarrassed laugh).
MARSHALL: OK I do actually like it. But I have got . . .
LANDLORD: . . . got others to see have you?
MARSHALL: Yes, two places. But I mean . . . have I got any competition? I mean, does anyone else want it?
LANDLORD: Well, the situation is that I came back at four o'clock. There's a chap coming round at six o'clock – between six and seven – and . . . um . . . being a bit of a racist . . . but he was Black – nice enough chap – but I thought he might create problems so I said look, I'd let him know.
MARSHALL: Would you not have a Black . . . ?
LANDLORD: No. He was a nice chap, you know. But, on the other hand, he was a big bloke and he'd be a bit of a handful. But I thought he might create problems you know . . .
MARSHALL: Damn. I don't know what to say. I don't want to lose it but I don't want to say yes for sure.
LANDLORD: Well, I've got another room . . . which I let as well.

MARSHALL: Well, I'll take my chances because you're saying the black
    guy is not going to get it?
LANDLORD: That's right.

On the way downstairs to show Marshall out the landlord continues his
justification for not wanting to let to the previous applicant, at one
point describing him as 'a bit arrogant'.

These two encounters were covertly filmed by the two prospective
tenants who were in reality making a television documentary (*Black and
White*, BBC Television, 1987). Armed with hidden microphones and
cameras they went looking for accommodation, jobs, and leisure
entertainment. The documentary was, in fact, a televised replication of
a well-known piece of research initiated by a committee appointed by
the British government in 1965. The brief of this research was to
investigate the nature and extent of discrimination against ethnic
minorities in Britain (Daniels, 1968). As in the television programme,
one of the research techniques was to dispatch three interviewers,
purporting to be genuine applicants, in search of housing, jobs, and a
variety of other services. In most respects the interviewers were similar
– similar age, appearance, qualifications – but there were some crucial
differences: the first applicant to any vacancy happened to have
somewhat darker skin than the other two because he was West Indian or
Asian; the second applicant's skin was white but he was from Hungary;
and the third applicant was always white and English.

The results were dramatic: out of 60 landlords approached, the West
Indian received identical treatment to the other two on just 15
occasions (Daniels, 1968). On 38 of the 45 other occasions he was told
that the flat had gone when both other applicants were told later that it
was still vacant. When applying for jobs equally stark discrimination
occurred: 40 firms were approached. As table 1.1 shows, on no less than
37 occasions the West Indian or Asian applicants were told that there was
no vacancy. The White English received only 10 and the Hungarian 23
such outright refusals. Direct offers of jobs or encouragements to apply
showed a similar bias.

It is tempting to dismiss such findings on grounds of their antiquity.
Surely, one might ask, after nearly three decades of successive race
relations and equal opportunities legislation it would be difficult to
witness such overt discrimination today? I would not be so sanguine.
There was, after all, that television documentary which revealed
repeated instances of differential treatment of the Black and White
reporters. That such discrimination lingers on is confirmed in three still

Table 1.1 Employment discrimination in Britain in the mid-1960s

Response	White English	White Hungarian	Asian or West Indian
Offers of jobs or encouragement to apply	15	10	1
'No vacancy at present' but details taken or asked to call back	15	7	2
'No vacancy'	10	23	37

Source: Daniels (1968), table 11.

more recent reports. One, from the Urban Institute in Washington, USA, using the same technique as Daniels (1968), showed that when differential treatment of applicants occurred, White job applicants in Washington and Chicago received three times as many job offers as equivalently qualified Black applicants. Hispanic applicants fared only slightly better, the equivalent comparison revealed Anglos receiving over two and a half the number of offers (Turner et al., 1991). The second, from the British Commission for Racial Equality, revealed that as many as 20 per cent of private accommodation agencies in 11 British towns and cities are still discriminating against ethnic minorities in the allocation of rented property although, fortunately, individual landlords and hoteliers were found to be somewhat less discriminatory (CRE, 1990). In the third, a small-scale study of discrimination against Asian doctors by British hospitals, it was found that a postal application from someone with an English-sounding name was twice as likely to be short-listed for a job interview than a closely matched applicant with an Asian name (Esmail and Everington, 1993).

And behind these statistics lies a grim reality of daily verbal abuse, harassment, and threat of physical attack for many members of minority groups. According to recent figures, there was an increase of over 50 per cent in the number of racial attacks in Britain reported to the police over the two-year period 1988–90 (CRE, 1993). Perhaps the following, pushed anonymously through the door of a British Black family, will serve as one last illustration to remind us that prejudice can sometimes – perhaps often – contain elements of overt hostility and violence:

> *Your going to learn a good lesson soon black bitch. Your kind are no good who go with white men. Go back to Africa, slag. You black bastard, if I can't get you I will get your kids.* (*Independent*, 13 February 1990).

These examples are all instances of a particular kind of prejudice, prejudice towards members of ethnic minorities. There are, of course, many other common varieties of prejudice – against women, against gay people, against disabled people – as will become clear in the pages of this book. But what exactly do we mean by the word prejudice? It is conventional at this point to refer to a dictionary in which we can find prejudice typically defined as:

> *a judgement or opinion formed beforehand or without due examination.* (*Chambers English Dictionary*, 1988)

Definitions like this have led many social psychologists to emphasize such features as 'incorrectness' or 'inaccuracy' in their attempts to define prejudice. Thus, for example:

> *Ethnic prejudice is an antipathy* based upon a faulty and inflexible generalization. *It may be felt or expressed. It may be directed toward a group as a whole or toward an individual because he is a member of that group.* (Allport, 1954, p. 10; my emphasis)

Or this:

> *the prior negative judgement of the members of a race or religion or the occupants of any other significant social role,* held in disregard of the facts that contradict it. (Jones, 1972, p. 61; my emphasis)

Or this, more recently still:

> *an* unjustified *negative attitude toward an individual based solely on that individual's membership in a group.* (Worchel et al., 1988, p. 449; my emphasis)

Such social psychological definitions have much to recommend them over more formal lexical accounts. In particular they accurately convey one essential aspect of the phenomenon of prejudice – that it is a social orientation either towards whole groups of people or towards individuals *because* of their membership in a particular group. The other common factor between these definitions is that they stress the negative flavour of group prejudice. Of course, logically, prejudice can take both positive and negative forms. I, for example, am particularly favourably disposed towards all things Italian: I love Italian food, Italian cinema, and lose no opportunity to try out my execrable Italian on anyone who will listen (much to the embarrassment of friends and family). However, such harmless infatuations hardly constitute a major social problem worthy of much of our attention as social scientists. Rather, the kind of prejudice which besets so many societies in the world today and which so urgently requires our understanding is the negative variety: the wary, fearful, suspicious, derogatory, hostile or ultimately murderous treatment of one group of people by another. Thus, in common with the above authors, I shall be concerned in this book with what governs variations in these different forms of antipathy.

However, I do not believe it is necessary to imply – as do these definitions – that prejudice must be regarded as a 'false' or 'irrational' set of beliefs, a 'faulty' generalization, or is an 'unwarranted' disposition to behave negatively towards another group. There are three reasons for taking issue with this point of view. First, because to say that an attitude or belief is 'faulty' in some way implies that we could have some way of establishing its 'correctness'. In some rather special circumstances it might be possible to do this, but only if the belief in question referred to some objectively measurable criterion (Judd and Park, 1993). But how often would this be possible? Prejudiced statements are typically couched in much more vague and ambiguous terms. Take the landlord quoted earlier in the chapter: how could we hope to establish the truth or falsity of his belief that Blacks are liable 'to create problems'? Devise some procedure to measure people's scores on this index against some normative standard of 'peaceableness'? Even to pose the question seems to me to highlight the insurmountable difficulties that would be encountered in trying to answer it. And even if such a comparative test were possible and, let us suppose hypothetically, it did show a greater incidence of 'problem creation' in Black populations, would this justify regarding that landlord's statement as unprejudiced? There are a myriad of possible explanations for the hypothetical statistic – for example, reactions to provocation by Whites, response to unjust social deprivation, and so on – any one of which would suffice to refute the imputation of Blacks' supposed propensity 'to create problems'. The fact remains that the sentiments expressed by that landlord – and their social consequences – are no less negative (and prejudicial) for having some alleged basis in reality.

A second problem with including any 'truth value' element in a definition of prejudice stems from the peculiarly relativistic nature of intergroup perception. It has long been observed – and we shall see ample confirmations in later chapters – that for groups, even more than for individuals, 'beauty is in the eye of the beholder'. In other words, what one group finds 'pleasant' or 'virtuous' or even self-evidently 'true' may be viewed very differently by another group. So, if one group regards itself as 'thrifty' is that view more or less at variance with reality than another group which regards them as 'stingy'? Of course, it is impossible to say. The important distinction between the two views lies not in their relative 'correctness' but in the implied value connotations.

A final point to make about some of these traditional definitions of prejudice is that they often seem to pre-empt the analysis of the origins and functions of prejudiced thinking. Thus, when Allport (1954) refers to an 'inflexible generalisation', or when Ackerman and Jahoda (1950) talk of prejudice serving an 'irrational function', they are presupposing more in their definitions than it may be wise to allow. It may well be, as we shall see in subsequent chapters, that much prejudice does have an apparently immutable and dysfunctional quality to it. But equally, as those chapters will also reveal, to think of prejudice as being impervious to change or as having no rational function for its adherents is to fail to do justice to the variety and complexity of the forms it can take, and its surprisingly labile quality in certain circumstances.

These considerations lead me, therefore, to adopt a less restrictive definition of prejudice than those we have encountered so far. For the purposes of this book prejudice will be regarded as any or all of the following: *the holding of derogatory social attitudes 'or cognitive beliefs, the expression of negative affect, or the display of hostile or discriminatory behaviour towards members of a group on account of their membership of that group.* Such a definition has much in common with those adopted by Secord and Backman (1974), Sherif (1966), and Aboud (1988) and by way of elaboration requires only two additional comments. The first is that in this rather wide sense in which I shall be using the term, prejudice can be regarded as roughly synonymous with a variety of other terms such as sexism, racism, homophobia, and the like. There are some who would restrict certain terms like 'racism' to ideologies or practices which are justified by reference to presumed biological group differences (for example, van den Berghe, 1967; Miles, 1989). However, from the social psychological perspective adopted here, I believe it is more useful to regard these as special cases of the more general phenomenon of prejudice. In this way we do not exclude from our discussion important intergroup prejudices such as some forms of religious bigotry which do not have any obvious biological component.

The second point is that prejudice is not to be regarded as just a cognitive or attitudinal phenomenon but can also engage our emotions as well as finding some manifestation in behaviour. Thus, I shall not be drawing any firm distinctions between biased attitudes, hostile feelings, and discriminatory or oppressive behaviour. Which is not to say that these different forms of prejudice are all identical or are necessarily highly intercorrelated; we shall review evidence which suggests that the relationship between them is often, in fact, quite complex. But still it is possible to say that they *are* all facets of a general prejudiced orientation. This multiple-level emphasis is deliberate and stands in contrast to some trends in modern social psychology which have tended to stress the cognitive aspects of prejudice and rather to have overlooked its affective and behavioural components (for example, Hamilton, 1981; but cf. Mackie and Hamilton, 1993). This cognitive analysis is undoubtedly important; indeed, I shall be devoting two whole chapters to it (chapters 3 and 4). However, to ignore the emotionally laden – one might even say saturated – nature of prejudice as it is actually perpetrated and experienced in everyday life is, it seems to me, to overlook something rather fundamental about it. Thus, in the pages which follow a recurring theme will be the interplay between the cognitive and more motivational processes implicated in prejudice.

A Social Psychological Approach

Having defined what I mean by prejudice I should say a few words about the general analytical approach I shall be adopting throughout the book. At this stage I shall outline the perspective only in rather broad terms without very much supportive evidence and argumentation. Its more detailed documentation will be left to subsequent chapters.

The first point to make is that I see prejudice as primarily a phenomenon originating in group processes. There are three closely related respects in which this is so. *Firstly* it is, as I have chosen to define it, an orientation towards whole categories of people rather than towards isolated individuals. Even if its target in any concrete instance is only a single individual (as in the example with which I began the previous section), nevertheless that person's individual characteristics matter much less than the markers which allocate him or her to one group rather than another – by name, by accent, by skin colour, and so on. The *second* reason prejudice should be regarded as a group process is that it is most frequently a socially shared orientation. That is to say, large numbers of people in any segment of society will broadly agree in their negative stereotypes of any given outgroup and will behave in a similar way towards them. Although, as we shall see in the next chapter, there are some grounds for believing that in its most chronic and extreme forms prejudice may be associated with particular types of personality, we cannot escape the conclusion that it is too widespread and too prevalent a phenomenon to be simply consigned to the province of individual pathology. The *third* reason follows directly from the first two. In so far as prejudice is usually directed *at* particular groups *by* some other groups we should not be too surprised to discover that the relationships between these groups play an important role in its determination. Thus, such intergroup relations as a conflict over scarce resources, or power domination of one group by another, or gross disparities in numerical size or status can all, as I will show in later chapters, have crucial implications for the direction, level, and intensity of prejudice which will be shown. Indeed, it is this *intergroup* nature of prejudice which really forms the leitmotif for the whole book.

The second general point about the perspective to be taken is that the focus of my analysis will predominantly be the individual. I shall be concerned, in other words, with the impact that various causal factors have on *individuals'* perceptions of, evaluations of, and behavioural reactions towards members of other groups. These causal factors may take a variety of forms. Some may themselves be individually located (as in the case of certain personality and cognitive processes – see chapters 2–4). On the other hand, many of the most powerful causal agents, as we shall see, stem from characteristics of the social situation in which people find themselves (for example, social influence from peers or the nature of intergroup goal relationships – see chapters 6 and 8). Still others may have their origin in the wider society as our discussion of socialization influences (chapter 5) and the analysis of new forms of prejudice (chapter 7) will reveal. But still, in all these instances, as a social psychologist my concern is with their implications for individual social behaviour.

Now since this seems rather to contradict my earlier claim that prejudice was essentially a group process a little further elaboration is necessary. Actually, as I have argued elsewhere, this contradiction is more apparent than real (Brown, 1988). To assert the causal importance and distinctiveness of group-based processes within social psychology is merely to recognize that individuals and individual behaviour can be transformed in group settings much as the behaviour of a metallic object can be affected by the presence of a magnetic field. The presence of the magnetic field – something external to the object itself – does not prevent us from describing and predicting what will happen to the object. In the same way it is possible to analyse individuals' behaviour as part of a coherent pattern of group processes.[1] Consider the actions of protestors during a gay rights demonstration or in an episode of ethnic conflict. To be sure, those actions – their form, direction, and intensity – are likely to be shaped by the norms and goals of those around them and the relationships between the groups concerned. However, those actions are no less incidences of social behaviour by individual persons for that, and as such fall squarely in the province of social psychology.

We can now see the resolution to the apparent contradiction between wanting to study prejudice simultaneously as a *group*-based phenomenon and also at the level of *individual* cognition, emotion and behaviour. The key is to recognize that I am not proposing the simultaneous study of individual behaviour and group behaviour in themselves; these are indeed rather different levels of analysis. Rather, I wish to distinguish between *individuals acting as group members* – that is, in terms of their group memberships – and *individuals acting as individuals* (Sherif, 1966; Tajfel, 1978). It is with the former class of behaviour – with people acting as 'women' or 'men', as 'gays' or 'straights', as 'Blacks' or 'Whites' – that I shall be mainly concerned throughout this book.

In arguing for this kind of social psychological approach I should immediately make it clear that I do not for one minute believe that social psychology has any privileged disciplinary position in providing explanations and remedies for prejudice. A complete understanding of the phenomenon is surely only possible if we also take due account of the complex mix of historical, political, economic, and social structural forces at work in any given context. Others, far better qualified than I, have argued persuasively for the importance of such macroscopic perspectives in the analysis of prejudice and I shall do little more here than to distil – albeit briefly and inadequately – what I see to be the essence of their arguments. (For a fuller exposition see the classic and contemporary contributions of Banton (1983), Cox (1948), LeVine and Campbell (1972), Miles (1982), Myrdal (1944), Rex (1973), Simpson and Yinger (1985), van den Berghe (1967)).[2]

History is important because it is this which bequeaths us our language, our cultural traditions and norms, and our societal institutions. All these play a significant part in how we come to construe our world in terms of different social categories, the first and indispensable precursor to all forms of prejudice (see chapter 3). Likewise, political processes cannot be ignored for these help determine a country's legislation on basic civil rights or its immigration policies (to name but two issues). Besides directly affecting the lives of minority groups (usually to their detriment) such policies contribute to the ideological frameworks in which various ethnic (and other) groups are differentially valued in society. Miles (1989), for example, has described how the European settlement of Australia and the subsequent development of a 'white Australia' policy in the early years of this century was historically accompanied by the emergence of various racial terms in both official and everyday language. It is something of a tragic irony that the 'success' of that 'white Australia' policy in perpetrating a systematic assault and oppression of the Aboriginal people has resulted in their virtual obliteration from all the official 'histories' of the continent (Pilger, 1989).

Economic factors can play an important – some would say an overriding – role in governing relations between groups in society. When one group has the means and the will to appropriate whole territories from another for the purposes of economic exploitation, as in the case of Britain's colonization of large parts of Africa, Asia, and Australia, then racist beliefs are often developed in justification (Banton, 1983). Alternatively, the demand for labour in an industrialized economy can transform previously accepted views on the capacities and rights of certain groups virtually overnight. This has been powerfully portrayed in the documentary film *Rosie the Riveter* which describes the sea-change in public attitudes towards women undertaking full-time employment – particularly in skilled engineering occupations – during the Second World War as a result of the conscription of men into the forces. The equally rapid reversal of these same attitudes and a corresponding pressure on women to remain at home as caregivers in the post-war era is a further confirmation of the influence of economic forces on intergroup attitudes and behaviour. In Simpson and Yinger's (1972) pithy summary: 'prejudice exists because someone gains by it' (p. 127).

Though not easily separable from the factors just discussed, the very structure of society, its organization into sub-groups and the social arrangement of those groups, can play their part in the manufacture and maintenance of prejudice. As an example, consider the difference between societies composed of groups which are of ever-increasing size and inclusiveness (family, village, region, and so on), and those in which groups cut across one another (for example, where norms prescribe that people must marry outside their immediate community thus creating an overlap between the family and village groupings). Drawing on extensive anthropological sources, LeVine and Campbell (1972) suggest that the latter type of society is less given to internal conflict because of the competing loyalty structures created by the criss-crossing of different groups (see chapter 3). Other kinds of societal analyses reveal how institutions and social practices can exist to regulate the access to goods and services by different groups in society. Such differential access can then perpetuate and perhaps even accentuate existing disparities which, in turn, can generate their own self-fulfilling justification for prejudice against particular groups. Take access to education. In Britain someone's chances of going to university are strongly related to their parents' social class. According to recent figures, over 65 per cent of acceptances of offers for university places were obtained by children of social classes I and II (who comprise only 30 per cent of the 18-year-old population). In contrast, less than 10 per cent of the offers were obtained by applicants of classes IV and V (who make up over 60 per cent of the same population) (UCCA, 1990; Redpath and Harvey, 1992). Such a skew in the class composition of university students results in similar imbalances in the recruitment to different occupations and the likelihood of unemployment. From there it is an easy step to the perpetuation of prejudiced images of working-class people as 'uneducated', 'stupid', and 'lazy'.

It is clear, then, that there are several different levels at which prejudice can be analysed and the social psychological perspective is but one of these. But if, as Allport (1954) elegantly put it, 'plural causation is the primary lesson we wish to teach' (p. xii), what is the relationship between these different causal factors? Can the different levels of analysis be reduced to some more fundamental perspective? Consider the following two social scientists' views. They are talking about war but it could as easily have been prejudice:

> To attempt to explain war by appeal to innate pugnacity would be like explaining Egyptian, Gothic, and Mayan architecture by citing the physical properties of stone. (White, 1949, p. 131)

> Dealings between groups ultimately become problems for the psychology of the individual. Individuals decide to go to war; battles are fought by individuals; and peace is established by individuals. (Berkowitz, 1962, p. 167)

Each is claiming the theoretical priority of one discipline over another. For White, an anthropologist, it is the societal analysis which is fundamental; Berkowitz, a psychologist, believes that a microscopic approach is ultimately more valuable. In fact, neither form of reductionism is necessary. It is possible, as LeVine and Campbell (1972) have persuasively argued, to pursue these various lines of enquiry more or less independently of one another in a spirit of what they call 'optional autonomy' (p. 26). In their view no one level of analysis can have any claim of superiority or priority over another. Disciplinary preference should simply be dictated by the nature of the problem with which one is confronted. Thus, to analyse the effect of discriminatory hiring practices on unemployment levels in different ethnic groups a macroscopic level of analysis is obviously appropriate. But if one's concern is with the actual intergroup dynamics of employment selection procedures then a social psychological approach would probably be more fruitful. Each analysis can be conducted relatively unencumbered by the other. However, this is not to propose a form of intellectual anarchy. In the last analysis the different approaches will have to be 'congruent' with one another, to use LeVine and Campbell's (1972) term again. That is, a valid theory of employment discrimination pitched at the economic or sociological level will have to be consistent with social psychological conclusions drawn from studies of individual social behaviour in job interviews, *and vice versa*.

This is the position I have taken in this book. By accident of training I am a social psychologist and it is that perspective I attempt to develop in the chapters which follow. But I hope that, by the time the final page is reached, it will be clear that social psychology, whilst it contains the potential to contribute significantly to both the dissection and the dissolution of prejudice, can never do more than explain a part – and perhaps only a small part – of the phenomenon as a whole.

Summary

1. Prejudice is often defined as a faulty or unjustified negative judgement held about the members of a group. However, such definitions run into conceptual difficulties because of the problems in ascertaining whether social judgements are faulty or at variance with reality. Instead, prejudice is here defined simply as a negative attitude, emotion, or behaviour towards members of a group on account of their membership of that group.

2. Because prejudice involves judgements by groups of other groups and can be shown to be affected by the objective relationships between those groups, it is appropriately regarded as a phenomenon originating in group processes. However, such a perspective is not incompatible with a social psychological analysis which is primarily concerned with individual perceptions, evaluations, and actions. Such an analysis sees individuals acting as group members, part of a coherent pattern of group dynamics.

3. A social psychological analysis is but one of a number of valid social scientific perspectives on prejudice. Each discipline can usefully pursue its own research problems more or less independently of the others although, ultimately, these diverse analyses will have to be compatible with each other.

Further Reading

Allport, G.W. (1954) *The Nature of Prejudice*, chs 1, 14, 15. Reading, Mass.: Addison-Wesley.

Brown, R.J. (1988) *Group Processes*, ch. 1. Oxford: Basil Blackwell.

Sherif, M. and Sherif, C.W. (1969) (eds) *Interdisciplinary Relationships in the Social Sciences*. Chicago: Aldine.

Notes

1. Actually the analogy with magnetic fields is not quite precise because, unlike inanimate objects, human beings have the ability to alter and recreate the group 'magnetic' fields in which they find themselves. But the point is that their attempts to do so can still be analysed as individual constituents of an organized system (Asch, 1952; Steiner, 1986).

2. This is obviously a rather selective and eclectic list of citations and hardly does justice to the large literature on race and other intergroup relations outside social psychology.

Prejudiced Individuals

2   British National Party supporter

Extremely prejudiced people are often thought of as having particular personality characteristics. This may only be part of the story however. Social and situational factors are often more important determinants of prejudice.

Not long ago one of my colleagues had a leaflet pushed through his letter box. It contained a few hundred vitriolic words complaining that the British Home Secretary had not prevented the visit to Britain of a Mr Sharpton, a Black activist from the United States. The gist of the leaflet was that Mr Sharpton was here to incite Black rioting and that the media were conspiring to give him free publicity. Here are a few selected but quite representative extracts from that leaflet:

Already Black violence is on a massive scale here with thousands of our women having been viciously raped and our elderly brutally attacked.

We know the Press is Jew-owned (Maxwell and Murdoch are Jews from Russia) and that a former Director of the BBC stated 'We are all Marxists at the BBC'. Also it is laid down Communist policy by Israel Cohen to incite Blacks against Whites. We know too that the Home Secretary is a stooge of the Board of Jewish Deputies.

We hope through this series of leaflets to alert you that millions of hostile racial aliens are not here by accident but that they are here through conspiracy; conspiracy against YOU.

Presented with such blatant and obviously offensive racism a common reaction is to label its author as a 'crackpot' or as having some kind of personality problem. Indeed, for many – lay people and psychologists alike – the phenomenon of prejudice is exactly this: a manifestation of a particular and probably pathological personality type. In this chapter I want to consider this hypothesis in some detail. I begin with the best-known version of it which proposes that the origins of prejudice can be sought in the psychological make-up and functioning of the individual, and this is thought to be the product of a certain familial history. A particular upbringing, so this theory claims, produces someone with a strongly deferential attitude towards authority, a rather simplistic and rigid cognitive style, and a strong tendency to be susceptible to right-wing and racist ideas. This theory can be extended to include a general syndrome of intolerance, whether on the left or right, and in a second section I examine approaches which have developed this thesis. I conclude by identifying a number of difficulties which both of these kinds of individualistic approaches run into, difficulties which I believe render them rather inadequate as accounts of the causes of prejudice.

The Authoritarian Personality

The best-known and most influential attempt to link prejudice to a particular personality type was provided by Adorno et al. (1950). This theory – a unique blend of Marxist social philosophy, Freudian analysis of family dynamics, and quantitative psychometric attitude research – quickly established itself as a reference point for a whole generation of researchers into the nature of prejudice.

Its basic hypothesis was simple. It was that an individual's political and social attitudes cohere together and are 'an expression of deep lying trends in personality' (Adorno et al., 1950, p. 1). Prejudiced people are those whose personalities render them susceptible to those racist or fascist ideas prevalent in a society at a given time. The theory did not try to explain the origins of those ideas at a societal level; this, asserted its authors, was a problem for sociological or political analysis. Rather, they were concerned to account for individual differences in the *receptivity* to those ideas.

According to Adorno et al. (1950), these personality differences can be traced to the family in which the child is socialized. Much influenced by Freudian thinking, they believed that the child's development involves the constant repression and redirection of instinctive drives by the constraints of social existence. The earliest and most powerful agents of this socialization process are, of course, the parents, and in the 'normal' case they strike a balance between allowing the child some self-expression – for example, tolerating occasional outbursts of temper or exuberance – whilst imposing some flexible limits of acceptable and unacceptable behaviour. The problem with prejudiced people, argued Adorno et al., was that they had been exposed to a family regime which was overly concerned with 'good behaviour' and conformity to conventional moral codes, especially as far as sexual behaviour was concerned. The parents in such families – especially the fathers – use excessively harsh disciplinary measures to punish the child's transgressions. As a result, or so Adorno et al. believed, the child's aggression towards the parents (one inevitable effect of its 'natural' urges being frustrated) is displaced away from them because of anxiety about the consequences of displaying it so directly, and *on to* substitute targets.

The most likely choice of scapegoats would be those seen as weaker or
inferior to oneself, for example anyone who deviated from the societal
norm. Ready candidates for this cathartic release of aggression were
thought to include members of minority ethnic groups or other socially
devalued categories, such as homosexuals or convicted criminals.

Adorno et al. proposed that this syndrome was not just reflected in
the direction and content of the person's social attitudes, it also
manifested itself in the cognitive style in which those attitudes were
constructed and expressed. On account of the parents' disciplinary zeal
and strictly conventional morality, Adorno et al. believed that the child
develops a simplistic way of thinking about the world in which people
and their actions are rigidly categorized into 'right' and 'wrong'. Such a
tendency was thought to generalize into a cognitive style which is
marked by the consistent use of very clearly demarcated categories and
an intolerance of any 'fuzziness' between them. Of course, such a way
of thinking also readily lends itself to the endorsement of distinctive and
immutable stereotypes about social groups.

The end result, therefore, is a person who is over-deferential and
anxious towards authority figures (since these symbolize the parents),
who sees the world – often literally – in black and white terms, being
unable or unwilling to tolerate cognitive ambiguity, and who is overtly
hostile to anyone who is not obviously an ingroup member. Adorno et
al. called this type of person the 'Authoritarian Personality', and the
author or authors of the leaflet with which we began this chapter would
constitute an excellent example of just such a type. The combination of
crudely anti-Black, anti-Semitic, and anti-Communist invective laced
with undercurrents of sexual violence and fear of powerful conspiracies
is precisely the kind of constellation of attitudes which the prototypic
authoritarian is thought to endorse.

To substantiate their theory Adorno et al. initiated a huge research
project which combined large-scale psychometric testing and individual
clinical interviews. The psychometric work was initially concerned with
designing some objective measures of various forms of overt prejudice
(for example, anti-Semitism, general ethnocentrism). This then evolved
into the construction of a personality inventory which, it was hoped,
would tap the central aspects of the underlying authoritarian personality
syndrome. This measure – the most famous to emerge from the project –
they called the F-scale, so labelled because it was intended to measure
'pre-fascist tendencies'. It consisted of 30 items which, after a careful
process of screening and pretesting, were all designed to reflect various
aspects of the authoritarian person's hypothesized make-up. For

example, there were questions concerned with authoritarian submission ('obedience and respect for authority are the most important virtues children should learn'), with aggression towards deviant groups ('homosexuals are hardly better than criminals and ought to be severely punished'), and with the projection of unconscious, especially sexual, impulses ('the wild sex life of the Greeks and Romans was tame compared to some of the goings-on in this country, even in places where people might least expect it'). The scale had good internal reliability and, just as its authors had predicted, correlated well with their previous measures of intergroup prejudice despite the fact that it contained no items specifically referring to ethnic groups.

In an attempt to validate the F-scale, small sub-samples of very high and very low scorers on it were selected for intensive clinical interviews which consisted of detailed questioning of the respondents' recollection of their early childhood experiences, perceptions of their parents, and their views on various social and moral issues of the day. These interviews did seem to confirm many of Adorno et al.'s theoretical suppositions about the origins and consequences of authoritarianism. For instance, high scorers on the F-scale tended to idealize their parents as complete paragons of virtue. Here is how one respondent described her mother:

> (she is) . . . the best in the world . . . she's good, in fact, the best. In other words, she's just tops with me. She's friendly with everybody. Never has no trouble. (Adorno et al., 1950, p. 343)

At the same time they recalled their childhood as a time of strict obedience to parental authority with harsh sanctions for any minor misdemeanours. As another high scorer remembered:

> Well, my father was a very strict man . . . His word was law, and whenever he was disobeyed, there was punishment. When I was 12, my father beat me practically every day for getting into the tool chest in the back yard. (Adorno et al., 1950, p. 374)

Their current attitudes corresponded well to their answers on the F-scale items: very moralistic, openly condemnatory of 'deviants' or social 'inferiors', and exhibiting sharply defined categorical stereotypes, often openly prejudiced. The low scorers, by contrast, painted a more equivocal and balanced picture of their early family life and typically presented a more complex and flexible set of social attitudes.

Whether due to the ambitiousness of its theoretical and applied goals or to the range of methodologies it employed, *The Authoritarian Personality* excited considerable interest amongst social psychologists in the 1950s. A review article which appeared just eight years after its appearance cited over 200 published studies investigating correlates of authoritarianism with such psychological phenomena as leadership, impression formation, problem solving, social acquiescence, psycho-pathology, cognitive style and, of course, prejudice (Christie and Cook, 1958). It is the latter two topics which are of interest to us here. What independent empirical support is there for Adorno et al.'s hypotheses that the authoritarian is characterized by an over-rigid cognitive style which does not easily accommodate ambiguities and equivocation and which, when translated into social attitudes, shows up as a stereotypical derogation of and hostility towards minority groups?

One of the earliest experiments to examine the association between authoritarianism and mental rigidity was by Rokeach (1948). His technique was to present subjects with a series of simple arithmetic problems. In the practice trials these problems required at least three separate operations for their solution. However, in the test trials the problems, though superficially similar to the practice sessions, could be solved by a simpler one-step procedure in addition to the previously rehearsed longer solution. The key question was whether subjects would solve these subsequent problems with the faster method or whether they would persevere rigidly with the less direct technique they had learned in practice. Rokeach also measured their ethnocentrism which normally correlates well with authoritarianism. Just as he (and Adorno et al.) had hypothesized, those scoring highly (that is, above the median) on ethnocentrism showed consistently more mental rigidity than those scoring below the median. However, after several unsuccessful attempts to replicate these findings, Brown (1953) concluded that the link between authoritarianism and rigidity only emerged when the testing situation was important for subjects. By experimentally manipulating the presumed social, scientific, and personal significance of the arithmetic problems, Brown found a clear-cut association between authoritarianism and rigidity only in the 'ego involving' conditions and not in the 'non-involved' group. Using a different technique Block and Block (1950) also found evidence that ethnocentric subjects were less tolerant of perceptual ambiguity than non-ethnocentric subjects. They exploited Sherif's (1936) autokinetic paradigm in which people are exposed to a tiny but stationary dot of light in a completely dark room. This produces an illusion in which the dot appears to move around haphazardly. After some dozens of trials observers normally start to show stability in their estimates of the extent of perceived movement, whether tested alone or with others. Block and Block observed how long it took for these subjects to stabilize their judgements, reasoning that the more quickly they did so the greater their intolerance of this highly ambiguous situation. When they compared the ethnocentrism of those who stabilized quickly with those who took much longer, Block and Block found that the latter's scores were reliably lower than the former's. In sum, therefore, there is at least some evidence from these early studies that more authoritarian (or more prejudiced) people do have a tendency to think in a particular way. I shall return to this issue later when we consider a more generalized conception of authoritarianism (see the next section).

What of the link between authoritarianism and prejudice? As already noted, Adorno et al. (1950) found substantial correlations (usually greater than 0.6) between their earlier measure of outright ethnocentrism and the F-scale, thus confirming their hypothesized link between prejudice and personality. Subsequent investigations have borne out this relationship. For instance, Campbell and McCandless (1951) found a similar-sized correlation in a sample of US students between authoritarianism and their own measure of xenophobia which tapped hostility towards the Blacks, Jews, Mexicans, Japanese, and English. Studies outside the US have also found associations between authoritarianism and prejudice. Pettigrew (1958) found reliable correlations (of between 0.4 and 0.6) between the F-scale and anti-Black prejudice, a point to which I shall return later. Some 30 years later in the Netherlands, Meloen et al. (1988) reported consistent and substantial correlations between authoritarianism and ethnocentrism, and similar relationships between authoritarianism, sexism, and support for extreme right-wing political groups. In India Sinha and Hassan (1975) found that religious prejudice against Muslims, caste prejudice against Harijans, and sexist prejudice were all predictable from the authoritarianism of some high-caste Hindu men. Moreover, the three indices of prejudice also correlated highly amongst each other, further supporting the idea of an underlying prejudiced personality. Also consistent with *Authoritarian Personality* are the correlations which have been observed between authoritarianism and attitudes towards stigmatized or deviant subgroups. For example, Cohen and Streuning (1962) and Hanson and Blohm (1974) all found that authoritarians were less sympathetic than non-authoritarians towards mentally ill people even when, as was the case in the former study, the respondents were actually staff in psychiatric institutions. In a similar vein, attitudes towards people with AIDS may be less positive amongst authoritarians (Witt, 1989). Finally, authoritarianism in men has been found to correlate both with sexual aggression towards women and with guilt associated with past sexual aggression (Walker et al., 1993).

Despite this range of supportive evidence, research on the link between authoritarianism and prejudice has not been entirely unequivocal. We can note to begin with that some of the observed correlations are not very strong, usually explaining less than a half and sometimes less than a fifth of the variance in prejudice scores. Thus, whatever the contribution of personality disposition to expressed prejudice there are clearly other processes at work too. A second problem is that occasionally zero correlations have been reported between authoritarianism and outgroup rejection. One interesting example is Forbes's (1985) study of the link between authoritarianism and intergroup attitudes in Canada. Amongst English-speaking respondents there was a significant correlation (as predicted) between authoritarianism and anti-French feeling, although this was very weak (< 0.2). However, the same group showed a *negative* correlation between authoritarianism and a measure of nationalism and no correlation at all with *inter*nationalism. Even more problematic were the consistent null relationships observed amongst the francophones.[1] A further anomaly was identified in two early studies of Perlmutter (1954, 1956). Perlmutter was interested in the opposite of xenophobia (or ethnocentrism) – namely, xenophilia: an *attraction* towards strangers and foreigners. Having devised a measure of this orientation, he correlated it with the F-scale. He found that xenophilic subjects tended to be *more* authoritarian than their less xenophilic peers, a curious result indeed in the light of Adorno et al.'s suggestion that authoritarians should in general be *rejecting* of outsiders and foreigners.

Ironically enough, the explosion of research interest stimulated by *The Authoritarian Personality* quickly identified a number of rather damaging methodological and theoretical flaws in the whole project (Brown, 1965; Christie and Jahoda, 1954; Rokeach, 1956). Since many of these criticisms are both well known and better articulated elsewhere, I shall do no more than rehearse what I see as the most damning of those early arguments, leaving for a later section a more general critique of the attempt to explain prejudice in personality terms.

At a methodological level most of the critical attention focused on the design and validation of the F-scale (Brown, 1965; Hyman and Sheatsley, 1954). Three problems in particular came to light. The first was that Adorno et al. had used rather unrepresentative samples of respondents on which to develop and subsequently refine their questionnaires. Despite the impressive size of some of these samples – over 2000 respondents in the test of the F-scale alone – they were drawn mainly from formal (and predominantly middle-class) organizations. These, Hyman and Sheatsley (1954) suggested, might well attract a particular kind of personality type and, in any case, hardly constituted a sound empirical base from which to construct a general theory of prejudice. A second and perhaps more serious problem concerned the construction of the F-scale itself. In common with other scales devised by Adorno et al., all the items were worded so that agreement with them indicated an authoritarian response. The obvious drawback of this, as Brown (1965) pointed out, was that any authoritarianism so measured cannot easily be distinguished from a general tendency to agree with seemingly authoritative sounding statements. This confounding was highlighted by Bass (1955) when he constructed a reversed F-scale in which all the original items had had their meaning inverted. In theory, these two scales should be perfectly and negatively correlated; in fact, Bass found that the interscale correlation, while negative, was rather modest indicating that some respondents had, indeed, simultaneously agreed with several authoritarian statements *and* their opposites. This defect, at least, has been corrected in later authoritarianism measures (Altemeyer, 1988; Lee and Warr, 1969). Finally, the steps taken to validate the F-scale through those in-depth clinical interviews with high and low scorers left much to be desired. Particularly worrisome was the fact that the interviewers knew in advance the score of each respondent, thus raising the possibility that, unconsciously or not, they could have influenced the answers they elicited. As psychology was later to discover, even the behaviour of laboratory rats can be affected when one's research assistants are aware of the experimental hypotheses under test (Rosenthal, 1966). How much more likely would such experimenter effects be when working with cognisant – and possibly acquiescent – human subjects?

. There were other more substantive criticisms to be made of *The Authoritarian Personality* project. One centred on the correlations which Adorno et al. reported between authoritarianism and such variables as intelligence, level of education, and social class, correlations which were observed still more strongly in later research (Christie, 1954). The theoretical significance of these correlations is that they suggest an alternative explanation for the genesis of authoritarianism. Perhaps the latter simply reflects the socialized attitudes of particular sub-groups in society and does not, as Adorno et al. contended, have its origins in personality dynamics deriving from a certain kind of family upbringing (Brown, 1965). Perhaps this explains why Mosher and Scodel (1960), when they measured the ethnocentrism of children and their mothers, and also the mothers' attitudes towards authoritarian child-rearing practices, found a reasonable correlation between the two measures of ethnocentrism but absolutely no association at all between the mothers' child-rearing attitudes and their children's prejudice level. This strongly suggests some direct socialization of attitudes rather than an indirect shaping of a prejudiced personality by parenting style. However, as we shall see in chapter 5, even the direct socialization model is not without its problems. A second theoretical criticism of *The Authoritarian Personality* was that it dealt with only one variant of authoritarianism – namely, right-wing authoritarianism. Could it not be that people with other political views are also authoritarian and hence also prejudiced? This argument was made most forcibly by Shils (1954) drawing from historical and political sources, but it was properly developed and generalized into a more systematic psychological theory by Rokeach (1956, 1960).

Prejudice on the Left and Right

Rokeach's (1956) analysis began by distinguishing between the *content* of what a prejudiced person believes in – that is, the specific constellation of intolerant attitudes and the outgroups to which these are directed – and the underlying organization or *structure* of those beliefs. According to Rokeach, Adorno et al.'s theory and associated measuring instruments really only deal with prejudice amongst right-wingers towards conventional conservative targets such as Communists, Jews, and other 'deviant' or minority groups. Perhaps, argued Rokeach, it would be possible to find manifestations of outgroup rejection amongst left-wingers as well, albeit towards different targets. The virulent rejection of Trotskyists and other so-called revisionists by supporters of Stalin would be a case in point (Deutscher, 1959). Rokeach's main hypothesis was that what these apparently very different kinds of prejudice had in common was a similar underlying cognitive structure in which different beliefs or belief systems were well isolated from one another so that mutually contradictory opinions could be tolerated. Furthermore, such belief systems would be rather resistant to change in the light of new information and would be characterized by the use of appeals to authority to justify their correctness. He labelled this syndrome of intolerance the 'closed mind' or dogmatic personality, in contradistinction to the 'open minded' or non-prejudiced person (Rokeach, 1960).

To substantiate his theory Rokeach (1956) devised two new scales. One was the Opinionation Scale which consisted of a series of rather extreme social attitude statements worded in both a right-wing and a left-wing direction. This was designed to be a measure of intolerance. The other was the Dogmatism Scale which, while intended to be closely related to Opinionation, aimed to tap general authoritarianism. Although some of the items of this scale bore a marked resemblance to the earlier F-scale items, and shared the latter's positive response set, it was Rokeach's hope that the Dogmatism measure would be a more content-free index of authoritarianism than Adorno and his colleagues had been able to devise. As we shall see, there are grounds for doubting whether he was successful in this.

Using standard psychometric procedures Rokeach (1956) established that these scales were internally reliable. He then attempted to demonstrate their validity. This he did in a variety of ways with, it has to be said, mixed success. In two small studies he compared the Dogmatism scores of groups of students judged by their professors or their peers to be especially dogmatic or very open-minded. Using the professorial judgements as the criterion, there were no reliable differences between the groups on measured dogmatism although the scale did prove more discriminatory when using peer ratings as the bench-mark (Rokeach, 1960). In further studies Rokeach (1960) compared the Dogmatism scores of groups which, on *a priori* grounds, he considered to be more dogmatic than average (for example, avowed Catholics, members of left- and right-wing political groups), with those he considered less dogmatic (for example, non-believers, political liberals). At the same time he also measured their authoritarianism and ethnocentrism using the instruments devised by Adorno et al. (1950). Some of these comparisons did indeed support his contention that dogmatism was a more general measure than authoritarianism. For instance, his (admittedly rather small) group of Communists scored the same as Conservatives on dogmatism but considerably lower on authoritarianism. On the other hand, these same Communists scored marginally higher than Liberals on dogmatism but lower than them on authoritarianism, thus suggesting that it might be possible to distinguish general intolerance from a right-wing political position in a way that the

F-scale seemed not to do. This was further supported by correlational evidence from several studies in which Dogmatism consistently correlated with both left *and* right Opinionation and, of course, authoritarianism and ethnocentrism (Rokeach, 1956). The latter two measures, however, only correlated with right Opinionation. Against this generally supportive pattern of evidence, though, were the comparisons amongst religious groups, some of which failed to show the expected differences in Dogmatism (Rokeach, 1956).

What are the origins of the dogmatic personality? Here Rokeach followed Adorno et al. (1950) in believing that they lay in early family socialization experiences and particularly the relationships with the child's parents. He thus expected 'closed minded' (or dogmatic) people to display the same exaggerated glorification of their parents and to manifest other symptoms of repressed anxiety (for example, nail-biting, nightmares, and so on) that Adorno and his colleagues had described in their portraits of authoritarians. Consistent with this, Rokeach (1960) did find that 'open-minded' students were more likely to describe their parents in equivocal or ambivalent terms and to recollect fewer symptoms of childhood anxiety. However, somewhat surprisingly, it was the 'intermediate' rather than the extremely 'closed-minded' group who showed the biggest contrast with this group.

How useful is the concept of dogmatism for predicting prejudice? Unfortunately the amount of research addressing this question is rather sparse, especially when compared to the enormous literature on authoritarianism and prejudice. Rokeach himself, as we have seen, demonstrated that dogmatism was correlated with the generalized rejection of outgroups measured by the Ethnocentrism scale.[2] Maykovich (1975) also found that a measure of dogmatism[3] was correlated with Whites' anti-Black attitudes in the US, even after the effects of major social variables such as geographical region, education, and socio-economic status had been accounted for. In another context, that of fundamentalist religious groups in Israel, dogmatism was found to be correlated with anti-Arab prejudice although not strongly (Kedem et al., 1987). However, another study of religious groups, this time churches in Northern and Southern US states, provided rather less support for Rokeach. Although dogmatism was significantly correlated with three different kinds of prejudice (anti-Semitism, anti-Black, and anti-mentally ill), when respondents' concern for their social status was statistically controlled these correlations dropped markedly and, in the case of anti-Black prejudice at least, became non-significant (Hoge and Carroll, 1973). Finally, in a rare experimental study, Dion (1973) found dyads composed of high-dogmatic subjects showed no greater discrimination towards a rival dyad in a 'gaming' experiment involving the contingent distribution of money, and nor were their intergroup evaluations any more biased than dyads of less-dogmatic subjects. In this experiment the mere fact of division into groups seemed more important than the personality compositions of those groups, a phenomenon to which we shall return at some length in chapter 3.

Another attempt to link personality to prejudice but to separate it from political conservatism was made by Eysenck (1954). Like Rokeach, Eysenck proposed that people's disposition towards intolerance was independent of their endorsement of left- or right-wing ideology. He called this tendency tough-mindedness (as opposed to tender-mindedness) and suggested that it was associated with the personality trait of extraversion. According to his more general theory of personality, extraverts differ constitutionally from introverts in their susceptibility to stimulation and in their conditionability (Eysenck, 1952, 1967). When translated into the social domain, Eysenck argued that this meant that 'tough-minded' people (that is, extraverts) were more resistant to social conditioning by family and other societal influences and hence would be more likely to endorse and adopt extreme (that is, unconventional) social and political attitudes. At the same time, these attitudes would probably be tinged with strong elements of punitiveness or aggression (since these tendencies, too, would be less restrained than they would be in more 'normally' socialized individuals). Thus, for Eysenck, very conservative people, though they differ markedly from extreme left-wing individuals in the actual views they endorse, nevertheless have some personality characteristics in common.

In later work Eysenck somewhat modified and then extended this thesis. Perhaps because very conservative (and prejudiced) attitudes were not always positively correlated with extraversion – indeed, in one study a significant *negative* correlation was observed (Wilson, 1973) – Eysenck subsequently proposed that psychoticism and not extraversion was the main personality characteristic underlying 'tough-mindedness' (Eysenck and Wilson, 1978). Then, pursuing his biological argument still further, he suggested that people's social attitudes – including their levels of prejudice – could be genetically determined (Eaves and Eysenck, 1974; Martin et al., 1986).

As we shall see shortly, there are serious grounds for doubting the plausibility of such a genetic theory of prejudice, but what of the more general claim, proposed by both Rokeach and Eysenck (albeit from different premises), that extremists of the left and right do share some personality attributes?

The data from Rokeach's and Eysenck's own research are not very convincing. In the case of the former, the key study comparing respondents at opposite ends of the political spectrum is based on some very small samples indeed (for example, just 13 Communists) and, perhaps because of this, none of the crucial 'extremist' vs 'centrist' comparisons on dogmatism are actually statistically significant (Rokeach, 1960). In the case of Eysenck's (1954) research, although the data base is much larger, the findings purporting to show that extreme left- and right-wingers are equally 'tough minded' have been hotly disputed, not least by Rokeach himself (Rokeach and Hanley, 1956; see also Eysenck (1956) and Brown (1965)). More recently, McFarland et al. (1992) were able to study the levels and correlates of authoritarianism in the former Soviet Union and in the United States. Although the Russian respondents tended to score lower in authoritarianism than the American samples, the pattern of correlations suggested that authoritarianism was *positively* correlated with an endorsement of Communist ideals in the former group and negatively correlated in the latter. Other supportive evidence for the idea that ideologies of left and right share similar psychological characteristics has been provided by Tetlock (1983, 1984). Analysing the rhetoric of both Conservative and Socialist politicians in the US and Britain, he has shown how their arguments tend to be less complex than their more centrist counterparts, thus supporting the idea that they may see the world in more stark and rigidly defined terms. Whether this difference in cognitive style can be attributed to personality functioning is arguable, however, since it is possible that at least some of it may be determined by whether their party is in government or opposition. When in opposition politicians tend to make speeches which are less qualified and circumspect than when they are in power (Tetlock et al., 1984).

Perhaps the most trenchant criticism of attempts to equate extremists of different political persuasions has been made by Billig (1976). He points out that measuring instruments adopted in this kind of research, far from being politically neutral (and thus able to detect purely psychological distinctions), actually contain items which are ideologically heavily laden. He concludes that any differences – or similarities – observed between groups are thus attributable to the aggregation of political attitudes elicited by the particular mix of items on any given scale. To demonstrate this point, Billig and Cochrane (1979) showed how members of the Communist and National Front parties in Britain *could* be clearly distinguished by a careful analysis of the individual items they endorsed on Rokeach's (1973) Value Survey instrument, thus contradicting the idea that they could be regarded as belonging to a common psychological category.

The Limitations of a Personality Approach to Prejudice

Let me now turn from the discussion of particular theories and consider the wider argument that it is possible to explain the variation and occurrence of prejudice by reference to individual differences in personality. There are, it seems to me, four major limitations to this thesis (see also Billig, 1976, for a similar critique).

The first is that it underestimates – or, even, in its strongest form completely ignores – the power and importance of the immediate social situation in shaping people's attitudes. It is by now almost a truism in social psychology that our opinions and behaviour are strongly influenced by such factors as the attitudes of others around or near to us, the norms of our group, and the relationships between our group and others (Brown, 1988). So it is with the expression of prejudice. Take, for example, a study by Levinson and Schermerhorn (1951) which was concerned to evaluate the effects of a six-week human relations workshop on its participants. At the start of the workshop the participants had broadly similar F-scale scores to other samples but by its end their authoritarianism had declined significantly by over a third of a scale point. An even more dramatic demonstration of the situational lability of authoritarianism was provided by Siegel and Siegel (1957). In one of social psychology's rare 'true' field experiments, Siegel and Siegel were able to observe the change in authoritarianism over a one-year period amongst two groups of American women students. One group had been residents in very conservative and traditional sorority housing whilst the other had lived in dormitories where more liberal norms prevailed. The beautiful feature of this study from a methodological point of view was that these housing assignments had been made on a properly random basis, thus ensuring that at the beginning of the year the two groups would be equivalent in terms of personality and other characteristics. True to form, those who had been exposed to the more progressive group norms showed a marked decline in their authoritarianism whilst the sorority group changed hardly at all (see table 2.1).

Table 2.1 Changes in authoritarianism after exposure to liberal or conservative group norms

	Time 1	Time 2 (one year later)
Conservative sorority	103.0	99.1
Liberal dormitories	102.1	87.3

Source: Siegel and Siegel (1957).

The doubly ironic feature of both of these studies is that their measure of prejudice which proved sensitive enough to detect changes in the respondents' attitudes as a result of their group experiences was, in fact, the F-scale, supposedly an index of people's temporally and situational *stable* personality!

Further evidence on the situational specificity of prejudice emerged from Minard's (1952) study of a West Virginian mining community in the USA. He noted how the strict segregation and discrimination which existed in the town evaporated once the miners were at work underground. Apparently, the situational norms and the strong inter-dependence engendered by the hazardous nature of their work were a more critical influence than any enduring personality dispositions. Another confirmation of the importance of the situation was provided by Stephan and Rosenfield (1978) in their study of American children's interethnic attitudes following school desegregation. The most powerful predictor of positive attitude change was the increase in the amount of intergroup contact. Much less powerful (and mostly only marginally significant in a statistical sense) was the authoritarian nature of the children's parental background. Once again, a situational factor (amount of contact) proved more important than a personality variable.

The second limitation is an extension of the above argument to a broader cultural or societal level. The seminal study here is the cross-cultural research of Pettigrew (1958) which examined prejudice in South Africa and the US. Unsurprisingly, he found that White South Africans showed very high levels of anti-Black prejudice, as did Whites from the southern US. However, whilst there was a correlation at an individual level between authoritarianism and prejudice in both places, the overall sample means for authoritarianism were no higher than in other less-prejudiced groups. In other words, in terms of their overall distribution of personality types they were rather similar to 'normal' populations, despite their overtly racist attitudes. Pettigrew's conclusion was that the origin of this racism lay much more in the prevailing societal norms to which these respondents were exposed than in any personality dysfunction. This conclusion was reinforced by the consistently high correlations he observed between prejudice and measures of social conformity.

Over the years South Africa has been a particularly significant context in which to study the determinants of prejudice because of its institutionally racist structure during the apartheid era. The apartheid system, founded as it was on the twin premises of ethnic segregation and white supremacy, provided a fertile breeding ground for the generation and transmission of racist ideas. Following Pettigrew's (1958) research, several other studies have examined the origins of prejudice there. In general, the existence of an intra-individual correlation between authoritarianism and prejudice has been confirmed, although not always strongly (Colman and Lambley, 1970; Duckitt, 1988; Heaven, 1983). Perhaps more important, however, is the finding that socio-demographic variables have been consistently good predictors of levels of prejudice, independently of levels of authoritarianism. For example, Afrikaans-speakers and lower socio-economic status groups have tended to be more prejudiced than English-speaking or middle-class groups (Duckitt, 1988; Pettigrew, 1958). The existence of these large sub-cultural differences further strengthens the argument that social norms rather than individual personality dynamics determine overall levels of prejudice in particular groups.

The third difficulty with any personality account is its inability to explain the uniformity of prejudiced attitudes across whole groups of people. The very nature of such theories – explaining prejudice via individual *differences* among people – makes them particularly unsuited to explain how prejudice can become virtually consensual in certain societies. In pre-war Nazi Germany or, until very recently, in modern-day South Africa consistently racist attitudes and behaviour were observable amongst hundreds of thousands of people who must surely have differed on most other psychological attributes. For a contemporary and more systematic illustration of the pervasiveness of prejudice, albeit in a milder form, Davey's (1983) study of interethnic attitudes amongst English children will serve well. Part of this research involved having children share out some sweets between unknown members of different ethnic groups shown in photographs. As can be seen in table 2.2, of the 500 or so children participating, fully 50 per cent were ethnocentric in their distribution of sweets – that is, they gave more to

Table 2.2 Ethnic discrimination in English children: percentage of allocation strategies adopted

| Pattern of sweets allocation[a] | Ethnic origin of children | | | |
	White	West Indian	Asian	All
Ethnocentric	59.8	41.4	39.8	50.2
Fair	24.7	36.0	25.8	27.8
Outgroup favouring	0.4	0.8	1.6	0.8

Note: [a] 'Ethnocentric' was defined as those children who gave at least three out of the four sweets to their own group; 'Fair' as those who distributed two sweets to each of the ethnic groups; 'Outgroup favouring' as those who predominantly favoured another group at the expense of their own.

Source: Davey (1983), table 9.2.

the ingroup photographs than to other group members. Of the white children, nearly 60 per cent showed this discrimination. It is difficult to imagine that so many of these children, coming as they did from a variety of perfectly ordinary backgrounds, had all been exposed to the kind of special family dynamics alleged to give rise to the prejudiced person (see also chapter 5 for further findings from Davey's research).

A fourth problem concerns the historical specificity of prejudice. If uniformities of prejudice are hard to explain with a personality model, the sudden rises and falls of prejudice over time are equally problematic. For instance, the growth of anti-Semitism under Hitler occurred over the space of only a decade or so, much too quickly for a whole generation of German families to have adopted the child-rearing practices necessary to engender authoritarian and prejudiced children. The attitudes of Americans towards the Japanese before and after the bombing of Pearl Harbor in 1942 would be another even more telling case (Seago, 1947). The changes here, at both a personal and an institutional level, including the establishment of large prison camps for Asiatic Americans, took place over a matter of months (Nakanishi, 1988).

Two more recent and systematic studies underline this point. The first was conducted over a 15-year period between 1973 and 1987 with successive cohorts of Canadian undergraduates (Altemeyer, 1988). Using a modified authoritarianism scale, corrected to avoid the response biases inherent in the F-scale, Altemeyer observed a steady increase in authoritarianism over this period. Significantly, from the aetiological point of view, the parents of those same students changed in their levels of authoritarianism hardly at all over the same period. Even more impressive were the results of a longitudinal study of over 900 Dutch adolescents (Vollebergh, 1991). Tracing the changes in authoritarianism over a two-year period, Vollebergh observed a small but highly reliable decrease in authoritarianism. Moreover, this could be observed at each of the five age levels she studied. Temporal changes such as these are, as I have already noted, rather awkward for explanations which trace the origins of prejudice to family dynamics. They are even more damaging – fatally so – for a theory like that of Eaves and Eysenck (1974) which proposes an inherited basis to prejudice. It is simply untenable to suppose that any significant genetic change could have taken place over time periods which, in an evolutionary time frame, correspond to less than the blink of an eye.

These historical changes pose a still more critical problem for the personality approach because they suggest that authoritarianism may actually be an effect of changing social conditions rather than deriving from particular child–parent relations. If this is so, then, as every introductory statistics student is constantly reminded, the commonly observed correlation between authoritarianism and prejudice, rather than indicating a causal relationship between them, may actually stem from their joint dependence on these wider societal factors.

This interpretation is rendered more plausible by a series of archival studies which have examined historical correlations between various economic indices and several societal indicators of authoritarianism. The first of these was conducted by Sales (1972) who proposed that an important source of authoritarianism – in adults as much as in children – is the existence of threatening factors in society. Chief amongst these are the prevailing economic conditions: when times are hard people will feel under greater threat than they will in periods of prosperity. He reasoned that such feelings of threat would manifest themselves in people's attraction towards more authoritarian forms of religion. When he examined conversion rates to various American churches between 1920 and 1939, a period spanning the boom years of the 1920s and the great depression of the 1930s, he found some support for his hypothesis. There were reliable negative correlations between income levels and conversion rates to 'authoritarian' religions like Catholicism and Seventh-Day Adventism, but positive associations for 'non-authoritarian' churches like Presbyterians. Thus, to paraphrase Marx's famous dictum: it is especially authoritarian religions which are the 'opiates of the people' in times of economic recession. Sales (1973) then extended his analysis by ingeniously devising some other indicators of authoritarianism. For example, he suggested that in a threatening climate popular cultural icons like comic strip characters should emphasize power and toughness, there should be a growth in the popularity of astrology and other superstitious beliefs, and people's choice of pet dogs should veer towards the aggressive hunting breeds such as Dobermann Pinschers and German Shepherds and away from lap dogs like miniature poodles. All these indices showed reliable associations with economic variables. Similar archival studies of Germany in the pre-war period and the US in the 1970s and 1980s have largely supported Sales's conclusions (Doty et al., 1991; Padgett and Jorgenson, 1982).

Adorno et al., Rokeach, and others set out to discover why so many people are prejudiced. They believed that the answer lies in the personality structure of the individual: children experiencing particular upbringings would grow up to be deferential towards authority, be dogmatic and rigid in their thinking, and above all be hostile towards minority groups. However, as we have seen, such a personalistic approach runs into severe problems accounting for both the pervasiveness of prejudice in some times and places, and its almost complete absence in others. If personality factors are important at all, then it is probable that they are so for those at the two extremes of the distribution of prejudice: the perpetually tolerant and the unremitting bigot. For the remaining large majority, personality may be a much less important determinant of prejudice than the many and varied *situational* influences on behaviour. Furthermore, for these people it may even be more appropriate to regard personality as itself an effect of those same social and cultural variables rather than as a causal agent in its own right.

Summary

1. A common explanation of prejudice is to attribute it to some special type of personality. The most famous example of such an explanation within psychology is the theory of *The Authoritarian Personality* (Adorno et al., 1950). This proposed that certain family conditions, particularly the experience of excessively harsh and moralistic parenting,

produces an outlook on life which is overdeferential towards authority, socially conservative, hostile towards minority or 'deviant' groups, and dominated by a simplistic and categorical perceptual and cognitive style. This approach, whilst historically influential in stimulating empirical research, has been widely criticized on methodological grounds.

2. An extension of *The Authoritarian Personality* approach is the hypothesis that intolerance and mental rigidity are not the exclusive prerogative of the political right but can be observed in extreme left-wingers also. The best-known example of this approach is Rokeach's theory of dogmatism. This theory, too, is not without its empirical difficulties.

3. All personality accounts of prejudice are limited because of their tendency to downplay or ignore situational factors and to neglect the influence of societal or sub-cultural norms. Furthermore, they cannot readily explain the widespread uniformity of prejudice in some societies or groups. Nor can they easily account for the historical changes in the expression of prejudice and the correlation of these changes with socio-economic variables.

Further Reading

Billig, M. (1978) *Fascists: A social psychological view of the National Front*, ch. 3. London: Harcourt Brace Jovanovich.

Brown, Roger (1965) *Social Psychology*, ch. 10. London: Macmillan.

Notes

1. Given the size of the samples (both > 600) it seems unlikely that the absence of any strong relationships in this study can be attributable to a lack of statistical power.

2. Somewhat surprisingly the work on prejudice for which Rokeach is most well known did not employ dogmatism as an independent variable. This is his Belief Congruence Theory which is dealt with more fully in chapter 3.

3. It is not clear whether this was Rokeach's scale since the measure Maykovich used is not described in the paper. Nor is Rokeach's theory referred to directly there.

Social Categorization and Prejudice

3   Women queuing at post office

In any situation there are usually several ways people can be categorized: by age, ethnicity, gender and so on. The categories most likely to be chosen are those which best match the situation and which are most easily accessible to the perceiver.

Already in the first two chapters we have encountered several examples of prejudice which, though they have all differed widely in their intensity and mode of expression, have all had one thing in common: they all involved some negative sentiment directed *towards a particular group of people, or at least representatives from that group.* It will be recalled from chapter 1 that this is one of the defining characteristics of the kind of prejudice I am concerned with in this book: that it has this categorical basis, as opposed to other forms of antipathy which may be more interpersonal or idiosyncratic in character. Viewing prejudice in this way is important because it emphasizes its social consequences for those who are its target. Prejudice is not something that happens to isolated individuals; potentially it can affect *any* member of the outgroup in question.

Such a categorical definition is important for another reason. It underlines the fact that the perpetrators of prejudice are very likely to have engaged in a certain kind of cognitive activity before, or perhaps as, they formed their prejudiced judgement or performed their discriminatory deed. When someone makes a racist or sexist remark of the type, 'Blacks are . . .', or 'Just what you would expect of a woman . . .', or when an employer chooses to employ a majority group applicant in preference to someone equally well qualified from a minority, they have mentally invoked one or more social categories. They have then used that categorization as the starting point to infer some attributes about the people in question and then, often, to justify their actions towards them. Indeed, so central is the categorization process to the operation of prejudice that some have argued that it is the *sine qua non* without which prejudice could not exist (Allport, 1954; Tajfel, 1969a).

In this chapter, the first of two devoted to cognitive processes underlying prejudice, I begin by considering the most direct consequences of categorization, that of intercategory differentiation and intracategory assimilation. As we shall see, these effects occur not just at a perceptual and judgemental level but have behavioural implications also. In subsequent sections I consider what happens when more than one categorical dimension is psychologically salient. In the first of these I show how and when the differentiation and assimilation processes combine and cancel out in situations where the categories cut across each other. I then focus particularly on the intracategory assimilation process, a process which leads to members of the same group being seen as more similar to each other than they really are. In intergroup contexts this process seldom operates symmetrically; usually one group is seen as more homogeneous than the other. Next I consider what factors govern the choice of different available categorizations for making sense of any given situation. Finally, and by way of a direct contrast, I consider a theory which proposes that category differences are less important for intergroup attitudes than is commonly supposed. Instead, according to this theory, similarities and differences in belief are the crucial factor.

Categorization: a Fundamental Process

The idea that social categorization is a necessary precursor of prejudice is crucial because it emphasizes the latter's ordinary or common-place nature (Allport, 1954). Categorization is a cognitive process which does not just occur in bizarre circumstances or in certain pathological cases. It is, as Bruner (1957) suggested some years ago, an inescapable feature of human existence. Why is this? It is so because the world is simply too complex a place for us to be able to survive without some means of simplifying and ordering it first. Just as biologists and chemists use classification systems to reduce nature's complexity to a more manageable number of categories linked together in scientifically useful ways, so too do we rely on systems of categories in our everyday lives. We simply do not have the capability to respond differently to every single person or event that we encounter. Moreover, even if we did have that capacity, it would be highly dysfunctional to do so because such stimuli possess many characteristics in common with each other, as well as attributes which distinguish them from other stimuli. By assigning them to categories based on these similarities and differences we can deal with them much more efficiently. This is one reason why human languages are all replete with complex systems of categories and sub-categories; they permit ready reference to whole classes of people and objects without the constant need for particularistic description. In Allport's memorable phrase, categories are 'nouns that cut slices' through our environment (Allport, 1954, p. 174).

To give an example I have used before (Brown, 1988): suppose I visit some foreign city and I need to find my way to some famous landmark.

It is much more useful for me to be able to recognize particular categories of people (for example, police, taxi drivers, local residents) to ask for directions than simply to ask the first person I meet (usually an equally lost fellow tourist). What is a matter of mere convenience in this mundane example can become literally a question of life or death in more threatening environments. To be able to recognize and behave appropriately towards members of 'our' and 'their' side in the streets of Beirut can make the need for fast and accurate categorical judgements more than a little important for one's personal survival.

Differentiation and assimilation

If social categories are to be useful simplifying and ordering devices then it is important that they help us discriminate clearly between those who belong and those who do not. One of the first people to recognize this important point was Campbell (1956) who, in a rarely cited paper, observed that an important facet of stereotyping was an enhancement of contrast between groups. He then demonstrated that this was a rather basic consequence of categorization by eliciting such a contrast effect in a simple physical judgement task. He asked his subjects to learn the physical location of some nonsense syllables. (On every trial a given syllable was always presented in the same position along a horizontal line.) Within the stimuli there were two implicit categories of nonsense syllable, one in which the central letter was always 'E', the other which always ended in an 'X'. The 'E' group were always presented towards the left, the 'X' group to the right, although they overlapped in the middle. Campbell found that subjects made consistent errors in estimating the position of these overlapping syllables – the 'E' stimuli being moved to the left, the 'X' stimuli to the right – so that the physical locations of the two categories of stimuli were more clearly separated.

This principle was later formalised by Tajfel (1959) into two hypotheses on the cognitive consequences of categorization. The first of these was that if a category is imposed on a set of stimuli – whether these be physical objects, sensory events, or people – such that some of the stimuli fall into class A and the remainder into class B, then this will have the effect of enhancing any pre-existing differences between the two categories. The second hypothesis, really a corollary of the first, was that differences *within* the categories will be attenuated. Or, put less formally, members of different groups will be seen as more different from each other than they really are whilst members of the same group will be seen as more similar.

The first direct test of these hypotheses was carried out by Tajfel and Wilkes (1963). Like Campbell (1956), Tajfel and Wilkes studied judgements of physical stimuli. They simply asked their subjects to estimate the length of each of a series of lines, presented one at a time. There were, in fact, eight different lines each differing from its neighbour by a constant amount (a bit less than 1 cm). This is an easy enough task and, sure enough, subjects in the control conditions made estimates quite close to the actual lengths of the lines. However, in the experimental conditions one small new piece of information was made available to the subjects as they made their judgements. On each card containing the stimulus line the letter 'A' or 'B' appeared. It so happened (though the subjects were never told this) that the four shorter lines were labelled 'A', the four longer lines 'B'. The addition of this simple A/B categorization had a curious effect on the subjects' judgements: most of their estimates remained accurate with the exception of the perceived difference between the longest 'A' line and the shortest 'B' line (that is, the two lines at the boundary of the A/B dichotomy). Consistently this difference was seen by the subjects to be twice its actual size (around 2 cm). In other words, just as Tajfel had hypothesized, the perceived difference between the two categories had been exaggerated. However, contrary to his second hypothesis, there was much less evidence that the differences *within* the categories were reduced. Only towards the very end of the series of trials was there any noticeable intracategory assimilation.

Stimulated by these experiments, others have confirmed the category differentiation effect in a variety of different tasks including sound patterns comprising speech phoneme categories, judgements of area, estimates of temperature in different months of the year, impressions of faces, and the evaluation of attitude statements (see Doise, 1976; Eiser and Stroebe, 1972; Krueger and Clement, 1994). The latter judgemental tasks are interesting because they are more social in content and hence imply that the effects of the categorization process may, as Campbell (1956) had surmised, apply in a rather wide range of situations. Eiser (1971) devised something of a replication of Tajfel and Wilkes's (1963) experiment by asking subjects to judge the permissiveness of a series of attitude statements concerned with the recreational use of drugs. In the experimental condition half the statements were attributed to one newspaper (*The Gazette*), the remainder to another (*The Messenger*). Imposing a category in this way had the same effect as it had in Tajfel and Wilkes's line estimation experiment. The judged difference between the 'permissive' and the 'restrictive' statements was consistently greater than it was in the control condition where no newspaper labels were present. Once again, however, there was little sign that the addition of the category caused statements from the same newspaper to be seen as more similar to each other.

However, later experiments have confirmed the existence of the intracategory assimilation effect also. McGarty and Penny (1988), using a similar attitude judgement paradigm to Eiser (1971), found evidence of both category differentiation *and* assimilation. And Doise et al. (1978), using a still more realistic task, also found both effects. In this experiment schoolchildren were presented with photographs of three boys followed by photographs of three girls and asked to tick off which of a series of 24 trait adjectives applied to each photograph. Half the children knew in advance they would be judging both boys and girls and hence the gender category was somewhat salient for them; the remainder were unaware whilst rating the first three photographs that there would be three others of the opposite sex to follow. The judgements in the two conditions showed consistent differences. When the gender category was salient there were reliably more *different* adjectives used to describe the male and female photographs, and correspondingly more *identical* adjectives used to describe photographs of the same gender.

Social categorization and intergroup discrimination

So far we have seen that psychologically introducing a category into an otherwise undifferentiated situation has some fairly predictable distorting effects on people's perceptual and cognitive functioning. But, it might reasonably be objected, surely most of these phenomena are rather far removed from the kinds of social judgements and behaviour involved in intergroup prejudice? Is there any evidence that social categorization has any more meaningful consequences for people's attitudes and behaviour towards members of their own and other groups? Indeed there is. We shall encounter several other instances in later sections where categorization processes are seen to have some quite complex and profound effects on intergroup relations, but before dealing with these there is one further consequence of the mere fact of categorization itself which needs describing. This is that it seems to provide the sufficient circumstances for people to begin to favour their own group over others, whether this favouritism be in the form of biased evaluative judgements or as some kind of concrete behavioural discrimination.

One of the first studies to demonstrate this was by Rabbie and Horwitz (1969). Dutch school children who were strangers to one another were randomly divided into groups of four, labelled 'green' and 'blue', allegedly for administrative reasons. They then worked on their own on some irrelevant tasks for a few minutes. Then, depending on experimental conditions, one of two things happened. Some of the children learned that one of the groups was to receive a reward (some new transistor radios) for helping with the research, whilst the other would not, apparently due to a shortage of resources. This 'common fate' would be decided by the toss of a coin. However, for other children – in the control condition – this piece of information was omitted and so they had nothing more in common with each other than their colour label. The participants were then asked to rate each other on a number of socio-metric scales. The question was: would these impressionistic ratings of what were more or less complete strangers be influenced by those flimsy labels 'green' and 'blue'? The results showed that in the conditions where the children experienced some interdependence – that unexpected and arbitrary reward or deprivation – there was clear evidence that those from the ingroup were rated more favourably than those coming from the other group. In the control condition, on the other hand, the ratings appeared to show no such bias. Rabbie and Horwitz initially concluded that mere classification itself was not sufficient to influence people's intergroup judgements; what seemed to be necessary was some additional feeling of interdependence. Actually, as they later conceded, that conclusion was premature (Horwitz and Rabbie, 1982). In a follow-up study, where they increased the size of that control group, they did find some (statistically significant) evidence of ingroup–outgroup differentiation. Here, then, was the first evidence that simply placing people into one of two, albeit pretty meaningless, categories could have predictable effects on their judgements of real peers (and not just of physical stimuli or hypothetical others).

This conclusion was confirmed in an even more dramatic fashion in a series of experiments initiated by Tajfel et al. (1971). They set out to discover if simply belonging to a group, and nothing else, might be enough to instigate a rudimentary form of behavioural prejudice – that is, the differential treatment of ingroup and outgroup members. To this end, they devised what has come to be known as the Minimal Group

Paradigm, so called because it sought to create groups which had been stripped bare of all the usual concomitants of group life – face-to-face interaction, an internal group structure, a set of norms, relationships with other groups, and so on (see Brown, 1988). All that remained, in fact, was the knowledge of having been placed in one category rather than another. To achieve this rather bizarre situation experimental participants are usually invited to take part in a 'decision-making' experiment, the first part of which consists of showing them some pairs of abstract paintings and getting them to indicate which of each pair they prefer.[1] Supposedly on the basis of these preferences, each person is then allocated to one of two groups; in the original experiments these were called Klee and Kandinsky, named after the painters of the pictures. An important feature of this group allocation procedure is that it is done privately; nobody knows who else is in their (or the other) group. In this way the anonymity of the groups is preserved and possible contaminating factors like having particular friends in one of the groups are avoided. The next part of the 'decision-making' experiment is then introduced. This consists of the subjects allocating money to various other people, identified only by code numbers and their group membership, using specially prepared booklets of reward matrices[2] (see table 3.1). To eliminate self-interest as a motive the subjects are never able to award money to themselves directly.

What strategies might they use? An examination of table 3.1 reveals that there are a number of possibilities. One perfectly reasonable objective might be always to try to give the two anonymous recipients as near as possible the same amount on the grounds that there was really nothing to choose between them – who *were* numbers 72 and 47 after all? Another rational strategy would be to choose the box that totalled the highest sum with the aim of maximizing the amount that would eventually be dispensed to everyone. Still another possibility would be to choose at random since the whole situation was so devoid of cues for action that this is as sensible as anything. Or, finally, one could choose to discriminate systematically between the recipients on the basis of their group membership.

In fact, the evidence shows that only the first and the last of these strategies are used with any regularity (Branthwaite et al., 1979; Turner, 1980). The usual pattern is for people to make some effort to be fair in their allocations but, at the same time, to show a reliable tendency to award more money to ingroup members than to outgroup members. Thus, in the original experiments, in Matrix 1 in table 3.1 over 70 per cent of subjects made choices favouring their own group with a mean

Table 3.1 Two sample matrices from the minimal group paradigm

Reward numbers

Matrix 1

Member 72 of Klee group	18	17	16	15	14	13	12	11	10	9	8	7	6	5
Member 47 of Kandinsky group				5	6	7	8	9	10	11	12	13	14	15	16	17	18

Matrix 2

Member 74 of Klee group	25	23	21	19	17	15	13	11	9	7	5	3	1
Member 44 of Kandinsky group				19	18	17	16	15	14	13	12	11	10	9	8	7

Notes:
1 On each page subjects must choose one pair of numbers which stand for real monetary rewards.
2 These are two of several types of matrix used. Matrix 1 was designed to measure general group favouritism, while Matrix 2 was designed to measure the tendency to maximize the difference between ingroup and outgroup recipients. In the experiment, these matrices would be presented to each subject at least twice: once as above, and once with the goup affiliations of the two recipients reversed.

Source: Tajfel et al. (1971).

response from people in the Klee group (say) of between the 14/9 and 13/10 boxes (Tajfel et al., 1971). This was true even when, in absolute terms, that ingrouper would be worse off. For example, in Matrix 2 the mean response from those in the Kandinsky group was somewhere between the 13/13 and 12/11 options (Tajfel et al., 1971). Note that this choice results in the Kandinsky recipient receiving 6–7 points less than s/he might otherwise have done but, crucially, thereby receiving *more* than the Klee recipient. This 'maximizing difference' strategy, as it is known, has been a consistent feature of findings from minimal group studies (Turner, 1983).

Such intergroup discrimination in minimal group settings has proved to be a remarkably robust phenomenon, having been replicated more than 20 times in several different countries using a wide range of experimental subjects (Brewer, 1979; Tajfel, 1982). In a later chapter (chapter 6) I shall return to these experiments to consider various explanations for the findings they have generated, but for now it is worth noting that this apparently spontaneous discrimination is entirely consistent with the more general differentiation phenomena associated with the categorization process (Doise, 1976). Consider the situation confronting the experimental participants. For the few minutes of the experiment there is little to distinguish their fellow subjects. The code numbers are apparently random and hence uninformative. Faced with this ambiguity they latch on to the only other available piece of information – the Klee and Kandinsky category memberships – and then use this to make sense of the situation. Once that particular (and only) classification has been adopted the inevitable category differentiation occurs, and occurs in the only way possible here: by allocating different amounts to ingroup and outgroup recipients. That is why it is so significant that subjects often seem to be as concerned with maximizing the differences between the categories as they are with favouring the ingroup in an absolute fashion. Here at a socially meaningful behavioural level is apparently the same phenomenon that can be observed in physical and social judgements.

This is an important conclusion because it suggests that at least some of the origins of prejudice are to be found in the operation of a normal cognitive process. This idea of prejudice as essentially normal or ordinary is, of course, in marked contrast to the approaches considered in chapter 2 where the emphasis was much more on prejudice as a deviant or pathological syndrome. As I argued there, the personality perspective, while potentially useful to explain prejudice in some of its more extreme forms, was limited precisely because of its inability to account for its more common-or-garden everyday manifestation. However, let me hasten to add, this recognition of the 'ordinariness' of prejudice should not lead us too quickly to assume its inevitability. Whilst it is true that the world is replete with categories of different kinds – men and women, employed and unemployed, old and young, Black and White – as we shall see later, there are still complex issues to unravel in ascertaining which of these categories will come into play when; and what happens when different category systems operate simultaneously.

Crossed categorizations

I have a friend who works in a Canadian university. Naturally she has both male and (though rather fewer) female colleagues. As in many Canadian public institutions, both English and French may be used in the teaching and administration of the university and, in fact, both anglophones and francophones[3] work there. Let us imagine a hypothetical committee of academics at this university evaluating some job applications for a research position. The composition of this committee, let us assume not too implausibly, is almost entirely male anglophones. How, we may ask ourselves, might they react were they to be confronted with a succession of candidates, some of whom were anglophones, some of whom were francophones, some male and some female?

In due course I shall present some empirical data which we collected to answer just such a question as this, but let us first analyse this situation theoretically from what we know of the operation of categorization processes. As we saw in the previous section, we should expect an enhancement of the between-category differences and a diminution of the within-category differences. Doise (1976) has argued that in the case where two categories cut across one another (in our example, gender and language preference) any differentiation in terms of the original categories will be reduced because of the simultaneous operation of the between- and within-category effects on both dimensions. As figure 3.1 illustrates, the differentiation and assimilation processes should effectively cancel each other out and the end result should be lessened, or perhaps even completely abolished, bias in terms of gender or language.

There is a good deal of evidence which supports this hypothesis. Social anthropologists, for example, have often noted how societies which are characterized by cross-cutting kinship and tribal systems seem to be less prone to internal feuding than those with a more pyramidal structure. Gluckman's (1956) analysis of the Nuer people from the Sudan illustrates this well. Drawing on Evans-Pritchard's (1940) famous ethnographic data, Gluckman shows how the Nuer's kinship system reduces the likelihood of severe intergroup conflict. For example, marriage rules prohibit intermarriage with any relative closer than seven generations distant, thus effectively requiring people to marry outside their immediate community. Such exogenous marriage conventions create a complex web of loyalties between neighbouring groups, since any village is likely to contain relatives by marriage. Of course, not all is perfectly harmonious. Gluckman notes that while cross-cutting structures may alleviate *internal* tensions, they can heighten aggression towards 'real' outsiders (those with no kinship ties at all). Thus, Nuer rules of warfare carefully constrain the kinds of weapons and limits of violence between tribes, but contain no such prescriptions where 'foreigners' are concerned. Quantitative analyses comparing 'matrilocal' societies (such as the Nuer) with other types of arrangement confirm this correlation between crossed categorizations, internal cohesion, and external aggression (LeVine and Campbell, 1972).

The first attempts to examine this same idea experimentally told a similar story. In one study, Deschamps and Doise (1978) asked some teenage girls to rate 'young people' and 'adults', and 'males' and 'females' on a number of stereotype traits. Half rated these as dichotomous pairs.

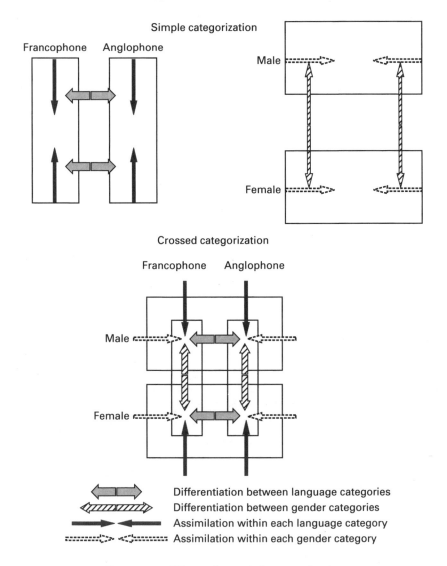

Figure 3.1 Effect of crossed categorizations

This was the Simple Categorization condition. The remainder rated the categories in conjunction: 'young females', 'male adults', and so on. This was the Crossed Categorization condition. In the latter the perceived differences between both the age and the gender categories were consistently smaller than in the Simple case. An even more dramatic result emerged from a second study. Here young girls and boys worked on a number of games. In the Simple condition they were seated around a rectangular table such that the boys occupied two sides, the girls the other two sides. In the Crossed condition, before starting the games the boys on one side of the table and the girls on the adjacent side were given red pens, and the other boys and girls given blue pens, the experimenter casually remarking that now 'we have a group of Blues and a group of Reds'. The children's estimations of each other's performance were radically altered by this intervention. In the Simple condition both boys and girls believed that their own gender had performed better than the other; in the Crossed case, however, this gender bias completely disappeared. In fact, even those of the opposite gender *and* in the other colour group were rated as favourably as those in the same category on both criteria.

These experiments stimulated a number of others. Brown and Turner (1979) pointed out that the two categories employed in Deschamps and Doise's studies might not have been of equal significance. Using two artificial categories we found evidence of the maintenance of some bias in the partially overlapping case (that is, when one membership is shared but not the other). More importantly, in the completely non-overlapping case (that is, sharing neither category) the bias was magnified. It is fair to say that the former result has not generally been replicated, whilst the latter has. Perhaps the most definitive set of laboratory studies on the criss–cross effect has been done by Vanbeselaere (1991). Using two equally important categorizations he confirmed Deschamps and Doise's (1978) original findings that bias against those who share at least one category membership is virtually eliminated. However, in accord with Brown and Turner (1979), against those who share neither category the bias seems to increase (see also Diehl, 1990).

These laboratory findings are interesting because of their potential significance for policies aimed at reducing prejudice. They suggest that if we can arrange social situations so that at least two (and perhaps even more) categorical dimensions cut across one another then, in principle, the likelihood of persistent prejudice between groups along any one of those dimensions should be reduced. Unfortunately, in the world

Table 3.2 Effect of cross-cutting gender and ethnicity in Hong Kong

Ethnicity	Same-sex targets	Opposite-sex targets
Cantonese	3.2	2.5
Shanghai	3.0	2.4
American	2.8	2.2
Indian	2.5	1.9

(Scale 1–4)

Source: Brewer et al. (1987), table 1 (collapsing across boys and girls).

outside the laboratory such a neat panacea for prejudice is not always so effective.

In a study in Hong Kong, for instance, Brewer et al. (1987) asked some Cantonese boys and girls to express their liking for each of eight hypothetical peers. These 'stimulus' children were either male or female and were from one of four different ethnic groups: Cantonese (like themselves), Shanghai, American, and Indian. The children's responses showed two things very clearly (see table 3.2). First and foremost, they preferred those of their own gender. This was the strongest single effect in the data. They also showed a clear preference for the two Chinese groups over the other two, but this preference was slightly stronger when evaluating same-gender targets than opposite-gender targets. Brewer et al. interpreted their findings as showing that for these children gender assumed greater importance than ethnicity and that, unlike in Deschamps and Doise's (1978) laboratory experiment, the addition of the second (ethnic) dimension was not enough to eliminate that potent gender bias. Notice that even Cantonese (ingroup) children of the opposite gender are viewed no more favourably than Indian children of the same gender.

This tendency for one categorical dimension to dominate in real-life contexts was confirmed in a study conducted amongst Bangladeshi Muslims and Hindus (Hewstone et al., 1993). Here the cross-cutting categories were religion (Muslim vs. Hindu), nationality (Bangladeshi vs. Indian) and, in a second study, language use (Bengali vs. other languages). In the Hong Kong study gender had dominated; here it was religion. If people were seen as sharing the same religion they were always evaluated positively. If not, the ratings dropped sharply, no matter if they were of similar nationality or spoke the same language.

Across the border in India religious distinctions also tend to dominate. In the early 1990s there was significant civil unrest in several cities in India, sometimes sparked off by disputes over the ownership of particular religious sites. The nature of the religious prejudice under-lying this unrest is well caught in this extract from an interview with a middle-class Hindu Indian:

> To be honest, Muslims who stayed behind in India at the time of partition were riff-raff. There are exceptions, of course, but in general Indian Muslims are not very intelligent. The elite went to Pakistan. And in Bombay, Muslims are the underworld, the mafia, if you like. They are the gold smugglers, the drug dealers, the illegal currency, that sort of criminal thing. And they think of themselves as Muslims first and Indians second – never the other way round.   (Independent, 13 December 1992)

Similar sentiments were recorded, if somewhat less vividly, by Hagendoorn and Henke (1991) in their study of religious and caste/class attitudes in Northern India. Upper class/caste Muslims and Hindus tended to derogate those from a different religion, especially if they came from a lower-status group. However, the lower-status groups (of both religions) were much less affected by either religion or status and, indeed, seemed to show something more nearly resembling the original criss-cross effect observed in the laboratory.

These field studies serve as important reminders that which category dimension will assume pre-eminence in any situation is very dependent on particular local circumstances. In Northern Ireland, the Lebanon, and the Indian sub-continent religion is often crucial. Elsewhere, however, religion can pale into insignificance against other more powerful social divisions. The fact that Iranians and Iraqis share the same (Muslim) religion did not prevent them killing each other in large numbers in their war during the 1980s. In this case the national conflicts of military and territorial interests overrode any psychological affili-ations deriving from their shared religious category membership (see chapter 6).

Thus the complexities of intergroup situations in the real world, particularly where the groups are of different size or status and where they may be co-operatively or competitively interdependent, should lead us to be cautious about the efficacy of criss-cross arrangements for reducing prejudice. As one final illustration of this, let me return to the Canadian personnel selection situation with which I began this discussion. In the course of a survey of university academics we included a hypothetical scenario in which six candidates (described in brief curricula vitae) were applying for a research assistantship (Joly et al., 1993). The CVs had been carefully prepared: four equally good ones

Table 3.3 Effect of cross-cutting categories in a Canadian university: recommended payment rates for research assistant candidates

'Strong' candidates				'Weak' candidates	
Female anglo.	Male anglo.	Female franco.	Male franco.	Male anglo.	Male franco.
5.7	5.4	4.9	3.8	3.6	2.8

Notes:
1 Scale 1–7, where 1 = $19 per interview, 7 = $25 per interview
2 Summed across M, F, anglophone and francophone respondents
3 Amongst the 'strong' candidates both the anglo vs. franco and the male vs. female differences are significant

Source: Joly et al. (1993).

differing only in gender and language preference, and two obviously inferior ones, both from men, one anglophone, one francophone. Our respondents, who also included both male and female anglophones and francophones, were asked to indicate their recommendation for a payment rate for these six candidates. Not surprisingly, the two weaker candidates were generally allocated lower salaries (see table 3.3). However, amongst the 'good' candidates there was some evidence of bias against francophones even, it has to be said, from the francophones themselves! (Breaking table 3.3 down into different types of respondent did not produce a markedly different picture.) Once again, then, the presence of two cross-cutting categories did little to diminish the historically rooted perception of francophones as a lower status group. In addition, and perhaps somewhat surprisingly, the female candidates fared slightly better than the male candidates, though this gender bias was less strong than the language bias.

Perceived intragroup homogeneity

The two fundamental effects of categorization are the exaggeration of intergroup differences and the enhancement of intragroup similarities. As the study of these effects was extended to a wider range of settings, particularly those involving the categorization of people, it became clear that they were not symmetrical; there were consistent differences in how the ingroup and the outgroup were perceived. In this section I want to focus on assymetries in the second effect: the assimilation of within-category differences, or perceived intragroup homogeneity.

Everyday observation suggests that if there is a bias in the perception of intragroup homogeneity it is in the direction of seeing the outgroup as more homogeneous, more alike one another, than the ingroup: 'they are all alike, *we* are all different'. Here is John Motson, a well-known (White) football commentator making a revealing remark during a newspaper interview:

> 'There's a nice ginger-haired boy there', he said pointing to the Brighton full back. 'Pity he's not playing in the final. Very easy to identify. Actually I'm glad Brighton aren't in the final. The three black lads up front would be very difficult to distinguish. *Though perhaps, I shouldn't say that.*' (*Independent*, 5 May 1992; my emphasis)

Hamilton and Bishop (1976) observed something similar in the White residents they interviewed in neighbourhoods in Connecticut into which a new family, which might have been Black or White, had recently moved. The respondents were more likely to mention the arrival of the new family if it were Black than if it were White. However, despite this greater awareness they seemed to know less about the new Black families. After one month only 11 per cent knew their last name compared to 60 per cent knowing the name of the new White family. Apparently the Black families were continued to be seen in categorical terms, as Blacks, with little to distinguish them, whilst the White families were more individually perceived.

One of the first attempts to study this phenomenon systematically was by Jones et al. (1981) who asked members of university clubs to rate members of their own club as to how similar they were on a number of trait dimensions. The exercise was repeated for the members of other clubs. Jones et al. found a consistent tendency for members of outgroups to be seen as more similar to one another than members of the ingroup. Similar results have been obtained in several other studies (see Quattrone, 1986). For instance, Linville et al. (1989), using more complex measures of perceived variability, found that members of an elderly persons' home and a younger student group each rated the other age group as more homogeneous than their own.

What is the explanation for this outgroup homogeneity effect (as it is known)? One view is that it stems from the different amount of information we have about ingroup and outgroup members (Linville et al., 1989). We usually know more individuals in our own group, we may interact with them more often and, as a result, be more aware of the differences among them. Members of the outgroup, on the other hand, because they are less well known are likely to be seen in a more global and undifferentiated fashion. This model, then, stresses the importance of differential familiarity with members of ingroups and outgroups. A second model adopts a slightly different perspective, suggesting that it is not information about a number of specific exemplars which is important, but the nature of the category as a whole (Park et al., 1991). According to this view, people hold in their heads, not a tally of specific ingroup or outgroup people known, but more abstract conceptions of the categories as a whole, modelled on the prototypical member of each and some estimate of the variability around this typical person. The reason that the ingroup may be seen as more variable is that the conception of that category is both more important (because it contains the self), more concrete (again because we have at least one case very well known to us), and more provisional (because of a presumed greater motivation to form an accurate impression about those close to us psychologically).

Although intuitively plausible, the first view – call it the familiarity hypothesis – does not have much empirical support. Linville et al. (1989) did find that over the period of a semester members of a university course rated their fellow class-mates as increasingly more variable, and then demonstrated in a computer simulation that greater perceived variability can be associated with changes in familiarity. However, these findings stand against a number of other studies which have either found no effects for familiarity, or even an inverse correlation. For example, in the Jones et al. (1981) study above, there was no association between the number of members known in each group and the estimates of that group's variability. Another problem for the familiarity hypothesis is that the outgroup homogeneity effect can still be observed in minimal group situations where there is equal and near zero information about both the ingroup and the outgroup because the groups concerned are anonymous (Wilder, 1984a). Even more problematic is evidence from some recent research of ours which examined variability judgements during the process of group formation (Brown and Wootton-Millward, 1993). We studied groups of student nurses over a year of their training. These groups were small (typically less than 20 in each) and their members had extensive daily face-to-face contact with one another. If Linville et al. are right, the greater mutual acquaintanceship afforded by this experience should have led to enhanced perceived variability within the ingroup over time, and thus a more pronounced outgroup homogeneity effect. In fact, there was *no* consistent tendency towards greater perceived ingroup variability over time and, still worse for the familiarity hypothesis, on at least two judgemental dimensions it was the ingroup, and not the outgroup, which was seen as more homogeneous.

In fact, this last finding was only the latest in a series of studies which have shown that the outgroup homogeneity effect is far from the universal feature of intergroup perception that it is sometimes claimed to be (Simon, 1992a). Curiously enough, one of the first – and often overlooked – studies of perceived homogeneity also found evidence of *ingroup* homogeneity (Stephan, 1977). Stephan studied the mutual perceptions of Black, White and Chicano school children in the South-West of the USA. Contrary to the many studies which came after, Stephan found that all three groups saw their own group in less differentiated terms than the other two groups. Noting that at least two of the groups in Stephan's study were minorities, we speculated that an ingroup's size relative to other groups might be an important factor in determining whether ingroup or outgroup homogeneity would be observed (Simon and Brown, 1987). Perhaps, we thought, where an ingroup is in the minority it may feel its identity to be under threat from the larger majority group. One response to such a threat might be a greater need to protect the cohesion and integrity of the ingroup by seeing it in more homogeneous terms, a kind of psychological closing of ranks. Using a minimal group paradigm we independently varied the size of both the ingroup and the outgroup and discovered, as we had expected, that those who found themselves in a relatively smaller group showed clear ingroup homogeneity; those in the non-minority groups showed the usual outgroup homogeneity effect (see figure 3.2). Two further details from the experiment confirmed our suspicion that people's identities might be involved in this reversal. One was the data from the control conditions in which exactly the same judgements were made but with one crucial difference – the subjects were not themselves allocated to a group and hence were acting as neutral 'observers'. These subjects showed no tendency to see smaller groups as more homogeneous, thus ruling out the possibility that our results could be explained as simply an effect of group size (see also Bartsch and Judd, 1993). A second and clinching point was the finding that those in the minority groups identified more strongly with their ingroup than members of larger groups.

The discovery that minority groups typically display ingroup homogeneity has been confirmed in several other studies both inside and outside the laboratory (Mullen and Hu, 1989; Simon, 1992a). Two examples will suffice here. One comes from an educational setting and exploits the fact that in most universities women form a distinctive minority (in this case being outnumbered by about 8:1; Brown and Smith, 1989). Judgements from male and female staff in the British university studied replicated the earlier Simon and Brown (1987) finding: men (the majority) showed outgroup homogeneity, women showed ingroup homogeneity. Similarly, in a study of heterosexual and homosexual men it was found that the latter saw their fellow gays as more similar to one another than the majority outgroup. Heterosexuals, on the other hand, generally showed outgroup homogeneity (Simon et al., 1991.) In neither of these two studies was there any consistent relationship between the number of group members' known and perceived homogeneity, once again contradicting the familiarity hypothesis.

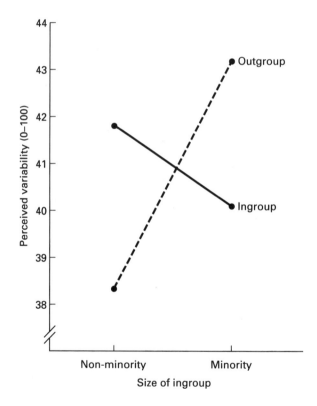

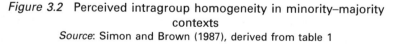

Figure 3.2 Perceived intragroup homogeneity in minority–majority contexts
Source: Simon and Brown (1987), derived from table 1

We have seen, then, that people's direct knowledge of ingroup and outgroup members cannot satisfactorily explain these differences in perceptions of intragroup homogeneity. Moreover, the existence of *ingroup* homogeneity in certain intergroup contexts also raises problems for the second explanation which posits more abstract conceptions of ingroup and outgroup (Park et al., 1991). What other explanations might there be? One clue comes from that finding in the Simon and Brown (1987) experiment that identity was more important for minority group members. Turner et al. (1987) have suggested that the process of identifying with a group involves the simultaneous operation of two processes: the matching of oneself to what are seen as the key defining, or 'criterial', attributes of the ingroup prototype, and the maximizing of the distance between this and the outgroup prototype. It is the first process which is of interest here. To the extent that people strive to make themselves more similar to some idealized conception of what a 'good ingroup member' should be, this will tend to induce an enhanced perception of ingroup similarity – at least along certain dimensions.

The dimensional specificity of homogeneity perceptions is by now well established. Kelly (1989) in her study of British political parties found that party members saw their own party as more homogeneous on those issues central to their party's ideology, but as less homogeneous on more generalized criteria. Similarly, in our study of student nurses, we found ingroup homogeneity on nurse-relevant dimensions ('care and understanding', 'communication') but the opposite on criteria more relevant to the doctor outgroup (for example, 'professional independence') (Brown and Wootton-Millward, 1993). Both of these studies replicate the same basic pattern found in more controlled laboratory conditions (Simon, 1992b). All in all, therefore, it seems reasonable to suppose that an important factor contributing to asymmetries in group homogeneity perceptions are processes stemming from people's identities as members of certain groups and not others (see chapter 6).

Factors Governing Category Use

As we have seen, in most social situations there is more than just one categorical dimension available to participants. When I bring to mind a typical lecture class, for instance, I recall that it consists of roughly equal numbers of men and women; there is a majority of White British students and a sprinkling of people from various other ethnic and national minorities; most are between the ages of 18 and 21 but there is usually a handful of older students, often noticeable because they sit together; I remember, too, that not all are studying for psychology degrees since our courses are routinely taken by students from other disciplines; there may be a couple of my colleagues sitting in on the lecture as part of the new university appraisal system; finally there will be a diversity of different sartorial styles – an occasional jacket and tie, maybe a 'punk' or two, both making a striking contrast to the jeans and t-shirts worn by the more conventionally attired students. Which of these categories shall I be most likely to use as I give my lecture and what factors govern that choice?

The first point to note is that there are different *levels* of categorization, some more inclusive than others. In the example above, the most inclusive category would be 'student' or, perhaps, if I wished to include my colleagues and me, 'members of the university'. Several other categories would have been much less global and might consist of combinations or partitions of categories – for instance, 'mature psychology students'. According to Rosch (1978), when people categorize the physical world of objects they are most likely to use what she calls 'basic' level categories – for example, 'chairs' and 'tables' – rather than 'superordinate' or 'subordinate' levels (for example, 'furniture' or 'bar stool' respectively). Extending this argument to the social domain, Turner et al. (1987) suggest that, in general, the basic level for categorizing people is that of the social group, whatever that happens to be in any situation. The corresponding superordinate and subordinate levels are 'human being' and 'individual differences'.

Shortly I shall examine some of the factors that determine which of the available groupings are selected on any particular occasion but for now it is worth emphasizing that there is growing evidence that what constitutes commonly used basic social categories are often, in fact, not broad undifferentiated groups but, rather, sub-types within these. Brewer et al. (1981) asked (young) college students to sort some photographs into piles in any way they wished. The set of photographs contained various pictures of elderly people and some of people their own age. Analysis of the sorting strategies used by the students indicated that these typically did not comprise a simple 'old' versus 'young' dichotomy but were responsive to apparent sub-divisions within the elderly category (for example, 'senior citizen', 'elder statesmen'). As we shall see in chapter 5, this use of sub-sets of a larger category is also prevalent in younger children.

This tendency to use sub-types was confirmed by Stangor et al. (1992) using a less direct method. In their experiments they showed subjects a series of photographs of Black and White men and women. Associated with each photograph was a statement which that person had purportedly made. The subjects' job was subsequently to recall which statement had been made by whom. If they used either of the ethnic or gender categories to assist them in this memory task one would expect systematic confusion errors amongst members of the same category – for example, thinking that 'Mark' had said something which had, in fact, been attributed to 'David' – but fewer errors between different categories – for example, confusing 'Mark's' statement with 'Joan's'. The pattern of errors showed clearly that both principal categorizations were used (though gender more strongly than ethnicity), but they seemed to be used in conjunction to form sub-categories (for example, 'White women', 'Black men', and so on). This was revealed by the fact that the highest number of errors was made in the within-sex within-ethnicity combination, roughly twice as many as in the other combinations. This happened even when subjects were either implicitly or specifically instructed to pay attention to one of the categorical dimensions. There was one further interesting result from this research: more-prejudiced subjects (as determined by a pretest on a prejudice scale) were slightly more inclined to make within-ethnicity confusion errors than less-prejudiced subjects, suggesting that for the former ethnicity was a particularly important category. I shall return to this finding in a moment since it bears on the question of which categories are chosen when.

Knowing that people prefer to use more refined groupings than simply 'old' and 'young', 'Black' and 'White', does not in itself help us to predict which of the many possible ways of carving up the world will actually be chosen on a given occasion. To do this we need to know more about the people perceiving the situation (What are their habitual ways of seeing things? What are their needs and goals?), and more about the situation they are confronted with (What are the actual similarities and differences amongst the people in it? What happened immediately before which might have 'triggered' one set of categories rather than another?). These insights were provided by Bruner (1957) who suggested that the categories most likely to be used are those which are most 'accessible' to a person – this is short-hand for the first set of questions – and those which best 'fit' the stimuli he or she is faced with – the second set of questions (see also Higgins, 1989).

To illustrate these ideas of 'accessibility' and 'fit' let me return to my (not so) hypothetical classroom context. In that situation, as we saw, there are a multiplicity of categories and cues associated with them. As a teacher perhaps the most obvious thing I will do is to classify the room into 'students' and 'staff'. This division might be particularly likely on this occasion because I am uncomfortably aware of the presence of my two colleagues at the back of the room. Because I am being evaluated that day my self-awareness as a teacher and my need to perform well are especially salient to me. On other occasions, however, the student/staff division may be less useful to me. Perhaps in the usual run of things I am more attentive to national differences in the class, simultaneously monitoring the level of understanding amongst those for whom English is not their first language and the level of boredom amongst the native English speakers (should I go too slowly or repeat myself too often). I might make further divisions. In an earlier chapter I confessed my affinity for things and people Italian. This could lead me to identify the two or three students from Bologna amongst the larger group of foreign students, perhaps addressing an example or joke (in my bad Italian) in their direction. My habitual or 'chronic' interest in this domain makes that particular category especially likely to be used by me. Moreover, a remark of mine like that will probably draw my audience's attention to the same group division, even if only temporarily.

But whatever categories I bring with me to the classroom because of my idiosyncratic predispositions or temporary task goals, they will only be useful to me if they match the actual people in front of me in some way. It is thus rather unlikely that the categories Catholic and Protestant will be used. As far as I am aware, few of my students are religious and this particular categorization simply would not discriminate amongst them.[4] On the other hand, a categorization by gender or nationality does actually correspond to some real differences amongst the class members. Of course, some of these differences are more clear-cut than others. Campbell (1958) and Rosch (1978) have pointed out that most stimuli in our environment do not form themselves into perfectly defined groupings but nearly always have an element of approximation or 'fuzziness' about them. Campbell (1958), in particular, has identified some of the factors which seem to lead to discrete entities (that is, people) being seen as groups, a property he call 'entitativity'. These are common fate, similarity, and proximity. People who move around together or to whom similar things happen (common fate) can be said to form a category as much as, to use Campbell's example, the close spatial and temporal interdependence of the molecules of a stone lead to it being seen as a single object. Likewise, people who are similar to one another in some respects (for example, they speak the same language) are likely to be classified together. Those who are often physically near one another (proximity) – the mature students in my example – may also be regarded as a group for some purposes. In sum, there are some real physical, psychological, and cultural differences between people to which categories must correspond, even if only approximately, if they are to be functional for us.

'Accessibility' and 'fit' are not independent of one another. Since, as we shall see, which categories are most accessible can change from situation to situation this has implications for their 'fit' with real differences amongst those being perceived. Also, not all categories are psychologically equivalent to us: we are members of some and *not* members of others. Turner et al. (1987) have noted that this introduces an element of asymmetry into the accessibility X fit combination. According to Turner et al., the categorization which is more likely to be adopted in any situation is that which simultaneously minimizes the difference between self and the most prototypical member of the ingroup category and maximizes the difference between that proto-typical ingrouper and the prototypical outgroup member. This they have formalized into what they call the optimal 'metacontrast ratio', and the important point they stress is that it is not a fixed formula for the perceiver in any situation. If a different ingroup identity becomes salient for whatever reason, a different metacontrast ratio becomes operative. As we saw above when discussing accessibility, my identity in that class-room might switch from 'teacher' (vs. student) to 'English' (vs. 'foreign'), depending on immediate contextual needs and cues.

Let me now examine some of the empirical research which has investigated this question of the choice of categorization. First I deal with three features of the immediate situation which have been found to be important: the entitativity of potential category members, their perceptual distinctiveness, and the recent external evocation of a category. These are all directly relevant to the 'fit' component of Bruner's (1957) theory. Then I turn to the 'accessibility' component by considering some aspects of the perceiver which have also been found to determine category usage.

Category fit

As we have seen, Campbell (1958) suggested that the way people (as stimuli) actually stand in relation to one another influences whether they are perceived as members of the same group. One of the clearest demonstrations of this was provided by Gaertner et al. (1989) in a study investigating how ingroup bias can be reduced. Gaertner et al. reasoned that if members of two categories could be perceived as belonging to a single superordinate group or, alternatively, simply as separate individuals, then any ingroup bias associated with these categories would be reduced. Accordingly, in three different experimental conditions they sought either to maintain a two-group division, to subsume it in a larger category, or to eliminate group cues altogether. Using artificial group labels (different colour tags), six subjects were initially assigned to one of two groups and had to work together in those groups. The two groups were then brought together to work on a further task and the nature of this encounter was systematically varied. In the 'two-group' condition the members of the group sat opposite each other at a table, keeping their original group labels, and interacted mainly amongst each other with a view to winning a prize for the best single solution to the task. In contrast, in the 'one-group' condition the members of the two groups sat in alternate places around the table, devised a new group label for the larger entity formed by the joining of the groups, and worked with each other to win a prize for the best joint group solution to the task. And in the 'individual' condition each person sat at a separate table, was asked to think up an idiosyncratic name, and worked towards the best individual solution. Notice how this experimental manipulation incorporated all three of Campbell's (1958) criteria for entitativity: physical proximity (where they sat), similarity (the labels), and inter-dependence of fate (the reward outcomes). Table 3.4 shows how the manipulation affected subjects' perception of the situation. It is clear (from the percentages along the upper left to lower right diagonal) that it had a marked effect on the way subjects categorized each other. And, as expected, these altered perceptions also were associated with differences in ingroup bias, least being observed in the 'one-group' case, most in the 'two-group' condition. (I shall return to this experiment in chapter 8.)

Another situational factor which some have argued may determine which categories get cognitively 'triggered' is the perceptual distinctive-

Table 3.4 Situational effects on perceived entitativity (% of subjects in each condition choosing each cognitive representation of the situation)

	Experimental condition		
Cognitive representation	Two Group	One Group	Separate Individuals
Two groups	80.0	21.7	16.7
One group	18.9	71.7	15.8
Separate individuals	1.7	6.7	67.5

Source: Gaertner et al. (1989), table 1.

ness of certain people. Kanter (1977), for instance, has suggested that people who constitute a numerical minority in an organization can become the focus of attention from the majority. Kanter herself was particularly interested in how women were perceived and treated in predominantly male work situations. She describes how in one company, where women were outnumbered by 15:1, such 'token' representatives of the category 'woman' seemed to be easily noticed and were sometimes the object of exaggerated sex-role stereotyping from their male colleagues. Kanter's data were somewhat impressionistic but they were followed up by some experimental studies by Taylor and her colleagues (Taylor, 1981; Taylor et al., 1978). In these experiments subjects listened to a tape-recorded discussion of six people whose pictures were shown during the recording to coincide with their oral contributions. The composition of the group was systematically varied. In one experiment it consisted of one Black and five Whites, five Blacks and one White, or three of each (Taylor, 1981). In another, gender was the categorization variable and the group consisted of single-sex participants and all other possible sex ratios (Taylor et al., 1978). Both studies provided some, but not unequivocal, evidence of the cognitive drawing power of numerical distinctiveness. Taylor (1981) reports how memory for the solo Black person's contributions was better than for the Black people in the balanced 3 vs. 3 group. The 'solo' was also thought to be more influential than his counterparts in the balanced group though he was not seen in a particularly (Black) stereotypical fashion. Similarly, Taylor et al. (1978) found that 'solo' men and women were seen as more assertive than in a balanced group. However, they were not seen in more sex stereotyped ways – the relevant statistical interaction was non-significant – which would have been a more unambiguous indication that the gender category had been evoked.

A further investigation of the alleged distinctiveness of 'solos' was reported by Biernat and Vescio (1993). In two studies using the same paradigm as Taylor et al. (1978) with Black and White participants they found only ambiguous results for the hypothesized category distinctiveness of the 'solo' person. The pattern of memory errors seemed to indicate that the Black–White category was actually more likely to be evoked in the 'balanced' conditions since the difference between 'within-race' and 'between-race' errors – a key indicator of category usage – appeared to be greater there than in the 'solo' conditions (see Oakes, 1994; Biernat and Vescio, 1994). Indeed, in one of the experiments, one of the 'solo' conditions failed to show any reliable 'within' versus 'between' differences in recall errors. On the other hand, in those 'solo' conditions the lone Black person was more positively evaluated than the Blacks in the other conditions though, again, not especially along ethnic stereotypical lines.

Thus, it seems that just being in a minority is not a very reliable or potent source of distinctiveness. There are other sources, however. People with a physical disability or some visible bodily disfigurement often complain about how frequently they are stared at. One reason for this may be that for most people the sight of a disabled person may be a fairly novel event and this novelty may itself catch people's attention. So argued Langer et al. (1976) when they arranged for various photographs of disabled and non-disabled people to be displayed in a public foyer. They unobtrusively measured how long passers-by stopped and looked at the pictures and found that those of people with a physical disability (a woman in a leg brace or a hunch-backed man) were consistently looked at longer than those of non-disabled people.[5] In a follow-up study Langer et al. (1976) also found that subjects chose to sit further away from a physically disabled person than from a non-disabled person. This difference disappeared if they had had a prior opportunity to view the disabled person, thus presumably reducing her novelty for them.

It is not just the stimulus properties of the situation which can activate one category rather than another. If some event has occurred very recently which is evocative of a particular categorization then it is likely that subsequent events or situations will also be interpreted in terms of that same category system. Thus, if we see a news item alleging some racial harassment by the police, this heightens our sensitivity to ethnic issues in subsequent reports of police malpractice. We may be more ready to look for evidence of racial discrimination than had the prior report not come to our notice. In technical terms this is known as 'priming'. The powerful effects of priming were shown in two experiments by Skowronski et al. (1993). They studied the effects of two types of prime on people's recall and impressions of a person described in a short story. The primes used were adjectives or labels designed to evoke the category 'mentally handicapped', and hence to influence the judgements made about the person. One type of prime was adminis- tered covertly by having words like 'stupid' and 'dumb' embedded amongst a large number of neutral words shown to the subjects before they read the story. The other kind of prime was a much more overt label, 'mentally retarded', that was used to describe the character in the story. Because it was so much more obvious, this second type of prime might have been expected to elicit more socially desirable responses in the subjects than the covert one. Indeed, this is what happened. With the addition of explicit labels subjects tended to remember more items from the story that were stereotypically *incongruent* for mentally handicapped people and to evaluate the principal character more positively. With the more subtle primes, however, the effects generally went in the opposite direction: so long as there was no overt label, subjects recalled more stereotypical attributes about the person and generally evaluated him more negatively (see figure 3.3).

There is even some evidence that the activation of a category by a prime can occur below the level of conscious awareness. Devine (1989) presented subjects with various words that are stereotypically associated with the category Blacks (for example, 'niggers', 'lazy', 'athletic'), but she did so only very briefly by means of a tachistoscope. The exposure time was only 80 ms and each word was immediately 'masked' by a string of meaningless letters. Under such conditions it is virtually impossible to detect the words and, indeed, subsequent checks revealed that subjects could not recognize the primed words at better than chance levels. Some subjects were presented with a high proportion (80 per cent) of ethnically associated words, others a much lower proportion (20 per cent). Following this priming experience the subjects read a brief scenario in which a person performed some actions that could be interpreted as more or less hostile. They were asked to make some judgements about the person. Devine reported that those subjected to the higher proportion of ethnic primes rated the person significantly more negatively (for example, more hostile, unfriendly, and so on) than those exposed to only 20 per cent of ethnically associated primes. Devine concluded that in the more concentrated priming conditions the category 'Blacks' had been subconsciously activated and that this category was then used to interpret the ambiguous behaviour in the scenario in a manner consistent with the prevailing Black stereotype (that is, 'aggressive'). Devine had also pretested the subjects for their levels of prejudice but apparently this made little difference to their susceptibility to the priming stimuli.

However, there are now grounds for doubting this last finding as we have recently discovered in a series of experiments (Lepore and Brown, 1994a, b). High- and low-prejudice subjects reacted differently to both subliminally and supraliminally presented ethnic outgroup labels: the more-prejudiced subjects subsequently evaluating the target person more negatively, the less-prejudiced subjects rating him more positively (see also chapter 7).

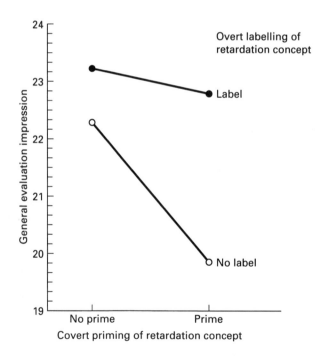

Figure 3.3 Effects of overt and covert primes on a social judgement
Source: Skowronski et al. (1993), figure 2

Category accessibility

If transitory situational factors can influence the categories which best 'fit' a given set of stimuli it is no less true that some attributes of the perceiver can also contribute to the ease or difficulty with which categories are accessed. Three in particular have been found to be important: the current task or goal of the person doing the categorizing, his/her ingroup–outgroup relationship to the target people, and the extent to which certain categories are chronically accessible for the person, either due to some personal or social needs or because of a specially high frequency of prior usage (Higgins, 1989).

The importance of task demands for category selection was demonstrated by Oakes and Turner (1986). Using the same paradigm as Taylor et al. (1978) that I described earlier, they showed how giving subjects certain instructions can override any distinctiveness properties associated with 'solo' stimuli. Like Taylor et al., Oakes and Turner varied the sex composition of a tape-recorded discussion group. Half the listeners were warned, as in Taylor et al.'s experiment, that they would be asked to describe just a single person; the remainder were told to concentrate on the group as a whole. In the latter conditions, reasoned Oakes and Turner, the sex category would be the most likely to be used, not in the 'solo' case, but in the 'balanced' (3M vs. 3F) groups where it would be a better fit for the task at hand. This, indeed, seemed to be the case. The evaluation of the same male target was more stereotyped in the 'balanced' than in the 'solo' conditions, implying that the sex category had been more readily accessed there. It is noteworthy that Biernat and Vescio (1993), in the experiment described earlier, used similar task instructions to Oakes and Turner and also found evidence of greater sex category usage in the balanced group conditions.

A further and more direct demonstration of the importance of the perceiver's task was provided by Stangor et al. (1992). Presented with a series of men and women, some dressed casually and some more formally, subjects' recall errors showed, as usual, that the sex category had been used (since many more 'within-sex' than 'between-sex' errors were made). Style of dress (formal vs. casual) was used as a secondary classification. However, when this same procedure was posed as a personnel selection task for choosing a 'media representative', the subjects used the dress style category significantly more. Nevertheless, there are limits to the extent that experimental instructions like this can influence people's use of categories. In the two other experiments by

Stangor et al. (1992) in which the most functional categorizations were ethnicity and sex, both very well learned and presumably habitually used categories, attempts to change subjects' category usage by direct instructions or indirect means (a prime) proved ineffectual. I shall return to this issue again shortly.

A second factor influencing category usage is the potential intergroup relationship of the target person to the perceiver. Here the issue is not which category system is likely to be used but into which category will the target person be placed – the perceiver's own, or another? Introducing this factor reminds us that *social* categorization is crucially different from the categorization of the physical world. For when we categorize in the social domain we ourselves are often implicated in the outcome in a way which is not true when we classify different kinds of fruit or pieces of furniture. Leyens and Yzerbyt (1992) have suggested that one consequence of group membership is that we can become especially vigilant about who else is classified with us; psychologically we find it easier to misclassify a real ingrouper as a member of an outgroup than to run the risk of 'letting in' a member of the outgroup. They call this the 'ingroup over-exclusion' effect and demonstrated it in an experiment conducted amongst French-speaking Walloon subjects in Belgium. In Belgium there has been a long history of tension between the Walloons and their Flemish-speaking compatriots. Setting their study in this Walloon–Flemish context, Leyens and Yzerbyt presented their subjects with profiles of a number of people. The way they did this was, for each target person, to present one piece of information at a time (to a maximum of ten items). The subjects were asked to stop the presentation whenever they felt they had enough information to classify the person as a Walloon. The information had been carefully pretested so as to be either positive or negative, and confirmatory or dis-confirmatory of the Walloon stereotype. Their results showed that subjects seemed to need consistently more confirmatory (and positive) information before classifying the target as a fellow Walloon than they did when the information was clearly disconfirming (and negative), which quickly led them to categorize the target as Flemish. This phenomenon was confirmed in another study using language as the categorical cue (Yzerbyt et al., in press). This time the Walloon subjects listened to Walloon- or Flemish-speakers reading sentences in both French and Flemish[6] and the key measure was how long they took to recognize the true identity of the speaker. Not surprisingly, they were quickest to classify a Walloon speaking French. However, they were much slower (by nearly half a second) to classify the same person when s/he spoke Flemish. The same difference was not apparent when classifying the Flemish outgroupers, whatever language they spoke. Once again, where there is any ambiguity about including a person as a member of the ingroup, the subjects seemed to be more reluctant to do so than when placing them into the outgroup.

The ingroup over-exclusion effect may only be visible under ambiguous conditions, however. Notice that in both the above studies the phenomenon was found when there was conflicting information (that is, traits confirmatory or not of the ingroup stereotype, people speaking the 'wrong' language). When the categorization task is more clear-cut such ingroup over-exclusion may not occur; indeed, one can even find the opposite. Such anyway might be the conclusion from Zarate and Smith's (1990) experiments in which subjects shown photographs of Black and White men and women simply had to respond 'yes' or 'no' to a categorization query (for example, 'does the label "woman" currently describe the photograph?'). In general, there was no ingroup over-exclusion observed for the ethnic stimuli since both Black *and* White subjects took longer to classify the Black photographs. For gender there seemed to be something of an ingroup over-inclusion effect because photographs of the same sex as the subjects were consistently categorized faster by gender than those of the opposite sex.

Thus far, we have considered some general factors which seem to affect the accessibility of categories. However, it is also the case that there are some people for whom a given categorization is perpetually or 'chronically' accessible. This is particularly likely to be the case for those with especially high prejudice levels; for such people almost any situation will be interpreted via their particular favoured categories (Lepore and Brown, 1994b). Evidence for this comes from a number of sources. Allport and Kramer (1946) presented equal numbers of photographs of Jewish and non-Jewish people to subjects who had been pretested on a measure of anti-Semitism. The more anti-Semitic subjects identified a greater number of photographs as Jewish than the less-prejudiced subjects, and were also more accurate. In our terms, ethnicity was a chronically accessible categorization for the prejudiced subjects and, as a consequence, they applied it more readily – and, it seems, more precisely – than the less-prejudiced subjects. This experiment has been replicated several times since, though not always with the same results (Tajfel, 1969b). Nevertheless, one consistent finding has been the tendency for more-prejudiced people to be more willing to classify people as belonging to the outgroup, even if sometimes erroneously. This is still further evidence of the ingroup over-exclusion effect.

This was most elegantly demonstrated by Quanty et al. (1975) who applied a signal detection analysis to the facial recognition paradigm. Like Allport and Kramer (1946), they asked high- and low-prejudiced people to classify photographs as Jewish or non-Jewish. In an interesting variation they then promised some of the subjects a financial reward either for correctly identifying Jewish faces or for correctly identifying non-Jewish faces. The remainder received no incentives for accuracy. Once again, high-prejudiced subjects classified more photographs as Jewish as revealed by their generally lower threshold criteria levels than the low-prejudiced subjects. Interestingly, only the latter group were affected by the different task incentives (see table 3.5). For them, the accessibility of the Jewish/non-Jewish category could be affected by different perceptual goals; for the more-prejudiced subjects apparently ethnicity was sufficiently chronically accessible as to be unaffected by such a temporary task set.

Another demonstration of chronic category accessibility was provided by Pettigrew et al. (1958). They ingeniously adapted a piece of equipment used for visual perception research, the stereoscope. This permits two images to be presented separately but simultaneously to each eye. Depending on the nature of the stimuli, the two pictures either fuse into an amalgam picture, or one picture dominates the other.

Table 3.5 Influence of temporary and chronic factors on use of a categorization: criterion levels (B') for classifying photographs as Jewish

		Task incentives	
Prejudice level	None	Identify Jewish	Identify non-Jewish
Low	0.39_a	-0.01_b	0.39_a
High	0.05_b	0.05_b	0.03_b

Note: Different subscripts significantly different, $p < 0.05$.

Source: Quanty et al. (1975), experiment 2.

Note: B' levels indicate the threshold for classification; the higher the number the less likely that photographs would be classified as Jewish.

Pettigrew et al. conducted their experiment in South Africa and used pictures which conformed to the four official ethnic group classifications defined by the ruling White government of the time: 'European', 'Indian', 'Coloured', and 'African'. The pictures were presented in pairs, either matching two faces from the same category or two from different categories. The subjects themselves were also drawn from the same four groups. Of particular interest were the White subjects because, it could be argued, they might have been particularly prone to categorize the world in a simple 'Black' vs. 'White' manner because of the greater salience – or, as we would say, 'accessibility' – of that division for those probably quite prejudiced people. There was some evidence of this greater ease of accessibility. Across all stimulus pairings White subjects were more likely to report seeing a 'European' or 'African' image than were the other three groups. In the pairing where the two images maximally conflicted (for example, 'European' and 'African') this difference between the Whites and the others became still more marked and most extreme of all amongst the Afrikaaner subjects who were traditionally more prejudiced than English-speaking Whites in South Africa. Parenthetically we can also note that this is a vivid illustration of the effects of a political ideology on social cognition. The apartheid system which proscribed by law the physical mixing of different ethnic groups seems here to have achieved a similar effect at a perceptual level: an inhibition of the 'mixing' of 'European' and 'African' photographic images.

It is not only ethnicity which can be chronically accessible. Stangor (1988) showed that gender, too, can be a more readily available category for some people than for others. Stangor first assessed people's general tendency to use gender concepts in the descriptions of others. On the basis of this, pretest subjects were classified as 'chronically accessible' for gender (or not). In a subsequent memory task in which male and female targets were seen to perform various behaviours there was clear evidence that the 'chronically accessible' subjects made more 'within-sex' than 'between-sex' recall errors than the less gender-prone subjects. (This anticipated a similar result in Stangor et al. (1992) described earlier (pp. 61), where, it will be recalled, ethnically prejudiced subjects made more 'within-race' errors than less-prejudiced subjects.) Similar effects on memory tasks involving gendered stimuli have been observed using degree of sex-typing as an index of chronic accessibility (Frable and Bem, 1985; Taylor and Falcone, 1982; although cf. Beauvois and Spence, 1987).

Categorization versus Belief Similarity as a Basis for Prejudice

The final issue to be considered in this chapter is whether we have not exaggerated the importance of categorization as the basis for different kinds of prejudice. Perhaps, after all, despite all the theory and evidence which I have discussed above, the perception of someone as belonging to a different group to ourselves matters less than some other factor in paving the way for negative intergroup attitudes and discrimination. Such was the claim of Rokeach (1960), who argued that the crucial 'other factor' was the degree of similarity or 'congruence' between our belief system and that of the other person. Following Festinger (1954), Rokeach believed that similarity of opinion between two people leads to mutual attraction because of the validation that such agreement provides. On the other hand, disagreement leads to dislike because of the threat to our belief system that is posed by that discord (see Brown, 1988, for a more extensive discussion of this perspective). Rokeach then extrapolated from this well-founded hypothesis and proposed that various group prejudices have less to do with people's memberships of those groups, and their associated norms, stereotypes, and intergroup relations, but are principally the result of 'belief incongruence', a perception that the people concerned hold belief systems incompatible with our own. To quote him directly, 'belief is more important than ethnic or racial membership as a determinant of social discrimination' (Rokeach, 1960, p. 135).

To test this idea Rokeach et al. (1960) devised an experimental paradigm in which group membership and belief congruence are independently varied. Thus, subjects typically have to express their liking for various people who are alleged to belong to either the same or a different group from themselves and who are also seen to hold similar or different beliefs. In a number of studies using this basic technique the belief factor usually emerges as a more powerful determinant of attitude than the categorical variable. Thus, White subjects will often say that they prefer a Black person with similar beliefs to a White person with dissimilar beliefs (for example, Byrne and Wong, 1962; Hendrick et al., 1971; Rokeach and Mezei, 1966; Rokeach et al., 1960). The exceptions to this conclusion appear to be for rather stronger measures of attraction (for example, desire to have a close friendship) where several studies have found that the category difference assumes greater importance than belief dissimilarity (Insko et al., 1983; Stein et al., 1965; Triandis and Davis, 1965).

Despite the empirical support for Rokeach's theory, there are several grounds for doubting whether it offers an adequate account of prejudice, at least in the strong form in which he originally formulated it. To begin with, we should note that the theory involves some sleight of hand in explaining the occurrence of any kind of intergroup prejudice. If it is the case, as Rokeach argued, that we dislike people (that is, are prejudiced against them) because we perceive them to hold different beliefs from us, why should we assume that members of outgroups hold those different beliefs? Surely, if social categories are unimportant, then our liking for a person should be on a case-by-case basis, decided by that person's similarity to us. There should be no *a priori* reason why a whole group of people (for example, Blacks if we happen to be White) should share the same beliefs. And yet, prejudice *is* manifestly patterned along categorical lines, as the dozens of examples we have already encountered in this book testify so clearly. Thus, for Rokeach's theory to hold water we need to add the extra and *category-based* assumption that members of another group are likely to believe in different things from us. In fact, there is some evidence that this is exactly what people do perceive, but, note, such a perception is first predicated on the psychological reality of the ingroup–outgroup category difference (Allen and Wilder, 1979; Wilder, 1984a).

A second difficulty with Rokeach's theory is that it is limited by an important qualification. From the beginning he wished to exempt from the belief-congruence explanation those situations in which the prejudice has become institutionalized by law or social custom, or where there exists significant social support for its expression. There, he conceded, people's respective group memberships would override belief congruence as the basis for prejudice (Rokeach, 1960, p. 164). Thus, for many of the most widespread and virulent manifestations of prejudice – against Blacks in South Africa and in many parts of Britain and the USA; between different religions in Northern Ireland, India and the Lebanon, and so on – it seems that Rokeach's theory is simply inapplicable.

A third criticism of the belief-congruence approach hinges on the typical experimental methodology used to substantiate it. I have presented this critique in more detail elsewhere (Brown, 1988; Brown and Turner, 1981) so here I will do no more than briefly reiterate the main argument. The central point of this critique is that the race-belief paradigm (as it has come to be known) does not usually present a proper intergroup situation to the experimental participants. Typically, subjects are confronted with a series of individuals (real or hypothetical) who just happen to endorse this or that set of beliefs and who, almost incidentally, share a category membership (or not) with the subject. In such circumstances, I have argued, it is little wonder that one of the major determinants of *interpersonal* attraction (that is, attitudinal or belief similarity) comes to the fore as the principal causal factor. On the other hand, where the group-like nature of the situation is given equal weight to considerations of interpersonal similarity, the evidence for Rokeach's theory is much less strong.

Perhaps the direct example of this comes from an experiment by Billig and Tajfel (1973) which employed variants of the minimal group paradigm I described earlier in the chapter. Their objective was to examine the effects on intergroup discrimination of different methods of group formation. In one condition the subjects were informed only that some recipients were more similar to them than others because they had preferred the same kind of painting in the pretest. There was no mention made of groups. This, therefore, constituted a 'pure' similarity condition. In a second condition, by contrast, there was no mention of any similarity; subjects were simply told that they had been assigned to two groups by the toss of a coin. This was a 'pure' categorization condition. In a third variant the first and second conditions were combined so that similarity of picture preferences formed the basis for categorization. Finally, in a control condition there was neither similarity nor categorization. The first two conditions are the critical ones. If Rokeach is correct, one would expect discrimination in the first and not the second. If, however, categorization does have an independent influence, then one would expect more discrimination in the second than the first. Table 3.6 summarizes the main results and it is clear that the latter interpretation received more support: in the two conditions where a categorization was present ingroup favouritism in the reward allocations was visible. The main effect of the similarity variable, although statistically significant, was much weaker than the categorization effect.

Other experiments using the minimal-group paradigm have also generated findings which are difficult to reconcile with belief-congruence theory. Allen and Wilder (1975) independently varied the similarity of the ingroup and the outgroup to the subject, apparently on the basis of artistic and political beliefs. Varying the perceived similarity of the outgroup had no effect on the level of intergroup discrimination;

Table 3.6 Categorization versus similarity as determinants of intergroup discrimination

	No categorization	*Categorization*
No similarity	−0.2	+2.0*
Similarity	+1.0	+3.9*

Note: Discrimination could range from −12 to +12, positive scores indicating ingroup favouritism. Asterisk indicates that score was significantly greater than zero.

Source: Billig and Tajfel (1973), figure 1.

subjects were as strongly biased against a 'dissimilar' outgroup as they were against a 'similar' outgroup. More problematic still were the findings from two experiments reported by Diehl (1988). In the first, Diehl varied the similarity between the individual subject and *one member* of the ingroup and of the outgroup. In this interpersonal situation there was some limited support from Rokeach's position since those who were similar were liked, regardless of group membership. Nevertheless, on the measure of discrimination (allocation of monetary rewards) the similarity of the outgroup had little effect on the amount of bias displayed. Then, in the second experiment, Diehl varied the extent of perceived similarity between *the groups as a whole*, thus reducing the interpersonal nature of the situation. In these conditions similarity had exactly the opposite effect to that predicted by Rokeach: there was more discrimination against the 'similar' outgroup than against the 'dissimilar' outgroup.

It seems clear, therefore, that the original form of Rokeach's (1960) hypothesis is not tenable as an explanation for prejudice. In situations in which group memberships are psychologically salient which, as I argued in chapter 1, are exactly those which are of most interest to students of prejudice, the idea that dissimilarity of beliefs is a more potent force than categorical differences simply cannot be sustained. Nevertheless, there is a weaker version of Rokeach's theory which may be more consistent with the evidence. In this form, some division into ingroup and outgroup is taken as read and what is then at issue is the effect of different degrees of intergroup similarity (Brown, 1984b). Do people typically display less prejudice against outgroups which are seen as endorsing similar attitudes to those which prevail in the ingroup than against outgroups which seem to believe in quite different things? The answer to this question is, I believe, a qualified 'yes'. However, to understand how I arrive at this conclusion requires some consideration of the consequences of group membership for a person's social identity. Since this is not treated until chapter 6, I shall postpone further discussion of the alternative form of Rokeach's theory until then.

Summary

1. A fundamental aspect of human cognition is people's need and ability to categorize the world. This arises because of the enormous amount and complexity of information with which we have to deal. This is as true of the social world as it is of the physical world. Associated with this simplification function of categorization are a number of biases and other outcomes which have important implications for under-standing prejudice and how it can be reduced.
2. One direct outcome of categorization is a cognitive accentu-ation of differences between categories and a diminution of the difference within categories. These differentiation and assimilation processes have been shown to affect intergroup perceptions, attitudes, and behavioural discrimination.
3. When two or more systems of categorization operate simul-taneously the effect can be to reduce the biases associated with any one of the categorizations in isolation. This is most evident in laboratory settings. In naturalistic contexts often one categorization will dominate over the other(s).
4. Once a given categorization comes into play differences within groups are attenuated. This is usually not a sym-metrical process – some groups may be seen as more homogeneous than others. Often the outgroup is seen as more homogeneous although in certain intergroup contexts – particularly those involving minorities – and along value discussions central to a group's identity, the reverse is observed.
5. The adoption of a particular categorization in a given situation depends upon the ease of its cognitive *accessibility* to the person concerned and the degree of *fit* between that

category system and the actual differences and similarities between people in that situation. Factors affecting accessibility and fit include the person's needs, goals and habitual dispositions, and features of the stimuli such as visibility, proximity, and interdependence.

6. Some have claimed that categorical differences are less important basis for prejudice than perceived differences in beliefs. This claim is only tenable in those situations where group memberships are not psychologically salient. Otherwise, the evidence shows that categorization factors are more important than interpersonal difference in belief. A more limited role for belief dissimilarity at the intergroup level is, however, possible.

Further Reading

Diehl, M. (1990) The minimal group paradigm: theoretical explanations and empirical findings, in W. Stroebe, and M. Hewstone (eds) *European Review of Social Psychology*, vol. 1. Chichester: John Wiley.

Doise, W. (1976) *L'Articulation psychosociologique et les relations entre groupes*, pt II. Brussels: A. de Boeck. Also in English as *Groups and Individuals* (1978). Cambridge: Cambridge University Press.

Fiske, S. and Taylor, S. (1991) *Social Cognition*, 2nd edn, ch. 7. New York: McGraw-Hill.

Tajfel, H. (1981) *Human Groups and Social Categories*, chs 4–6. Cambridge: Cambridge University Press.

Wilder, D. (1986) Social categorization: implications for creation and reduction of intergroup bias, in Berkowitz, L. (ed.) *Advances in Experimental Social Psychology*, vol. 19. New York: Academic Press.

Notes

1. This is but one of a variety of different procedures which have been used for allocating people to groups. Others include: musical preferences (Brown and Deschamps, 1980–1), dot estimation tasks (Tajfel et al., 1971), and even, most minimally of all, the simple toss of a coin (Billig and Tajfel, 1973).

2. The techniques for scoring these matrices and the various measures which can be derived from them are described by Bourhis et al. (1994).

3.   The terms 'anglophone' and 'francophone' refer to people whose preferred language is English and French respectively.

4.   Of course, if I am giving the lecture in Northern Ireland the same dichotomy might be much more functional!

5.   This difference was eliminated in one experiment by making the passers-by aware that they were being observed. Apparently, then, the 'attention grabbing' properties of novelty can be easily counteracted by social desirability factors.

6.   According to Yzerbyt et al. (1995) this paradigm was inspired by a significant event in Belgian history. Apparently, in the middle ages there was a Flemish rebellion against the French, and as a method for detecting French spies, the Flemish rebels asked strangers to pronounce two Flemish words. Those who failed to pronounce them correctly were instantly killed, a rather macabre example of the 'ingroup over-exclusion effect'.

Stereotyping and Prejudice

4 Traditional roles

Men and women's occupation of different social roles provides a 'kernel of truth' for conventional gender stereotypes.

The observation in the last chapter that perceived differences amongst members of the same category often become blurred leads naturally to a phenomenon at the heart of the study of prejudice, that of stereotyping. To stereotype someone is to attribute to that person some characteristics which are seen to be shared by all or most of his or her fellow group members. A stereotype is, in other words, an inference drawn from the assignment of a person to a particular category. Despite its popularity in everyday and scientific usage the word 'stereotype' has a curious origin. It actually derives from an aspect of the printing process in which a mould is made so as to duplicate patterns or pictures on to the page. It was Lippmann (1922), a political journalist, who first saw the aptness of the term to describe how people use cognitive moulds to reproduce images of people or events in their minds – the 'pictures in our heads' as he called them (Lippmann, 1922, p. 4).

In any discussion of stereotypes three questions invariably arise: Where do they come from? How do they operate and with what effects? How can they be changed? Accordingly, I have organized this chapter around these same three themes. Because we are interested in the implications of stereotyping processes for prejudice I shall naturally concentrate mainly on unfavourable group stereotypes. But this is by no means a universal feature of them. Just as the categories on which they are based are not, in themselves, positive or negative, so too it is perfectly possible for stereotypes to have positive, negative or even neutral overtones.

Origins of Stereotypes

During the height of the debate over the Maastricht Treaty and the future of the European Community in 1992 a student of mine gave me a cartoon cut from a German newspaper. Surrounding the circle of twelve stars (the logo of the Community) there is the caption, '*Der perfekt Europäer ist . . .*' and then there are twelve images, each capturing or humorously contradicting some well-known national stereotype:

'*kocht . . . wie ein Engländer*' (cooks like the English), '*übt Selbstbe-herrschung . . . wie ein Italiener*' (is self-controlled like an Italian), '*humorvoll . . . wie ein Deutscher*' (has the humour of a German), and so on (*Lippische Landeszeitung*, 28 October, 1992). A few days later another newspaper reported the results of a cross-national survey conducted in six European countries. It recorded how the respondents viewed Germans as above average in the traits of 'hardworking', 'aggressive', 'ambitious', 'successful' and 'arrogant', but below average in 'humorous' and 'untrustworthy'. The British, on the other hand, were depicted as 'boring', 'arrogant', but 'humorous', whilst not faring so well in 'ambition' and 'hard work'. The latter defects were also perceived in Italians (together with 'untrustworthiness'), somewhat compensated for by their 'stylishness' and 'humour' (*The European*, 12–15 November, 1992). Such are some of the 'pictures in the heads' of late twentieth-century Europeans. Where do such images come from?

The simplest answer is that they are embedded in the culture in which we are raised and live, and that they are conveyed and reproduced in all the usual socio-cultural ways – through socialization in the family and at school, through repeated exposure to images in books, television and newspapers (just like those I have just quoted from). Allport (1954) was in no doubt that these were potent sources of prejudicial stereotypes, devoting no less than four chapters of his classic book to the societal socialization and perpetuation of prejudice. I shall examine some of these influences in the next chapter, but for now we can note that one of the strongest pieces of evidence for this socio-cultural view of the origins of stereotypes comes from their persistence over long periods of time. This was demonstrated by some research inspired by one of the earliest studies of ethnic and national stereotypes (Katz and Braly, 1933). Katz and Braly's technique was simple in the extreme. They asked their subjects (Princeton University students) to indicate for each of ten groups how many of a long list of attributes seemed 'typical' of the group in question. They found that for each group there were three or four adjectives which were ticked by a quarter or more of their respondents. In some cases there was remarkable consensus. For example, 78 per cent and 65 per cent respectively believed that Germans were 'scientifically minded' and 'industrious'; 84 per cent and 75 per cent rated Negroes as 'superstitious' and 'lazy'. Some 20 and then 40 years later the same procedure was used with subsequent cohorts of Princeton students (Karlins et al., 1969; Gilbert, 1951). The results from these follow-up studies simultaneously revealed evidence of change and stability in the endorsement of group stereotypes. The clearest sign of change was the greatly reduced consensuality of the most obviously negative stereotypes. For example, those percentages seeing Negroes as 'superstitious' and 'lazy' declined to 13 per cent and 26 per cent by 1967. There were also changes in the content and complexity of some stereotypes. Some previously dominant images were replaced by others and typically more traits were included in each group's stereotype. However, despite these changes, it was noteworthy how many of the same attributes recurred in the later studies. For example, the 'scientific/ industrious' German stereotype was still very much in evidence in 1967, with 47 per cent and 59 per cent respectively endorsing the two traits. Recall, too, that in the survey data with which I began this discussion 'hard-working' was still regarded as a typical German trait amongst Europeans in 1992. The persistence of these stereotypes over several generations seems most plausibly attributed to some process of socio-cultural transmission.

But what of the changes that Gilbert (1951) and Karlins et al. (1969) reported? As I shall show later in this chapter and elsewhere (chapter 6), there are good reasons why we should expect stereotypes to change in response to different intergroup situations or disconfirming informa-tion. However, one other obvious explanation for the changes observed in those Princeton studies is simply that the normative climate in American society changed over the years. Thus, what might have been socially acceptable to express publicly in the pre-war years – for example, 'Negroes are lazy' – became progressively less acceptable in the decades after the war which were marked by anti-discrimination legislation and desegregation social policies. Indeed, both Gilbert and Karlins et al. note anecdotally that some of their respondents resisted having to attribute traits wholesale to a group. Thus, we must leave open the possibility that at least some of the changes in group stereotypes recorded by these relatively simple techniques are attributable to social desirability factors rather than to internalized changes in attitude. I shall return to this issue in chapter 7.

A second explanation for the origin of stereotypes is that they derive, however tenuously, from some aspect of social reality. By this is not meant that any particular stereotype of an outgroup is in some way objectively 'true' in the sense of accurately describing that group's actual characteristics. Rather, the suggestion is that a group's culturally distinctive behaviour patterns or the particular socio-economic circum-stances in which it finds itself could provide the seed-bed in which certain stereotypical perceptions about it could readily flourish. This is sometimes known as the 'grain of truth' theory of the origin of stereotypes (Allport, 1954; Brewer and Campbell, 1976).

How might this work? Let us suppose that a given ethnic group occupies an economically disadvantaged position in society. It has poor wage levels, high unemployment, crowded and impoverished housing conditions, low levels of educational achievement, and shows similar deviations on other indices. It is not too difficult to see how these visible and objective indicators of a group's social position could rather easily get translated into perceptions of that group as 'poor', 'lazy', and 'stupid'. Given what we now know about the cognitive differentiation effects associated with categorization (see chapter 3), it is then but a short step to those attributes becoming exaggerated still further to form the full-blown stereotypes that constitute prejudice. Some evidence for this socio-economic basis for stereotypes was obtained by Brewer and Campbell (1976) in their ethnographic study of 30 ethnic groups in East Africa. One of the more economically developed of these groups, the Kikuyu tribe in Kenya, was consistently described by other groups in the area as 'intelligent' and 'progressive' or, less flatteringly, as 'pushy' and 'proud'.

A variation of this same theme explains the origins of stereotypes by reference to the over-representation of different groups in certain socially prescribed roles. Eagley and Steffen (1984) have argued rather convincingly that some gender stereotypes seem to derive more from the requirements of fulfilling the traditional feminine roles of 'home-maker' and 'caregiver' than from any inherent properties of women themselves. They showed this by demonstrating that the consensual stereotypes of women as being more 'kind', 'warm', and 'understanding' than men (but as less 'active', 'self-confident', and 'competitive') could be eliminated and even reversed if a woman was described as also being an employed person. Similarly, men were seen as just as interpersonally 'sensitive' as women if they were described as 'homemakers'. In a similar demonstration, Eagley and Wood (1982) showed how the common view of women as being more compliant than men stemmed from a perception of them as typically occupying subordinate status positions in employment settings. A woman described as a 'manager', on the other hand, was seen as just as independent as her male counterpart. It seems, therefore, that people draw inferences about men's and women's attributes by observing them in their typical roles. Note, too, that this role 'typicality' is not itself spurious; in most industrialized countries more women than men do actually have responsibility for child care and other domestic work, and if they work outside the home they are more likely to do so in jobs where they will be taking orders from men – as secretaries, nurses, and the like.

The fact that groups occupy very different positions in society, some having manifestly more wealth, power and privilege than others, suggests a third origin of stereotypes. This is that they can serve an ideological function, to justify – or to criticize – the status quo. For, to depict a deprived minority group as 'lazy' or 'stupid' helps to rationalize the social system which may have created that deprivation in the first place, and simultaneously endorses the dominant group's right to its privileged position (Devine and Sherman, 1992). This implies that stereotypes are rooted in the web of social relations between groups and do not derive solely or even mostly from the workings of our cognitive systems (Tajfel, 1981b). This viewpoint has been argued forcibly by Oakes et al. (1994) and it is one to which we return in chapter 6.

The fact that at least some of our stereotypes may have some distant basis in real – albeit illegitimate – differences between groups should not come as too much of a shock. A recurring theme of the previous chapter was that the human brain is rather adept at simplifying and making sense of the vast and complex array of social information confronting it. It would be rather surprising – and not a little discomforting – if all the inferences it allowed us to draw were completely at variance with reality. Nevertheless, it is not a perfect system and in those inferential processes biases and distortions do occur. I shall catalogue these in some detail in the next section but one such cognitive bias is of interest here because it points to a fourth origin of stereotypes.

Stereotypes as illusory correlations

The bias in question is a peculiar sensitivity we seem to have towards statistically infrequent events or attributes. Things which are less common than average or which happen only rarely seem to attract a disproportionate share of our attention and may be remembered more readily than more commonplace occurrences. The discovery that the psychological distinctiveness of infrequency could give rise to stereotyping was first made by Hamilton and Gifford (1976). Drawing on some earlier work of Chapman (1967) which reported that people over-estimated the degree of association between words which were paired together infrequently, Hamilton and Gifford presented to their subjects a number of sentences in which individuals belonging to one of two groups ('A' and 'B') were described as performing desirable or undesirable behaviours. In the stimuli there were always twice as many people in group 'A' as in group 'B' so the latter was a minority group. Similarly, desirable behaviours outnumbered undesirable behaviours by just over 2:1. The upper portion of table 4.1 shows that in the stimuli there was no correlation between group membership and the behaviours; the likelihood of a group B person performing an undesirable act was the same as a group A person. When asked to recall the frequency with which different behaviours had been performed by members of the two groups, the subjects were fairly accurate in assigning the positive behaviours but showed a consistent tendency to attribute too many of the less-frequent undesirable behaviours to the numerically smaller – and hence more distinctive – group B, and too few to group A (see lower half of table 4.1). In other words, they formed an 'illusory correlation' between group membership and undesirable behaviour. If we extrapolate this phenomenon outside the laboratory it suggests that in a predominantly White country people will more readily remember relatively rare anti-social behaviours (for example, physical assaults) committed by Blacks (the minority group) than they will the same acts perpetrated by Whites. In this way an incorrect stereotypical perception of a correlation between aggressiveness and skin colour could arise.

In this first demonstration of illusory correlation the stereotype formed of group B was a negative one because the undesirable attributes happened to be the infrequent ones. Of course, statistically speaking this need not be so and in a subsequent experiment Hamilton and Gifford (1976) confirmed that the same effect could be found with positive

Table 4.1 Statistical infrequency as a source of illusory correlation

	Group	
	A	B
Distribution of behaviours between two groups in the stimuli		
Desirable	18.0 (67%)	9.0 (33%)
Undesirable	8.0 (67%)	4.0 (33%)
Distribution of behaviours between two groups as perceived by subjects		
Desirable	17.5 (65%)	9.5 (35%)
Undesirable	5.8 (48%)	6.2 (52%)

Source: Hamilton and Gifford (1976), table 1.

attributes. Other studies, too, have replicated the effect in a variety of contexts suggesting that it is a fairly general phenomenon (see Hamilton and Sherman, 1989). In a study we conducted in a university setting, where 'women' and 'senior academic staff' were the two rare occurrences, we too found that people consistently over-estimated the number of senior women staff (Brown and Smith, 1989).

Nevertheless, despite these demonstrations that the illusory correlation effect can be observed for positive as well as for negative traits, thus suggesting the operation of some affectively neutral information processing bias, the phenomenon may not be quite so simple. Schaller and Maass (1989) pointed out that in most real-life settings people are not detached observers recording and recalling information about groups; typically they belong to one of the groups in question. Schaller and Maass argued that such group affiliations would motivate people to be more likely to perceive illusory correlations if these would result in a favourable stereotype of their group, but be less susceptible to the phenomenon if the ingroup stereotype would be unfavourable (for example, if one was a member of group B in table 4.1). In a series of experiments they showed this to be the case; the size of the perceived correlations could be predictably exaggerated or attenuated by the simple device of assigning subjects to one of the two groups in the usual experimental paradigm and varying the relative frequency of the desirable and undesirable traits (Schaller, 1991; Schaller and Maass, 1989).

In another experiment Stroessner et al. (1992) induced positive or negative mood states in their subjects prior to presenting them with the usual stimulus materials. They argued that the arousal of affect in this way would interfere with people's attentional processes so that they might be distracted from noticing the perceptually distinctive 'rare' behaviour undertaken by the minority group. The result, they predicted, would be a disruption of the normal illusory correlation effect. This was exactly what happened. Compared to 'control' conditions, where no unusual mood was induced, the size of the perceived correlations between minority group and infrequent behaviour was noticeably smaller in the two mood conditions, even though the subjects were no more accurate in their recall judgements. In other words, the emotionally aroused subjects made just as many errors in remembering which behaviours to attribute to which group, but these errors did not form the usual systematic illusory correlation pattern. Thus, the arousal of affect (whether positive or negative) may be able to inhibit the *formation* of a stereotype which is based on the biased processing of differentially frequent events or information. This is an interesting conclusion because, as we shall see shortly, once a stereotype is actually in place, being in a particularly good or bad mood may increase the likelihood of it being used.

So far I have presented the illusory correlation phenomenon as being caused by some psychological bias in favour of 'distinctive' stimuli, whether at the level of initial attention or subsequent recall. However, it is possible that neither of these two processes is involved and, moreover, that perceptual 'distinctiveness' does not underlie the bias at all. Fiedler (1991), for example, has proposed that the illusory correlation phenomenon can be more persuasively traced to the statistical properties of skewed contingency tables than to the alleged psychological distinctiveness of infrequency. In one experiment, Fiedler rearranged the usual presentation of stimuli so that some cells of the objective frequency table contained zeros. Despite the fact that these stimulus events could not have been psychologically distinctive (since they never actually occurred), subjects still overestimated their frequency.

A further challenge to conventional wisdom has been offered by McGarty et al. (1993). They have discovered that it is possible to obtain the illusory correlation effect *without first presenting the stimulus materials to the subjects*. All that is required, apparently, is to inform subjects *either* that there will be twice as many statements about group A as about group B *or* that half the statements will describe positive behaviours performed by group A. Then, when asked to attribute some behavioural sentences to group A or group B, the subjects display an illusory correlation effect at least as large, if not larger than, those obtained in the conventional recall paradigm (McGarty et al., 1993, experiment 1). This is puzzling indeed for the accepted explanation that is based on differential ease of attention or recall, for there were no stimuli to attend to or recall. McGarty et al. argue that what causes the illusory correlation effect is not, in fact, the 'distinctiveness' of one cell of the 2 × 2 contingency table; rather, it is a result of the subjects' categorization activity. What happens, they suggest, is that subjects use the group labels 'A' and 'B' to try to make sense of the stimuli. Since there is, in fact, a greater absolute number of positive statements associated with group A they form an initial hypothesis 'group A is good'. Then, through the usual process of trying to optimize the meta-contrast ratio between group A and group B (see chapter 3), they bias their attribution of statements to 'A' and 'B' so as to sharpen the differences between the two groups. According to this view, the formation of stereotypical associations between groups and attributes is a result of subjects' attempts to impose some order on the stimuli by categorization rather than an automatic property of the stimuli themselves.

Stereotypes in Use

Once a stereotype has been acquired what are its effects on people's judgements about the social world and, more important still, on their behaviour towards others? What factors seem to inhibit or encourage their use? To answer these questions I want first to examine the large literature which has been concerned with the expectancies and biases which have been observed to be associated with stereotypes. These include both overt judgements and perceptions, presumably made under conscious control, and more subtle effects which may occur even without our awareness. I shall also examine how the stereotypes we have of various groups – our own and others – are described in rather different linguistic forms. I then discuss some of the psychological and contextual factors which have been shown to lead to increased or reduced stereotype use. Many of these effects occur in people's heads – as biases in perception, cognition, memory or causal attribution – but it is also important to recognize that they have behavioural consequences too. As we shall see in the final part of this section, in everyday social situations the operation of stereotypes can have very real implications for those who are their targets.

Stereotypes and social judgements

A stereotype, whether prejudiced or not, is a cognitive association of a social category with certain characteristics. Most straightforwardly, then, we might expect that someone who possesses a stereotype about a group will, when encountering a particular individual from that group, attribute to that person the relevant stereotypical characteristics. On the basis of that attribution we might anticipate further consequences: the person concerned might be evaluated differently (consistent with the stereotype) and hence be judged to be a more or less suitable employee, tenant, or whatever.

The matter is a little more complicated than this, however. When we meet a real person we have at our disposal not just our preconceptions about their group membership but also information about the way they actually appear, dress, and behave which may not be consistent with the group stereotype. How do we integrate these different pieces of information? This was one of the questions which Locksley et al. (1980) set out to investigate. They presented their subjects with a transcript of a telephone conversation between two people, one of whom came across from his/her remarks as either decidedly assertive or as someone lacking in confidence. The sex of this target person was also varied. Subsequently the subjects were asked for their impression of the target's personality and to predict how they might behave in some other hypothetical situations. Locksley et al. reasoned that if the subjects' sex stereotypes were operative, their judgements of the target should be affected simply by switching the target's sex (it is a widely held stereotype that men are more assertive than women). Rather surprisingly, altering the alleged sex of the target had almost no effect whatsoever on the subjects' judgements of him/her. The overriding factor was the behaviour of the person implied by the telephone conversation: in the 'assertive' condition the person was subsequently rated as more assertive and more masculine, *irrespective of their sex*, and to be more passive and feminine in the 'passive' condition. In a subsequent experiment they again elicited judgements of assertiveness in different experimental conditions. In one, the only information available was the target's sex; in another some additional information was also provided but this had nothing at all to do with assertiveness; in the third, the additional information did refer to the target's assertiveness (or passivity). Again, the target's sex was varied. Consistent with the first experiment, Locksley et al. found that the sex label had no effect on judgements in that third condition. In the first two, however, the presumed sex of the target did influence judgements in the direction of the conventional stereotype. Locksley et al. optimistically concluded that in real situations where we have 'individuating' information about the person, 'social stereotypes may not exert as pervasive or powerful an effect on social judgements of individuals as has been traditionally assumed' (Locksley et al., 1980, p. 830).

However, there are several grounds for doubting the generality of this conclusion. First, the absence of stereotypical effects in Locksley et al.'s study may have been specific not only to the judgemental context they employed but also to the kind of measures they used. Nelson et al. (1990), for instance, found that people's estimates of heights of men and women portrayed in photographs were reliably influenced by the sex of the person depicted, even when there was no actual sex difference in height in the stimulus photographs themselves. Indeed, so powerful was this particular – and, at other times, usually rather accurate – stereotype that it persisted in experimental conditions where the researchers took pains to point out the absence of an overall sex difference in height in the stimuli and exhorted them to judge each photograph as an individual case even, in another condition, promising a substantial cash prize for the most accurate judge. In another experiment using a similar paradigm these authors also suggested that the apparent absence of a stereotype effect reported by Locksley et al. (1980) might have been due to different judgemental standards being employed for rating men and women (Biernat et al., 1991). They showed how the sex stereotype effect on height judgements could be eliminated by replacing an objective height judgement (in feet and inches) with the instruction to estimate the photographs *in comparison to others of the same sex*. It is possible that a similar within-sex subjective standard was used by subjects to estimate assertiveness in Locksley et al.'s experiment.

Secondly, Krueger and Rothbart (1988) point out that the absence of stereotypical effects in the Locksley et al. study might have been due to their pitting rather strong individuating information about the assertiveness of each person against the weaker information about assertiveness conveyed by the gender stereotype. It would be strange, indeed, if we did ignore very clear-cut information about people in forming impressions of them. However, if the relative potency, or what Krueger and Rothbart call the 'diagnosticity', of individuating and group stereotypical information is changed then we should find that their effects on judgements vary accordingly. They found that estimates of the aggressiveness of a target person, as derived from a brief behavioural description, of course correlated strongly with the content of that description (that is, whether it depicted more or less aggressive actions), but also varied according to the category label applied (for example, male versus female), particularly when the individuating information only weakly implied aggressiveness.

Finally, there are several studies which have clearly demonstrated how stereotypes do affect judgements even when information is available about the individual characteristics of the person being judged. Grant and Holmes (1981) presented Canadian subjects with mini-character sketches of a person whose nationality (as Chinese, Irish, or Somalian) was also evident. The portraits implied someone who was either somewhat like the Chinese stereotype ('scientific', 'ambitious') or like the Irish stereotype ('happy go lucky', 'talkative'). Grant and Holmes found that merely altering the presumed nationality of the person had a significant influence on the judgements made about him, even if the character sketches themselves had an even more powerful independent effect (Locksley et al., 1982). Glick et al. (1988) also found a reliable sex stereotyping effect in a more realistic personnel selection context. Business managers were asked about the likelihood of inviting a candidate for interview for certain jobs based on a brief curriculum vitae. The CV implied a predilection for traditionally masculine, feminine (or neutral) activities and independently identified the person as male or female. As expected, the individual characteristics of the applicants influenced the managers' views on the suitability of individuals for different jobs but so too did their sex: male applicants were more likely to be short-listed for a sales manager job and females for a dental receptionist position.

Perhaps most vividly of all, Darley and Gross (1983) found that social class stereotypes can influence people's judgements of children's academic performance. In their experiment subjects were first shown a videotape of a nine-year-old girl (called Hannah). This depicted her as either coming from a deprived working-class background or as enjoying a more privileged middle-class environment. This was designed to generate negative and positive expectancies respectively of her academic performance because of the well-known correlation between class and educational achievement. The impact of these stereotypical expectancies was assessed in two separate conditions: one in which no further information was available; the other in which a second tape was shown in which Hannah undertook some tests but which presented a rather ambiguous and inconsistent picture of her abilities. In all cases subjects were asked to predict Hannah's likely future performance in different academic domains. In the second condition subjects had some further and potentially individuating information, and so, if Locksley et al. (1980) are right, we should expect to find less impact of the social class stereotype amongst them. In fact, as figure 4.1 shows, exactly the opposite happened. Those who had access to the additional information contained in the second tape projected their class stereotypes on to Hannah's future performance more strongly than those who only ever saw the first tape. For the former subjects, 'middle-class' Hannah was estimated to achieve a whole grade point higher than 'working class' Hannah.

Darley and Gross (1983) concluded from their experiment that we do not use stereotypes in an undiscriminating or unthinking way; rather, stereotypes serve as tentative hypotheses for which we then seek out further information. Without that further information, as in the 'no

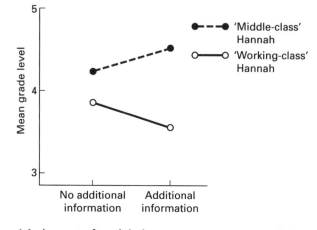

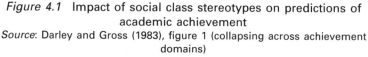

Figure 4.1 Impact of social class stereotypes on predictions of
academic achievement
Source: Darley and Gross (1983), figure 1 (collapsing across achievement
domains)

information' conditions of their experiment, we hesitate to apply them too firmly (see also Leyens et al., 1992, 1994).

The idea of stereotypes as 'hypotheses' about the world is an appealing one and in itself would not be a cause for concern. After all, some philosophers of science have long advocated that an optimal strategy for scientists is to derive hypotheses from their theories and then set about trying to falsify them by reference to empirical data (for example, Popper, 1963). What more could we ask of lay people going about their daily lives? Unfortunately, neither scientists nor ordinary people often follow such Popperian ideals. Instead of attempting to falsify their hypotheses it seems that people usually seek out information that will confirm them. This was observed some time ago in research on logical reasoning (Wason and Johnson-Laird, 1972). It turns out that in our social reasoning such confirmatory biases are also the norm (Snyder, 1981; Stangor and Ford, 1992).

One of the most compelling demonstrations of this phenomenon was by Snyder and Swann (1978). They led subject interviewers to believe that the person they were about to interview was an extravert or an introvert. Then, during the interview itself the subjects could select from a range of questions in order to discover whether the target person really did fit the designated personality type. Those holding the 'extravert' hypothesis systematically chose more questions likely to reveal extravert tendencies (for example, 'What would you do if you wanted to liven things up at a party?'); those holding the alternative hypothesis chose more questions indicative of introversion (for example, 'What factors make it hard for you to really open up to people?'). Such confirmation-seeking tendencies persisted even when, in another experiment, subjects were offered a substantial reward for the most accurate diagnosis. And, perhaps most disturbing of all, in a further study the interviewees themselves started to display the very extravert or introvert tendencies that their interviewers had been primed to expect, even though, of course, everyone (both interviewers and interviewees) had been randomly assigned to the different expectancy conditions. I shall return to this self-fulfilling characteristic of stereotypes shortly.

However, whilst stereotypical expectancies can often mislead us by biasing our search for and receptiveness to new information, they may also be very functional in allowing us to perceive some things more readily or, equally usefully, by freeing up cognitive resources to concentrate on other more pressing concerns. This renewed emphasis on the cognitive benefits of stereotyping has been given recent prominence in an ingenious series of studies by Macrae and his colleagues (Macrae et al., 1994a, b). In one experiment the task facing subjects was to recognize words as they became progressively less degraded by reducing the density of a covering mask. The set of words contained traits stereotypical (and, counter-balancingly, non-stereotypical) of two categories of social deviants: child abusers and soccer hooligans. Prior to the word-recognition task subjects were primed for one of these two categories by being asked to generate a list of characteristics of the typical abuser or hooligan. This prior procedure facilitated their subsequent recognition of the stimulus words that were stereotypical of their primed category (Macrae et al., 1994b). In other experiments it has been shown that the presence of an activated stereotype on one task permits an improved performance on a simultaneous task (Macrae et al., 1994a). A typical experimental procedure asks subjects to undertake an impression formation task (i.e. recalling as many attributes as possible about a variety of stimulus people) whilst *at the same time* monitoring some factual geographical information presented to them aurally. Half the subjects are given a category label alongside each stimulus person (and, of course, several of the attributes are stereotypical for that category); the remainder do not have this label. Macrae et al. argued that the presence of the category label would activate a stereotype which would mean that the relevant traits would be more readily assimilated. This then would allow them to concentrate better on the contemporaneous task. Indeed, this seemed to be the case. Those in the 'category label' condition recalled significantly more of the geographical information than those in the 'no label' conditions. This also happened in a second experiment even when the labels were presented subliminally.

Stereotypes influence not only our expectations for the future but they can bias our recall of the past as well. This was shown by Hamilton and Rose (1980) who presented subjects with a series of slides depicting some occupational groups (for example, stewardess, salesman) associated with some traits (for example, attractive, talkative). In the slides each trait appeared with each occupation exactly the same number of times. However, when asked to recall what they had seen, subjects erroneously remembered more stereotypical associations (for example, 'attractive stewardess') than non-stereotypical pairings (for example, 'attractive salesmen'). Information consistent with their occupational stereotypes was more readily remembered – even over-remembered – than inconsistent information. Although this finding fits well with the idea of stereotypes as hypotheses waiting to be confirmed, in one sense it is slightly counter-intuitive. One could argue that it is stereotype *inconsistent* information which should be recalled better because it is more distinctive and hence more likely to attract our attention (Wyer and Gordon, 1982). Recent reviews of the by now large literature on person memory have, in fact, found that in general there is a consistent memorial advantage for information which is incongruent with prior expectation (Rojahn and Pettigrew, 1992; Stangor and McMillan, 1992). However, a more careful examination of this body of work reveals that the better memory for inconsistent information is usually associated with memory for individuals and their associated attributes; when groups are the targets, people recall stereotype-consistent information better (Stangor and McMillan, 1992; but cf. Rojahn and Pettigrew (1992), who reached a slightly different conclusion). One reason for this individual–group difference could be that people may expect at least some individual variation within a group and hence the 'inconsistent' pieces of information can more easily be overlooked; within a single person, on the other hand, we may expect greater coherence and so any 'inconsistencies' are more remarkable (Fiske and Taylor, 1991).

The selective effects of group stereotypes on memory occur even in the most primitive conditions. Howard and Rothbart (1980) asked subjects to recall various statements about behaviours which had previously been associated with members of two experimentally created groups. The subjects themselves had been assigned to one of these two groups also. The behaviours to be recalled were both favourable and unfavourable and, of course, both types were exactly balanced between the two groups. However, the subjects' memories were not so well balanced. While they were equally good at recalling the group origin of the favourable behaviours, when it came to the unfavourable behaviours they were much better at recalling those associated with the outgroup than the ingroup (see figure 4.2). Just like the line from that old Simon and Garfunkel song, 'a man hears what he wants to hear and disregards the rest', it seems that having a few minutes' minimal psychological investment in a group is enough to bias what we remember about it. How much stronger would such an effect be with a lifetime's identification with a religious or ethnic group?

This experiment of Howard and Rothbart reminds us that the stereotypes we hold of different groups are often not evaluatively neutral but are biased in particular directions. Indeed, the central interest of stereotypes to students of prejudice is precisely because of this. There is now mounting evidence that such biases may be almost automatic in their operation; quite literally, we may not even need time to think to

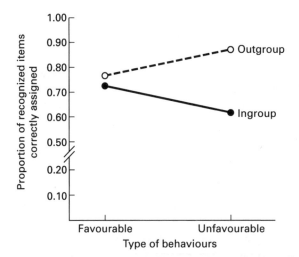

Figure 4.2 Selective recall for ingroup and outgroup information
Source: Howard and Rothbart (1980), figure 1

display some kinds of differential reaction to group-associated stimuli. The first hint that this might be so came from two experiments by Gaertner and McLaughlin (1983) which measured how long (White) subjects took to decide whether two strings of letters presented on a screen were real words. Some of them were actually nonsense syllables (for example, KUPOD, ZUMAP), but others were real words including BLACK, WHITE, three positive adjectives (for example, CLEAN), and three negative adjectives (for example, STUPID). The key question was how long subjects would take to acknowledge the pairing of BLACK and WHITE with these negative and positive words. In the event there was no difference in reaction time to the negative pairings with the ethnic labels, but real *positive* words associated with WHITE were responded to consistently faster than when they were associated with BLACK. Notice that the task was very easy: the subjects were not required to say that they endorsed any of the word pairings, only to identify them as real words or not. And this was easier when there was the familiar and psychologically comfortable association between the ingroup and things positive. This was subsequently confirmed by Dovidio et al. (1986) who again presented White subjects with the words BLACK and WHITE. This exposure lasted only a couple of seconds after which it was replaced by a second word, and subjects had to indicate if the second word 'could ever be true' of the group or was 'always false'. The subsequent words were positive or negative and more or less stereotypical for Blacks and Whites. In general there were faster reaction times to the stereotypically consistent pairing than to incon-sistent associations and, once again, White-positive pairings tended to elicit quicker responses than Black-positive pairings. To complete the picture, negative-White pairings showed up with longer latencies than negative-Black ones. A similar effect, using a slightly different pro-cedure, was observed by Lalonde and Gardner (1989) in a Canadian context, with the added twist that, in general, outgroup stereotype labels were applied more quickly than ingroup labels.

Perhaps most intriguing of all is a study by Perdue et al. (1990) which suggested that these differential associations of ingroup and outgroup with positive and negative attributes is both a rather generic cognitive tendency and one which may occur subconsciously. In their experiment they first presented some pronouns with ingroup or outgroup connota-tions (for example, 'we', 'us', 'they', and so on). But this time the exposure was so brief (55 ms) and immediately overwritten on the screen by another word that few would have been able to detect what had actually been presented. Now the subjects' task was simply to indicate quickly whether the second word was a positive or a negative description. Only that. The rather dramatic finding was that subjects' reaction times to make that decision were systematically affected by that first subliminally presented pronoun. As can be seen in figure 4.3, reaction times for positive words were noticeably faster when they had been primed by 'we' or 'us' than they were for negative words with the same primes. The subconscious priming of the implied outgroup labels had less effect, a finding confirmed in a subsequent experiment.

Stereotypes and social attributions

The idea of stereotypes as hypotheses about the characteristics of groups, albeit biased and confirmation-seeking hypotheses, suggests another important function that they serve, that of influencing people's explanations of social events (Tajfel, 1981b). Let us suppose we witness

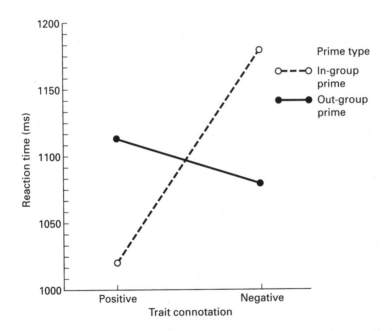

Figure 4.3 Reaction times for positive and negative words when preceded by subliminal ingroup/outgroup primes
Source: Perdue et al. (1990), figure 2

a Black person in the street giving someone a push. How should we interpret that action? Was it a friendly shove or was it more aggressively intended, a prelude to some more violent interchange? Further, should we infer that the perpetrator of the act consistently behaves like that or, alternatively, was provoked by some temporary situational factor? These, of course, are the classic questions with which attribution theory has been concerned, although not often from the standpoint of intergroup prejudice (see Hewstone, 1989, for an exception). What role might group stereotypes play in the attribution process? In the example above there is an obvious possibility: if, as is the case in Britain and the USA, one of the prevailing stereotypes of Black people is that they are aggressive, this might lead more readily to an interpretation of the action as hostile, perhaps deriving from a dispositional (that is, internal) tendency to get involved in fights.

This, anyway, was Duncan's (1976) hypothesis when he prepared two similar videotapes showing a heated argument between two men that culminated in one of them shoving the other. In half the tapes the perpetrator was Black, in the remainder he was White. The ethnicity of the victim was also varied. White observers of this scene, believing it to be a real exchange, were asked to interpret what had happened. In the versions with a Black perpetrator over 90 per cent of the subjects judged the action to be 'violent' or 'aggressive' and tended to attribute it to some internal cause; in the White perpetrator versions less than 40 per cent coded it as violent or aggressive and were more inclined to believe in some situational cause for the action. Similar, if slightly less startling, results were obtained by Sagar and Schofield (1980) when they presented some short vignettes to Black and White schoolchildren. The vignettes described a number of ambiguous dyadic interactions involving all combinations of Black and White 'instigator' and 'victim'. The consistent attribution, made by both Black and White children, was that the behaviour involving the Black instigator was more 'threatening' than the same behaviour by a White.

The influence of stereotypes on attributional judgements has been observed in other intergroup contexts. Macrae and Shepherd (1989) found that people's explanations for two criminal actions (assault and embezzlement) varied according to whether they were allegedly performed by a labourer or an accountant. In each case the action was attributed more internally if the criminal stereotypically fitted the crime (for example, the accountant embezzling) than if the two were inconsistent. In another study these same authors found that attributions for actions consistent with a group stereotype were made faster than those for actions which fitted less well, suggesting that less cognitive work was needed (Macrae and Shepherd, 1991). Finally, Furnham (1982) found that employed people were most likely to believe that those out of work do not try hard enough to get jobs or are unwilling to move to do so, an internal attribution consistent with the stereotype of the unemployed as lazy propagated by some popular newspapers and right-wing politicians. Not surprisingly, unemployed workers them-selves were more likely to attribute their plight externally (for example, to 'an influx of immigrants').

The fact that people on different sides of an intergroup divide often offer very different explanations for the same phenomenon was noted by Pettigrew (1979). Drawing on Ross's (1977) idea of the 'fundamental attribution error' in which people tend to assume internal causes for others' behaviour but external causes for their own, Pettigrew suggested that group members were susceptible to an 'ultimate attribution error'. The gist of this notion is that negative behaviours (for example, some aggressive action) by outgroup members will be seen as internally caused ('they are like that'), while the same behaviour from the ingroup will be justified with reference to some external cause ('we were provoked'). Positive behaviours will tend to be explained in just the opposite fashion: some charitable action by an ingroup person? ('obviously we are a generous lot'); the same action by a member of the outgroup renowned for its meanness? ('well, I guess there are exceptions to every rule').

Several studies have supported this hypothesis. Taylor and Jaggi (1974) presented Indian (Hindu) office workers with some scenarios in which a Hindu or Muslim behaved in a desirable or undesirable manner. When Hindus were depicted in a positive light the behaviour was mainly attributed internally; the same behaviour by Muslims was attributed externally. For negative behaviours the reverse occurred. A similar phenomenon was observed in Northern Ireland by Hunter et al. (1991). Catholics' and Protestants' explanations for various violent events in the region were the mirror image of one another, each attributing violent acts by their own group externally but outgroup aggression internally. Nevertheless, despite the commonness of this 'ultimate attribution error' effect, it is far from universal. Some research by Hewstone and his colleagues in Bangladesh and South-East Asia has revealed that such intergroup attribution biases may be most typical of dominant or majority groups (Hewstone and Ward, 1985; Islam and Hewstone, 1993). For example, Islam and Hewstone found that whilst Muslims (a majority group) in Bangladesh consistently attributed positive ingroup and negative outgroup outcomes more internally, the same was not true of the Hindu minority.

It is not just the content of causal attributions which may alter according to whether we are explaining positive or negative ingroup or outgroup behaviours; the very language we use may also change. Maass et al. (1989) asked members of rival quarters (*contrade*) of an Italian city to describe what was happening in some cartoons depicting members of their own and the other *contrada*. The studies were conducted in the weeks prior to an annual horse race involving intense competition between the *contrade*. When the descriptions were analysed linguistically it became apparent that positive ingroup behaviours were described using words more indicative of enduring dispositional states than were the same behaviours by outgroup members. The latter tended to be depicted in more concrete and situationally specific terms. For negative behaviours exactly the opposite occurred. A similar phenomenon was observed in newspaper reports of an anti-Semitic demonstration at an international basket-ball match between an Italian and an Israeli team (Maass et al., in press). Jewish newspapers' accounts of the demonstrators were more likely than non-Jewish reports to use more abstract descriptions implying some deeper-rooted and less-transitory explanation for the event. As Maass et al. (1989) point out, these linguistic biases in people's intergroup accounts may have important implications for stereotype maintenance and change. For, by their nature, more-abstract and general conceptions are typically quite resistant to modification in the light of new information, unlike very concrete representations which may be disconfirmed by a single or a few contrary instances. To the extent that positive ingroup and negative outgroup stereotypes veer in the direction of abstraction whilst negative ingroup and positive outgroup images are usually more concrete, the outlook for attempts to change mutually derogatory intergroup stereotypes does not seem very optimistic. I shall return to this issue of stereotype change in a later section.

Factors affecting stereotype activation and use

Thus far, we have considered the various ways that stereotypes influence our judgements or recollections of social situations. From the ease and frequency with which such influences have been observed it would be easy to conclude that, in any context in which social categories are psychologically available, stereotypes will come into play more or less automatically. Though plausible, such a conclusion may not quite do justice to the complexity of people's social cognitions. I want now to consider some of the factors which inhibit – or encourage – the reliance on stereotypic expectancies.

One such factor is the extent of our mental preoccupation with other concerns; what Gilbert and Hixon (1991) have called 'cognitive busyness'. Since one primary function of stereotypes is that they act as mental short-cuts to save us the trouble of having to investigate and apprehend each person we encounter in depth, one simple hypothesis is that the more we are distracted with some other cognitive task the more we will need to rely on those stereotypical short-cuts in our social judgements. This was Macrae et al.'s (1993) prediction when they showed their subjects a short videotape depicting a woman talking about her life-style and interests. Half the subjects believed the woman was a doctor, the remainder were told she was a hairdresser. In addition, some subjects were given a distracting task to perform (rehearsing and then recalling an eight-digit number); others were not. When asked to remember as much as they could about what the woman had said, the subjects with the additional mental task recalled more items which were consistent with her occupational stereotype than those which were not. They also rated her in more stereotypical terms. Those without the distracting task showed exactly the reverse pattern.

While these data perfectly support the notion of the stereotype as 'the (mental) sluggard's best friend' (Gilbert and Hixon, 1991, p. 509), there is one further wrinkle to the story. Gilbert and Hixon point out that cognitive busyness will lead to more stereotyping only if some appropriate category has actually been engaged; prior to this – let us say in the first few moments of an interaction – such cognitive distraction might actually prevent a stereotype being activated. In an elegant experiment they provided some evidence that this might be the case. The experiment began with an Asian or a White woman (depending on experimental condition) holding up cards on which some word fragments were printed (for example, POLI-E, N-P) and subjects had a few seconds to think of as many words as possible that the fragments could be. Half were distracted by having an eight-digit number to remember. The word completions revealed an intriguing pattern: when the stimuli were presented by the Asian confederate the *non-distracted* subjects were more likely to dream up words associated with the Asian stereotype (for example, 'polite', 'nip') than when the White confederate presented them. The distracted subjects, on the other hand, were unaffected by the ethnicity of the confederate. Then, in a second task, both groups of subjects listened to apparently the same confederate talking about her daily life and, again, half of each group were distracted by some other task during this monologue. In the subsequent ratings of the confederate only one sub-group of subjects rated the Asian confederate as more stereotypically Asian than the White confederate. This was the group who had initially not been distracted (thus allowing the stereotype to be *activated)* but who were distracted in the second phase (thus encouraging the stereotype to be *used*).

The result is reminiscent of the experiment by Stroessner et al. (1992) discussed earlier. It will be recalled that they observed that emotional arousal can disrupt stereotype formation, in their case by interfering with the perception of an illusory correlation. It turns out that emotions also play a rather important role in stereotype use, in an exactly analogous way to the effects of cognitive busyness. In short, when we are upset or anxious about something we are more likely to fall back on familiar, and hence readily available, stereotypes in our social perceptions. Stephan and Stephan (1985) were among the first to draw this to our attention. They pointed out that interactions between members of different groups can sometimes be anxiety-provoking affairs, whether because of pre-existing conflict between the protagonists or merely due to tension born out of ignorance, embarrassment and misperception. Drawing on the well-established research finding of the disruptive effects of emotion on information processing ability (Easterbrook, 1959), they suggested that encounters between members of different groups can become breeding grounds for the growth of stereotypical judgements. In support of this idea they found that in a sample of Hispanic college students those who reported more anxiety in dealing with interethnic interactions were also more likely to see the Anglo outgroup in more stereotypical terms.[1] Other studies of interethnic relations have underlined this important role that affect plays in intergroup situations. Dijker (1987) found that the anticipation of meetings with ethnic minority people was associated with feelings of anxiety and irritation in a sample of Dutch respondents. Similarly, contact between Hindus and Muslims in Bangladesh was found to be correlated with feelings of anxiety which, in turn, was associated with greater perceived outgroup homogeneity and negative outgroup attitudes (Islam and Hewstone, 1993). This apprehension, which can be associated with intergroup contact, has important implications for attempts to reduce prejudice, a point to which I return in chapter 8.

Laboratory studies, too, confirm how heightened emotionality can increase the likelihood of stereotypical judgement. Wilder and Shapiro

(1989a,b) used a variety of techniques to make their participants anxious – for example, leading them to believe that they would be required to be photographed in baby clothes or that they would shortly experience an uncomfortable electric shock.[2] Prior to this discomforting experience they viewed a tape of a discussion group which portrayed the majority behaving in a particular way, thus creating a temporary group stereotype. One member of the foursome always deviated from this normative position and it was the evaluation of this 'deviant' which was of interest to Wilder and Shapiro. Consistently this target person was rated more similar to his peers (that is, more in line with the group stereotype) by those observers who had been made anxious. The control subjects, who had escaped the anxiety induction, veridically saw the target as clearly differentiated from the rest of the group. Significantly from the perspective of intergroup contact policies, one effective way of reducing anxiety, and hence stereotyping, was by having subjects anticipate a co-operative (as opposed to a competitive) intergroup encounter (Wilder and Shapiro, 1989b; see chapter 8). Mackie et al. (1989) also found that mood states – both positive and negative – affected the stereotypical nature of people's recall judgements in a similar paradigm to that used by Hamilton and Rose (1980) and which I described earlier.

The extent to which people are cognitively or emotionally preoccupied is an incidental feature of social situations. To that extent such factors offer little promise for consciously altering people's reliance on prejudiced stereotypes in their judgements. However, there is a third factor which may affect the likelihood of stereotype use, and that is the degree to which they and the target of judgement are positively interdependent. Put less formally, if one person depends on another for the achievement of something they may be more inclined to look for information specific to that person and be less reliant on a group stereotype. Some preliminary – although, as yet, far from conclusive – evidence for this has been provided by Neuberg and Fiske (1987). They led subjects to believe that they would shortly be interacting with a former schizophrenia sufferer. It had previously been established that this category of mental illness was on the whole disliked and also liable to arouse some anxiety among students. The interaction anticipated was described as one in which they would be outcome-dependent (or not) with this stigmatized person to win some monetary prize. The effect of varying the interdependency between them in this way seemed to make subjects pay greater attention to information about the person and, sometimes, to anticipate liking him more, though it has to be said that the observed effects were not always very strong or consistent. Moreover, subsequent research by Pendry and Macrae (1994) suggest that the possibly individuating effects of interdependence are easily disrupted by cognitive distraction. Nevertheless, as we shall see in a later chapter, there are other benefits accruing from co-operative intergroup encounters like this which are broadly consistent with these findings (see chapter 8).

Stereotypes as self-fulfilling prophecies

Thus far, I have been solely concerned with the effects of stereotypes on us the perceivers; how and when they influence our perceptions, recollections, and evaluations of others. To conclude this section I want to consider their effects on those being perceived. I shall show that they are not merely hypotheses for which we selectively seek out confirmatory evidence; they may themselves create the very conditions in which that confirmatory evidence is more readily forthcoming (Darley and Fazio, 1980; Snyder, 1981). This altogether more dynamic view of stereotypes as self-fulfilling prophecies has support from a number of studies.

Take, for example, an early experiment of Word et al. (1974). Here, White subjects had to role-play the position of a job interviewer. Half the interviewees were White and half Black, but in either case they were confederates of the experimenters who had carefully trained them to react in a standardized way throughout the interview. Careful observation of the interviewers' behaviour revealed that they acted in a subtly different way with the Black as compared to the White interviewee: they sat further from them and tended to lean further back in their seats; the interviews were also fully 25 per cent (or three minutes) shorter and contained more speech disfluencies (for example, stuttering, hesitations). One can easily imagine what effect these differences in non-verbal behaviour might have on a real job interviewee but Word et al. did not leave this to our imagination. In a second experiment they reversed the roles. This time the *interviewers* (always White confederates) were trained to act in one of two ways: *either* to sit closer to the interviewee, make fewer speech errors, and make the interview last longer, *or* do the opposite. These were, of course, the very differences in behaviour elicited by the Black and White confederates in the first experiment. This time it was the behaviour of the interviewees, again all White, which was carefully monitored and evaluated by independent judges. The striking finding was that their behaviour seemed to reciprocate that of the interviewers: when they were sat closer to and talked to more fluently they responded in the same way, and noticeably differently from the other experimental condition. As a result, they were judged to be reliably calmer and also to be more suitable for the 'job' they were being interviewed for. A similar self-perpetuating effect was observed by Snyder et al. (1977). They led male subjects to believe that the person they were speaking to on the telephone was either an attractive or an unattractive woman. The men's image of their partner seemed to elicit different behaviours from her: her interaction style was subsequently judged by independent observers to be more friendly, likeable and sociable in the 'attractive' than in the 'unattractive' conditions (see Snyder, 1981, for other examples of this phenomenon).

Such findings are not restricted to the artificial confines of the social psychologist's laboratory. The self-fulfilling nature of stereotypes has also been observed in naturalistic contexts with very real and profoundly important consequences for those concerned. Some of the most compelling evidence has come from school settings, a line of research inspired by Rosenthal and Jacobson's (1968) famous experiment in an American elementary school. In this school, like others around the country, the children were regularly assessed with various intelligence and achievement tests. In the year of the study Rosenthal and Jacobson obtained permission to add a new measure to the battery of tests, the Harvard Test of Inflected Acquisition. Despite its rather grandiose name, it was actually a perfectly ordinary and well-standardized non-verbal intelligence test. However, the true nature and results of this test were only ever known by Rosenthal and Jacobson. After the first administration of the test the researchers randomly selected around one-fifth of the children in each year and designated them as children who would be likely 'to show a significant inflection or spurt in their learning within the next year or less than will the remaining 80 per cent of the children' (Rosenthal and Jacobson, 1968, p. 66). The names of these likely 'bloomers' were then passed on to the teachers (and only the teachers) with a brief explanation sheet outlining the researchers' (bogus) expectations. One year later, Rosenthal and Jacobson retested all the children with that same Test of Inflected Acquisition. The results which captured the imagination of social psychologists and educators then and since are shown in figure 4.4. In the first two grades the 'experimental' children – those arbitrarily labelled as showing special promise – did actually significantly increase their scores on the intelligence test.[3] For the remaining grades the comparisons between the 'experimental' and 'control' children showed negligible differences. What was so remarkable about these increases was that they could only be attributable to the teachers' expectations, for it was only they in the schools who knew the identities of those allegedly 'bright' children; the children themselves had not been informed of their 'superior' ability.

The small numbers of children involved, the lack of consistent IQ gains in the older grades, and a variety of methodological difficulties with the study have meant that Rosenthal and Jacobson's findings have not always been universally accepted (Elashoff and Snow, 1971; Thorndike, 1968). Nevertheless, since that pioneering effort other research has confirmed that teachers' expectations do have a consistent and measurable effect on student performance. One of the most convincing demonstrations of this was Crano and Mellon's (1978) cross-lagged panel analysis of some longitudinal data collected from 72 British junior schools, involving over 5000 children. The logic behind cross-

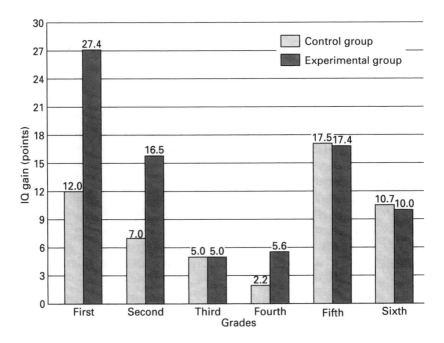

Figure 4.4 Effects of teacher expectations on student achievement levels
Source: Rosenthal and Jacobson (1968), figure 7.1

lagged analysis is simple. Suppose we have two variables – in the present case teachers' expectations (E) and pupil performance (P) – and we find that they are positively correlated. As we have all had drummed into us a hundred times, correlation does not imply causality and hence we cannot infer that E is giving rise to P; it would be equally plausible to conclude that the students' performance was actually responsible for the teachers' future expectations of them. However, suppose we obtain our measures of E and P at two points in time (t_1, t_2). If E is genuinely causing P rather than the other way around, then we should expect the correlation between E_1 and P_2 to be greater than the equivalent correlation between P_1 and E_2. This, then, was the basis of Crano and Mellon's analysis. They had access to teachers' evaluations of their charges on some behavioural, motivational, and academic criteria; they also obtained the scores of those same students on a variety of standardized achievement tests. And both kinds of data were available at two points in time, separated by a year. The pattern of correlations Crano and Mellon obtained was very clear. Of 84 possible comparisons between the correlations $E_1 P_2$ and $E_2 P_1$, nearly three-quarters of them revealed the former to be higher than the latter, clear evidence of a *causal* effect of expectations on subsequent performance.

A similar conclusion was reached by Jussim (1989) in a study of American teachers and students in the domain of mathematical achievement. Even when statistically controlling student motivation levels and prior achievement scores, teachers' evaluations of their students were significantly correlated with those students' subsequent scores in two maths tests. However, Jussim also pointed out that these correlations were generally smaller in magnitude than those between student *prior* performance on teacher evaluations. In other words, and somewhat reassuringly for the educational profession and parents alike, teachers' estimates of their students' abilities are not completely arbitrary but are based somewhat on how well they do.

Nevertheless, even if relatively modest in size, these self-fulfilling expectancy effects are potentially important for the preservation of prejudiced stereotypes. Eccles Parsons and her colleagues have pointed out that parental expectations of their children's competencies are influenced by the child's sex, even when taking into account the child's actual capabilities, and these expectations are related in turn to the children's own self-perceptions of their abilities in different domains (for example, girls seeing themselves as better at English but worse at mathematics; Eccles Parsons et al., 1982; Eccles et al., 1990). It is then but a short step to the children self-selecting academic and career options consistent with these self-concepts, thus perpetuating gender stereotypes about the relative linguistic and technical disabilities of men and women.

Institutional practices within schools may compound expectancy effects and may even create some of their own. For instance, in many schools there is streaming by ability. In such situations students from socio-economically disadvantaged backgrounds, which will often include disproportionate numbers of ethnic minorities, are usually over-represented in the lower ability groups. There is thus some correspondence between the academic categorization ('slow' band) and other category labels (for example, 'working class', 'Black'), thus helping to preserve the negative stereotypes of intellectual inferiority associated with the latter. This problem is well illustrated by the evidence from Epstein's (1985) study of a large number of American schools which found that teachers with more negative ethnic attitudes were also more likely to use some kind of 'tracking' system in their classrooms. Such practices would inevitably place more Blacks (and other minority groups) in the 'slower' tracks, thus conveniently bolstering the teachers' prejudiced beliefs.

As a final example of stereotypes as self-fulfilling prophecies let us consider a cross-cultural study by Levy and Langer (1994). Levy and Langer are interested in the cognitive capacities of elderly people. A 'common-sense' view, at least in many western cultures, is that as we get older our various physical and intellectual capabilities irreversibly decline: we become less active, more forgetful, and so on. Accepting that, of course, there are biological changes associated with ageing, Levy and Langer speculated that at least some of these deficits can be attributable to culturally prevalent stereotypes associated with elderly people. Perhaps, they argued, society *expects* a deterioration in old age and helps to contribute towards that deterioration by not permitting elderly people to remain as physically and mentally active as they are able. Furthermore, the elderly themselves may internalize that same stereotype and come to model their own behaviour on what they see as the group prototype (Turner et al., 1987). To assess the extent of this social contribution to cognitive decrements associated with ageing, Levy and Langer (1994) compared the memory performance of six different groups: a sample of hearing American adults, a sample of Americans with a profound hearing disability, and a sample of Chinese adults. Half of each sample were 'young' (15-30 years), half 'old' (59-91 years). In addition the subjects were also tested for their stereotypical attitudes towards elderly people. The selection of the hearing-disabled and Chinese samples was important because in each of these two groups there is a markedly different stereotype of old people. In China, for instance, old people are revered and expected to contribute much more fully to social and political life than is common in the West. Deaf people, too, have an independent value system, relatively insulated from mainstream cultural beliefs, and tend to hold old people in high esteem. Levy and Langer's results certainly bore this out. Both these groups had significantly more positive attitudes towards ageing than the American hearing sample. Furthermore, the elderly subjects (but not the young) in the same two groups outperformed the elderly American hearing group on four memory tasks. Finally, to show the link between the stereotypical attitudes and memory, the correlations were positive in the elderly subjects (the more favourable the attitude the better the memory performance) but negative amongst the young.

Stereotype Change

In this chapter I have tried to emphasize the view of stereotypes as guides to judgement and action. I have argued that they, and the categories with which they are associated, are indispensable cognitive devices for understanding, negotiating and constructing our social world. If this is the case they would be poor guides indeed if they were completely immutable, unable to change in response to new and maybe contradictory information. In this final section, then, I want to discuss some of the factors which give rise to stereotype change. This will not be an exhaustive treatment, however, since I want to return to this issue in more detail in chapter 8 when I consider how prejudice can most successfully be reduced. The focus there will be on the situational variables and social practices which are most likely to lead to a diminution of negative stereotypes and intergroup discrimination. Here I want to concentrate on how people deal with information which is inconsistent with their stereotypes. When does this lead to a revision of those beliefs and when, on the other hand, is it simply ignored or otherwise assimilated to leave the prejudiced ideas intact?

In the week in which I am writing this the British Open Golf tournament is being held at Sandwich, a few miles from my office. The particular course on which it is being played, the Royal St George, is one of the several golf clubs around the country to which women are still not permitted to belong. The proximity of this bastion of male

chauvinism and the temporal coincidence of an all-male sporting event
– belying the supposedly 'Open' nature of its title – suggested to me that
an example from the world of golf would be an appropriate way to
begin this discussion. Here is Bill Raymond, a male golfer with some
very clear ideas about men's and women's abilities at the game:

> *Women don't play golf, they play at it . . . the average woman doesn't need 14*
> *clubs. They could hit any of the bloody clubs from 100 yards. The average lady is*
> *much worse than the average man. They play a different game. They can't play as*
> *quickly or as accurately. Everything's got to be right from the head gear to the furry*
> *golf covers.*   (*Independent*, 19 December 1990).

The question I want to consider is this: what kind of information
about women's golfing capabilities would it take to modify Mr
Raymond's belief in their inferiority?

Gurwitz and Dodge (1977) raised two possibilities. On the one hand,
they suggested, he might encounter many women golfers each of
whom failed to confirm his stereotype in some respect. Perhaps one
might be a prodigious hitter; another might be able to hit her three-
irons to land on a sixpence; another might care little for her appearance
and break par on every round. The accumulation of such inconsistencies
with his derogatory stereotype of women golfers might eventually lead
him to change his view. On the other hand, another force for change
might be for him to meet just a few very striking counter-examples to
his stereotype; two or three champion golfers who can hit the ball long
and straight, always break par, play quickly, and dress conventionally.
Perhaps such obvious contradictions would compel him to revise his
stereotype. Gurwitz and Dodge found some evidence for the latter
process. In the context of stereotypes about college sorority members,
they presented subjects with information about three sorority members
and asked them to predict what a fourth friend of these would be like.
In the experimental conditions of interest to us here, several pieces of
information about the friends were presented which disconfirmed the
traditional sorority stereotype. This information was either 'dispersed'
amongst all three friends or 'concentrated' in just one of them. The
subjects' ratings of the missing fourth woman were significantly less
stereotypical in the latter case, suggesting that the 'glaring exception'
can, indeed, induce a change in a group stereotype.

This will not always be the case, however, as was demonstrated by
some subsequent experiments by Weber and Crocker (1983). Following
Rothbart (1981), they called the change induced by a few strong

exceptions 'conversion', and the change induced by many discrete disconfirmations 'book-keeping' (since it implied that stereotypes were modified by simply adding up the amount of inconsistent information). To these two models they added a third, 'sub-typing', which they suggested could act to promote *or* to inhibit change in an overall group stereotype. To illustrate this let us return to our beleaguered Mr Raymond one last time. Suppose he does indeed witness some outstanding golfing feats by two women players. One convenient strategy for him is to place those two players in a special sub-group – perhaps 'professional women golfers' – which then allows him to leave his more general stereotype of 'ordinary women golfers' intact. In a typically apt phrase, Allport (1954) called this process 'refencing' and suggested that it was a common cognitive device which permits people to sustain their prejudiced beliefs even when confronted with contradictory evidence. However, sub-typing can also have positive effects on stereotype change. Suppose Mr Raymond is continually faced with dozens of women golfers who do not fit his stereotype. Perhaps he sub-types some of them as 'professionals', others as 'low-handicap golfers', others as 'good around the greens', and perhaps even some as 'sensibly dressed'. The proliferation of sub-types, necessitated by his exposure to a wide range of counter-examples, begins to render his original superordinate category of the 'woman golfer' (who dresses inappropriately and cannot play well) rather less useful to him. As a result, the global and negative stereotype becomes fragmented and hence less potent.

Weber and Crocker (1983) modified Gurwitz and Dodge's (1977) procedure for providing disconfirming information – this time about two occupational groups – which was either 'concentrated' in a few members or 'dispersed' across several. They also varied the size of the sample of evidence from each group, six members in one condition, thirty in another (notice that both are larger than the group of three which Gurwitz and Dodge had used). In their subsequent judgements of the occupational groups, the subjects were clearly influenced by the size of the sample, and hence the absolute amount of disconfirming information. However, this cannot have been a simple 'book-keeping' type of change since an even more significant factor was *how* the information was distributed across the sample. When it was dispersed across many members it produced a less stereotypical view of the occupational group than when it was concentrated, even though the gross amount of inconsistent information was the same in each case (see figure 4.5). This result was later confirmed by Johnston and Hewstone

(1992) and was directly contrary to what Gurwitz and Dodge had found. Weber and Crocker also showed that sub-typing could help to explain the changes they observed. In a subsequent task subjects were asked to sort the 'stimulus persons' who had comprised the sample into groups. In the conditions where the disconfirmations were all concentrated into a few cases, subjects typically only ever formed one sub-group (consisting of those counter-examples); in the 'dispersed' conditions by contrast, between two and four sub-groups were formed.

In another experiment Weber and Crocker (1983) further clarified the role that this sub-typing process plays in stereotype change. They varied the representativeness of the disconfirming group members. Some were seen as highly typical of the group, despite manifesting counter-stereotypical characteristics; the others were seen as unrepresentative. The

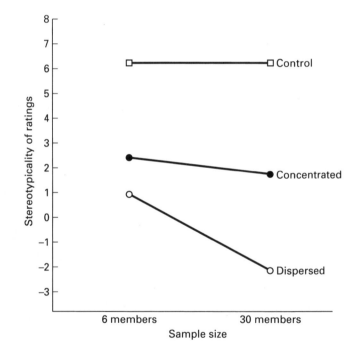

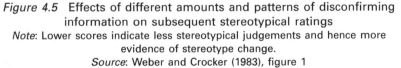

Figure 4.5 Effects of different amounts and patterns of disconfirming information on subsequent stereotypical ratings
Note: Lower scores indicate less stereotypical judgements and hence more evidence of stereotype change.
Source: Weber and Crocker (1983), figure 1

former case produced more evidence of stereotype change than the latter, a finding replicated in other research (Johnson and Hewstone, 1992). I shall return to this issue in chapter 8 where it will be seen that the typicality of outgroup members with whom we have contact plays an important role in modifying our intergroup attitudes.

Gurwitz and Dodge (1977) found that concentrating all the contradictory information into one highly salient counter-example was more effective than dispersing it; Weber and Crocker (1983) and Johnston and Hewstone (1992) showed the opposite. What could account for this discrepancy? One obvious factor is the size of the sample from which the consistent and inconsistent information is drawn. In Gurwitz and Dodge's case it was only three; in the other studies it varied between six and thirty. It seems, then, that the 'conversion' mode of stereotype change is only likely when we have relatively few examples on which to make up our mind (notice that in figure 4.5 the 'benefits' of dispersed information are most noticeable in the large sample). Another factor which could favour the 'conversion' process is if the target group in question is also highly homogeneous (as well as being small). In that case, one or two striking counter-examples seem to be particularly effective in inducing stereotype change (Hewstone et al., 1992).

One other source of stereotype-disconfirming information may be a group's success or failure in achievement situations. Mackie et al. (1992; in press) have identified an interesting bias which people seem to show when making inferences from a group's performance. A group's outcome – that is, whether it 'passes' or 'fails' some test – seems to exert a greater influence over people's judgements about that group's capabilities than its actual performance. So a group which wins some tournament with a score of (say) 70 may actually be evaluated more positively than another group which just fails to win but nevertheless scores the same (or, perhaps, we might speculate, even a little more). Using both occupational and ethnic groups, Mackie et al. (1992) showed how these favourable evaluations are not restricted to the particular group achieving the positive outcome; they may also be generalized to the wider category to which the group belongs. Such a finding could have potentially important implications for the success of affirmative action programmes in employment and education. To the extent that minority or disadvantaged groups can be seen to achieve successful *outcomes* (for example, obtaining more senior posts or gaining access to higher education), then this itself may result in some changed perceptions of that group, whatever the paper qualifications or scholastic achievement test scores of those groups.

Until now we have only considered how the amount and patterning of disconfirming information can affect the revision of stereotypes. To conclude we ought also to note that some stereotypes are easier to change than others. Rothbart and Park (1986) asked people to estimate how many instances of observable behaviour it would take to confirm or disconfirm that somebody (or some group) possessed each of a large list of traits. They also had to rate the favourability of each trait. One of the clearest findings which emerged from their study was that the more favourable a trait was the greater number of occasions it would need to confirm it but the correspondingly fewer occasions to *disconfirm* it. The opposite held true for unfavourable traits. In other words, as Rothbart and Park (1986) put it, 'unfavourable traits are easier to acquire and harder to lose than are favourable traits' (p. 135). If we put this assessment together with Maass et al.'s (1989) linguistic analysis of ingroup and outgroup descriptions that we discussed earlier – recall that they discovered that descriptions of negative outgroup characteristics tended to be couched in rather general and hence not easily falsifiable terms – then we are forced to a rather sobering conclusion about the difficulty of changing prejudiced outgroup stereotypes. If we restrict ourselves solely to the cognitive level of analysis – how social information is attended to, processed, and recalled – then such pessimism seems inescapable. Fortunately, however, as we shall see in chapters 6 and 8, other social and motivational processes can be brought to bear on intergroup relations which offer a more positive prospect for stereotype change.

Summary

1. A stereotype is the perception that most members of a category share some attribute. Stereotyping arises directly out of the categorization process, particularly the consequent assimilation of within-group differences.
2. Stereotypes can originate from the culture in which people are socialized, from real cultural and socio-economic differences between groups, and also from a cognitive bias which seems to result in an illusory correlation between minority groups and infrequently occurring attributes. The source of

this bias may lie in the 'distinctiveness' of such infrequent conjunctions but recent evidence suggests that it may derive as much from a categorical differentiation process.

3. Stereotypes can influence people's judgements of individuals but this depends on the relative importance or salience of individuating and group based information. A useful way of viewing stereotypes is as hypotheses in search of confirmatory information. Much evidence exists for this confirmation-seeking nature of stereotypic expectancies.

4. Stereotypes are usually not evaluatively neutral because they are often associated with ingroups and outgroups. There is evidence that the differential value associated with ingroup and outgroup stereotypes can affect judgements even below the level of conscious awareness.

5. Stereotypes also influence attributional judgements about the causes of ingroup and outgroup actions. A typical finding is that positive and negative behaviours by the ingroup are attributed internally and externally respectively; for outgroup behaviours the reverse applies.

6. Stereotypes may be used more if people are cognitively or emotionally preoccupied with other concerns. The reason for this is that such distractions are thought to consume cognitive attention, thus paving the way for the labour-saving afforded by stereotyping.

7. Stereotypes can have self-fulfilling properties, creating in the targets of their focus the very attributes hypothesized to exist. Such self-fulfilling prophesies have been observed in educational contexts.

8. Stereotypes change in response to disconfirming information, but the patterning of that information (concentrated in a few exemplars or dispersed across many) and the valence of the stereotype undergoing revision are important factors in determining the extent of change.

Further Reading

Bar-Tal, D., Graumann, C.F., Krulanski, A.W. and Stroebe, W. (1989) (eds) *Stereotyping and Prejudice: Changing conceptions*, chs 2, 3, 4, 10. New York: Springer Verlag.

Expectancies and Social Issues (1990) *Journal of Social Issues*, *46*(2) (whole issue).

Hewstone, M. (1989) *Causal Attribution: From cognitive processes to collective beliefs*, ch. 6. Oxford: Basil Blackwell.

Leyens, J.-P., Yzerbyt, V.Y. and Schadron, G. (1994) *Stereotypes and Social Cognition*. London: Sage.

Oakes, P.J., Haslam, A. and Turner, J.C. (1994) *Stereotyping and Social Reality*, chs 3–8. Oxford: Blackwell Publishers.

Notes

1. The causal links here may also be reciprocal. That is, those who saw the outgroup most stereotypically may well be more anxious over the contact. I am grateful to Tom Pettigrew for pointing this out.
2. Probably much to the relief of the subjects none of these events actually transpired.
3. These findings have always seemed particularly compelling to me. Some years ago I taught in a secondary school. My subject then was mathematics which, at that school, was streamed by 'ability' after the first year. An abiding, and still saddening, memory from that experience was to witness the systematic decline in numeracy over the different year groups. The contrast between the least-able members of the first year mixed-ability class – always trying, always believing they would eventually master the subject – with their elder peers in the fourth- and fifth-year 'bottom' sets – sullen, bored, convinced of their ineptitude – was striking indeed. The label that they were 'no good at maths' had stuck with them and also with us, their teachers, and we all – students and teachers alike – behaved accordingly.

The Development of
Prejudice in Children

5   Black child bathing dolls

'Which doll looks most like you?', 'Which is the nice doll?', 'Which doll would you like to play with?'

Children's answers to questions like these can shed important light on the development of their ethnic identity and attitudes.

In an earlier chapter I examined a theory which traces the roots of adult prejudice back to childhood socialization experiences (see chapter 2). The thrust of that approach, as we saw, was to identify certain patterns of family dynamics which would give rise to an authoritarian or dogmatic personality. Notwithstanding the historical importance of that psychodynamic perspective, from the point of a developmental social psychology of prejudice it suffered from two crucial weaknesses. One was that it was essentially a theory of the deviant personality. Only some children, those unfortunate enough to have been brought up in a particularly strict family with dominant and moralistic parents, were thought likely to be predisposed to develop into prejudiced adults in later life. The remainder – presumably the majority? – because they were not so afflicted, were eased out of the theoretical field of view. The second drawback was that despite its interest in the childhood origins of prejudice, remarkably little of the research it inspired actually studied children themselves. With the exception of Frenkel-Brunswik (1949, 1953) and one or two others, most work in this tradition studied adults and relied heavily on their retrospective reports of their childhood. However interesting these may be, they are no substitute for the direct observation of children's attitudes and behaviour.

In this chapter, therefore, I want to turn the spotlight fully on children, particularly in the first ten years of their lives. What is known about prejudice in children and what can this tell us about prejudice in us adults? Are children bound simply to reproduce the racist, sexist, and ageist norms of the society into which they are born, little chips off their prejudiced elders' blocks? Or, instead, might they contribute something themselves, developing some attitudes and stereotypes of their own from their categorical attempts to systematize and control their social environment? These are some of the questions I shall be pursuing in this chapter.

Following Goodman's (1952) lead, I have divided the chapter into three main sections dealing respectively with children's awareness of social categories, their identification with and preference for some of those categories rather than others, and then their full-blown intergroup attitudes and behaviour. In a final section I discuss the origins of these phenomena, debating the extent to which this aetiology should be regarded as unidirectional (that is, from society to child) or, alternatively, as a more reciprocal process in which children play their part too.

Awareness of Social Categories

A little girl of about nine or ten years of age looks at the dozen photographs of children spread out in front of her and sorts them into three piles because they look alike to her. When asked why she sorted them as she did she replies, 'They're girls, they're boys, and they're handicaps' (Maras, 1993, p. 140). For her, the way to impose some order on to that array of strange faces was to classify them by sex and disability. In order to do that she clearly must have been *aware* of the existence of those particular categories.

This issue of category awareness has always been a central preoccupation of researchers interested in children and prejudice. In part this is because, as we saw in chapter 3, any kind of prejudiced perception, attitude, or action necessarily implies the prior application of some categorical distinction. One cannot be sexist (say) without first having categorized people as men and women. This in itself makes the phenomenon of awareness of interest to prejudice researchers. What gives it added importance has been to discover the age at which social categorizations emerge reliably for the first time and to ascertain how their usage develops over the course of childhood. To the extent that such categories can be observed very early in life, then the idea of *tabulae rasae* on to which are written adult ideas becomes difficult to sustain.

One of the earliest attempts to study category awareness was by Clark and Clark (1947). They developed a paradigm which was taken up by generations of subsequent researchers in the field. It involves presenting the child with two (or more) dolls, one of which is 'white' in colour and has yellow hair, the other 'brown' with black hair. The child is asked a series of questions about these dolls and the two most relevant to ethnic awareness are those which simply ask the child to give the researcher the one 'which looks like a white (or coloured) child'. Clark and Clark posed this question to Black children from three to seven years of age and found that even at the youngest age over 75 per cent of the children correctly identified the ethnicity of the doll.[1] By the age of five, well over 90 per cent were doing so.

One might quickly object that presenting a child with such a forced choice between just two predetermined categories does not very sensitively assess their spontaneous awareness and use of different categories. Fortunately, however, such an objection can be quickly countered by other studies which have used different techniques and have produced broadly similar findings. Horowitz and Horowitz (1938), for instance, presented White American children with a whole series of five pictures of which three were similar on two criteria and the remaining two differed on one of the criteria. For example, three White males, one Black male, one White female: which is the odd one out? The children's choices give us a clue as to which category is most salient for them. By combining ethnicity, sex, age, and socio-economic status in different ways Horowitz and Horowitz were able to discover which category predominated. Ethnicity seemed to be dominant in most of the combinations in which it occurred. Sex was the second most potent category, and socio-economic status generally the least important. Williams and Morland (1976), reviewing several studies using photographic stimuli in which more than just one Black and one White person are portrayed, also confirmed the presence of considerable ethnic awareness in children as young as four years, although this was somewhat higher for Whites than for Blacks.

Research with that other major social category, gender, has produced similar results. Thompson (1975) found that over 75 per cent of the two-year-olds he studied could correctly classify photographs as male and female, a figure rising to 90 per cent by age three. Similar findings with slightly different techniques have been obtained by other researchers, showing that by two and a half, and certainly by three years of age, gender labels can be readily and correctly used (Duveen and Lloyd, 1986; Slaby and Frey, 1975; Yee and Brown, 1994).

Other studies have examined category awareness in more open-ended tasks and in these, too, clear evidence of the early availability of ethnic and gender concepts has been found. A popular technique has been to present children with a series of photographs and ask them to sort them into groups according to how they 'belong together' or 'look alike'. Sometimes the task is constrained by forcing the child to classify sequentially into dichotomous clusters; others allow the child to use as many categories as he or she wishes simultaneously. Within the stimulus photographs there are usually several cues which the child could use as sorting criteria − for example, there may be adults and children, males and females, different ethnic groups, and so on. Davey (1983) used sex, age, ethnicity, and style of dress (to convey socio-economic status) in his study of 7–10-year-old British children. By far and away the most frequent sorting criterion was ethnicity, used first by nearly half the children. Sex was the next most popular, and dress style used very rarely.

We used a similar technique with White children aged from three to nine years (Yee and Brown, 1988). Within the photographs we systematically varied sex, ethnicity (Asian Indian and White) and age, and there were also some other possible sorting criteria (for example, hair colour). The youngest children tended simply to place all the photographs in a single large category but by the age of five ethnicity was clearly emerging as a criterion (used by over a third of that age group) and completely predominated in the two oldest groups (used by two-thirds of them). More detailed analysis of the sorting strategies used by these older children revealed that, indeed, ethnicity was the primary dimension – the children usually placed all the Indian photographs together – and then there were some subdivisions within the White stimuli (for example, by dark and light hair). This is strongly reminiscent of the outgroup homogeneity phenomenon that I discussed in chapter 3: the Indian outgroup is perceived as a single category; the White ingroup is seen in more differentiated terms.

In these two studies, although gender was clearly available as a categorization to the children, it was seldom used. This might suggest that it is generally less potent a social cue than ethnicity. However, such a conclusion may be premature. Changing the context – for example, the micro context of the categorization task or the broader cultural milieu in which the research is conducted – can dramatically affect the likelihood of which different categories are used. Davey (1983), for instance, followed up his open-ended task with a more structured series of questions in which the children had to 'match' two pairs of photographs 'to play together'. Faced with this task the children used sex rather than ethnicity as the predominant category: they were much more likely to match up two pairs of girls (or boys) than they were to put together children from the same ethnic group. As we shall see later in the chapter, such gender segregation is a remarkably pervasive and precocious feature of children's play behaviour.

In different contexts different categories may assume importance. This was revealed by Ferraresi (1988) in a study of 4–5-year-old Italian children using the same photographs as Yee and Brown (1988). Here, ethnicity was used much less frequently than had been the case with British children. If anything, the children tended to sort the photographs by hair colour and secondarily by gender. Maras (1993) employed a similar technique to explore children's awareness of disability. This time only photographs of the same (White) ethnicity were used and several of them had various kinds of obvious physical and learning disabilities. Asked to sort these, the children (aged 5–10) invariably categorized by gender and disability and tended to make few distinctions amongst the children with disabilities, despite the fact that these were clearly visible (for example, two were in a wheelchair, two had hearing aids, and so on).

Because all of these studies were concerned with children's awareness of social categories and their ability to use and articulate that awareness verbally, the age groups studied were seldom younger than $2\frac{1}{2}$–3 years. However, there is some evidence which suggests that even infants of a few months old are capable of categorical distinctions among human stimuli. Fagan and Singer (1979) employed a habituation paradigm with babies 5–6 months. In a habituation paradigm one stimulus is shown to the infant repeatedly for two fixed periods (for example, 30 seconds). The idea is to get the baby used (or habituated) to that stimulus. Then that stimulus and the 'test' stimulus are presented together and the time the baby stares at each one is measured. If they fixate the test stimulus for longer than the original it is assumed that they see something novel in it and hence have discriminated between them. Fagan and Singer carefully matched photographs of a man and a woman, or an adult and a baby, so that they were as similar as possible on a number of facial features (for example, hair length and texture, separation of the eyes, thickness of lips). They also matched *same* sex or age photographs that were actually *less* similar to one another than the male–female or adult–baby pairs (that is, they had fewer facial features in common). The infants spent consistently longer looking at the test photograph when it was of different sex or age (despite being objectively more similar) than when it was of the same sex or age as the control photograph. Interestingly, one of the female–female pairs which the infants did not differentiate actually contained a White and a Black woman. Thus these infants were capable of gender and age, but not ethnic, differentiation. Such social categorical abilities parallel their achievements in physical domains, where there is evidence that by six months they are capable of making distinctions amongst different phonetic, colour, and shape categories (Small, 1990).

Still more incredibly – and somewhat controversially – it may be that very young babies are also sensitive to some of the same cues that adults use in evaluating people's physical attractiveness. Langlois et al. (1987) asked adult judges to rate a series of White female faces for attractiveness. This allowed Langlois et al. to designate half the photographs as 'attractive' and half 'unattractive'. When they presented one member of each of these groups in pairs to infants of 2–8 months, they found that they spent consistently longer fixating the 'attractive' faces. This was as true for the youngest infants (2–3 months) as it was for the older group

(6–8 months). They replicated this finding in three subsequent experiments with six-month-old children (Langlois et al., 1991). In one they extended the paradigm to include male stimuli, and found, again, that attractive photographs (of either sex) elicited longer fixation times. There was also a serendipitous finding that the babies tended to stare longer at two photographs of the same sex as themselves (irrespective of attractiveness), although this was more pronounced in the male than in the female babies (see figure 5.1). This confirms the earlier Fagan and Singer (1979) finding that very young children are indeed able to make sex discriminations. The two remaining studies, one using Black female faces, the other infant faces, also found infants staring longer at 'attractive' than at 'unattractive' photographs (Langlois et al., 1991). Although these findings for attractiveness are not, strictly speaking, evidence of categorical differentiation, since the original photographic judgements were dimensional rather than classificatory, such data do suggest that the ability to detect socially valued cues emerges really quite early in life.

In sum, then, the evidence from this wide variety of studies shows quite clearly that children from an extremely early age are alert to the categorical divisions current in their social environment and can be quite adept at using them. Although not conclusive, this capability so early in the child's life does seem to suggest that such distinctions are not simply or directly

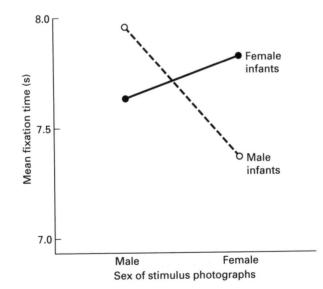

Figure 5.1 Primitive gender categorization in six-month-old infants
Source: Langlois et al. (1991), table 2

imposed on children by adults but are picked up by the children themselves. Furthermore, the sensitivity of children's preferred categorizations to both task and cultural variations suggests that they are used by them in an active and strategic manner. This is consistent with our earlier discussion of the important social psychological functions of categorization (see chapter 3). Adults use categories to simplify and make sense of their environment; apparently children do the same.

Category Identification and Preference

So far, we have only considered the onset and development of children's *awareness* of different social categories. However, awareness does not necessarily imply an identification with or a preference for some categories over others. In this section, therefore, I examine what is known about the development of children's category preferences, concentrating mainly on ethnicity and gender since these have been the focus of most research attention. As we shall see, there is a wealth of evidence which indicates that children from as young as three years of age (and possibly even earlier) identify with these categories and express clear evaluative preferences for one over another. However, the nature and direction of those preferences seems also to depend on the social standing of their group in the wider society: children from dominant or majority groups often respond quite differently from those belonging to subordinate or minority groups.

Ethnic and national categories

Researchers investigating ethnic identification have used similar techniques and materials to those I described in the first section. Typically, children are shown pictures or dolls which are chosen to represent different ethnic groups and are asked which one most closely resembles them, which they would like to play with, which one 'looks nice/bad', and so on. The early research by Goodman (1952) and Clark and Clark (1947) provided the inspiration for literally dozens of subsequent studies. Questions about self-identifications revealed that a majority of children at the ages studied (between 3 and 7 years) identified themselves with the doll appropriate to their ethnic group – that is, Black children identified with the darker coloured stimuli, White children with the lighter ones. However, beneath this general trend lay some important differences. Perhaps the most important was what seemed to be an asymmetry between the identification of the minority (Black) children and those from the White majority. Clark and Clark (1947) found that only about two-thirds of the Black children identified with the darker doll. Goodman (1952) found a similar percentage but a much higher figure (over 95 per cent) of the White children identifying with the White stimuli. In addition to these ethnic group differences there were some developmental effects, particularly amongst the Black children. Clark and Clark (1947) observed that over 60 per cent of the three-year-old Black children actually identified with the *lighter doll*, a figure in striking contrast to the 87 per cent of seven-year-olds identifying with the darker doll.[2]

These findings on identification were underlined by some even more marked ethnic differences to questions about play preferences and evaluative judgements. In one of the earliest studies Horowitz (1936) found that in four different samples of White children there was a consistent preference for White photographs in response to the question 'show me the one you like the best' (the children had to rank order a series of 12 photographs of Black and White children). This preference, already evident in kindergarten children, seemed to increase with age, levelling off at around ages 9–10. However, the few Black children in Horowitz's study also preferred the White photographs. The percentage of pro-White preference was lower than amongst the White children but was still reliably above a chance (or no preference) level. This finding was confirmed by Clark and Clark (1947). At every age group of the Black children they studied there was a majority showing a preference to play with the *White* doll and also indicating that this was the one which 'looked nice'. These differences were not always significantly different from the chance level but they were highly consistent and, because they favoured the 'outgroup', radically different from the pro-ingroup preferences shown by the White children in the Horowitz (1936) study.

In the following three decades similar results were reported from a number of studies in the United States. Using a variety of different techniques – for example, actual photographs rather than line drawings, or more complex tasks than simple binary choices – a consistent pattern emerged: White children showed a very strong and definite preference for stimuli which represented their own ethnic group whilst Black children seemed to be much more ambivalent, often showing a preference for and, in some cases, an identification with the outgroup – that is, with Whites (see Brand et al., 1974; Milner, 1983; Porter, 1971; Williams and Morland, 1976). The prevalence and strength of this outgroup preference amongst Black children has been a matter of some debate, and it is true that in some of the studies the Black children's choices did not deviate significantly from 50 per cent chance level (Banks, 1976). But what is beyond doubt in these early studies is the clear discrepancy between the Black and the White children's responses: the strong ingroup preference in the latter and no preference or outgroup preference in the former. A study by Asher and Allen (1969) conducted in the mid-1960s captures this well. They tested a large number of Black and White children aged from three to eight years using both Black and White researchers to control for any possible experimental demand effects. Adopting a similar 'doll methodology' to that devised by Clark and Clark (1947), they found a clear preference for the lighter-coloured puppet in *both White and Black children* (see figure 5.2). In addition to these overall strong pro-White preferences Asher and Allen observed some age effects. In both groups the pro-White bias seemed to increase from 3–4 years to reach a peak at 5–6 years and then decline again in the older 7–8 year olds. As we shall see, this curvilinear pattern with its maximum around the age of six may be developmentally quite significant.

Thus far, I have concentrated on research carried out with Black and White American children between the 1930s and the 1960s. However, the patterns of children's ingroup and outgroup favouring preferences observed in those studies are by no means restricted to those ethnic groups or that country. In several other societies, too, researchers noted a consistent tendency for (dominant) majority group children to show strong ingroup identification and preference whilst (subordinate) minority group children's identification with their ingroup was much weaker and was often paralleled by evaluative preferences for stimuli symbolic of the majority group. Vaughan (1964a, b) studied the ethnic attitudes of Maori and Pakeha (White) children (aged 4–12) in New Zealand using the conventional doll choice technique and also pictures to which various positive and negative traits had to be attributed. Over 60 per cent of the minority (Maori) children 'correctly' identified themselves with the ingroup picture but this was considerably lower than the 90 per cent of White children who did so. On the stereotypical traits the difference between the majority and minority children was even more marked. At every age group the Pakeha children made clear ingroup-favouring attributions and (except in the two oldest groups studied) in consistently greater numbers than the Maori children, most of whom clearly favoured the outgroup. As in other studies, the peak for pro-White preference seemed to be in the 6–8 age range, declining somewhat as the children grew older.

A similar pattern has been found in Britain amongst West Indian and Asian children, although somewhat more strongly for the former than the latter (Jahoda et al., 1972; Milner, 1973). Another British study was interesting because it attempted to assess preferences among more than two categories (Richardson and Green, 1971). In this research the children were asked to rank order six pictures depicting a Black and a White child with no physical disability, and four White children with various stigmata or disabilities (for example, facial disfigurement, amputated arm). Although the design was not complete (since there were no Black children with disabilities), it was clear that all children rank ordered the pictures showing children without handicaps higher than those depicting some disability. In this study, physical disfigurement or disability was liked even less than minority group membership. As

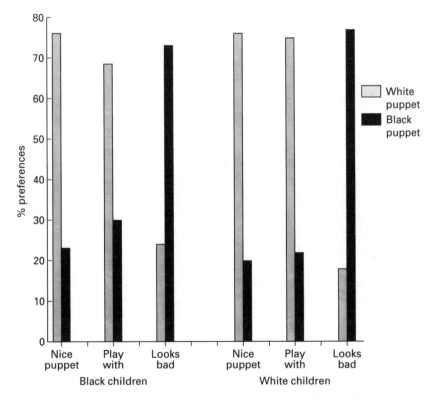

Figure 5.2   Black and White preferences for black and white puppets in the mid-1960s
Source: Adapted from Asher and Allen (1969), table 1

usual, however, when considering just the Black and White non-disabled pictures the White children showed clear ingroup preference (over 70 per cent) and the West Indian children were more equivocal (just over 50 per cent favouring the Black picture).

Aboud (1977) investigated ethnic identification and attitudes amongst some Canadian preschool children of White, Native Indian, and Chinese origin. Three quarters of the White children applied an appropriate ethnic label to themselves but only about a half and a third respectively of the Chinese and Indian children did so. On a different measure there was once again a general pro-White preference in all children (though reportedly reversed amongst the Indians). Finally, Morland (1969) found evidence of both pro-ingroup and pro-White preference in Chinese children in Hong Kong aged 4–6 years. The pro-ingroup preference was determined in the usual way by asking which of a pair of photographs (Chinese or White) the child would like to play with. Around two-thirds chose the Chinese photograph, a clear manifestation of ingroup preference although much lower than is typically observed amongst comparable White children elsewhere (over 80 per cent). On another question, 'Which child would you rather be?', there was again a majority (54 per cent) pro-ingroup response. However, fully 28 per cent indicated that they would rather be the child of the other (White) ethnicity. Once again, the contrast with the lower outgroup choice proportion in White children (typically, 15 per cent) is striking. Whilst the Chinese population in Hong Kong are clearly not a numerical minority, at that time they were subject to colonial rule by Britain and in that sense could be regarded as a subordinate status group like the others we have already considered.

So far we have reviewed work on ethnic categories and, as we have seen, there is ample evidence that children value these categories differently, suggesting that ethnic prejudice emerges at quite an early age. What of nationalism: do children show a similar preference for their own nationality? Does it emerge at as early an age? The answer to the first question is an unequivocal 'yes' although, again, the strength of the preference varies somewhat with countries. Regarding the second, it is harder to judge because most of the relevant studies have used slightly older children (six years and upwards). Nevertheless, the degree of own nationality preference does show a similar developmental pattern of initially increasing and then levelling off and declining.

Piaget and Weil (1951) unearthed some of the first evidence. Reasoning that the development of such social attitudes might correspond to the development of cognitive abilities, they identified three stages in children's thinking about countries. In the first (5–6 years), they believed that children would be unlikely to have a coherent concept of their country because of their difficulty in dealing with part–whole relationships (for example, is Geneva part of Switzerland or vice versa?). A little later on – say, around eight years – once children have a better cognitive grasp of certain concepts, they will develop a strong affinity to their own country but will fail to grasp that members of other countries may not share that ethnocentric perspective. Finally, by age ten or older, the children arrive at the third and properly 'mature' stage of cognitive ability which should allow them to have some under-standing of the nature of countries as social categories and the possibility of reciprocal attitudes between members of different categories. Piaget and Weil provided little quantitative evidence for the existence of these stages but some of the verbatim comments from their respondents are revealing none the less. Here are two children talking about Switzerland (their own country):

> DENISE (aged 6): I like Switzerland because it has such pretty houses.
> PIERETTE (aged 8): I like Switzerland because it's my own country. My mummy and daddy are Swiss, so I think Switzerland is a nice place. (Piaget and Weil, 1951, pp. 566–7).

Nor were they simply pro-Swiss. Some of them had decidedly negative ideas about other countries too:

> MURIELLE (aged 8): (Q Have you heard of foreigners?) 'Yes there are Germans and French.' (Q Are there any differences between these foreigners?) 'Yes, the Germans are bad, they're always making war. The French are poor and everything's dirty there. Then I've heard of the Russians too, they're not at all nice.' (Piaget and Weil, 1951, p. 569)

Piaget and Weil's suggestion that six-year-old children were unlikely to have any well-articulated views about their own and other countries has not been substantiated by subsequent research. One of the landmark studies was the cross-national project by Lambert and Klineberg (1967). They surveyed over 3000 children of ages varying from 6 to 14 years in 11 countries. One of the early questions in the interview was 'What are you?' The most common response to this open-ended question was to mention their gender; ethnicity or nationality were mentioned only rarely on the whole. The use of social categories in these self-definitions seemed to increase somewhat with age between six and ten years, then to level off. Despite the low frequency with which ethnicity and nationality were mentioned spontaneously – a finding confirmed by others (Jahoda, 1963; McGuire et al., 1978) – when the children were specifically asked about their own and other national groups they were able to answer quite easily, even when as young as six. In the vast majority of countries the children used positive adjectives to describe their own country (two exceptions being the Japanese and Black South Africans). Furthermore, when asked which nationality other than their own they would most and least like to have there was a remarkable consensus across the 11 countries: the preferred nationalities were American, British and French (in that order). The only noticeable variation came from the Black South Africans who most often mentioned 'White' as their preferred alternative nationality. The *least* preferred nationalities were Russian, African, Chinese and German although there was less consensus over these. Once again, the Black South African children stood out as being the most prominent rejectors of their own ethnic group; 35–55 per cent of this sample mentioned African tribal nationality as their least preferred choice. The parallels between these reactions and those of subordinate group children in the doll and picture preference studies discussed earlier are striking.

Further evidence for the existence of pro-own nationality preferences in children was obtained by Tajfel et al. (1972). They asked 6–11-year-olds in Scotland, England, and Israel to do two things. One was to allocate a set of photographs to two categories according to their perceived nationality (for example, English and Scottish, Oriental and European). The other was to place those same photographs into four boxes according to how much they liked the look of them. These two tasks were a week or two apart and the order counterbalanced. The results showed clear evidence of own national preference because there was a correlation between the children's decisions in the two tasks: photographs perceived to be of one's own nationality were consistently placed in the boxes marked 'more liked'. However, the Scottish children showed this tendency only very weakly, and amongst 'oriental' Israeli children there was a significant preference for 'European'-looking photographs. It is significant, I think, that both these groups could at that time be regarded as of lower status in their respective societies.

Nearly all the work we have looked at so far was conducted in the 30 years before 1970. As we have seen, a fairly consistent finding was of a strong pro-(White) ingroup identification and preference amongst White children, and a more ambivalent attitude from minority group children, sometimes showing neither ingroup nor outgroup preference, sometimes showing a reliable pro-outgroup orientation. The following decade, however, saw the publication of a number of studies reporting a noticeable change in this pattern: the pro-ingroup preference amongst Whites persisted but the former ambivalence of Black and other subordinate group children gave way to consistent ingroup preference amongst them too. One of the clearest examples of this emerging trend was a study by Hraba and Grant (1970). Using the standard doll-choice technique they found that both Blacks *and* Whites made pro-ingroup choices, and this increased with age from four to eight years. Figure 5.3 displays their findings and, since the methodologies were so similar, a comparison with Asher and Allen's (1969) earlier finding shown in figure 5.2 is instructive. Note especially the different pattern of results from the Black children. These historical changes were confirmed in other studies at about the same time which also observed pro-ingroup preferences in both majority and minority children (Aboud, 1980; Braha and Rutter, 1980; Epstein et al., 1976; Stephan and Rosenfield, 1978; Vaughan, 1978). As we shall see later in this chapter when we consider various theories, these historical changes may be particularly significant. However, for the moment, let them just serve as a reminder that social psychological phenomena are rarely immutable, unaffected by socio-political developments in the wider society.

Before we leave this issue there is one matter which deserves further discussion. This concerns just how we should interpret these findings on ethnic preferences: does a consistent preference for one group imply a derogation of the other? It will be sensible to consider this question separately for dominant and subordinate group children.

Taking the dominant group first, that is, White children in most studies. We must immediately recognize that in a binary choice task ('Which of these two pictures do you prefer?') we cannot infer that a preference for one stimulus implies the active rejection of the other. Thus, one reading of the substantial pro-ingroup preference shown by these children in nearly every study is simply that they feel more positive about their own group and either only slightly less positive or, at worst, neutral about the other. This, then, would not indicate the existence of any overt prejudice on their part. However, some attitudinal and behavioural data that I shall be presenting in the next section suggests that this may be too benign a conclusion. This caution is reinforced by anecdotal evidence reported in some of the studies we have already looked at. Consider the following observations from Goodman (1952) who reported that around a quarter of the four-year-olds she studied made clearly prejudiced comments:

STEFAN: All I like is the white one [girl in picture]. Not the black one – the white one.

NORMAN: He's a freshie! Look at his face – I don't like that kind of face.

BILLY (looking at two pictures): A good man – and a black one. (Goodman, 1952, p. 47)

Or these, from Milner (1973, p. 290), in response to questions as to why a particular choice was made: 'He shoots people'; 'He fights rough'; 'He takes money away from the white man'.

When we consider the subordinate group children we must first remember the greater variability of their responses, ranging from strong

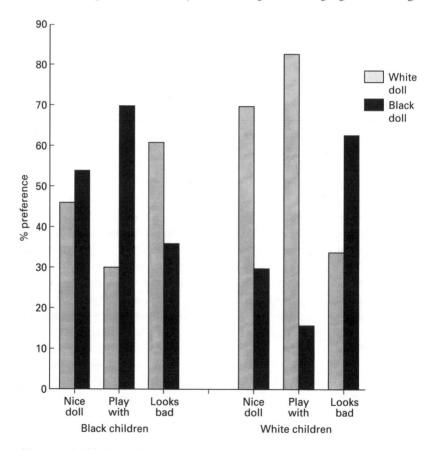

Figure 5.3 Black and White preferences for black and white dolls in the late 1960s
Source: Hraba and Grant (1970), table 1

ingroup preference to almost as strong a preference for the outgroup. It is the latter response which excited the most controversy amongst psychologists and educationalists because it seemed to imply a mis-identification with their ethnic group, perhaps even some kind of 'self-hatred'. Once again, the binary choice preference data by themselves do not support this idea though it is noteworthy that the proportion of minority group children showing ingroup preference is nearly always considerably smaller than that shown by the majority group. The difficulty with the 'self-hatred' thesis was underlined by Stephan and Rosenfield (1978) in their study of inter-ethnic attitudes and self-esteem amongst White, Black and Mexican-American elementary school children. All three groups were ethnocentric, the Whites somewhat (though non-significantly) more so than the other two groups. The White and Black children had roughly equivalent levels of self-esteem while the Mexican-Americans were lower, perhaps as a result of social class. In other words, there was little sign of a general minority 'self-rejection'. Nevertheless, there was a correlation between self-esteem and ethnocentrism among the Black children: the less ethnocentric they were (that is, the less they favoured Blacks relative to Whites) the lower their self-esteem.

Still, some anecdotal evidence suggests that outgroup preferences may indeed imply ingroup rejection, at least for some children. Here are some of the reasons Black children gave for not choosing the Black doll in Clark and Clark's (1947) study: 'Because he's ugly'; 'Because it don't look pretty'; ''Cause him black' (p. 316). And, even more strongly, from a four-year-old black girl in Goodman's (1952) research: 'Black people – I hate 'em' (p. 46). Maya Angelou, the celebrated Afro-American writer, recalls that one of her earliest childhood fantasies was

> to look like one of the sweet little white girls who were everybody's dream of what was right with the world.   (Angelou, 1969, p. 4)

And, saddest of all, are reports that Black children have occasionally been observed attempting to 'wash themselves clean' of their skin colour. This has been related to me on more than one occasion by people who have had first-hand experience of looking after Black children and was recounted again in a recent popular magazine article on racism in Britain where an Asian woman is quoted as saying, 'my nine year old daughter goes into the bathroom and scrubs her skin until it bleeds because the neighbours say she's dirty' (*Living*, June 1992, p. 25).

It would be a mistake to generalize from these fragmentary observations and conclude that minority group children have always had, and will always have, a negative view of themselves and their group; it is clear that there have been important cultural and historical variations in these self-perceptions. Nevertheless, the consistency with which differences in Black and White children's intergroup preferences have been observed does suggest that the experience and consequences of growing up as a subordinate and a dominant group member are not the same, and that our theories of prejudice development would do well to reflect this.

Gender identification and preference

With very occasional exceptions, the typical study of ethnic identification has presented children with just two target stimuli and asked them to make a choice between them. Most often the stimuli were implicitly of the same gender. Arguably, therefore, the children were more or less obliged to differentiate between them on ethnic grounds if they were to discriminate at all. Such a procedure also precludes the investigation of one other major social category – perhaps the most important category of all – that of gender. Thus, preference studies which include gender information in their stimuli are of particular interest because they permit an assessment of the relative importance of gender and ethnicity (or other category) for that particular sample of children. One such study was by Katz and Zalk (1974) which asked the usual questions of 4–5-year-old children about *four* dolls: two Black and two White, two of each gender. Contrary to the studies reviewed earlier, Katz and Zalk found little ethnocentric preference from either the Black or the White children. On the other hand, there were some signs of own-gender preference, but only from the girls.

That gender identity and corresponding gender preferences are important for children from an early age has long been suspected (Kohlberg, 1966; Mischel, 1970). Indeed, as Maccoby (1988) has pointed out, it would be strange if gender was not frequently used as a social psychological construct in view of its ubiquity as a social category in just about every known language and culture. Certainly the empirical evidence, albeit mainly from western societies, bears this out. Thompson (1975) found that while two-year-olds were still uncertain of their gender identity (only about half correctly answered that they were a boy or a girl), by $2\frac{1}{2}$–3 years gender identity was much more firmly established (well over 80 per cent were correct at these ages). However, knowing one's gender at this age does not imply a full understanding of the gender concept. Kohlberg (1966) reasoned that children's thinking about gender would parallel their thinking in other domains. He suggested that just as children below the age of five or six can be easily misled by the physical appearance of things – for example, believing that a tall thin glass contains more liquid than a short wide glass – so, too, might their perceptions of gender be rather unstable. Slaby and Frey (1975) showed this rather convincingly by asking 2–5-year-olds a number of questions about the ramifications of being a boy or a girl. After establishing, like Thompson (1975), that the vast majority (over 90 per cent) knew their own gender, they went on to ask such questions as what would happen if they wore clothes normally worn by the opposite sex, or if they played games typical of the opposite sex. Slaby and Frey found that there was a clear age progression in the acquisition of what they called 'gender constancy': the younger children could not easily understand that changing one's clothes did not mean that one underwent a sex change! It was not until age five or older that significant numbers of children demonstrated complete constancy (see also Yee and Brown, 1994). Interestingly, the level of constancy attained was predictive of the children's preference for attending to same-sex adults portrayed in a short film clip. Those at a higher level of constancy attended more to the same-sex models.

In fact, children show a preference for their own sex well before they have a clear sense of gender identity. Anyone who has worked in a preschool nursery or primary school will tell you that boys prefer to play with boys and, perhaps even more noticeably, girls with girls. This early gender segregation has been observed in several studies. One of the most intensive was conducted in a Montreal day-care centre and involved the careful observation of the affiliative behaviour of children from 18 months to 5½ years (La Freniere et al., 1984). Figure 5.4 shows how the percentage of same-sex affiliative acts increased with age. With the youngest children there is little gender segregation, but already by just over two years the girls are showing a clear same-sex preference, directing twice the number of affiliative acts toward their fellow girls as they do towards boys. By the age of three the boys have 'caught up' and thereafter both boys and girls continue to display marked own-gender preference.

In an earlier laboratory study Jacklin and Maccoby (1978) had also found own-gender preference in their observation of same-sex and opposite-sex pairs of strangers of just under three years, even where all the children were dressed alike in gender-neutral clothes. There was always more social interaction in the same-sex pairings, and this was somewhat more true of the girls than the boys. In a further study of children's free play these same researchers found still more evidence of gender segregation, although these children were a little older ($4\frac{1}{2}$–6-year-olds) and, perhaps because of this, they did not find any sex difference in the degree of own-gender preferences (Maccoby and Jacklin, 1987).

There is nothing sacred about the age of three to four for the onset of gender segregation however. In other cultures with different patterns of family life and social norms it may occur at a different age. Harkness and Super (1985), for example, found that gender segregation in a rural Kenyan community did not occur until 6–9 years. They attributed this later appearance to the greater family and economic responsibilities which typically fall on these children's shoulders: they routinely assist with child care, cattle supervision and other domestic chores, and these activities

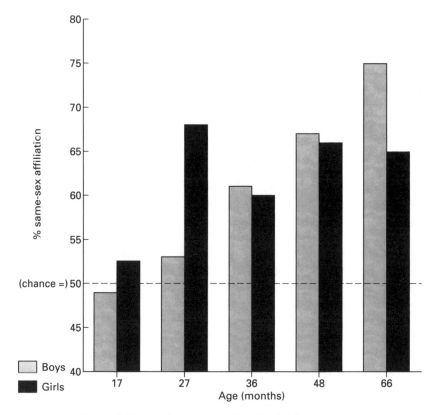

Figure 5.4 Gender segregation in children at play
Source: La Freniere et al. (1984), adapted from figure 1

usually take place in mixed-sex groups. Once they approach or reach adulthood, often marked by some formal ceremony, then the division of labour and social interaction along gender lines becomes much sharper.

Nor is gender segregation immutable. Serbin et al. (1978) showed how positive reinforcement by nursery school teachers could alter the frequency with which 4–5-year-old children engaged in cross-sex co-operative play. During the two-week 'intervention' phase of the study teachers systematically praised those children found playing co-operatively with a member of the opposite sex. This had the effect of increasing the amount of time the children played like this. However, they reverted to their preferred same-sex activities immediately after the intervention period was over.

Hayden-Thompson et al. (1987) used a different methodology. They asked children to 'post' photographs of known class-mates into one of three boxes according to how much he or she liked each peer. On each box was a picture: either a happy face (for children they liked a lot), a neutral face, or a sad face (for those they did not like). The children regularly posted more of their same-sex peers into the 'happy' box and, in one of the studies at least, the girls showed this gender bias earlier (at the kindergarten age) than the boys. Extending the number of faces to seven (see figure 5.5), we asked 3–9-year-old children what they thought of boys and girls (Yee and Brown, 1994). We also asked them to think of some 'nice' and 'not so nice' things about each gender. Both in these spontaneous comments and on the more structured 'smiley faces' scale, clear own-gender bias was evident. Here are some of the things that one little girl said:

About girls (+): 'They play with you; they don't quarrel; they let you be first with their own elastic; they share.'

(−): 'You say, "can I look at that"? and then they say "can I have it back?" and they snatch it . . .'
'They don't like you, they go off and talk about you and be horrible and they gang against you.'

About boys (+): 'Because they share and are kind; help you a lot.'

(−): 'Horrible, they push you and they fight; don't share; don't let people go first, go first themselves.'

As can be seen in figure 5.5, by age five both boys and girls are showing massive favouritism for their own gender. Note that the ratings for the outgroup are well below the notional mid-point of the scale

(= 4). Note, too, that the girls (though not the boys) showed this bias even as young as three.

In sum, then, there is ample evidence testifying to the psychological importance of gender categories for young children. They very quickly learn which gender they are and, although that identity is not secure

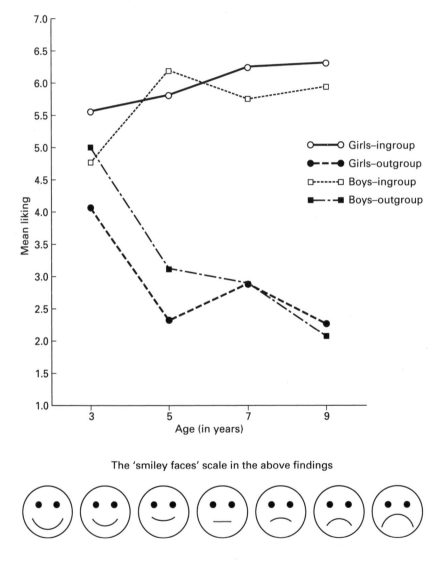

The 'smiley faces' scale in the above findings

Figure 5.5 The development of own-gender bias
Source: Yee and Brown (1994), adapted from table 1

until age five or six (at least in western children), they show very consistent preferences for peers of the same gender as themselves from an earlier age than this. This gender prejudice – if that is what we want to call it – seems to reach its peak at around five or six and maintains that level until early adolescence.

Intergroup Attitudes and Discrimination in Children

In the last section I reviewed the evidence on the ontogeny of children's identification with and preference for various ingroup categories. Inevitably much of that data was comparative in nature, children expressing more positive orientations towards one group than towards another. In this section I want to develop that theme further and examine more generalized intergroup attitudes and stereotypes in children and, wherever possible, explore the implications of these for behavioural discrimination. Just as in the previous section, two themes will recur in this discussion: one is the comparatively early age at which biased attitudes and behaviour can be observed in children; the other is an apparently 'critical' period between five and eight years during which they seem to become especially group-centric.

It may be recalled from chapter 2 that a particularly convincing demonstration of the pervasiveness of discrimination in children was provided by Davey (1983). There I reported how, in a study of over 500 British primary school children, over half showed evidence of ethnocentrism in the distribution of sweets to (unknown) children of their own and other ethnic groups. Running alongside this ingroup favouritism were some equally biased stereotypes of the groups concerned. The children were asked to post cards on which various positive and negative attributes were written (for example, 'these are clever people', 'these people are lazy') into one of four boxes: three of the boxes were identified by photographs of adult members of the three ethnic groups involved in the study, one box was labelled 'nobody'. As can be seen in table 5.1, the children's stereotypical views were nearly always more positive about the ingroup than about one or both of the other groups – sometimes attributing as much as twice as many positive traits to it than to the others – and were correspondingly less negative about it than the others. Davey (1983) also reports that these discrepancies between ingroup and outgroup images were greatest in the younger children (aged 7–8) than in the older respondents (aged 9–10), at least for the White and West Indian groups.

Table 5.1 English children's ethnic stereotypes

Respondents	Traits	Target groups			
		Whites	West Indians	Asians	Nobody
White	+	38*	19	18	5
	–	10*	18	21	48
West Indians	+	30	34*	15	8
	–	14	11*	27	46
Asian	+	33	14	31*	6
	–	11	29	12*	45

Notes
Figures are the mean percentage allocations of traits to each of the four groups.
* Ingroup perceptions for each group

Source: Davey (1983), tables 9.3, 9.4, and 9.5.

Similar evidence of children's propensity to favour their own ethnic group was provided by van Avermaet and McLintock (1988), this time in the context of different-language speakers in Belgium – the Dutch-speaking Flemings and the French speaking-Walloons. The study was conducted with Flemish children aged 6–10 and began with a short video (without sound) of another class of children who were alleged to be either Dutch- or French-speakers. This provided a pretext for the children to distribute some rewards (some jars of attractive colour pens) to their own class and to the other. In the first intergroup evaluations the children were fairly positive about the other class of children but were invariably more positive about it when it was alleged to be Dutch-speaking (like themselves). This ingroup bias was most evident in the middle age group studied (eight years). In their subsequent reward distributions they were also biased against the other class, keeping six jars of pens for themselves and giving only just over two to the other group. This unequal distribution was affected by how well they thought the two classes had done in the task, giving more to the other group if it had done better. However, such equitable behaviour was much less likely to be displayed if they thought that the other class was French-speaking.

This issue of the balance between equity and ingroup favouritism was explored in an experiment we conducted with young girls and boys (Yee and Brown, 1994). In the context of a competition to make collages out of scrap materials, we showed two collages to the children and elicited their preference for one or the other. According to experimental condition, this preferred collage was alleged to have been made by a team of girls (or boys), the other, less preferred, picture having been made by a team of the opposite sex to the first. The children then allocated prizes to the two teams, some toys whose attractiveness each child had previously rank-ordered for us. As can be seen in figure 5.6, the boys seemed to use some kind of equity principle in their allocations, giving more attractive prizes to the 'better' team. The girls, on the other hand, always gave the girls' team the better prizes however well it had done. One other finding from this study was of interest. The extent of the gender bias in these prize

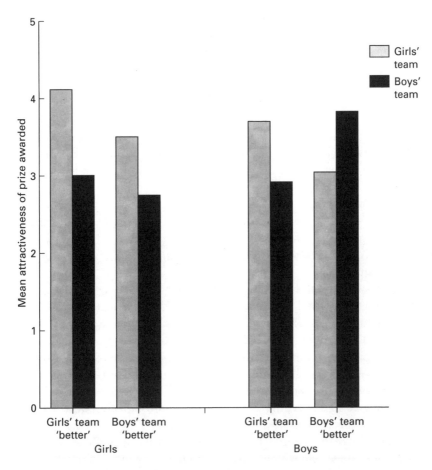

Figure 5.6 Gender discrimination in young children
Source: Yee and Brown (1994), adapted from table 3

allocations was positively correlated with one component (stability) of gender constancy as, indeed, was the bias in their gender attitudes reported in the last section (figure 5.5).

That girls may be more gender-biased than boys was also found by Zalk and Katz (1978). They presented 7–10-year-old American children with a number of dichotomous choices in which they had to decide which of two hypothetical children, identified by gender-specific names, had performed some desirable or undesirable behaviours. By counting the number of times the child nominated the target person of his/her own sex for the different kinds of behaviour a gender-bias score was computed. In general, the children all showed evidence of own-gender bias, though this was stronger for girls than for boys and also stronger for younger children (around seven) than for the older ten-year-olds.

The finding that young children can be more biased than their older peers is, as we shall see, significant for various theoretical explanations of the development of prejudice. Such age effects crop up time and again in research on children's intergroup attitudes and were prominent in a study of gender stereotypes by Berndt and Heller (1986). They presented students from six years to college age with pairs of activities (for example, mending a bicycle, home baking) and asked which of each pair of activities a given actor would be most likely to perform. The sex of the actor was, of course, systematically varied and in the control conditions this was the only information available to the subjects. In two other conditions they were also given information about two pieces of prior behaviour by the actor. This information suggested that the actor typically behaved *either* in sex stereotypical ways (for example, liked to make model aeroplanes if he was a boy), *or* counter-stereotypical ways (the activities would be reversed). At all ages those in the control conditions predicted that the actor would make sex-typed choices of activity. This sex-typing was magnified in the additional stereotypical information condition and was generally reduced (or even eliminated altogether with the oldest subjects) in the counter-stereotypical condition. However, there was an important exception to this general trend: for the eight-year-olds, not only was their degree of sex-typing greater in the control group but it persisted even into the counter-stereotypical condition. Despite being told that the girl (boy) in question had previously chosen masculine (feminine) activities, these eight-year-olds continued to believe that the actor would choose activities stereotypical for their own sex in the future. A similar 'resistance' to individuating information in young children was observed by Biernat (1991), although she did not find this to be abnormally high at the third grade, as Berndt and Heller had done.

It is not just the major social categories of ethnicity and gender which elicit biased evaluations from children. Stigmatized groups – for instance, people with disabilities – may also be devalued relative to the non-stigmatized majority. Clear evidence of this was provided by Maras (1993) in a large-scale study of children's attitudes towards disabled peers. The children (aged 5–11), all from mainstream British primary schools and not obviously handicapped in any way, were asked how much they would like to play with different children, some of the same sex, some of different sex, some with disabilities (for example, hearing impairment, physical handicap), some without. In effect this was a criss-cross categorization arrangement similar to those discussed in chapter 3. Just as we noted there for other naturally occurring crossed categorization situations, there was little evidence that the criss-crossing eliminated bias along either categorical dimension. As can be seen in table 5.2, as usual boys preferred to play with boys, and girls with girls. However, they both preferred to play with non-disabled rather than disabled peers. The net result of these two prejudiced attitudes – one for gender, one for disability – was that the disabled peer of the opposite sex was rated lowest of all and well below the mid-point of the scale. Age had some influence on these attitudes. If anything older children (8–11) showed stronger gender bias than younger (counter to other trends we have noted), although bias in terms of disability was not affected by age.

Powlishta et al. (1994) examined the relationship between three different forms of prejudice in a large sample of Canadian children (aged 5–13). These were: gender bias, bias towards people speaking another

Table 5.2 Children's preferences for peers with and without disabilities[a]

| | Stimuli | | | |
| | Non-disabled | | Disabled | |
Respondents	Girl	Boy	Girl	Boy
Girls	3.8	2.5	3.0	2.2
Boys	2.4	3.8	2.2	2.7

Note: [a]Answers to the question 'How much would you like to play with . . . ?' (scale 1–5).

Source: Maras (1993), table 9.6.

language, and bias towards obese people. In each domain they found considerable evidence of bias in favour of the child's own group and this was greatest in the younger two age groups studied (aged 5–9) than in the older children. Once again girls showed more gender bias than boys although this sex difference did not generalize to the other categories. Most interesting, however, were the generally zero correlations between prejudice in one domain and that in the others. In other words, there was no evidence at all of consistent individual differences in generalized prejudice. This is contrary to what one would expect from a personality account of prejudice (see chapter 2).

In most of these studies the attitudes were elicited in response to photographic or pictorial stimuli. A still more compelling demonstration of how children's attitudes and behaviour can be altered by the perception that a peer belongs to a stigmatized category was provided by Harris et al. (1992). Testing the self-fulfilling prophecy hypothesis (see chapter 4), they paired elementary school boys with other boys that they did not know to work on two tasks. Half the boys were led to believe that their partner suffered from some hyperactive behaviour disorder and were warned to expect that he might be difficult to play with; the remainder were given no such expectancy information. In fact, unbeknown to these subjects, only half of their partners – but equally in *both* conditions – had been diagnosed as having the disorder; the other partners were 'normal'. These expectancies had a powerful influence on the boys' attitudes and behaviour. Those told they were interacting with a hyperactive partner (whether or not they actually were) found the task harder than those given no expectancy information. They were also less willing to give their partner credit for doing well and, from observations of their actual behaviour, acted in a less friendly way towards him. The 'target' children's attitudes were the mirror image of this. Those designated as hyperactive (especially when, in fact, they were not) enjoyed the experience less than those not so stigmatized, presumably in response to the perceivers' unfriendly behaviour.

All the intergroup phenomena we have discussed thus far have been associated with real-life categories such as ethnicity, gender, and disability, all of which are imbued with deeply ingrained cultural values and meanings. How general are these effects and, in particular, is it possible to disentangle them from the particular social relationships in which they occur? To answer these questions it can sometimes be helpful to create *ad hoc* groups and observe people's – in this case, children's – affiliations and behaviour. One such attempt was made by Vaughan et al. (1981). They adapted the minimal-group paradigm (see chapter 3) for use with 7- and 11-year-old children. After the normal picture preference task – only this time with children's paintings rather than those of Klee and Kandinsky – the children were divided into two groups. They then allocated money to these groups (but never to themselves personally). These reward allocations showed the usual intergroup discrimination: they gave more to their own group than to the others, particularly when this would establish a *relative* difference between the groups. There were no consistent age effects. A similar minimal-group paradigm was adopted by Wetherell (1982) comparing the responses of eight-year-old European, Maori, and Polynesian children in New Zealand. Like Vaughan et al. (1981) she observed intergroup discrimination in all three groups. However, there were some interesting cultural differences. The Polynesian and Maori children were more generous to members of the outgroup than were the Europeans, and the Polynesians especially seemed to favour allocation strategies in which *both* groups benefited rather than where the ingroup gained relative to the outgroup.

Those cultural differences notwithstanding, these studies show that children as young as 7–8 show similar propensities for ingroup favouritism following mere categorization as do adults (see chapter 3). However, in the classical minimal-group paradigm the two groups are of equal status and such parity seldom exists in the real world. What of children's reactions to being in a 'better' or 'worse' group? This was the issue we addressed in an experiment which exploited that game much-loved by organizers of children's fêtes and parties, the egg-and-spoon race (Yee and Brown, 1992). Each child was first given a practice session at egg-and-spoon running and given some performance feedback (the same for all children). They were then allocated to one of two teams of same-sex but unknown children. According to experimental condition, they were put in a team full of children who were obviously egg-and-spoon experts since they had all apparently done as well or better than the child him/herself, and clearly better than the rival team. Alternatively, they were put in the other, less good, team. When asked to evaluate the teams' likely performance in a forthcoming egg-and-spoon race the children's ratings were strongly affected by their team assignment. As can be seen in figure 5.7 (top half), those in the so-called 'fast' team all had a more favourable opinion of their own team than of the other.

The interesting findings came from the 'slow' team (bottom half of figure 5.7). Now most of the children reversed their ratings, evaluating the outgroup more favourably than the ingroup. But there was one

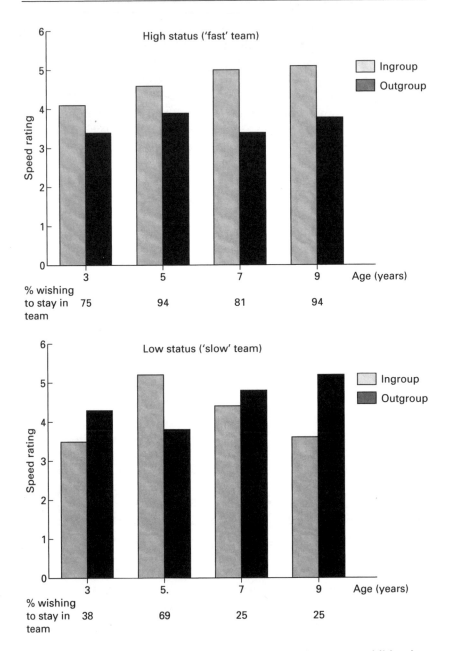

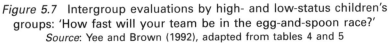

Figure 5.7 Intergroup evaluations by high- and low-status children's groups: 'How fast will your team be in the egg-and-spoon race?'
Source: Yee and Brown (1992), adapted from tables 4 and 5

important exception. The five-year-olds (actually nearer to $5\frac{1}{2}$) maintained and even increased slightly their ingroup favouritism, despite being told that they were in a less-good team! The group morale measure ('Do you want to stay in your team or move to the other?') told a similar story: over 80 per cent of those in the 'fast' team were happy to stay where they were; on the other hand, 70 per cent of the 'slow' teams (excluding the five year olds) wanted to change teams. Not the five-year-olds however: over two-thirds of them wanted to remain in that lower-status team.

For me, two things stand out from this experiment. One is that even very young children (of three years) are apparently able to make the necessary social comparisons to utilize information about the relative standing of their group. This is important theoretically because some have argued that at this age children are either not able or not disposed to make such comparisons (Ruble et al., 1980; Suls and Sanders, 1982). However, as we saw earlier with studies of ethnic preference, and now here with artificial groups, the evidence seems to be that such children are sensitive to intergroup status differences. The second salient feature of the results was the apparently very group-centric character of the 5–6-year-olds, even to the point of being resistant to apparently 'objective' information about their group's capabilities. This confirms similar hints noted elsewhere in this chapter that the period between five and eight years seems to be a particularly significant one for the development of intergroup attitudes. In the next section I shall return to this 'critical period' when I examine different explanations for the appearance of prejudice in children.

Understanding the Development of Prejudice in Children

'Don't you simply hate being a girl?' asked George.
'No, of course not', said Anne. 'You see, I do like pretty frocks and I
have my dolls and you can't do that if you're a boy.'
Enid Blyton, *Five on a Treasure Island* (1942;
1989 recording by EMI Records Ltd)

The most obvious explanation for the appearance of prejudice in children is that it is acquired through direct socialization by their parents and from other sources such as peer group influence and the usual channels of cultural transmission. This, one would suppose, would be the hypothesis of learning theories of child development and, very probably, of many lay people's accounts too (for example, Bandura, 1977; Mischel, 1966; Sears et al., 1957). Superficially, such an explanation would have much to commend it. Few would deny that the home environment has some influence on the development of the child, even if arguments still rage as to the exact nature and extent of this influence (see the debate initiated by Plomin and Daniels, 1987). The frequent depiction of men and women and certain minority groups in stereotypical roles in the media and in children's literature is, by now, a well-documented phenomenon (Durkin, 1985; Milner, 1983). I am sure I cannot be the only parent who, while reading his children their favourite bed-time stories, has winced at the crude reproduction of conventional stereotypes which seem to pervade their pages (see the epigraph above). What more natural conclusion to draw than that all these socio-cultural influences should directly determine our children's social attitudes?

Unfortunately, the truth is not so simple. True, such a conclusion is reinforced by empirical studies which have provided evidence of direct parental socialization of children's attitudes or which have observed correlations between exposure to mass media sources and children's prejudicial and stereotypical thinking. One of the earliest of these was the pioneering research of Horowitz and Horowitz (1938). In addition to their findings on ethnic awareness (see p. 122), they carried out interviews with both parents and children. Some of the published extracts from these give a revealing, if anecdotal, picture of direct parental socialization of racist attitudes in a southern state in pre-war America. Here, for example, is a seven-year-old White girl discussing her playmates:

> 'Mother doesn't want me to play with colored children, 'cause they colored men. Might have pneumonia if you play with them. I play with colored children sometimes but mamma whips me.'
>
> (Horowitz and Horowitz, 1938, p. 333)

Such direct control was openly admitted by some parents:

> 'T always played with other children. Yes, I used to tell her not to play with some. Just told her, never gave her any reasons. She never played with negro children, I didn't have to tell her that.'　(Horowitz and Horowitz, 1938, p. 335)

However, more systematic research has not always confirmed these early observations. It is true that Bird et al. (1952) and Mosher and

Scodel (1960) found correlations between the ethnocentrism of White parents and children's negative attitudes towards ethnic groups consistent with the idea of a direct transmission between the generations. The correlations were, however, not very strong. Similarly, Spencer (1983) found some relationships between Black children's ethnocentrism and their mothers' knowledge and beliefs about such issues as civil rights, Black history and integration. On the other hand, Branch and Newcombe (1980), adopting a similar approach of correlating parental and child attitudes in Black families, found some rather surprising inverse relationships: for the 4–5-year-olds there was a negative correlation between parental ethnocentrism (that is, pro-Black attitude) and the child's pro-Black choices on doll-choice type tasks. Only for the 6–7-year-olds did this relationship become positive, and then only weakly (and non-significantly). Likewise, Davey (1983), in the study already discussed (pp. 141–2), found little evidence of a strong link between the intergroup attitudes of parents (which were superficially tolerant) and those of the children which, as we saw, were quite prejudiced.

In the domain of gender attitudes a similar ambiguity exists. It is, of course, well known that from birth onwards boys and girls receive very different treatment from their parents and caretakers (Maccoby, 1980). What is less clear is whether these different experiences involve or result in the direct transmission of gender attitudes from parents to child. One study which *did* find a relationship between parental (sex role) attitudes and children's tendency to show gender stereotyping in toy preferences and occupational choices was by Repetti (1984). The mother's and father's femininity and masculinity respectively were positively correlated with their children's stereotyping. One other finding of interest was that whilst the *total* amount of television the children watched was completely unrelated to their stereotypical judgements, the amount of *educational* television was negatively related to their stereotyping. I return to the possible effect of the media shortly.

In contrast to Repetti's findings, other research has found little or no evidence of direct parental socialization. Perhaps the most systematic work has been done by Maccoby and Jacklin (1974, 1987). In their earlier review of sex differences in behaviour they found very little relationship between parental own-sex typing and that of children, suggesting that the acquisition of sex differences by child–parent imitation was not a straightforward affair (Maccoby and Jacklin, 1974). Their later studies of gender segregation in pre-school children cast further doubt on the influence of parents. Two findings, in particular, were significant (Maccoby and Jacklin, 1987). One was that although same-sex play preferences were widespread, these were not very stable across time for each individual child. That is, the degree of own-gender favouritism shown by one child from one week to the next varied considerably. This would be unlikely if certain children had been strongly influenced by their parents to adopt particular gender attitudes. The second finding was the lack of any strong evidence showing a link between parental behaviour and the children's preference for gender-segregated play. The only correlation was between the roughness of fatherly play with their daughters and the latter's preference for female playmates. Admittedly, these findings of Maccoby and Jacklin (1987) were 'null results' and hence are inherently uninterpretable and, moreover, were based on rather small samples. Nevertheless, they do cast some doubt on the idea that parents transmit gender attitudes to their children in any direct fashion.

Of course, parents are not the only influences in the child's life. In many parts of the world children grow up immersed in ideas and images from books, comics and, especially, television. The evidence for the effects of these media on children's prejudice is also equivocal. One of the first studies was by Himmelweit et al. (1958) which focused on the 10–14 age group. Because it was conducted in an era when television was nowhere near as widespread as it is now it was possible to achieve a good matching of 'viewing' and 'non-viewing' children and compare these two groups on a number of measures. One set is of interest to us here because they are concerned with children's ideas about foreigners and ethnic groups. Three slightly contradictory findings emerged. One was that viewers' judgements about outgroups were more objective and factual and less value-laden than the 'controls'. On the other hand, in another part of the study, there was evidence that viewers saw some foreigners (though not all) in more stereotypical terms (for example, the French as 'gay and witty'). Finally, more viewers than controls disagreed with the xenophobic statement 'My country is always right'. Perhaps one reason for the conflicting nature of these results is that the researchers restricted their sample to homes which could only receive one channel (BBC) which, at that time, carried a number of documentaries depicting life in other countries. This could have had the effect of providing factual information about those cultures and, simultaneously, reinforcing certain popular stereotypical images.

Subsequent research on the effects of television on children's social attitudes tended to confirm this ambiguous conclusion. Zuckerman et al. (1980) correlated parental reports of their children's television watching with measures of ethnic and gender prejudice. For the sample as a whole there were few reliable correlations. However, when girls and boys were examined separately there were significant correlations for the girls between amount of television watched, ethnic prejudice, and anti-*female* prejudice. There were no reliable relationships for the boys. Morgan (1982) also observed very different results for boys and girls in his longitudinal study of three cohorts of middle-school children. When each cohort was looked at separately there were a few (weak) correlations between television watching and sexist stereotyping, but these tended to all but disappear when such variables as intelligence and socio-economic status were controlled for. However, when looked at longitudinally, which allows stronger inferences about causality, the effects of television on sexism were apparent only for the girls: the amount of television watched in the preceding year was related to their subsequent levels of sexism. For boys this causal direction was inverted; for them, their initial levels of sexism predicted how much television they subsequently watched. Williams et al. (1986) studied the impact of introducing television into a community for the first time and observed significant increases in both boys' and girls' sex-role differentiation after a two-year period. Finally, in a unique intervention study, Johnston and Ettema (1982) examined the effects of a thirteen-week educational television series whose explicit aim was to promote counter-stereotypical images of males and females. The series significantly altered elementary school children's sex-role attitudes in the direction of making them less stereotypical, and some of these changes persisted for as long as nine months. However, the most marked changes were observed in the children who watched the programmes in school and where the viewing was followed by a class-room discussion with their teachers. For those who simply viewed the programmes, whether at home or at school, the attitude changes were smaller in magnitude. In sum, therefore, as Durkin (1985) has concluded, the effects of the mass media on children's stereotypes, whilst undeniable, are seldom straightforward unidirectional relationships, the one directly giving rise to the other.

In fact, I believe this is also the conclusion to which we are forced when considering the whole class of explanations which assume some kind of simple socialization of children's prejudice by social agencies, whether these be parents or wider cultural influences like the media. There are at least four facts which point to this conclusion.

The first is the very early appearance of social-category awareness and use by children. Recall that on pp. 121–6 we noted how children as young as $2\frac{1}{2}$–3 years, and occasionally even younger, show evidence of being aware of gender (especially) and ethnic differences and of discriminating between them behaviourally. Whilst not conclusive in themselves, such precocious signs of social differentiation are suggestive that the children themselves are contributing something to the process.

The second is the apparently non-linear trajectory of the growth of prejudice in children. As we saw earlier, there are several studies which point to an apparently critical period between five and eight years during which ingroup favouritism of various kinds seems to reach a peak, then to decline in the pre-adolescent period. If the socialization of prejudice simply involved the incremental acquisition of ideas and values from the child's social environment, one would not anticipate such an inverted U-shape for its developmental time course.

Thirdly, as Aboud (1988) has noted, there have been some marked changes in measured prejudice levels in adults over the past 40 years and yet recent studies of children's ethnic prejudice have shown that children below the age of ten still continue to manifest various kinds of bias and discrimination. The same argument can be made for gender where, again, it seems that levels of overt sexism have fallen in adults (Kahn and Crosby, 1985; Sutton and Moore, 1985), but not apparently in children, as we saw on pp. 137–44. As I shall discuss later (chapter 7), there may be more to these changes in adult attitudes than meets the eye but, still, the discrepancy between the generations remains a problem for the linear socialization model.

Finally, and related to the third point, are the generally low correlations which have been observed between parental and child intergroup attitudes. If the transmission was as direct as assumed by a simple socialization model, one would have hoped to explain more than 10 per cent or so of the variance that is implied by the typical correlations of 0.3 or less.

Partly in response to these kinds of problems, social psychologists have started to develop theoretical models which link the development of prejudice to more general cognitive social and affective changes which occur in children in the first ten years of their life (Aboud, 1988; Katz, 1983; Maccoby, 1988; Maccoby and Jacklin 1987; Vaughan, 1987). Although there are undoubted differences in emphasis between these various theories, they have in common the assumption that the child plays a more active role in the developmental process than the traditional socialization explanation allowed. In particular, all attribute primary importance to the cognitive capacity for categorization, both in assisting children to make sense of their environment and in locating themselves in that environment by providing them with various social identities.

Aboud's (1988) theory is a good example of this approach. She posits a three-stage model in which the early years (up to about five) are dominated by perceptual and affective processes. Children classify the world crudely into broad categories – male and female, familiar and strange – and associate these categories with different emotional responses, presumably derived from a mixture of their own personal experiences and the vicarious observation of the experiences of others. They also quickly learn to classify themselves as belonging to some categories and not to others. Thinking at this stage is egocentric and dominated by perceptual cues, the appearance of things and people (Piaget, 1954). The combination of these affective and cognitive processes could provide the basis for the early emergence of own ethnic (and presumably other) group preferences. From 5–7 years, however, children's thinking becomes more sophisticated as it progresses through the concrete operational period (Piaget, 1954). The immature concepts of groups which have been hitherto dominated by physical attributes such as clothing and skin colour and which manifest themselves in uncertainty about the possibility of changing sex and ethnicity, give way in this second stage to cognitions in terms of more abstract and internal attributes. At this point, paralleling the achievement of conservation in the physical domain, children recognize that many major social category memberships are relatively stable and do not change with superficial changes of appearance or with age. At about this same time (5–7 years) children's social orientations also undergo a shift from the earlier egocentric preoccupation with the self to a strong group focus, often coinciding with the transition to formal schooling. Thus, early group preferences in terms of simple like–dislike evolve into fully fledged stereotypes in which less obviously observable attributes and traits are associated with particular categories. According to Aboud, the coupling of these social and cognitive changes is likely to facilitate a particularly high degree of ethnocentrism among 5–7 year olds. Finally, as the child acquires properly operational thinking there is a recognition of the possibility of individual variation within groups, and the initially rather rigid stereotypes become more flexible and amenable to change in response to counter-stereotypic or individuating information. One might add, too, though this is not much emphasized in Aboud's account, that as children mature they become more sensitive to the norms of adult society and hence more aware of the social undesirability of expressing certain kinds of prejudice too overtly. Taken together, these last changes would produce a reduction in prejudice and discrimination.

Although Aboud (1988) was specifically concerned with ethnic prejudice, there seems no reason to suppose that similar socio-cognitive processes might not underlie the development of gender (and other kinds of) prejudice too, especially in view of the many similarities between them (Katz, 1983). Certainly one of its key predictions – the 'peaking' of stereotyping and prejudice around the concrete operational period – has, as we have seen, some empirical support (Asher and Allen, 1969; Berndt and Heller, 1986; Lambert and Klineberg, 1967; Powlishta et al., 1994; Vaughan, 1964a, b; Yee and Brown, 1992; Zalk and Katz, 1978).

Further evidence for the link between cognitive development and the development of prejudice comes from those studies that have found reliable correlations between measures of conservation – that is, the veridical perception of certain invariant properties of objects and people despite changes in appearance – and children's ethnic attitudes. Clark et al. (1980) and Aboud (1984) found that measures of physical conservation and measures of ethnic constancy were quite highly correlated. Clark et al. (1980) also included a measure of ethnic preference and found the usual curvilinear effect of strongest pro-White preference in their (White) children aged 5–7. The conservation measure was related to the ethnic preference measure, but only when a Black tester was used: 'conserving' children tended to be less ethnocentric than 'pre-operational' children. This effect of the experimenter's ethnicity, occasionally found in other studies also (for example, Katz and Zalk, 1974), underlines the importance of incorporating a social desirability component into any socio-cognitive model. However, such an addition may not be a simple one because the evidence on social desirability, conservation, and intergroup attitudes is rather mixed. Doyle et al. (1988) found conservation to be positively associated with more flexible ethnic attitudes, and the latter were only very weakly related to social desirability.

These studies found a negative correlation between conservation and ingroup-favouring biases. This may not always be the case, particularly if the sample studied is heavily weighted with children in the crucial 5–8-year age range. Corenblum and Annis (1993) found *positive* correlations between measures of cognitive development and positive ingroup attitudes in their study of 6–8-year-old Canadian children. Similarly, Yee and Brown (1994) found positive correlations between a component of gender constancy and two measures of gender bias, again with about half the sample in the 5–8 age bracket.

While Aboud's model seems to provide a plausible account of the development of ethnic attitudes, there are two issues which remain to be resolved before it can satisfactorily explain children's intergroup attitudes in general. One concerns its utility to account for the development of gender attitudes and, in particular, what appears to be precociousness in girls in demonstrating own-gender favouring preferences (see pp. 136–41, and Katz, 1983). Maccoby (1988) has suggested that gender should be treated as something of a special case in children's social development because of its universal prevalence as a social category and because of its functional utility for many social situations in which children find themselves. Also stressing the importance of cognitive factors (for example, self-categorization by gender, gender constancy, and so on), she argues that the very early emergence of gender segregation can be additionally traced to the different play styles of boys and girls and the distinctive cultures of boys' and girls' groups that this gives rise to (Maccoby and Jacklin, 1974). If each sex finds its own way of playing more compatible than that of the other sex then this behavioural differentiation could form the basis of subsequent evaluative biases at the attitudinal level also. The fact that girls sometimes show gender segregation earlier than boys might be attributable to a 'defensive' reaction by the girls against the typically more boisterous rough-and-tumble play of their male peers (Maccoby and Jacklin, 1987).

The second issue concerns the applicability of a cognitive developmental model like Aboud's to children from minority (or subordinate) groups. Three phenomena, in particular, are somewhat troublesome for the theory. One is the difference between their typical preference and identification data and that from dominant-group children. As we saw on pp. 126–30, there is an accumulation of evidence from a variety of different societal contexts that whilst dominant-group children almost always show strong ingroup favouritism, subordinate-group children show a much more diverse pattern ranging from outgroup favouritism, through 'fairness', to ingroup favouritism as well. The two other phenomena are related to this heterogeneity: the frequent 'peaking' of ethnocentrism in majority children between five and seven years seems either to be delayed by a year or two, or not to happen at all, in subordinate-group children (see Aboud, 1988, p. 127); and at least some of the variation in these children's ethnocentric preference seems attributable to cultural and historical variables. Recall that several of the studies showing pro-ingroup preference in Black American children were conducted post-1968; many of those showing pro-outgroup preferences were conducted before that 'watershed' (see pp. 132–3).

A partial explanation of some of these anomalies has been provided by Vaughan (1987). To the cognitive developmental account we have already considered, Vaughan adds the process of social comparison. Drawing on Tajfel and Turner's (1986) Social Identity Theory (see chapter 6), Vaughan argues that children's understanding and evaluation of their identity – be this ethnic, gender, or any other salient ingroup category – stems in large part from their comparison of that ingroup with relevant outgroups. When such a comparison reveals their group to be superior, or at least roughly equal, to others then the child can accrue some positive self-regard from its ethnicity (or other group membership). Such is usually the case for dominant-group children. On the other hand, for subordinate-group children such comparisons may be invidious in the sense that their own group appears obviously inferior on a number of dimensions. One of Goodman's (1952) Black respondents saw it so clearly: 'The people that are white, they can go up. The people that are brown, they have to go down' (Goodman, 1952, p. 45). Then the child's self-concept is also likely to be negative and it is not difficult to see how a negative identity could manifest itself in attitudes and preferences *against* their own group and *towards* the dominant, and apparently favoured, outgroup. The significance of incorporating this social comparative element into any cognitive-developmental model is that it can help us to understand why during certain historical periods there can be dramatic shifts in subordinate-group children's responses. The advent of such political movements as Black Power in the United States and Brown Power in New Zealand, both around the end of the 1960s, helped to create an ideological framework for African-Americans and Maoris in which their previously perceived 'inferiority' could be transformed into ingroup pride and the possibility of social comparability with the dominant (White) group (Vaughan, 1987).

In summary, then, what can we say of prejudice in children? Obviously much remains to be understood but at least this much is clear: children cannot be regarded as empty vessels into which the prevailing prejudices of adult society are steadily poured. Such a view simply is not compatible with the very early emergence of category awareness and use, the curvilinear nature of the growth of prejudiced thinking in childhood, and the weak evidence for unidirectional parent–child or society–child transmission of intergroup attitudes. Instead, the work I have reviewed in this chapter points to a much more dynamic developmental process in which children, just like their parents, are actively seeking to understand, evaluate, and control their social world with the (sometimes limited) cognitive means at their disposal. Since that world is itself partitioned in socially meaningful ways – for example, by gender, ethnicity, or age – it should not surprise us too much if the children's beliefs and behaviour become patterned along these same lines. Thus, the biases and preferences which we can so easily observe are not the result of some passive indoctrination by the adult world but the natural outgrowth of an interaction between that world and the psychological processes of categorization, identification, and comparison in the minds of our children.

Summary

1. Prejudice presupposes the awareness and use of social categories in perception, judgement, and behaviour. There is evidence that children from as young as three years of age are aware of two of society's major social categories, gender and ethnicity. Primitive behavioural discriminations in terms of gender may even be made in infancy.
2. From three years and upward children also readily identify with some categories rather than others and demonstrate clear attitudinal and behavioural preferences among these categories. Generally speaking they prefer members of their own group to those belonging to other groups. This has been demonstrated most clearly with gender, but also with ethnicity, nationality, and stigmatized groups such as disability.
3. There are some important variations in this own-group preference phenomenon. One is the tendency for members of ethnic minorities to show it much less strongly than members of dominant and majority groups. Indeed, in a number of studies conducted in the immediate post-Second World War period members of minority groups demonstrated a clear *outgroup* preference.
4. Children also manifest more generally prejudiced attitudes and discriminatory behaviour towards outgroups. Again, gender and ethnicity have been the most frequently studied categorical bases for this favouritism, although it has also

been found with *ad hoc* groupings. Results indicate that girls may show own-gender-favouring biases earlier and more strongly than boys. Also, a common finding has been a 'peaking' of group-centrism around the period 5–7 years, declining somewhat after this.

5. Explanations for the growth of prejudice in children which assume a passive absorption by them of the prejudices in the adult society are not easy to reconcile with the early appearance of category differentiation, the non-linear nature of prejudice development, and the weak or inconsistent correlations between parental and child attitudes or between exposure to mass media and prejudice.

6. A more promising explanation may lie in linking the development of prejudice to other aspects of the child's social and cognitive development. Such an approach, with its emphasis on the child's changing abilities to categorize and understand the world, regards the acquisition of prejudice as a more dynamic process: an interaction between children's developing socio-cognitive capacities and the socially structured environment which they have to deal with.

Further Reading

Aboud, F. (1988) *Children and Prejudice*. Oxford: Basil Blackwell.
Maccoby, E.E. and Jacklin, C.N. (1987) Gender segregation in childhood. *Advances in Child Development, 20*, 239–287.

Notes

1. Note that in this task, as in many others reported in this chapter, when one is presented with a binary choice like this there is a 'chance' level of responding of 50 per cent. Nevertheless, with the sample size used by Clark and Clark (1947) the 77 per cent rate of 'correct' responding by even the youngest children was significantly above this chance level.

2. It is worth noting that these findings of Clark and Clark (1947) were cited directly in a footnote to the famous 1954 US Supreme Court decision outlawing segregated schools. This must be one of the few occasions where social psychology can fairly claim to have had an influence on public policy.

Prejudice and Intergroup Relations

6   Anti-European demonstration

The threat to national identity was a powerful motive behind anti-European attitudes in Britain in the 1990s.

In 1994, the year in which I am writing this chapter, the world seems as riven as ever with intergroup hatred and bloodshed. In just the first six months we saw literally tens of thousands slaughtered in Rwanda as members of the Tutsi and Hutu tribal groups contest the right to govern that country. The killing in former Yugoslavia continues unabated as warring Croats, Serbs and Muslims dispute ownership of Bosnia. And, on a smaller but no less tragic scale, dozens of Palestinians were shot dead in a Hebron mosque by an Israeli soldier, and several Irish people were murdered in a bar in County Down, Northern Ireland, as they watched their team play in the World Cup. The awful irony of these events is that they take place in a year otherwise marked by some momentous examples of intergroup conflict resolution: the first free election in South Africa in which Nelson Mandela and his African National Congress party swept to power; the implementation of the peace accord between the Israeli government and the Palestinian Liberation Organization over the occupied territories of the West Bank. The histories of all these intergroup contexts are as many and as various as the situations themselves but they all have one thing in common: they can all be viewed as the playing out of the material interests of the groups involved. Whether the outcome is peace or war, tolerance or bigotry, it is often possible to trace that result to the groups' respective economic, political and geographical concerns at the time.

This idea forms the starting point for this chapter in which we consider prejudice as originating in the social relationships between groups. The first section, therefore, concentrates on objective goal relationships: What are the interests of the groups concerned? Are they in conflict or do they coincide? Viewed from this perspective, the rise and fall of prejudice in different eras and in different places immediately becomes comprehensible. However, as we shall see, such variations may not be completely explicable from a consideration of groups' objective interests; we may need to take account of their social psychological interests also. One important factor in this respect turns out to be a group's social standing in relation to other groups. Such intergroup comparisons can take place on many different dimensions, both concrete (for example, wealth) and less tangible (for example, friendliness). These intergroup relations are important because they have implications for the social identities of the group members concerned. Where these identities are secure and positive, often because the group has sufficient status and distinctiveness, then the consequential inter-group attitudes and behaviour are likely to be very different than if they are ill-defined or threatened in some way. These processes of maintaining or achieving satisfactory social identities provide the topic of the second section. In the third section the theme of intergroup comparisons continues as we consider their implications for people's sense of deprivation. Here the discussion returns to material issues such as income levels and living standards but viewed firmly from a *relative* rather than an absolute perspective. The conclusion from this section on relative deprivation is that prejudice springs as much from how badly off we *think* we are as from conditions of objective oppression and disadvantage.

Conflicting Group Interests

The idea that it is possible to analyse intergroup behaviour – and in prejudice we surely have an example *par excellence* of intergroup behaviour – by identifying the nature and compatibility of group goals has a long and distinguished history in the social sciences. In an influential article Campbell (1965) surveyed a number of theories in sociology, anthropology, and social psychology, dating at least from the turn of the century (Sumner, 1906), which are based on this premise. Noting that a common theme of these approaches is the idea that some group conflicts are 'rational' or 'realistic' in the sense that they are based on a real competition for scarce resources, Campbell (1965) labelled the perspective the Realistic Group Conflict Theory. The principal hypothesis of this theory is that intergroup attitudes and behaviour will tend to reflect group interests. Where these are incompatible, where what one group gains is at the expense of another, then the social psychological response is likely to be negative: prejudiced attitudes, biased judgements, hostile behaviour. Where they are compatible – or, even better, complementary – so that one group can only gain with the assistance of another, then the reaction should be more positive: tolerance, fairness, amicability. Campbell's anthropological colleague LeVine summed it up thus:

> *Describe to me the economic intergroup situation, and I shall predict the content of the (intergroup) stereotypes.*   (As recalled by Tajfel, 1981a, p. 224)

Within social psychology the most influential proponent of this Realistic Group Conflict Theory is Sherif (for example, 1966). Like Campbell, Sherif was concerned to rebut the idea that prejudice could be understood primarily as a problem of individual psychology (see chapter 2). Instead, he placed the causal emphasis squarely on to the nature of intergroup goal relationships. Prejudice, in his view, had its roots in the real or perceived conflicts of interests between one group and others. To demonstrate this thesis Sherif, together with his colleagues, conducted a series of justly famous field experiments which have come to be known collectively as the 'summer camp studies', so called because they were run under the guise of a summer holiday camp for boys (Sherif and Sherif, 1953; Sherif et al., 1955, 1961). The participants in the studies were some 12-year-old boys who had initially been screened to ensure that they all came from stable and non-deprived family backgrounds and that none of them know each other prior to the camp. These rather elaborate procedures were designed to ensure that their subsequent behaviour could not be attributed to any pre-existing deprivation or personal relationships amongst the boys.

In the first stage of the experiments the children were split up into two groups, care being taken to match these as closely as possible. In two of the experiments it was also arranged that the majority of each boy's friends, those that had been made in the first day or two of the camp, should be in the outgroup. In the third experiment the boys never actually met initially but were simply in their groups from the very start, camped some distance from each other and unaware of the other group's existence. For a few days the children participated in some activities in these groups but the groups themselves had little to do with each other. Despite this independence the observers did record some instances of comparisons between the group in which, according to Sherif (1966, p. 80), 'the edge was given to one's own group'. Moreover, in the third study, on learning of the existence of the other group, several boys spontaneously suggested that the other group be challenged to some contest. It is significant that these instances of intergroup rivalry occurred *before* any explicit competition between the groups had been introduced.

The researchers then implemented the second stage of the study. They organized a series of competitions between the groups (for example, softball, tug-of-war) and announced that the overall winner of these would receive a cup, and that each member of this successful group would also get an attractive new penknife. The losers would receive nothing. Thus, an objective conflict of interest was introduced since what one group gained, the other lost; the groups had moved from a state of independence to being negatively interdependent. This innovation produced a dramatic change in the boys' behaviour. From their initial peaceful coexistence they quickly became two hostile factions, constantly berating and sometimes even physically attacking the other group. Their perceptions and judgements of the two groups showed marked evidence of ingroup bias, and friendships became almost exclusively confined to members of their own group. Such favouritism is all the more noteworthy when it is recalled that in two of the studies the boys' friends had been placed in the *other* group. This was a vivid illustration of the power of a single intergroup relationship to transform a number of interpersonal relationships almost at the drop of a hat.

Having so easily generated animosity between the groups, Sherif and his colleagues then attempted to reduce the conflict. Starting from the same Realistic Group Conflict premises which had led to the design of the second stage of the experiments, they reasoned that to reduce the hostilities the groups must move from being negatively interdependent on one another to a state of *positive* interdependence. Accordingly, they created a series of situations in which the two groups had a *superordinate goal*, a goal which both desired but neither could attain on their own (Sherif, 1966). For example, one such occasion was when the camp truck was made to break down some miles from the camp. It was too heavy to be 'bump started' by one group of boys on its own; together they could (and did) get it started. After a series of such scenarios – apparently occurring naturally but, in fact, carefully engineered by the researchers – the two groups became much less aggressive towards each other and their perceptions and attitudes much less prejudiced.

On the face of it, the summer camp studies seem to provide some powerful evidence for the Realistic Conflict explanation of prejudice. Here were some ordinary children whose behaviour could be shown to vary predictably simply by changing the intergroup goal relationship. Such social psychological changes were too generic and too rapid to be attributable to some personality variable (see chapter 2), and neither could the prejudice be explained by belief dissimilarity between the participants (see chapter 3). The groups were carefully composed to be as similar as possible with, if anything, the outgroup members being more similar to each boy than his fellow ingroupers.

In the decades following Sherif's pioneering research, laboratory studies of intergroup relations largely confirmed his basic findings.

When the interdependence between groups is experimentally controlled to be either negative, neutral, or positive then the results are
quite consistent: one observes more ingroup bias, less intergroup liking,
and stronger intergroup discrimination when the groups are objectively
in competition than when they must co-operate over some joint goal
(Brown, 1988; Doise, 1976; Turner, 1981).

Findings from outside the laboratory have also been generally
supportive of the Realistic Group Conflict approach. Prevailing national
stereotypes often undergo sharp changes for better or worse according
to developments in international relations as new alliances are forged or
wars declared. I well remember how, in a few short weeks following
Argentina's military excursions to the Malvinos Islands in the South
Atlantic in 1982, popular British stereotypes of Argentinians quickly
became suffused with derogatory and bellicose imagery. Occasionally,
social psychologists have been on hand to record such changes more
systematically. Seago (1947) found that American college student
stereotypes of Japanese people became very much less favourable after
the Japanese attack on Pearl Harbor in 1941. Such negative attitudes
presumably greatly facilitated the American government's decision to
intern tens of thousands of Japanese-Americans in prison camps for the
duration of the war, an action whose consequences are still being felt
today (Nagata and Crosby, 1991; Nakanishi, 1988). During the Gulf
War of 1990–1 Haslam et al. (1992) recorded Australian students'
perceptions of the United States, which is apparently a rather negative
outgroup for this particular sub-group. Between September 1990, just
after Iraq invaded Kuwait, and February 1991, when they finally
withdrew, the stereotypes of Americans became significantly less
positive, particularly on such traits as 'arrogant' and 'scientifically
minded'. However, it was interesting that this change was also
dependent on the context in which the ratings were elicited. When the
questionnaire only mentioned Australia, Britain and the USA as possible
stimulus groups, thus underlining the 'outgroup' character of the
American category, the negative stereotype change over time was the
most pronounced. On the other hand, where (with another group of
respondents) Iraq and the Soviet Union were included as well, the
stereotypes of the USA remained more stable. Haslam et al. (1992)
argued that the inclusion of these two other outgroups shifted the
categorical frame of reference to incorporate the America into the
'friendly' ingroup against the 'enemy' outgroup Iraq.

More general ethnocentric attitudes may also be related to economic
and political relations between groups. Brewer and Campbell (1976)

conducted an ethnographic study involving 30 tribal groups in East Africa. Of these, 27 rated themselves more favourably than any other single group. The degree of this bias was related to the proximity of the groups being rated: nearby outgroups were derogated somewhat more than more distant groups. Such a correlation is consistent with Realistic Group Conflict Theory since neighbouring groups are more likely to become embroiled in disputes over grazing land, access to water and other scarce resources. The matter is complicated, however, because there are also more likely to be trading links between nearby groups which would give rise to *positive* interdependence and hence greater intergroup attraction (as indeed, Brewer and Campbell also found). Both patterns, found as they were by aggregating across all groups, become comprehensible once one analyses *specific* intergroup relationships amongst neighbouring groups which can vary from strong alliance to intense conflict in particular cases (Brewer, 1986).

A final illustration of the importance of conflicting group interests is provided by Struch and Schwartz (1989). They examined the attitudes of some Israeli citizens towards an ultraorthodox religious sect. Two types of attitudes were measured. One was concerned with aggression towards the sect and incorporated, at the mildest pole, some social distance items (for example, willingness to have as neighbours), some items concerned with electoral opposition to projects of special interest to religious groups and, strongest of all, the endorsement of certain actions aimed directly at penalizing the sect (for example, boycotting their stores). The second set of attitudes were more conventional ingroup and outgroup ratings from which measures of ingroup bias were derived. The clearest results were obtained for the aggression measure, where by far the strongest single predictor were respondents' answers to two questions concerning conflicts of interests between their own group and the sect: the more conflict they perceived the more aggression they expressed. However, some other results were also of interest. One was that perceptions of intergroup value dissimilarity were positively correlated with aggression. As we shall see in the next section, this is of some significance to other theories of prejudice. Another finding, of interest for the same reason, was that correlations between conflicting interests and aggression were significantly higher amongst those respondents who themselves identified strongly with some religious (but not ultraorthodox) group. In other words, the social identity of group members had an effect on how much psychological impact the conflict of interests between the groups had. Finally, and of no little interest in its own right, these same variables which had predicted intergroup aggression so strongly (accounting for nearly 40 per cent of the variance) showed almost no correlation with the intergroup bias measures. Moreover, ingroup bias and intergroup aggression were themselves completely unrelated. Such an empirical independence between these different indicators of intergroup orientation should warn us not to assume that prejudice is a unidimensional construct.

The Realistic Group Conflict Theory, as we have seen, provides a powerful explanation for many examples of prejudice. Moreover it has the advantage, conspicuously lacking in some theories (see chapter 2), of being able to account for the ebb and flow of prejudice over time or across different social contexts; these can often be attributed to changing economic and political relations between the groups concerned. Nevertheless, despite its undoubted merits there are, as Turner (1981) has noted, a number of empirical and theoretical difficulties with the perspective which mean that it is unlikely by itself to provide a complete explanation for all forms of prejudice.

One problem is that while it is clear that when groups are competing over some scarce resource they are likely to harbour more negative and biased intergroup attitudes than when they are co-operating with one another, such biases do not disappear altogether in the latter kind of situation. A number of experiments have demonstrated that ingroup favouritism is remarkably hard to eradicate even when groups have a material interest in its elimination (for example, Brown, 1984a; Ryen and Kahn, 1975).

A second difficulty, closely linked to the first, is that an explicit conflict of interests may not be necessary for the arousal of ingroup favouritism and competition. Ironically enough, one of the first hints of this was provided by Sherif himself. Recall that observation of his in one of the summer camp studies that even before they had explicitly introduced the competition phase of the experiment the boys had shown an interest in trying to 'best' the other groups in various activities. Such apparently gratuitous intergroup rivalry was demonstrated still more conclusively in the minimal categorization experiments described in chapter 3 (Rabbie and Horwitz, 1969; Tajfel et al., 1971). The main finding from those studies – that people will readily favour members of their own group as a consequence of mere categorization – poses a serious problem for Realistic Group Conflict Theory. For here is evidence that neither an immediate objective conflict of interests nor a prior history of intergroup competition are, in fact, necessary for the arousal of a rudimentary form of prejudice.

A final ambiguity in the theory concerns whether the negative interdependence which it assumes to underlie prejudice need always be based on real conflicts over such concrete things as land, money or political power. Perhaps, instead, it could derive from perceived conflicts of interests of some kind or, even, merely from a competition over some rather less tangible assets such as prestige or 'to be the winner'. Sherif himself was deliberately vague on this point, defining group interests as

> *a real or imagined threat to the safety of the group, an economic interest, a political advantage, a military consideration, prestige, or a number of others.*
>
> (Sherif, 1966, p. 15)

Allowing perceived conflicts to have similar causal status to actual conflicts helps to explain why some manifestations of racism (for example) take the form of 'they (immigrants) are taking all our jobs/houses and so on' even though unemployment and homelessness rates amongst immigrant groups are frequently higher than those of the host community. The cognitive beliefs may be more important than the demographic facts.

However, sensible though such a broad interpretation of conflicting interests may be, it does pose a theoretical problem to us students of prejudice. If perceptions of competing goals can underlie prejudice, and if such perceptions are not always correlated with the groups' actual relations, where do they come from? One obvious explanation is that such beliefs stem from ideological attempts by powerful interest groups to manufacture social divisions, presumably as part of some long-term 'divide and rule' political strategy (Billig, 1976; Reicher, 1986). Although such an argument has a ring of plausibility about it, particularly in relation to some real world intergroup tensions which do not seem to be founded in objective conflicts, it is not one for which it is easy to find conclusive empirical support. Moreover, the occurrence of such 'non-realistic' perceived conflicts, even in the rather more ideologically aseptic environment of the laboratory, suggests that there may be additional social psychological origins for such subjective competitive orientations. It is to those that we now turn.

Social Identity

What social psychological processes might give rise to prejudice independently of and in conjunction with the objective factors just considered? Some obvious candidates are the cognitive processes considered in chapters 3 and 4. As we saw, there are good reasons for supposing that social categorization and its biproducts of differentiation and stereotyping underlie much prejudiced thinking and judgement. The fact that categorization is such an all-pervading and necessary feature of human cognition points still more strongly to it as the guilty party. However, despite the undoubted importance of these cognitive processes, there is one feature of most intergroup phenomena which they cannot readily account for: there is usually an asymmetry in people's attitudes and behaviour such that the ingroup (and not the outgroup) comes off best. Theoretical models based solely on the cognitive activity of the person can explain why groups are perceived as more different from each other than they really are and why they may be seen in crude and over-simplified terms. But they cannot so easily account for why those perceptions have a consistently positive flavour when they refer to the ingroup and a negative or, at least, a less positive hue when they focus on the outgroup. To understand that pervasive ingroup bias we must turn to a further concept, that of social identity.

The concept of identity

What do we mean by 'social identity'? According to the architects of the theory which first gave it prominence in the field of intergroup relations, social identity 'consists . . . of those aspects of an individual's self image that derive from the social categories to which he perceives himself belonging' (Tajfel and Turner, 1986, p. 16). In other words, we invoke a part of our social identity whenever we think of ourselves as being of one gender/ethnicity/class rather than another.

Tajfel and Turner (1986) further assume that people generally have a preference for seeing themselves positively rather than negatively. Since part of our self-image is defined in terms of our group memberships, this implies that there will also be a preference to see our ingroups in a positive light in relation to those groups to which we do not belong. It is this general tendency to make biased intergroup comparisons which serves as the motivational core of Tajfel and Turner's theory. From it they derive their key hypothesis that the achievement or maintenance of a satisfactory identity requires that group members will search out various forms of positive distinctiveness for their ingroup. Where this is not possible they may seek alternative group memberships which offer greater scope for positive self-evaluation.

These, then, are the bare bones of Social Identity Theory. Before we examine it in more detail and explore its implications for understanding different kinds of prejudice, let us look at some research which has substantiated these basic tenets. First, take the idea that group membership has implications for people's self concept, particularly if the group is perceived to have done well (or badly) in relation to other groups. An early study by Zander et al. (1960) showed this quite well. They created cohesive and non-cohesive laboratory groups and set them to work on a fashion design task. Subsequently half the groups were deemed (by the experimenters, not in reality) to have done well relative to other groups, while the remainder were alleged to have performed badly. For the cohesive groups – those which mattered to their members (that is, they identified with them) – the group's apparent success or failure resulted in raised or lowered levels of self-esteem in its members. Moreover, their anticipation of their individual competence to perform some future and unrelated task on their own was also reliably affected by their group's achievement. This phenomenon of 'basking in the reflected glory' of one's group was also demonstrated in a clever field study by Cialdini et al. (1976). They observed college football supporters on the days immediately following intercollegiate games. If their college had won, college scarves and insignia were much more in evidence around campus than if it had lost. The students' willingness to be identified as belonging to the group seemed to be associated with the group's fortunes in intergroup encounters. Snyder et al. (1986) replicated this result in a laboratory study.

What of the proposition that people evaluate their group mainly by means of intergroup comparisons? As we shall soon see, there is no shortage of research demonstrating people's readiness to engage in comparisons of this sort when asked to do so, and they are often manifestly biased as the theory predicts. However, there is a surprising dearth of studies which have attempted to examine the prevalence of *spontaneous* (that is, unbidden) comparisons. An exception was a survey of international attitudes by Haeger (1993) conducted in six European countries. The very first substantive question in this survey invited respondents to write down whatever came into their mind when they thought of their own country. Analysis of these spontaneously generated images revealed that some 20 per cent of them contained comparative references to other countries. Here some examples: 'high standard of living: at the moment there is a glaring contrast because of war and famine in Somalia and elsewhere'; 'people are free and have a comfortable standard of living compared to other countries'; 'because we have the best kitchen of the world, the nicest beaches of the world and the most corrupt government of the world' (Haeger, 1993, appendix 2). Interestingly, a further 10 per cent of respondents made another kind of comparison, a comparison in time (either with the past or the future): 'right-wing radicalism has increased a great deal in the last few years'; 'future: looking grim' (ibid.). I shall return later to this issue of people's readiness to make different kinds of comparisons but, for now, these findings provide some preliminary evidence that intergroup comparisons do figure in people's conceptions of their own group.

Of course, once other groups are clearly in people's psychological field of view then biased intergroup comparisons are remarkably easy to observe (see reviews by Brewer, 1979; Messick and Mackie, 1989; Mullen et al., 1992; Turner, 1981). Rather than retread the ground covered by those reviews let me take two exemplary studies at opposite ends of the spectrum of artificiality.

One is the by now familiar minimal group paradigm of Tajfel et al. (1971) (see chapter 3). How does the concept of social identity help to explain the persistent tendency for people to display intergroup discrimination, even in as barren a social context as this? Consider again the situation: subjects have been placed in one of two trivial groups. They know next to nothing about those groups except that they are in one and that others (identified only by code numbers) are similarly categorized. Given this anonymity, the only possible source of identity, primitive though it might be, is the group they have been placed in (Klee or Kandinsky). However, that group is not easily distinguishable from the other and hence is contributing little positive to its members' self-concepts. It is for this reason that pressures for group distinctiveness are presumed to come into play as the group members try to differentiate their ingroup positively from the outgroup by allocating more money or points – it doesn't matter which (Turner, 1978a) – to fellow ingroupers than to outgroupers.

In this explanation there is a presumed link between discrimination and the identity and self-esteem of the group members showing it. The nature and empirical substantiation of this link has proved to be a controversial issue, which I shall discuss later. However, in the second study that I want to consider the connection between ingroup bias and group identification was examined more directly. This was a study of intergroup attitudes amongst members of different political parties in Britain (Kelly, 1988). Two of Kelly's measures are of interest: how much sympathy they had with each party's political views (a general evaluative

Table 6.1 Biased intergroup ratings in a British political context

Political party	Ratings of own party		Mean ratings of other parties	
	Evaluation	Liking	Evaluation	Liking
Conservative	5.6	4.9	2.2	3.0
Labour	6.0	5.8	2.1	2.9
Liberal	5.8	5.4	2.8	3.5
Social Democrat	6.1	5.3	2.7	3.0
Communist	6.7	5.8	3.2	2.9

Note: All ratings on a 1 (negative) to 7 (positive) scale.

Source: Kelly (1988), adapted from table 1.

measure), and how happy they would be at the prospect of spending an evening with a supporter from each party (a measure of liking). Table 6.1 shows how strongly they differentiated between their own party and all the others on these two indices.[1] Ratings of the ingroup were nearly all at 5 or above, while ratings of the outgroups were all well below 4 (the notional 'neutral' point of the scale). Kelly then correlated these indices of ingroup bias (ingroup–outgroup differences) with measures of group identification, perceived goal incompatibility between the parties, and the amount of interparty contact. Consistent with both the Social Identity and the Realistic Group Conflict approaches, levels of identification and goal conflict were independently and positively correlated with the amount of bias the respondents displayed. Contact was a much weaker predictor. In other analyses, their levels of self-esteem were also related to some of the indices of bias. Here, then, is some definitive evidence connecting biased intergroup judgements with social identity. I shall have occasion to return to this relationship later because it turns out that it may not hold true for all kinds of groups, but that is a complexity that can wait for the moment.

Threats to identity

Social Identity Theory, then, holds that an important motive behind intergroup attitudes and behaviour is the creation or maintenance of a satisfactorily positive identity. From this it follows that threats to people's social identities should be responded to by increased attempts to differentiate the ingroup positively from outgroups. If the threats are severe enough such differentiation may evolve from the mild expressions of bias that are typically observed in laboratory settings, where both ingroup and outgroup may be evaluated positively (only the former more so than the latter), to the more openly deogratory intergroup attitudes and behaviour that can properly be called prejudice. Such effects of threatened identity have been observed in a number of studies.

Perhaps the most obvious domain in which they can be seen is in the attempts by various ethnic and national groups around the world to maintain the integrity of their language (Giles, 1977). Going no further afield than Europe, the examples of the Flemings and Walloons in Belgium, the Catalans in Spain, Bretons in France, and the Welsh in Britain all spring readily to mind. According to Giles and his colleagues, the linguistic behaviour of these groups can be understood in terms of social identity processes (Giles and Johnson, 1981). In particular, they suggest that where these groups' ethnolinguistic identity is threatened – for example by gradual assimilation by the dominant language culture or, in extreme cases by outright rejection or suppression by the majority outgroup – then they will make increased efforts to re-establish distinctiveness, and one likely form of this is some kind of linguistic differentiation: speaking with a broader accent or switching into local dialect. Two experimental studies demonstrated this quite vividly (Bourhis and Giles, 1977; Bourhis et al., 1978). Both were carried out in a language laboratory and involved the language students being confronted with an outgroup speaker who threatened their linguistic identities by being very dismissive about their language. Clear evidence of language divergence by the students was found, either by broadening their accent or by switching languages altogether. In fact, in one of the studies covert recordings of their reactions captured muttered insults and obscenities directed toward the outgroup person, *but in the ingroup language.*

Similar strong reactions to threatened identity have been observed in other experimental contexts. In one experiment we conducted with school children we first divided them into two arbitrary groups, supposedly on the pretext of wanting to try out different versions of a reasoning test (Brown and Ross, 1982). The children received some feedback on their test performance (one group was alleged to have done better than the other) and then were given an opportunity to evaluate the capabilities of the two groups. These group evaluations were then fed back to the other group but in an experimentally controlled manner: unknown to the children, we arranged for a third of them to receive feedback which was rather derogatory in tone, casting aspersions as to their group's intellectual abilities in general. This was the High threat condition. A second set of subjects received slightly more conciliatory feedback, noting their group's apparent superiority/ inferiority in some aspects of intelligence but conceding (or claiming) parity in others. This was the Moderate threat condition. Finally, in a third condition the feedback message was not threatening at all since it conceded merit to the children's ingroup, however well it had done in the test. The reactions to these different levels of threat were quite consistent. Those in the High and Moderate threat conditions significantly increased their feelings of annoyance towards the outgroup; the Low threat subjects decreased. On other measures there were similar changes. For example, the so-called 'losing' group increased their levels of ingroup bias in direct proportion to the level of threat contained in the feedback from the outgroup. Grant (1992) has found similar strong reactions to identity-threatening communications in the context of male–female relations.

Breakwell (1978) studied threats to identity in a more realistic context. Some teenage boys, all professing to be avid football supporters, were described by the experimenter *either* as 'genuine' fans since they attended many of their team's games, *or* as only 'long range' (that is, non-genuine) supporters since they had, by their own admission, attended only a few matches. This description was backed up with some plausible-sounding official statements from well-known football managers. Breakwell reasoned that this second group would feel threatened because their identity as real football lovers had been called into question. Their reactions to some subsequent questions about the relative merits of their team's and other teams' supporters seemed to bear this out. As can be seen in figure 6.1, the 'threatened' group were more concerned to stress the superiority of their team's supporters on various dimensions of intergroup evaluation.

Breakwell et al. (1984) applied a similar analysis in their study of young people's attitudes towards unemployed workers. In most Western societies this category is a stigmatized group since such a high cultural premium is placed on having paid employment. Thus, young people who are out of work might be expected to feel that their occupational identity is somewhat threatened and might react to this by upgrading the status of 'unemployed'. This is what Breakwell et al. found.

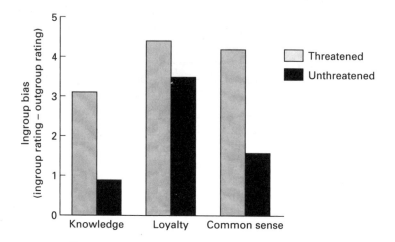

Figure 6.1 Reactions to a threatened identity
Source: Breakwell (1978), adapted from tables 7–9 (collapsing across threat conditions)

Compared to school children's ratings of the 'employed' and 'unemployed', the ratings of the latter category by unemployed people were significantly higher (though still lower than that of the 'employed'). As Breakwell (1986) later argued, such an attempt to change the status of one's (devalued) group are but one of several coping strategies that can be used to deal with threatened social identities. Let me now consider some of these.

Status relations as a source of threatened identity

Discussing the mutual attitudes of two groups such as the employed and the unemployed reminds us of an obvious fact: that most intergroup relationships are of unequal status and power.

What are the consequences for social identity of belonging to a dominant or a subordinate group and, most importantly for our present purposes, what implications do those have for people's intergroup attitudes?

Take the case of privileged groups first. Obvious examples of such groups would be White ethnic groups in many Western societies, people who work (compared to those who cannot), and people who have no obvious physical or mental disabilities (compared to those who have). On a whole host of comparative criteria such groups emerge as superior to other groups in society. Thus, if we follow the logic of Social Identity Theory, members of such groups have few identity problems. They can satisfactorily view their ingroups as enjoying the desired state of positive distinctiveness in relation to other groups, a perception which has comfortable ramifications for their own view of themselves.

At first glance, then, one might expect members of high-status or powerful groups not to need to manifest much evidence of intergroup differentiation. However, while this does follow strictly from the Social Identity hypothesis, there are other reasons why we should not expect this outcome. How are intergroup attitudes and behaviour usually elicited? Group members are typically asked to evaluate their own and other group(s) on a number of valued dimensions (for example, 'how intelligent/industrious/friendly are the groups?'), or are asked to allocate rewards between the groups. To such questions, which implicitly or explicitly refer to the comparative worth of the groups, members of high-status groups are likely to give answers which reflect their (to them) self-evident superiority. In other words, they are likely to show clear signs of positive ingroup bias. In fact, research on intergroup attitudes in hierarchical situations confirms that this generally happens. In a review of 42 separate studies we found that, indeed, high-status groups do tend to show more ingroup bias than low-status groups (Mullen et al., 1992). This effect was more pro- nounced in laboratory experiments where, usually, the status differences between groups can be more unambiguously measured or imple- mented. Also, in more naturalistic settings other important variables may be at work which, as we shall see, can radically interact with the effects of status itself.

To illustrate this general trend a study by Sachdev and Bourhis (1987) will serve us well. They modified the minimal-group paradigm so that the groups were of equal or unequal ability on a creativity measure. The subjects then had to evaluate the creativity of the groups on another task. As can be seen from figure 6.2, both the high- and equal-status groups showed very clear ingroup bias in their evaluations, while the lower-status groups tended to favour the outgroup. Notice, too, that the members' satisfaction with their ingroup (roughly equivalent to their strength of identification) was also correlated with status (lower part of figure 6.2). In a later study in which both the power and the status of the groups were manipulated, essentially the same findings emerged (Sachdev and Bourhis, 1991).

Why did the equal- and high-status groups in this study show roughly similar levels of ingroup favouritism? It is possible that the bias shown by these two groups may be serving rather different functions. For the higher-status group it may merely be a restatement of their socially defined superiority. The equal-status groups, on the other hand, may be attempting to *achieve* some positive distinctiveness. Indeed, it can be argued that the circumstances in which groups are very similar to each other in status is just where one might expect their identities to feel threatened and where they would therefore enhance efforts mutually to differentiate each other (Brown, 1984b; Turner, 1978b). In

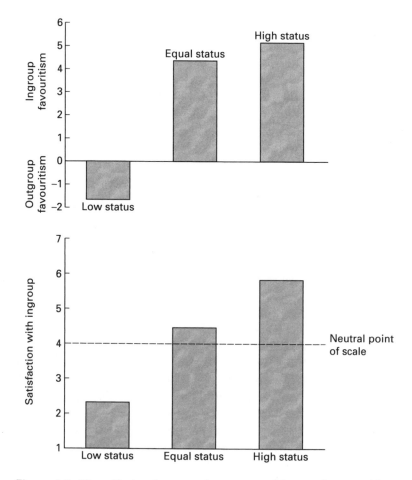

Figure 6.2   The effects of a group's status position on ingroup bias
and satisfaction with the ingroup
Source: Sachdev and Bourhis (1987), ingroup favouritism derived from three
measures of bias in table 1; 'satisfaction' from first three rows of table 2

the same way, two sports teams close to each other in a league will often show more rivalry than those at opposite ends of the table.

It was with this hypothesis in mind that I conducted a series of experiments on the effects of intergroup similarity (Brown, 1984a; Brown and Abrams, 1986). In these we led school children to believe that they were undertaking a task with members of another school. Depending on experimental condition, that school was alleged to be similar to them in status because they seemed to perform about as well as them academically, or was better or worse than them. In addition the prevailing attitudes towards different academic subjects in the two schools were depicted as being either similar or different. Both variables had effects on the children's intergroup attitudes. The outgroup thought to hold similar attitudes was generally liked better than the outgroup that was believed to be different (Brown, 1984a; Brown and Abrams, 1986; see also Grant (1993) for identical results in a different context). A second finding was that when the children believed they were about to co-operate with the other school, their levels of ingroup bias against the similar-status group were lower than the average of their biases against the higher- and lower-status group (Brown, 1984a). Both of these findings rather contradicted the Social Identity Theory prediction that similarity would provoke a greater search for positive distinctiveness. However, a third finding was more in line with that hypothesis. This was that where the outgroup was very similar indeed to the ingroup because it had similar attitudes *and* was similar in status, then the amount of bias increased (Brown and Abrams, 1986). It was as if a certain threshold of similarity had been crossed beyond which the ingroup felt threatened by the psychological proximity of the outgroup (see also Diehl, 1988; Roccas and Schwartz, 1993).

The discussion of ingroup similarity recalls a similar debate in chapter 3 where I examined the relative effect of categorization and belief similarity – the so-called race-belief controversy (Rokeach, 1960). However, note that there is an important difference in the studies we are now considering: in these experiments the question is not whether interpersonal belief similarity or sharing a common category membership is the more potent antidote to prejudice. Instead, the different category memberships are taken as given and the focus is on whether two similar groups enjoy friendlier relations than those which are different. On the whole, the evidence suggests that similarity (whether of status or attitudes) seems to promote attraction between groups. As we have seen, this has been found in some laboratory studies. It has also been observed in field studies of ethnic relations. For example, Brewer and Campbell (1976) found that ethnic groups in East Africa that were independently judged to be similar to one another tended to express friendlier attitudes towards one another than culturally more disparate groups. Similarly, Berry et al. (1977), in a large survey of Canadian interethnic attitudes, found a moderately strong positive correlation between respondents' evaluations of nine ethnic groups and their perceived similarity to themselves. Finally, as noted earlier, Struch and Schwartz (1989) found that religious groups in Israel that were seen to have similar values to the respondents' own groups were viewed with less hostility than those seen as dissimilar.

On balance, therefore, there is support for a weaker and modified version of Rokeach's (1960) Belief Congruence Theory. It is not the case, as he originally believed, that people's perception of interpersonal belief similarity can so easily override differences in category member-ship and reduce prejudice (see chapter 3). However, it may well be that outgroups which are seen as somewhat similar to the ingroup are treated more favourably than those which are perceived to be quite different. This runs rather counter to the idea derived from Social Identity Theory that intergroup similarity will be regarded as threatening and hence be reacted to aversely. There *are* circumstances in which this seems to happen – when groups have arrived at some extreme of similarity and find themselves literally too close for comfort. But at the more common intermediate levels of similarity groups seem to appreciate being able to have at least something in common.

So far I have considered high- and equal-status groups. What about groups of subordinate status? At first glance, members of such groups would seem to have an unenviably negative social identity. If, as Social Identity Theory suggests, they attempt to evaluate their groups in comparison to others in society they will frequently discover that they earn less (if they have a job at all), they live in poorer accommodation, enjoy fewer educational opportunities, and may be consensually derogated on a number of other criteria. Thus, materially and psychologically they will experience disadvantage, and such unfavour-able comparative outcomes should result in them having an unsatis-factory identity and, hence, lowered self-esteem.

Tajfel and Turner (1986) suggest that one response to this situation is for members of such groups to abandon their current social identity. Thus, in a spirit of 'if you can't beat 'em, join 'em', they may seek to leave their ingroup and join another apparently more prestigious group. Recall how the lower-status group members in Sachdev and Bourhis's (1987) experiment expressed markedly lower levels of satisfaction with their ingroup. This phenomenon of members of 'inferior' groups distancing themselves psychologically from their group is strongly reminiscent of some of the research findings on ethnic preferences among minority-group children that I reviewed in chapter 5. In many studies from Clark and Clark (1947) onward, minority (often Black) children showed a preference for the dominant (usually White) group stimuli.

Nevertheless, as we also saw in chapter 5, such a response is not inevitable. Members of subordinate groups may not always be so willing (or able) to reject their identity. For instance, if the boundaries between the categories are fixed and impermeable, as is the case with many ascribed group memberships like gender and ethnicity, then the option to leave the subordinate group may not be open.[2] Ellemers and her colleagues have shown that the mere knowledge that passage from one group to another is possible has the effect of lowering subordinate group members' level of identification with their group (Ellemers et al., 1988). In cases where such mobility is not possible Tajfel and Turner (1986) suggest that other tactics may be adopted. One is to restrict the comparisons made to other similar subordinate-status groups so that the outcome of those comparisons is more favourable to the ingroup. Rosenberg and Simmons (1972), for example, found that self-esteem amongst Blacks who made comparisons with other Blacks was higher than in those who compared themselves with Whites. On the other side of that ethnic divide, it is often reported that White respondents from poorer socio-economic backgrounds show more overt prejudice than more middle-class samples (Brown, 1965; Vollebergh, 1991). Such 'poor white racism', as it is sometimes called, may also be motivated in part by the desire to avoid identity-damaging comparisons with wealthier social classes and to seek positive distinctiveness in a relation to a similarly deprived group.

Another strategy is to side-step those dimensions of comparison on which the subordinate group is regarded as inferior and to find new dimensions, or new values of the old dimensions, so that the group can achieve some prestige. Lemaine (1966), in a study conducted – like Sherif's – in a children's camp, found that the potential losers in a hut-building contest discovered additional attributes to emphasise (for example, the hut's surrounding garden). The values and life styles of such varied sub-cultural groups as the 'beats' of the early 1960s, the Black Power Movement in the USA later in the same decade, 'hippies' in the 1970s, and 'punks' in the 1980s, all of which could be characterized by a rejection of the dominant society's cultural and moral norms, may be other examples of the same phenomenon.

None of these responses, with the possible exception of this latter one, are completely satisfactory for members of a lower-status group because they leave the unequal relationship between themselves and the dominant group essentially unchanged. Hence, the possibility of unfavourable comparisons with that group remains, with all the likely consequences for social identity that they entail. Why, then, do they not confront directly the dominant group's superiority by agitating for social and economic change and by refusing to accede to the consensually accepted definitions of their respective groups' worth? Such a directly competitive intergroup orientation would be the most obviously predictable reaction from the premise of Social Identity Theory that people generally strive for a positive identity and avoid a negative one. It turns out that subordinate groups *do* sometimes opt for this strategy – for instance, the various movements for civil rights in the 1960s instigated by Black people in the USA and followed by Maoris in New Zealand and aboriginal people in Australia and Canada and, most dramatically of all, the abolition of apartheid in South Africa brought about by the African National Congress in the 1990s. However, for this to happen it may be necessary that members of those lower-status groups can conceive of the existence of some alternatives to the current state of affairs (Tajfel and Turner, 1986). Until they can imagine that the old order is neither fair nor inevitable, they may be unlikely to engage in the psychologically risky comparisons with the 'superior' group. What are the circumstances which encourage the generation of these 'cognitive alternatives'? There are probably several but, to date, the three most powerful factors have been found to be, first, that the boundaries between the groups be relatively impermeable; second, that the status differences between them be somewhat unstable; and, third, that those differences be perceived as illegitimate, founded on unfair and arbitrary principles (Tajfel and Turner, 1986).

A recent experiment by Ellemers et al. (1993) provides a nice demonstration of the importance of all three variables. The experiment used a management–worker simulation. After being divided into two groups and taking a test of organizational problem-solving, the subjects were led to believe that one group had been allocated the higher-status management role, the other the worker role. (In fact, by some experimenter sleight of hand, all subjects were put into the latter lower-status group.) However, the basis for this allocation varied. Some groups were told that the assignment had been done fairly on the basis of their test performance and were also led to believe that their fellow group members accepted this as reasonable. Other groups were told a different story. They were told that the allocation had been made solely on the basis of the *number* of test items completed rather than their correctness and, moreover, it was indicated that their fellow group members thought this was a pretty unfair way to do things. In this way a legitimate or illegitimate status relationship between the groups was created.[3] Further information was then forthcoming. Half the groups were told that the status positions of the two groups could change later in the experiment ('unstable' condition); the remainder were told that they would not ('stable' condition). Finally, some subjects believed that if they performed exceptionally well individually they would have the opportunity to join the management group ('permeable' group boundaries); others believed that the group compositions would not alter ('impermeable' condition).

The effects of these different manipulations were remarkably consistent. Not surprisingly, those in the illegitimate conditions felt angrier than those in the legitimate conditions. However, it was the latter subjects who showed the most interest in finding some alternative criteria than the one used for evaluating the groups. This corresponds to the second of the identity-maintaining strategies that I noted earlier: the seeking out of new comparative dimensions when the current one is unfavourable to the ingroup. The group members' identification with their ingroup was affected by all three variables (see figure 6.3). Those in groups with impermeable boundaries showed higher identification than those who thought they could change groups. Those in 'illegitimately' inferior groups showed higher identification than those whose position was 'legitimate'. And stability, too, had an effect, albeit in conjunction with the other two variables. Highest identification was shown by those in the illegitimate, impermeable, and unstable condition, lowest by those in the legitimate, permeable, and stable condition. Faced with the identity-threatening prospect of having been assigned, apparently justifiably, to a subordinate group with little prospect of changing its position, group members who see the possibility of leaving it for another seem psychologically disposed to do so. At the other extreme, where the basis for their inferiority is obviously unfair, there is a real chance of the groups' positions reversing in the near future but no chance of escaping from their group (even if they wanted to); their identity needs are best met by sticking with their group and taking on the outgroup on its own terms.

Ellemers et al. (1993) were concerned mainly with the *intra*group reactions of subordinate group members to different socio-structural conditions. Their *inter*group measures showed generally rather weaker effects. However, other experiments, also concerned with the effects of illegitimate and unstable status relations, have consistently found that such changes elicit strong intergroup responses too, mainly in the form of greatly increased levels of ingroup favouritism (Brown and Ross, 1982; Caddick, 1982; Ng and Cram, 1988; Turner and Brown, 1978). One other noteworthy feature of these studies is that these effects are often observed as strongly in the 'superior' group as in the 'inferior' group, suggesting that destabilizing and delegitimating status relations present a threat to the higher-status group's identity and they react with enhanced attempts to defend their now fragile superiority.

These findings from the laboratory may help us to understand the historical changes in minority-group children's ethnic preferences reported in chapter 5. Most minority groups occupy a subordinate position in their respective societies. In North America (as in other countries) the 30–40

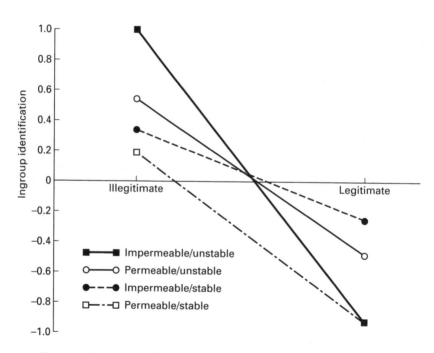

Figure 6.3 A subordinate group's reaction to status illegitimacy, instability, and permeability of group boundaries

Source: Ellemers et al. (1993), adapted from figure 1 (illegitimate and legitimate conditions only)[4]

year period prior to the 1960s can fairly be represented as one of stasis as far as their position was concerned. It is true that there was tremendous social and economic upheaval wrought by the Second World War but it must be remembered that in many southern states Black–White segregation in all spheres of life was widespread and officially sanctioned, and anti-Black racism was overt and often nakedly violent. In theoretical terms we might depict this situation as one in which the status relations between Blacks and White were legitimate and stable and where there was little chance of mobility between the groups (impermeable boundaries). Consistent with this analysis, most studies of ethnic preference in this period showed that minority-group children usually made *outgroup*-favouring choices and judgements. Contrast this to the turbulent period of the late 1960s and early 1970s. The Civil Rights Movement had been outstandingly successful in combating the worst excesses of institutionalized discrimination, there were several incidents of social unrest in cities as far apart as Los Angeles, Detroit, and Newark. And all of this was underpinned by an articulate ideology of Black consciousness which consistently rejected the values and legitimacy of the White majority. Such a situation could be described as *un*stable and *il*legitimate, though still with relatively impermeable social boundaries. Perhaps this was why it was in this period that several of the studies reporting *in*group-favouring choices and preferences amongst Black children were published.

The plausibility of this analysis was strengthened by the results of a study by Vaughan (1978). He examined changes in ethnic preferences amongst New Zealand Maori children as a function of urbanization and the rise of Maori consciousness. He argued that in rural areas the relationship between Maoris and the dominant Pakeha group was much more traditional and stable. On the other hand, in cities, particularly by 1970 when the Brown Power movement was well established, the intergroup relationship was much less stable and accepted. Corresponding closely to these socio-historical differences were some clear trends in Maori ethnic preferences: from a mere 30 per cent own-group choices in the earliest rural sample to 56 per cent own-group choices in the latest (1971) urban sample.

Social identity and prejudice: an evaluation

From the above I hope I have conveyed something of the contribution which Social Identity Theory is making to our understanding of intergroup relations, particularly in helping to explain variations in levels of ingroup-favouring biases in people's perceptions and judgements. Intuitively, too, it seems plausible to suppose that ethnic conflicts around the world are not *wholly* motivated by considerations of material gain, however important these undoubtedly are. What Muslims and Serbs are fighting for in Bosnia, or Catholics and Protestants in Ireland, or Christians and Shiites in Lebanon, is not just the military control of cities like Sarajevo, Belfast, and Beirut but also the very maintenance of themselves as distinctive ethno-religious groupings.

Nevertheless, despite all its unquestionable virtues, Social Identity Theory has not emerged unscathed from the two decades of research which it has inspired. Four problems, in particular, seem to me to be worthy of our brief consideration here.

The first concerns one of the central ideas of the theory, the presumed causal connection between intergroup discrimination and self-esteem. As Abrams and Hogg (1988) have pointed out, this link could take two forms. It could be that people show discrimination in order to raise their self-esteem simply because a positive self-concept is generally preferred to a neutral or negative one. Alternatively, it could be that prior low self-esteem, perhaps stemming from belonging to a low-status or stigmatized group, causes intergroup discrimination in order to raise it to 'normal' levels. The evidence for both of these processes is equivocal (Hogg and Abrams, 1990). It is true that two studies have found that, in minimal-group situations, subjects who were denied the usual opportunity to discriminate showed lower self-esteem that those who were not (Lemyre and Smith, 1985; Oakes and Turner, 1980). Moreover, Lemyre and Smith established that it was indeed intergroup discrimination which elevated self-esteem; control subjects who only distributed rewards between two ingroupers or two outgroupers showed lower self-esteem than those making intergroup allocations. On the other hand, Chin and McClintock (1993) were able to replicate these results in only one of their two conceptually similar experiments and correlations between the amount of ingroup bias and levels of self-esteem are sometimes close to zero (Hinkle et al., 1992; Hogg and Sunderland, 1991; Hogg and Turner, 1987). Studies investigating the opposite direction of causality have produced a similarly confusing picture. Hogg and Sunderland (1991) found that groups who had been told they had failed on a task did show lowered esteem and consequently greater discrimination. However, as we saw earlier, other studies have found that it is groups with *enhanced* status and power – and hence presumably *higher self-esteem* – who show greater ingroup favouritism (Luhtanen and Crocker, 1991; Mullen et al., 1992). At the very least, then, the available evidence suggests that the Social Identity hypothesis that self-esteem is an important variable determining or being determined by ingroup-favouring biases cannot be unambiguously sustained.

A second problem is related. If biased intergroup evaluations and decisions are motivated by social identity concerns then presumably one should expect to find a positive correlation between the strength of people's group identification and their levels of ingroup bias. However, when we have investigated this correlation empirically it has proved to be rather unstable (Hinkle and Brown, 1990). In fact, of the 14 separate studies which we were then able to locate, most of which involved sampling from more than one group of respondents, only nine revealed a positive median correlation between identification and bias, and many of these were quite weak (typically less than 0.3). Worse still for Social Identity Theory some of these positive medians disguised a considerable variation in direction and magnitude of the constituent correlations, some of these being significantly *negative*. In an attempt to account for this variability we have proposed that the psychological processes proposed by Social Identity Theory may not be operative in all groups. Instead, they may depend on prevailing levels of individualism or collectivism in the group (or its members) and their inclination (or not) to engage in intergroup comparisons (Hinkle and Brown, 1990). We argued then, and hence subsequently confirmed in three empirical studies, that one would only expect a strong link between group identification and ingroup favouritism in groups that can be simultaneously characterized as 'collectivist' – that is, where there is an emphasis on intragroup co-operation and group achievements – and 'relational' – that is, where there is a concern for one's group's standing or performance relative to other groups (Brown et al., 1992). It seems, therefore, that the hypothesized link between social identity and biased intergroup comparisons proposed by Tajfel and Turner (1986), while undoubtedly a potent motivator of intergroup behaviour in some contexts, may not be quite as generic as they had originally assumed.

A third difficulty concerns those unexpected effects of intergroup similarity that I discussed earlier. Except in cases where two groups perceived themselves to be very similar indeed, the hypothesized identity-threatening consequences of seeing another group as somewhat similar to one's own seem not to occur. A recent idea of Brewer's (1991) may help us with an explanation for this. Brewer suggests that individuals seek a compromise between needs for uniqueness and countervailing desires for assimilation. The former motive, she argues, can best be met in small groups which are highly distinctive from others in society; the latter implies the categorization of self as similar to a reasonably large number of others for reasons of affiliation and self-validation. The result is a choice of ingroups which provide the best trade-off between these two motives; what she calls the point of 'optimal distinctiveness'. It may be that this same compromise applies at the group level also. Perhaps people, as *group members*, want to be able to see that their group has sufficient in common with other groups to avoid feeling completely deviant and stigmatized but, at the same time, need to regard it as distinctive enough to retain its particular identity. This would suggest that prejudice will be least likely to be directed towards outgroups of intermediate similarity to the ingroup, groups that are neither so different as to have no points of contact with us nor so similar as to threaten our identity. Interestingly enough, such a hypothesis is exactly opposite to a predictions which can be derived from another quite different model, frustration–aggression theory (Dollard et al., 1939). By a careful analysis of the concept of 'displacement' in that theory, Brewer and Campbell (1976) derived an *inverted* U-shape curve for the hypothesized relationship between intergroup similarity and aggression towards the outgroup: highly similar or dissimilar outgroups should be preferred to those of moderate similarity. Doubtless, future research will reveal which of these contrary predictions best corresponds to reality.

The fourth problem is perhaps the most serious. Within the research instigated by Social Identity Theory the main focus has usually been on various measures of ingroup bias, whether in evaluative judgements or reward allocations. There is a good reason for this: since the theory posits a need for a *positive* and a *distinctive* identity, the obvious indices to choose from a research standpoint are those which reflect some positive intergroup differentiation on the part of one's respondents. The question is, however, do these commonly used measures of ingroup bias really represent prejudice as we are using the term (however loosely!) in this book? In chapter 1 I defined prejudice as 'the holding of derogatory attitudes or beliefs, the expression of negative affect, or the display of hostile or discriminatory behaviour towards members of a group'. How well does ingroup bias of the kind which we have discussed repeatedly in this chapter correspond with this definition? To begin with, we should note that 'ingroup bias' means a more favourable evaluation or treatment of the ingroup *than* the outgroup; in other words, it is an index of relative favouritism rather than one of absolute derogation of the outgroup. Indeed in many studies *both* ingroup and outgroup are evaluated (or treated) positively, only the former more so than the latter (Brewer, 1979). Moreover, ingroup and outgroup ratings may actually be positively rather than negatively correlated with one another (Turner, 1978b). A further complexity was added by the discovery that ingroup biases in evaluative judgements are usually not correlated at all with affective measures, that is, feelings of like or dislike for the outgroup (Brewer, 1979; Brown, 1984a; Turner, 1981). This was illustrated most clearly in the Struch and Schwartz (1989) study considered earlier. Intergroup aggression and ingroup bias seemed to be controlled by different variables and were themselves uncorrelated.

Further evidence for the independence of positive biases and more overt negative behaviour was provided by Mummendey et al. (1992). They adapted the classic minimal group paradigm so that, instead of allocating points or money, the subjects were asked to distribute (what they thought would be) durations of an unpleasantly high-pitched tone to ingroup and outgroup members. The use of this measure seemed to eliminate completely ingroup favouritism, and strategies of equalizing outcomes (fairness) or minimizing the total amount of aversive stimulation were much more in evidence. In a follow-up experiment the 'punishment' to be allocated was the time to be spent on a boring memory task. Again, fairness or joint minimization of misery were the prevailing strategies, although in certain experimental conditions some ingroup favouritism was visible – for example, when subjects were in a low-status minority group.

The explanation for these discrepancies between different intergroup indicators is still not clear. It could simply be that in the rather mild laboratory conditions in which much of our research is carried out there are strong norms against penalizing or harming a fellow subject. This would have the effect of raising the threshold for displaying ingroup favouritism on such measures (Mummendey et al., 1992). However, the fact that the indices of positive bias (that is, treating the ingroup better than the outgroup) and more overtly negative measure (that is, being derogatory or aggressive towards the outgroup) are often empirically unrelated both inside and outside the laboratory suggests that they may have different motivational origins. I want now to turn to the third major concept to be considered in this chapter, which may offer a clue as to what one of those different sources of prejudice might be.

Relative Deprivation

Between 1882 and 1930 there were 4761 reported cases of lynchings in the United States. Of these, over 70 per cent were lynchings of Black people – an average of 69 per year – and the majority occurred in southern states, for so long the heart of American slavery. Such a statistic is a sombre reminder of the awful extremes to which prejudice can sometimes go. Hovland and Sears (1940), who brought these grisly facts to the attention of social science, noticed that there was a considerable annual variation in these killings, ranging from a low of seven (in 1929) to a high of 155 (in 1892–3). They also observed that there was a remarkable correspondence between this variation and various farming economic indicators (farming being the principal industry in southern states): as the economy receded and times got hard so the number of lynchings increased (see also Hepworth and West, 1988, for further analyses of these data).

What might account for this covariation of economic recession with anti-Black violence? Hovland and Sears (1940) themselves believed that it was caused by frustration. Drawing upon Dollard et al.'s (1939) Frustration–Aggression Theory, they hypothesized that the hardships generated by a depressed economy raised people's levels of frustration which, in turn, generated increased aggression. Using the psycho-analytic concept of 'displacement' in the same way as Adorno et al. (1950) were to do ten years later (see chapter 2), Hovland and Sears suggested that the aggression would not be directed at the true source of the economic frustration (that is, the capitalist system which produced it) but would be diverted into more vulnerable and easily accessible targets such as members of deviant and minority groups (see Billig, 1976, and Brown, 1988, for more extended treatments of this argument).

Other attempts to confirm this so-called 'scapegoat'[5] theory of prejudice have had mixed success. Miller and Bugelski (1948) conducted an experiment with a group of young American men at a camp. One evening, when the men were eagerly anticipating a night on the town, the experimenters suddenly announced that the evening out was cancelled and the men would be required to undertake some uninterest-ing tasks instead. As it happened, they had also measured the men's ethnic attitudes towards Mexicans and Japanese both before this frustrating event and then again afterwards. Analysis of these attitudes revealed that they became significantly less favourable after the frustration; a control group experiencing no frustration showed no such change. This was a nice confirmation of the 'displacement' hypothesis since these two minority groups could have had no conceivable responsibility for the men's plight.

On the other hand, other experiments have yielded more equivocal results. For instance, Stagner and Congdon (1955) failed to find increases in prejudice in students following the frustration of failing some academic tests. Cowen et al. (1958), using a similar methodology, *did* find an increase in negative affect towards Blacks but this did not generalize to increases in more general ethnocentrism against other minorities. Even more problematically for the Frustration–Aggression Theory, Burnstein and McRae (1962) found *more* favourable evaluations of a Black team member following task failure, and this was particularly evident in highly prejudiced subjects who should have been the most eager to derogate him.

It was inconsistencies like these, as well as some other conceptual and empirical difficulties (Berkowitz, 1962; Billig, 1976), which led to the decline in popularity and utility of Frustration–Aggression Theory as an explanation of prejudice. In its place, and very much influenced by some of its central ideas (Gurr, 1970), emerged a theory which placed much less causal emphasis on *absolute* levels of hardship and frustration but stressed, instead, the importance of *relative* deprivation. The inspiration for this new approach – Relative Deprivation Theory as it is known – came from some serendipitous observations made in the course of a large-scale social psychological study of morale and social attitudes in the American army (Stouffer et al., 1949). They discovered that dissatisfaction was higher in certain sections of the military (for example, the air force) where prospects for career advancement were good, than in in others (for example, the military police) where the chances of promotion were poor. How so? Certainly not due to absolute levels of frustration because on that basis the military police should have been less happy than the air force. The answer, suggested Stouffer et al., may lie in the different levels of *relative* frustration (or deprivation): the air force personnel, although objectively better off, had a ready and superior comparison standard to hand (their promoted colleagues) and thus felt more aggrieved about their position; the MPs, with fewer such comparisons available, did not feel their deprivation so acutely.

This idea that deprivation is always relative to some norm forms the centrepiece of all theories of relative deprivation (Crosby, 1976; Davies,

1969; Davis, 1959; Gurr, 1970; Runciman, 1966). Gurr (1970), who has done much to formalize the theory and test its implications empirically, proposed that relative deprivation arises when people perceive a discrepancy between the standard of living they currently have and the standard of living they believe they *should* be enjoying. It is this gap between 'attainments' and 'expectations' that is thought to lie behind social discontent and prejudice.

Before we examine how this concept has been used to explain prejudice an important distinction must be clarified. In some versions of Relative Deprivation Theory – particularly those, like Gurr's (1970), which derive directly from the earlier Frustration–Aggression Theory – the stress is on the individual's direct experience of relative deprivation: what I enjoy/suffer relative to what I expect. However, there is another kind of deprivation, one which derives from people's perception of their *group's* fortunes relative to what they expect for their group. Runciman (1966) labelled this 'fraternalistic' deprivation to distinguish it from the other form, 'egoistic'. A nice illustration of this distinction was provided by Caplan (1970) who noted how many Black supporters of Black Power in the USA in the 1960s came from middle and upper income brackets rather than from the poorer (and most egoistically deprived) groups. Their own personal advantage relative to other Blacks did not prevent them from perceiving the relative *disadvantage* of Blacks, as a group, compared to Whites. As Walker and Pettigrew (1984) have pointed out, the fact that fraternalistic relative deprivation is based so firmly on group rather than individual outcomes makes it much more suitable a construct for the analysis of an intergroup phenomenon like prejudice.

What gives rise to relative deprivation? At the most general level, as just noted, relative deprivation is caused by a gap between expectations and achievements. Crawford and Naditch (1970) used a direct measure of this in their survey of Black residents in Detroit shortly after some rioting there. Respondents were asked to indicate on a vertical 11-step ladder where their present life style was in relation to their 'ideal life' (on the top of the ladder). The discrepancy between these two points was taken as a measure of deprivation. As can be seen from table 6.2, there was a clear relationship between the level of deprivation and their attitudes towards the riots and Black militancy. Those high in deprivation (putting themselves on step 4 or below) showed more sympathy with the objectives of Black militants than those scoring low (at step 5 or above).

Table 6.2 Black militancy and relative deprivation

Attitude item		Relative deprivation[a] (%)	
		Low	High
Do you think that riots help or hurt the Negro cause?	Help	28	54
	Hurt	60	38
Do you approve or disapprove of Black Power?	Approve	38	64
	Disapprove	36	22
Will force or persuasion be necessary to change White attitudes?	Force	40	51
	Persuasion	52	35

Note: [a] Perceived discrepancy between 'actual' and 'ideal' life.

Source: Crawford and Naditch (1970), table 1 ('don't knows' omitted).

The next question is: what determines people's aspirations for their ideal life? In Relative Deprivation Theory these are thought to derive from either or both of two kinds of comparisons. One is temporal in nature and involves a comparison with one's recent past. Davies (1969) proposed that people extrapolate from their own (group's) experience of affluence or poverty and expect the future to be similar. If living standards rise steadily over a period this will generate an expectation of future increases. From this Davies derived his famous J-curve hypothesis which suggests that dissatisfaction will be most likely not after a period of prolonged deprivation, but after a period in which people's living standards rise over a number of years followed by a sudden downturn. It is this sharp drop which produces the gap between actual and expected living standards necessary for the arousal of deprivation.[6] A second source of expectations are comparisons with other groups. When we perceive another group to be doing better or worse than our own, especially when that group is similar or in some way relevant to the ingroup, it is likely to generate expectations for how well we think our group should be doing. In turn, we will feel respectively deprived or gratified (Runciman, 1966). Again, the ingroup's absolute standing is not important; it is the relativity which counts.

A recent study of income distribution in Britain graphically illustrates both of these types of deprivation (Goodman and Webb, 1994). This charted the weekly income levels of the richest and poorest groups in society over a 30-year period. Figure 6.4 shows the results. Notice how the poorest group's disposable income rose slightly to 1981 and then fell in the following ten years. This should generate a mild form of temporal relative deprivation. 'Mild' because the initial increase in income may have been too slight to generate many rising expectations. Much more dramatic, however, is the fraternalistic relative deprivation. See how the gap between the rich and poor increases dramatically over time.

What are the effects of temporal and fraternal relative deprivation on prejudice? There has been very little research on the former. One of the few attempts to study variations in prejudice as a function of historical changes in prosperity was by Hepworth and West (1988). Using more sophisticated techniques, they reanalysed the same data set that Hovland and Sears (1940) had used nearly 50 years earlier. As well as confirming the correlations that Hovland and Sears had observed, albeit at a somewhat lower level, Hepworth and West also found a correlation

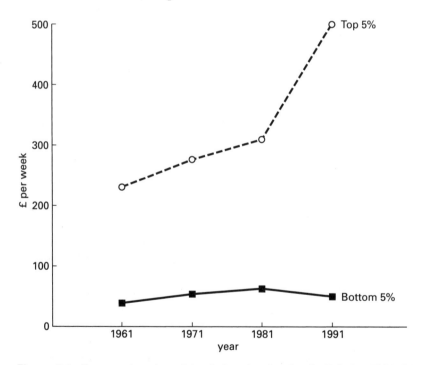

Figure 6.4 Temporal and social relative deprivation in Britain, 1961–91
Note: Figures show average weekly disposable income (after housing costs have been deducted) for a childless couple in the top and bottom 5th percentiles of UK income distribution.
Source: Goodman and Webb (1994)

between one year's lynchings and the *decline* in economic prosperity from the year previously. Davies (1969) himself tried to explain the incidence of Black urban rioting in the USA in the 1960s by reference to the rise and then fall of Black living standards in the previous two decades. However, Miller et al. (1977) disputed this analysis claiming both that the drop in Black prosperity that Davies noted occurred too early (in the late 1950s) to have generated the subsequent Black dissatisfaction and, moreover, that a more careful study of Black living standards revealed much greater variation over time than Davies had supposed (cf. Crosby, 1979; Davies, 1978, 1979; Miller and Bolce, 1979).

Much more attention has been paid to relative deprivation stemming from unfavourable social comparisons. A classic study demonstrating the link between relative deprivation and prejudice was that by Vanneman and Pettigrew (1972). They surveyed over 1000 White voters in four US cities and elicited their perceptions as to whether they felt they were doing better or worse economically than other White workers like themselves ('egoistic' deprivation). They also asked how those same respondents felt they were doing compared to Blacks ('fraternalist' deprivation). On the basis of these two measures Vanneman and Pettigrew divided their sample into four groups according to whether they could be described as 'gratified' (doing better than others), or 'deprived' (doing worse) in both the egoistic and fraternalistic sense (see table 6.3). On one direct measure of prejudice it was those who were fraternalistically or doubly deprived who showed the most prejudice. On a second measure, concerned more with attitudes towards race riots and measures to combat poverty and segregation, only the fraternally deprived scored highly. Notice that those who experienced only egoistic deprivation did not evince much prejudice at all; their discontent with their personal situation, since it was not combined with a group-based dissatisfaction, did not translate into intergroup prejudice. These attitudinal patterns were also reflected in electoral support for Black political candidates, the least support always coming from the fraternalistically deprived group.

These findings have been largely confirmed by other surveys in the US. Kluegel and Smith (1982) found that Whites' perceptions of being a group overlooked by government – arguably a form of relative deprivation – were correlated with beliefs that all groups in society had equal opportunities and a failure to recognize past discrimination against Blacks. Likewise, Bobo (1988a) found that Whites who believed that Blacks exerted too much political influence (compared to Whites)

tended also to differentiate positively between White and Blacks on a
'feeling thermometer'. On the other side of the ethnic divide Abeles
(1976) observed that Blacks' support for Black militancy was correlated
with fraternalistic deprivation. However, the moderately strong association that Abeles observed has not always been found amongst
minority-group respondents. McPhail (1971) in a survey of studies
which examined riot participation in the 1960s found that the statistical
relationships between measures of deprivation and participation were
often quite weak, the majority of the correlations being less than 0.2.
Furthermore, Spilerman (1970), using only aggregate economic and

Table 6.3 Fraternalistic and egoistic deprivation and prejudice

Type of deprivation	Prejudice measure[a,c]	Prejudice measure[b,c]
Doubly gratified (doing well personally *and* as a group	−20.9	−5.7
Egoistically deprived (doing poorly personally but well as a group)	−13.9	−14.1
Fraternally deprived (doing well personally but poorly as a group)	+14.3	+41.6
Doubly deprived (doing poorly personally *and* as a group)	+29.1	−9.0

Notes:

[a] Typical items included: 'would object if family member wanted to bring a Negro friend home for dinner'; 'would mind if Negro family with about the same income and education moved next door'; 'thinks white and black students should go to separate schools'.

[b] Typical items included: 'believes race riots caused by looters, agitators, militants, violent instincts, communist influence rather than bad conditions and racial discrimination' ; 'thinks most Negroes who receive welfare could get along without it if they tried'; 'believes busing school children harms their education'.

[c] On both measures the higher the score the more prejudice.

Source: Vanneman and Pettigrew (1972), table 9.

demographic data, found that the biggest single predictor of American civil disturbances in the 1960s was, in fact, the simple statistic of the size of the non-White population in any given city. Various indicators of relative deprivation (for example, relative income and employment rates) had no discernible influence once the non-white population size was controlled for.

The effects of relative deprivation are by no means confined to Black–White relations in the USA. Tripathi and Srivastava (1981) studied Muslim attitudes towards Hindus in India. Muslims are now a socially disadvantaged minority group in that country although prior to partition they were, in fact, the ruling group. This change in their status might be expected to lead to strong feelings of relative deprivation and, indeed, in another study they did show significantly higher deprivation levels than Hindus (Gosh et al., 1992). Tripathi and Srivastava (1981) divided their sample into high and low fraternalistically deprived groups and found, as expected, that the latter had much more positive intergroup attitudes than the former (see figure 6.5). In South Africa Appelgryn and Nieuwoudt (1988) found that relative deprivation was correlated with Black people's negative attitudes towards other ethnic groups. The same relationship was not found so strongly for white Afrikaaners' intergroup attitudes however.

National separatist attitudes have also been shown to be linked to fraternalistic deprivation. Guimond and Dubé-Simard (1983) found that

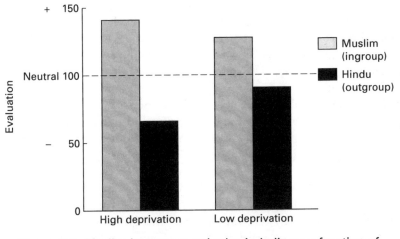

Figure 6.5 Muslim intergroup attitudes in India as a function of relative deprivation
Source: Tripathi and Srivastava (1981), table 1

French-speaking respondents (francophones) in Quebec perceived that francophones earned less than anglophones on average and that they were somewhat dissatisfied with this inequality. These feelings of dissatisfaction (or fraternalistic relative deprivation) were correlated with support for the Quebec nationalist movement. Personal dissatisfaction (egoistic deprivation) was much more weakly related to the same nationalist sentiments. Very similar results were obtained by Abrams (1990) among a large sample of Scottish teenagers. Their support for the Scottish Nationalist Party was predicted by fraternalistic deprivation (comparing Scotland with England), identification with Scotland, and their perception of income differentials between English and Scottish workers (another measure of fraternal deprivation). On the other hand, egoistic deprivation was mainly associated with personal feelings of unhappiness and stress. These very different consequences of fraternalistic and egoistic deprivation have also been observed in the domain of political activism: group-based deprivation is usually correlated with a desire for social change and militancy; egoistic deprivation with symptoms of depression (Koomen and Fränkel, 1992; Walker and Mann, 1987).

So far, all the work relating relative deprivation to prejudice that I have discussed has been carried out in field settings and mainly with ethnic groups. This has meant that the evidence has been correlational in nature with all the usual difficulties of causal interpretation which that implies. Moreover, in such surveys it is not always easy to investigate subtle interactions between variables especially if, as we have seen, some of the more direct relationships that are hypothesized sometimes fail to be observed. Then there is the question of how general the effects of relative deprivation really are; are they confined to ethnic groups or do they apply more widely? Experimental studies can often help to remedy these deficiencies.

It was with these issues in mind that a colleague and I set out to demonstrate unambiguously that fraternalistic relative deprivation did indeed cause prejudiced attitudes and derogatory intergroup behaviour (Grant and Brown, in press). Groups of women students worked on a task in which they had to come up with ideas for increasing the participation in senior university jobs. They each expected to receive around $10 for this task although they were warned that this payment would depend on the evaluation of their performance by another group. That evaluation, of course, constituted our experimental manipulation of deprivation: half the groups learned that the other group had given them a poor evaluation and recommended that they should only receive $4; the remainder were evaluated positively and were told that they would receive their expected $10.[7] The subjects reacted strongly to this manipulation. Compared to those who received what they expected, those who were relatively deprived showed markedly higher levels of ingroup bias against the other group, expressed consistently higher levels of dislike for them and, from careful observation of their videotaped interactions, expressed more derogatory remarks about them. Furthermore, they also seemed much readier to engage in collective protest against what they saw as an unfair decision – for example, by proposing to attack publicly the other group's views on equal opportunities or by giving them the 'cold shoulder' in a forthcoming intergroup encounter.

So far so good for the idea that feeling unfairly deprived will generate negative intergroup reactions. However, some other experiments indicate that it may not be as simple as that. One factor which may moderate the effects of deprivation is the degree of permeability of the groups' boundaries. We have already encountered this variable in our discussion of social identity processes where we saw that the possibility of 'escaping' to a higher status group does much to weaken the identity of the subordinate group (Ellemers et al., 1993; see pp. 182–4). Such a potential for social mobility may have similar effects on diluting the effects of deprivation, or so argue Wright et al. (1990). In their experiment they arranged for subjects to believe that they might have the possibility of joining a higher-status group depending on their performance in a decision-making task. There were to be real rewards associated with this superior group because members of it would be entered for a $100 lottery (instead of the paltry $10 they were currently enrolled in). Following the task the subordinate group members received some bad news. The superior group had decided that no one from the other group could yet join them. This rejection was accompanied by two other pieces of information. One concerned the likely number of subordinate group members who might eventually be admitted after subsequent tests. There were four quota levels: completely 'open' (that is, no quota), 30 per cent quota, 2 per cent quota, or completely 'closed' (that is, no lower-status members would ever be admitted). This, then, altered the permeability of the category boundaries between the two groups. In addition, the subjects learned how close they had come to joining the superior group. Half of them had apparently only just missed out, either because of they just failed the criterion level or because of the quota restriction; the remainder thought they were a long way from entry because their task performance was well below standard. These two variables – permeability and nearness to entry – had strong effects on the disadvantaged group's

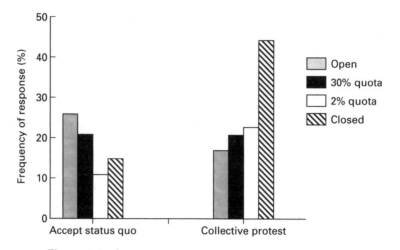

Figure 6.6 Group permeability and collective protest
Source: Wright et al. (1990), adapted from figure 3 (combining two types of collective protest)

reaction to its deprivation. A key question was whether they would simply accept the status quo or, alternatively engage in some kind of collective protest (for example, demanding a group retest, writing a collective letter of complaint). Figure 6.6 shows how the preference for these different responses varied with the different levels of group permeability. Those in the completely 'closed' condition showed the most evidence of collective protest. Even those whose chances of mobility were virtually non-existent (the 2 per cent condition) showed relatively little inclination towards collective discontent, an important caution as to the possible apathy-inducing effects of 'tokenism'. These tendencies were exacerbated still further by the 'nearness to entry' variable (not shown in figure 6.6): those near to entry showed most evidence of collective protest; those deemed to have little chance of mobility were the most accepting of their disadvantaged position.

A second factor which seems to be important in translating people's responses to inequality into collective action is the extent to which they believe that action is capable of effecting any change (Klandermans, 1984; McCarthy and Zald, 1977). However angry disadvantaged groups may feel, if they do not see some practical means of redress they may be unwilling to do or say much about their plight. It was to explore this tension between 'moral outrage and pragmatism' (to quote the title of their article) that Martin et al. (1984) designed their role-playing experiment which had women workers taking the part of a female sales manager in an oil company. This manager was described as being slightly, moderately, or greatly underpaid relative to male managers doing comparable jobs, thus creating three levels of relative deprivation. The workplace was also depicted as one in which this and the other female managers had (or had not) regular contact with each other, vital scarce skills which the company could not easily replace, and organized themselves into a formal group presumably with the aim of rectifying gender inequalities. In this way the experimenters hoped to create the impression that the disadvantaged group of women managers were (or were not) able to mobilize resources for changing their situation. Asked to imagine that they were such a manager, the subjects responded to the different levels of deprivation in an entirely predictable fashion: the larger the male–female pay inequality the more discontented they were. On the other hand, this variable had little effect on what kinds of protest they might engage in. This was determined much more by whether or not they believed that the collective efforts of women managers could be effectively marshalled. In short, some sense of perceived efficacy may be as important – if not more so – as a perception of being relatively deprived (see also Bernstein and Crosby, 1980; Major et al., 1991).

Theories of relative deprivation, then, offer several important insights into the genesis of prejudice. Of these, the most important is the observation that the objective conditions in which people live are a much less potent determinant of prejudice than their relative living standards – relative to other groups or to times past and future. Before we conclude the discussion two last comments are in order.

Relative Deprivation Theories, like Social Identity Theory, place a heavy emphasis on comparison processes. However, whether these comparisons lead to feelings of deprivation or gratification depends entirely on the type of comparison and the frame of reference that is chosen. Take that poorest sector of British society whose misfortunes were displayed in figure 6.4. If they made only temporal comparisons then they would have good reason to feel aggrieved, particularly if they focused on just the most recent ten-year period (when their real incomes fell). However, those with longer memories might look back to 1961 and reason that they are, in fact, 27 per cent better off than they were then and hence should feel more positive. But it is obvious that these feelings of temporal deprivation/gratification would pale into insignificance if they made social comparisons instead, especially comparisons with the richest 5 per cent in relation to whom the discrepancy is ever-widening. But are these the only intergroup comparisons that they can make? They could, alternatively, compare themselves with the unemployed, a group which itself greatly increased in size in Britain over the same period, and conclude that, in comparison to them, they were relatively *well* off. At present, Relative Deprivation Theories – and this is a weakness that Social Identity Theory suffers from also – do not readily allow us to specify which kind of comparison or comparison group will be chosen (although see Suls and Wills, 1991, for recent theorizing on this issue). Given that the outcomes of those comparisons are so crucial to the prediction of contentment, apathy, or protest, this problem is not, as Walker and Pettigrew (1984) have wisely observed, a trivial one.

The second concluding comment concerns the relationship between Relative Deprivation Theories, which we have just considered, and Social Identity Theory, discussed on pp. 169–89. Obviously there are several similarities between them. Both stress the importance of intergroup comparisons in the aetiology of prejudice although, as we have seen, some Relative Deprivation Theories do not distinguish between these and more interpersonal comparisons. Perceptions of injustice play an important role in both perspectives. Recall that perceived illegitimacy has been found to be an important factor determining people's reactions to identity threatening situations; likewise, in Relative Deprivation Theories there is an implied sense of grievance in the crucial psychological equation mapping 'expectations' to 'attainments'. If there are disparities between the theories they lie, I think, mainly in the different emphasis they give to certain social psychological processes and in the rather different outcomes which they predict. For Social Identity Theory group identification is the psychologically prior process: nothing can happen in the intergroup domain until and unless one has first identified oneself with a social category. This process is rather taken for granted in most versions of Relative Deprivation Theory, which are more focused on the outcomes of the social comparison process. This concern with the outcomes of intergroup comparisons is obviously shared by Social Identity Theory but, as noted on pp. 188–9, many of those outcomes – at least as studied by the majority of Social Identity Theory-inspired research – are in the cognitive-evaluative domain: how good do people *think* their group is compared to others? In contrast, the outcomes in Relative Deprivation Theory are markedly more affective in tone: how angry do people *feel* as a result of deprivation? Will this lead to violent protest? The two perspectives are then different, but in a complementary rather than a contradictory sense. And since, as I have been at pains to re-emphasize throughout this book, prejudice has both cognitive and affective components, it seems likely that both theories can contribute to its better understanding.

Summary

1. Prejudice can usefully be regarded as the outcome of conflicting group goals. Laboratory and field research findings converge to show that groups competing for scarce resources typically display more biased attitudes and greater mutual animosity than groups which are cooperating to achieve jointly desired objectives.

2. Conflicting interests are not necessarily for the arousal of mild forms of prejudice, however. Groups show a tendency towards intergroup discrimination in the most minimal group situations. One explanation of such spontaneous ingroup favouritism is based on the need for a positive social identity. Social identities are thought to be maintained by making positively biased intergroup comparisons.

3. If this is the case, then threats to social identity should generate prejudice. This can happen, particularly when group members feel the status position of the ingroup to be in some doubt because of structural instability or perceived illegitimacy. In general, groups with permeable boundaries seem to show less ingroup-favouring reactions than those with impermeable boundaries.

4. Not all threats to identity are reacted to adversely. Intergroup similarity – a potential threat to a group's distinctiveness – usually provokes positive reactions, except in cases of extreme similarity. Furthermore, some forms of prejudice cannot easily be explained in terms of social identity processes: ingroup bias is not always well correlated with group identification, nor is it usually associated with negative affective responses to the outgroup. The latter may be controlled by different processes.

5. Prejudice towards an outgroup can also be caused by a sense of relative deprivation. Relative deprivation refers to the perception that one's own group is not doing as well as

one believes it should be doing. Such expectations can derive from one's memory of recent gains/losses made by the ingroup or, more often, by comparing the ingroup's position to that of an outgroup. Field and laboratory research have largely confirmed the importance of relative deprivation in determining collective group reactions to felt injustice, although such factors as group permeability and efficacy are important moderating variables.

Further Reading

Abrams, D. and Hogg, M. (1990) *Social Identity Theory: Constructive and critical advances*, chs 1–4, 10–12. Hemel Hempstead: Harvester Wheatsheaf.

Olson, J.M., Herman, C.P. and Zanna, M.P. (1986) *Relative Deprivation and Social Comparison*, Hillsdale, NJ: Lawrence Erlbaum.

Sherif, M. (1966) *Group Conflict and Co-operation: Their social psychology.* London: Routledge and Kegan Paul.

Notes

1. There were some variations in the levels of bias shown against different outgroups but these need not detain us; and nor do they alter the main finding that the biases were generally strong and generic.

2. Except in relatively rare circumstances, such as choosing to have a sex change operation or artificially changing the colour of one's skin. In any case, such extreme 'passing' strategies can be fraught with difficulties (see Breakwell, 1986).

3. In fact, Ellemers et al. (1993) also included a third intermediate illegitimate condition where some justification for the status assignment was given. To simplify the presentation I have omitted this condition. The means from that condition were always approximately mid-way between the two other conditions.

4. Note that the vertical axis shows standardized factor scores and these do not correspond literally to positive and negative identification scores.

5. According to my dictionary this term stems from a Jewish religious custom in which a high priest symbolically laid the sins of a people on to a goat which was then allowed to escape into the wilderness (*Chambers 20th Century Dictionary*, 1979). How ironic, therefore, that Jews themselves have

so often become the scapegoats for the 'sins' of racist societies throughout human history.

6. The 'J' in the J-curve hypothesis comes from considering a graph of this rise and fall in standards. It resembles the curve of a letter 'J' laid upside down and at an angle.

7. We also included a second variable in the experiment in which we manipulated a threat to the group's identity. In the event this variable had only rather weak effects on the subjects' attitudes – for example, by increasing their ingroup bias – and no reliable effects on their behaviour.

Prejudice Old and New

7   Young women at bus station

Modern forms of prejudice sometimes take the form of increased social distance or mild aversion rather than outright hostility.

In this chapter I want to pick up two themes which have recurred in various places earlier in the book. The first is that prejudice is not a static phenomenon. As I noted in chapter 4 and again in chapter 5, there is a good deal of research to show that the plainly pejorative stereotypes of some minority groups that were commonplace 50 years ago are much less in evidence today. This is as noticeable from casual observation of people's everyday conversations as it is from the results of more systematic opinion surveys. The second theme is that prejudice is not a monolithic concept. This should already be clear from the different chapter headings which have identified its characterological, cognitive and social dimensions, but it emerged especially strongly in the last chapter where I noted that different measures of prejudice – ingroup bias, outgroup dislike, and so on – are often poorly correlated.

These two themes come together in this chapter as I consider first whether prejudice is really on the wane. As I shall demonstrate, there is much evidence that it is, at least in Western Europe and North America, where it has been most intensively studied, and at least at the level of publicly expressed attitudes. However, other evidence indicates that it is far from being extinct. Less-obtrusive measures still reveal that people's behaviour towards those in an outgroup, whether these be a different ethnic or gender group or people with disabilities, is often not the same as it is towards those in their ingroup. In the second part of the chapter I discuss various explanations which have been proposed to explain this disparity between overt and covert measures of prejudice. Although some of these are substantively different, what they all have in common is that new societal norms and changing political, economic and social relations between groups have combined to create a climate in which novel forms of prejudice can flourish. Underlying all these new kinds of prejudice is some residual negative affect associated with the outgroup in question.

Is Prejudice Declining?

It is relatively rare nowadays to hear prejudice in public, at least in circles in which I live. By and large, people's conversations and interactions

Table 7.1 Historical changes in White American ethnic stereotypes and attitudes

1 *Percentage of subjects selecting negative traits to describe Black Americans (student samples)*

	1933	1967	1990
Superstitious	84	13	3
Lazy	75	26	4
Ignorant	38	11	5
Stupid	22	4	3
Physically dirty	17	3	0
Unreliable	12	6	4

2 *Percentage endorsing prejudiced attitude statements (national surveys)*

	1963	1976	1985
Object to family member bringing home Black friend for dinner	52	26	20
Agree there should be laws against mixed marriages between Blacks and Whites	69	35	28
Think that Blacks and Whites should go to separate schools	38	20	7

Source: Dovidio and Fazio (1992), adapted from tables 1a and 2; and Dovidio and Gaertner (1986), figure 1.

give every appearance of being models of tolerance and understanding. So *un*accustomed am I to hearing sexist and racist comments being openly expressed that, on those infrequent occasions that I do, my first reaction is usually to think that their perpetrator is attempting some joke, albeit in dubious taste. Surveys over the past three decades suggest that this is not a completely subjective impression. They indicate that people's intergroup attitudes and stereotypes have indeed become more positive. Dovidio and his colleagues have done a useful job compiling some comparative historical data on American Whites' ethnic stereotypes and opinions (Dovidio and Fazio, 1992; Dovidio and Gaertner, 1986). Table 7.1 presents some of their findings and, on the face of it, it would seem that these really do show a progressive increase in tolerance over time. In the domain of gender, similar changes in attitudes towards women have occurred; research reveals less obviously sexist attitudes and greater support for gender equity in the work-place (Eagly et al., 1991; Kahn and Crosby, 1985; Sutton and Moore, 1985).

It seems to me that these are real advances. Whatever the reasons for the changes and however many doubts we may harbour about their genuineness (as we shall see), it is no small achievement of 40 years of anti-racist and anti-sexist campaigning and social reform that people are actually less openly bigoted and discriminatory than they used to be. If we couple these attitudinal changes with an apparent increase in the representation of women and minority groups in non-stereotypical roles in the media (Dovidio and Gaertner, 1986), and slight but nevertheless encouraging trends in their participation in professional occupations and managerial positions (Morgan, 1988; Pettigrew, 1985), then there is some reason not to feel completely pessimistic about the prospects for intergroup relations, at least in the domains of ethnicity and gender.

However, it would also be foolish to feel too complacent about these changes. Other research reveals that everything in the garden is far from rosy. To begin with, while it is true that some underprivileged groups have made advances in real terms in such areas as housing, education and employment, closer analysis reveals that in *relative* terms (that is, relative to some other groups – see chapter 6) inequalities are continuing and may even be increasing in some respects (Pettigrew, 1985; US Department of Labor, 1992). Secondly, it is possible that the decreases in prejudiced attitudes observed towards minority groups and women may not be mirrored in similar increases in tolerance towards other groups. A large survey carried out in 14 European countries in the early 1990s asked respondents the classic question, 'Would you object to someone like this as a neighbour?', following it with a number of category labels (*The European*, 9–12 July 1992). Consistent with the survey evidence presented above, only 10 per cent objected to potential ethnic minority group neighbours. However, other groups fared much less well. For example, 28 per cent objected to the idea of homosexuals living next door, 26 per cent to people with Aids, and 25 per cent to 'emotionally unstable' people. Another survey, conducted just in Britain, found that nearly two-thirds of the sample would rather not have 'gypsies' as neighbours, and 30 per cent or more preferred not to have Arabs or Pakistanis (*Independent*, 26 October 1993). In sum, the gains in public acceptance of some groups do not seem to have spread to others.

There are other reasons for concern. Some commentators, faced with the evidence of decreasing prejudice in surveys, have suggested that much of this decrease is more apparent than real (Crosby et al., 1980; Dovidio and Fazio, 1992). They point out that changes in societal norms and the existence of anti-discrimination legislation in many countries have made it increasingly unacceptable to express prejudice openly. Thus, the argument runs, people may only be paying lip-service to greater tolerance whilst really holding on to their prejudiced beliefs as fast as they ever did. There are four lines of evidence which point in this direction.

The first comes from research employing an experimental paradigm which was devised to reduce the social desirability effects which might be involved in responding to socially sensitive attitude or stereotype measures (Sigall and Page, 1971). The paradigm is known as the 'bogus pipe-line' because it involves connecting the subject via skin electrodes to an elaborate apparatus which supposedly can detect 'true' feelings. The experimenter goes to considerable lengths to convince the subject of the genuineness of the equipment which, in fact, is all a complete façade. Then, under the guise of wishing to validate the machine, the experimenter presents the subject with the critical measures and asks him/her to predict what reading the machine will give on each one. People's responses under this 'pipeline' condition are then compared to others' responses made without the benefit of all the technological trickery (control condition). The assumption is that subjects in the 'pipe-line' condition will be likely to 'predict' responses for the machine which are more in line with what they really believe than the responses of those in the control condition. To illustrate this effect, consider the six negative adjectives used to describe Blacks in table 7.1. Sigall and Page (1971) used these (and several others) to obtain stereotypical judgements about 'Negroes' and 'Americans' under 'pipe-line' and control conditions. Figure 7.1 presents the mean scores for just those six traits, showing how characteristic White American subjects thought they were of the two groups concerned. Notice that in the normal control condition they rated 'Americans' slightly more negatively than 'Negroes'. On the other hand, in the 'bogus pipe-line' condition the means were dramatically reversed: now 'Negroes' are reported as being more 'ignorant', 'stupid', 'lazy' and so on than 'Americans'. Other studies have found similar results (Allen, 1975; Carver et al., 1978).

A second body of research which suggests that intergroup attitudes measured with conventional techniques may not be all that they seem is that which has used unobtrusive methods to observe people's actual behaviour towards outgroup members. Crosby et al. (1980) collated a number of studies which had observed helping behaviour in interethnic settings. Many of these were naturalistic studies in which participants were unaware that they were taking part in an experiment. In just under a half of these, more help was given to a recipient of the same ethnicity as the donor than to an outgroup recipient. (This was equally true of Black and White donors). Thus, whatever these subjects might have *said* about Blacks and Whites as groups, significant numbers of them were *behaviourally* discriminating between 'needy' ingroup and outgroup members when it came to the crunch. Crosby et al. (1980) discovered one other interesting fact. When they examined only the studies using

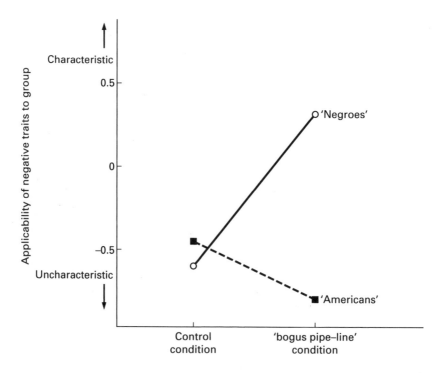

Figure 7.1 Measuring negative stereotypes with reduced social desirability contamination

Note: Figure shows means for the six negative traits given in table 7.1 (–3 to +3 scale).

Source: Sigall and Page (1971), adapted from table 1

White subjects there was a noticeable tendency for more intergroup discrimination in settings not involving direct face-to-face contact with the potential Black recipient. In these, three-quarters of the studies found significantly more help being given to fellow Whites. In contrast, when the situation involved more immediate contact between donor and recipient – and hence where, by implication, refusal to help would be more publicly visible – only about one-third of the studies found pro-White bias in helping. As we shall see, this difference between people's behaviour in immediate and more remote settings may be theoretically significant.

A third area of work relevant to this issue has focused on the relationship between people's public and presumably rather controlled responses on attitude scales and the like, and their more covert and perhaps more spontaneous non-verbal behaviours. One of the first attempts to study this in an interethnic setting was by Weitz (1972). Weitz had her White college students record a brief message for a later participant of whom they had been given a short description. This description contained information about the target person's ethnicity (Black or White) and also about his occupation (law student or petrol station attendant). Ratings of anticipated liking for this person were obtained together with a series of less-direct socio-metric measures (for example, choice of task with which to interact with the person, the tasks varying in intimacy). Weitz analysed the voice tone of the recorded message for such features as warmth and admiration and then correlated the presence of these paralinguistic cues with the other measures of friendliness. Some of these correlations were intriguing. For those subjects anticipating interacting with a Black person there were *negative* correlations between the verbal rating of friendliness and the other indices (for example, voice warmth and admiration, choice of task). The more friendliness they said they felt the less actually came across in their non-verbal behaviours.

A similar disparity between obtrusive and unobtrusive measures of interethnic proximity was observed by Hendricks and Bootzin (1976). In their experiment White women subjects arrived at the laboratory and were casually invited to take a seat in a room. One of the seats was already occupied by a Black or White confederate. The first and least obtrusive measure was simply which of the eight vacant seats was chosen by the subject. Then followed the more direct measure of proximity. The subject and the confederate had to stand at increasingly close distances from one another and rate how uncomfortable they felt.

On the latter measure, where social desirability norms were probably very salient, no effect was found for the ethnicity of the confederate. However, the more covert seating measure revealed that subjects chose to sit approximately one seat further away from the Black confederate than from the White confederate, a significant difference. Recall also that experiment by Word et al. (1974) that I described in chapter 4. There, too, Whites chose to sit closer to a fellow White interviewee, talked longer and with fewer speech errors, than they did to a Black interviewee.

A similar phenomenon has been observed in people's reactions to those with some kind of disability. Kleck et al. (1966) arranged for subjects to interact with a confederate who either had no obvious disability or appeared to be a leg amputee in a wheelchair (the same confederate was always used). The interactions with the 'handicapped' confederate were significantly shorter than those with the 'non-handicapped' confederate. Moreover, subjects in the latter condition were less anxious: their arousal levels, as measured by their galvanic skin resistance, were reliably lower than those interacting with the person in a wheelchair (see also Heinmann et al., 1981).

Consistent with these findings, some recent research using electro-myography suggests that people's attitudes may literally be only skin deep (Vanman et al., 1990). Electromyography is a technique in which electrical activity from muscle groups is recorded. According to Cacioppo et al. (1986), activity of different facial muscles gives a subtle and sensitive indication of people's likes and dislikes for various stimuli. Two areas of the face in particular are thought to be significant: the muscles above the eye which are used when we frown and the muscles in the cheek which are used in smiling, indicative respectively of negative and positive affect. Vanman et al. (1990) made recordings from these two muscle groupings whilst White subjects viewed slides showing White or Black people with whom they had to imagine interacting. After each slide subjects also rated the stimulus people on various scales, including how much they liked them. These self-report measures revealed a pro-Black bias; subjects professed to liking the Black stimuli more than the White. The electromygraphic readings told a different story, however. Whenever a Black photograph appeared there tended to be more activity from the 'frown' muscles and less from the 'smile' muscles, compared to the levels recorded for the White stimuli.

Fourth, there is the evidence, also presented in chapter 4, that certain of people's associative cognitive processes differentiate between Black and White stimuli. Of particular relevance are those studies which show that people's reaction times to category label and adjective associations are often reliably different according to the combination of category and valence of the adjective: typically, ingroup categories and positive word pairings elicit the fastest reactions, and ingroup–negative pairs the slowest (Dovidio et al., 1986; Gaertner and McLaughlin, 1983; Lalonde and Gardner, 1989; Perdue et al., 1990). Because these tasks do not usually require a considered evaluative judgement by subjects but instead call for a simple snap decision (taking only milliseconds), it seems unlikely that conscious attempts to inhibit socially undesirable responses come into play. And, indeed, the data, by demonstrating differential reactions to ingroup and outgroup stimuli, suggest that they have not.

What sense can we make of these discrepancies between direct consciously controlled attitude measures and more covert, perhaps more spontaneous, indicators of prejudice? Crosby et al. (1980) suggest two possible explanations. One comes from Campbell's (1963) model in which attitudes are seen as general dispositions to act. According to this view, we can only ever infer attitudes from people's behaviours, and these behaviours can be thought of as hierarchically arranged in terms of their costliness to the person. The attitudinal inferences we can sensibly make depend on whereabouts in this hierarchy the behaviour falls. Actions that are costly to the person and that could have been easily avoided tell us more about a person's attitude than low-cost behaviours that were unavoidable. Thus, a self-report on a prejudice scale – a typical low-cost behaviour which subjects may feel constrained by the researcher–respondent relationship to give – tells us less about people's disposition to be prejudiced than, say, someone's helping behaviour in a naturalistic interethnic setting where one could, if one really wanted, easily avoid giving help, and where, in addition, one has to expend time, effort or money on the recipient. For Campbell, therefore, conventional paper and pencil measures of intergroup attitudes are simply less good indicators of underlying orientations than other behavioural measures.

Although this theory sounds plausible, it is not without its difficulties. First, as Crosby et al. (1980) point out, it cannot always account for the observed findings – for instance, that difference in interethnic helping by Whites in face-to-face and less proximal situations. It is true that help in the latter contexts is easier to avoid giving (and hence should be a more reliable indicator) but, on the other hand, it is typically much less costly (which makes it a less good index of genuine intergroup attitudes). Second, it is not obvious how Campbell's model deals with the evidence from those studies which suggest that prejudice is sometimes revealed in spontaneous and automatic reactions. These are low-cost unavoidable behaviours. Does this necessarily render them poor indices of people's underlying disposition? If so, what should we make of their apparent inverse relationship to pencil and paper measures which are also, according to Campbell, only weakly valid measures?

A second and related explanation of the discrepancy between overt and covert measures draws on Kelman's (1961) distinction between compliance and internalization. For Kelman, people's behaviour in a situation can be mere conformity to immediately perceived rewards or costs or, alternatively, can reflect an internalized set of beliefs justifying their actions. If one changes the reward–cost ratio of performing certain deeds – for example, by introducing legal sanctions for race or sex discrimination and by promoting social values favouring tolerance – then one should expect greater compliance to non-prejudiced norms without, however, any internalization having occurred. However, such compliance will only occur in *public* where people feel under surveillance and hence where the costs of non-compliance are high. Without internalization, in more private contexts the prejudiced attitudes re-emerge. This could explain why interethnic helping is more discriminatory in distal than in proximal settings and why, too, overt controlled responses often correlate poorly with more automatic processes. From this perspective, then, the past 30 years have seen important changes in institutionalized norms and practices regarding ethnic and gender prejudice. These have exerted a strong influence on most people's compliant behaviour but may not have been internalized into everyone's own value systems.

The plausibility of this distinction between internalization and compliance is strengthened by some recent studies suggesting that even at automatic levels of responding one can detect differences between people who may dispositionally endorse different social values (prejudiced versus non-prejudiced). In chapter 3 I described a study by Devine (1989) in which people responded to subliminally presented stimuli consisting of the category 'Blacks' and stereotypically related traits by subsequently rating a stimulus person as more aggressive. Devine reported that this phenomenon was unaffected by prior prejudice level. However other research has found differential responding to both subliminal and supraliminal priming stimuli as a function of prejudice level (Augustinos et al., 1994; Lepore and Brown, 1994a; Locke et al., 1994). Using a variety of techniques these studies have all found that high-prejudice people typically display more negative reactions to outgroup-related primes than low-prejudice people. One interpretation of these findings is that high- and low-prejudice people have different internalized beliefs about ingroups and outgroups, and that these are revealed in experimental procedures which tap automatic processes.

The two explanations proferred by Crosby et al. (1980) to explain the historical changes in overt prejudice levels and the discrepancies between these and covert measures of prejudice propose that the basic nature of prejudice remains intact; it is only its outward manifestation that has changed with new societal norms outlawing public bigotry and discrimination, thus creating different social rewards and costs for its expression. I want now to consider some other theories which are also concerned with these contemporary forms of prejudice but which suggest that they may be qualitatively different from the varieties more common in the past.

New Forms of Prejudice

The observation that levels of overt prejudice were falling whilst other forms of discrimination were continuing has stimulated a number of new conceptualizations of prejudice over the past 20 years. These come in a multitude of guises: 'symbolic racism', 'modern racism', 'aversive racism', 'subtle prejudice', 'modern sexism', 'neo-sexism', and 'ambivalent sexism'. Although there are important differences between these various constructs, they have sufficient in common to justify my treating at least some of them together under the same headings. For simplicity's sake I have kept these to two.

The first focuses on those approaches which claim that 'old-fashioned' or 'red-neck' prejudice is gradually being supplanted by a 'modern' form in which the antipathy towards outgroups is symbolically or indirectly expressed. Although there is little consensus amongst the proponents of these new forms of prejudice as to their content or their origins, they do all share an individual differences perspective in the sense that the research goal has been to find reliable ways of distinguishing people who score high or low on some psychometric scale, and then to examine correlates of that distinction. The second cluster of approaches places more emphasis on situational factors. One of the main themes here has been that prejudice nowadays often takes the form of an 'aversive' response, sometimes as a reaction to anxiety-provoking situations. Thus, so long as there are no very explicit norms governing what should be said or done, people may display their prejudice by interacting in ways which subtly distance them from the outgroup person.

Modern prejudice

The first suspicion that some new kind of prejudice might be afoot came from a study of voting behaviour in the 1969 Los Angeles election for city mayor (Sears and Kinder, 1971). That election was essentially between a conservative White incumbent mayor and a liberal Black city councillor. Sears and Kinder found to their surprise that people's preference for the former candidate was not reliably correlated with their prejudice level as measured on conventional attitude items tapping beliefs in Black intellectual inferiority, opposition to school integration, and the like (see table 7.1 for typical items). On the other hand, some other questions, concerned more with the alleged economic and social advances made by minority groups and social policies aimed at the redressing of past inequalities were predictive of electoral preference for the more conservative politician.

Findings like these led Sears and his colleagues to propose that a new form of racism was supplanting the older and more blatant kinds of bigotry familiar from the 1930s and 1940s (McConahay, 1986; Sears, 1988). According to these authors there are several reasons for this. Changing societal norms have meant, as we have already noted, that open expressions of prejudice are now socially frowned upon. Thus, the predictive utility of traditional prejudice measures has been reduced because of these social desirability factors. Nevertheless, given the long history of racism in the United States (and elsewhere) it was assumed that some residual anti-Black affect would still comprise most Whites' socialization experience. In addition, the political demands of minority groups and the introduction of such policies as compulsory school busing and positive discrimination threatened traditional Western values of individual freedom of choice and equality of opportunity based on meritocratic principles. The perceived violation of these abstract values, then, was thought to be an important component of the new form of prejudice, especially when coupled with the culturally socialized negative affect towards Blacks. McConahay (1986) has summarized the modern racist's outlook on the world thus: discrimination no longer exists because all groups enjoy the same civil and economic rights; Blacks are making too many demands too quickly; these demands are unfair; therefore, any gains they have made are undeserved.

Before we examine how this construct has been measured, three further features of the approach should be mentioned. The first is that modern racists are to be distinguished from 'old-fashioned' racists mainly in their beliefs about the attributes of Blacks as a group. It is true that they share with 'old-fashioned' racists some negative feeling towards Blacks, but it is presumed that they do not endorse the traditional negative stereotypes of Blacks as 'stupid' and 'lazy', and nor do they agree with Deep South segregationist views about separate schools, mixed marriages and the like. The second is the importance that is attached to the violation of deeply held Western values in driving the modern racist's attitude. Indeed, it is the value conflict which is the core component of the ideology rather than any immediately perceived threat to personal interests. Thus, it is thought that what upsets modern racists is not so much that Blacks may be going to the same school as their (White) children, but that the educational policy of enforced busing to achieve better ethnic balances within city schools contradicts parents' 'right' to choose the school for their children. Finally, it is claimed that the techniques used to measure modern racism are less reactive than conventional instruments because they tap subtle and indirect aspects of prejudice rather than its more blatant features. This, it is felt, makes them less prone to the kind of social desirability response biases that I considered in the last section.

Some of the items used to measure modern racism are presented in table 7.2, contrasted with more traditional racism items. When factor analysed, it turns out that these two clusters of items tend to load on separate factors which supports the distinction between the two types of prejudice that modern racism theorists have made (McConahay, 1986). However, the separation is not complete and modern and old fashioned racism are usuallly substantially correlated with one another (ibid.). This correlation can be read two ways. It could mean that the two constructs are not as different as is claimed, or it could support the idea in modern racism theory that both types of prejudice share a common origin in negative feelings towards Black people. One way to decide which of these two interpretations is the most tenable is to see how well the different scales do in predicting other attitudes and behaviour that could

Table 7.2 Some items used to measure modern and old-fashioned racism

Modern racism

Over the past few years, Blacks have received more economically than they deserve.

Over the past few years, the government and news media have shown more respect for Blacks than they deserve.

Blacks are getting too demanding in their push for equal rights.

Discrimination against Blacks is no longer a problem in the United States.

Old-fashioned racism

If a Black family with about the same income and education as you moved next door, would you mind it a lot, a little, or not at all?

How strongly would you object if a member of your family had friendship with a Black – strongly, somewhat, slightly or not at all?

Generally, do you feel Blacks are smarter, not as smart or about as smart as Whites?

Generally speaking, I favour full racial integration (reversed item).

Source: McConahay (1986), tables 2 and 4.

reasonably be interpreted as prejudiced, or at least illiberal because of their implications for Black people.

One study to examine this question was by McConahay (1982). He used both kinds of measures to try to predict people's attitudes against compulsory busing in Kentucky, USA. In addition, he attempted to assess the extent to which respondents had a direct personal interest in the busing issue – for example, by having children of school age. The results were clear-cut. The largest single correlate of negative attitudes about busing was modern racism. Old-fashioned racism was also a reliable predictor, as was a simple feeling about Blacks 'thermometer' measure, but both of these correlations were much weaker than that obtained for the modern racism scale. Self-interest did not correlate at all. Essentially similar results were obtained by Jacobson (1985) who looked at people's attitudes towards affirmative action programmes in employment and education which are designed to give special consideration to previously disadvantaged groups such as women and ethnic minorities. The results from this large national survey again revealed that modern racism was the best predictor, followed by old-fashioned racism but more weakly, and that self-interest did not correlate at all with affirmative action attitudes (see also Kluegel and Smith, 1983, and

Kinder and Sears, 1981, for similar significant effects for modern-racism-type measures and much weaker or non-existent effects for self-interest indices).

Support for the concept of modern racism has also come from experimental studies. In two studies McConahay and his colleagues sought to examine the sensitivity of modern and old-fashioned racism scales to social desirability factors (McConahay, 1986; McConahay et al., 1981). This was achieved simply by varying the ethnicity of the researcher administering them (it was hypothesized that a Black experimenter might sensitize White respondents to respond more 'correctly' than a White experimenter). In fact, differences due to experimenter were only found on the old-fashioned racism measure; the modern racism scores did not change significantly. In another study modern racism was found to affect people's judgements in a simulated personnel selection task (McConahay, 1983). Here, the subjects were asked to indicate the likelihood that they would hire three candidates based on a brief curriculum vitae for each one. Two of the candidates were White, the third Black. The effect of modern racism was not simply to downgrade this latter candidate; rather, this depended on the order in which the black candidate's CV appeared. When it was first, high racists were indeed less likely to offer him a job than low racists. When it appeared last the opposite occurred. McConahay argued, not altogether convincingly in my view, that in the first decision context the ethnicity of the candidate was less salient than in the second, and hence norms to behave in a non-racist manner would have been less potent. Even if this was the case, it hardly explains the *positive* correlation between racism and hiring preference for the Black candidate in the second context.

The idea that prejudice may have developed new disguises is not confined either to the United States or to the Black–White context from which it originated. Workers in other geographical and social domains have also found that scales of modern prejudice have usefully predicted people's intergroup judgements. In Australia Augustinos et al. (1994) adapted McConahay's (1986) scale to focus on Whites' attitudes towards aboriginal Australians. They found that this measure correlated with the degree of endorsement of positive and negative attributes associated with Aborigines.[1] We, too, have developed a modern racism measure, this time for use in a British context, and have also found it correlates with various non-reactive measures of intergroup bias (Lepore and Brown, 1994b). In one study we asked subjects to make quick evaluative judgements of positive and negative trait words stereotypically associated with Blacks and Whites but, in fact, presented singly without any explicit associations with those two categories. High-racist subjects rated the 'White negative' words less negatively than did low racists. In contrast, low racists rated the 'Black positive' words more favourably than did high racists.

The village of Middlezoy in Somerset, Britain, is not perhaps the most obvious location to find contemporary examples of modern and old-fashioned prejudice. But a news report of a recent dispute there over the council's plan to build a campsite for travellers – or 'gypsies' as they are colloquially known – caught my eye as providing a nice illustration of the two phenomena (*Independent*, 13 June 1994). As elsewhere in Britain, antipathy towards travellers in Middlezoy is never far from the surface. Some, like the landlord of the village pub, express this hostility directly by refusing to serve people from the camp: 'I can refuse who I like can't I? I'm not saying I'm going to bar gypsies, that's more than I dare say, but I bar who I want to bar.' Others, however, find more apparently 'reasonable' grounds for their opposition. Here, for example, is the leader of the campaign to boycott the village school if travellers' children are allowed to attend it: 'People here believe primary education is very important, the formative years and they're frightened their children will pick up attitudes of, perhaps, the travelling fraternity who don't want to go to school.' Notice the appeal to the implied consensual value of the importance that 'our' children's education not be disrupted used to justify the exclusion of other children from the same social benefit.

A similar distinction to the modern vs. old-fashioned dichotomy has been proposed by Pettigrew and Meertens (1995). Their labels are 'subtle' and 'blatant' racism. The latter corresponds to old-fashioned prejudice. Subtle racism has much in common with modern racism since it, too, is comprised in part of a defence of traditional individualistic values together with beliefs that minority groups are in receipt of undeserved favours. However, Pettigrew and Meertens also propose that subtle racism includes an exaggeration of cultural differences between the majority ingroup and the minority outgroup (for example, in values, religion, and language), and a denial of any positive emotional response towards outgroup members. In contrast to blatant racists, subtle racists do not express overtly negative feelings towards minority groups, they merely withhold any positive feelings. Based on a large survey in four European countries, Meertens and Pettigrew found some support for their hypothesized distinction. Their scales of blatant and subtle racism were, as usual, quite well correlated but did seem to load on two separate[2] factors in a factor analysis. Both scales were positively correlated with general ethnocentrism, support for racist political organizations, and fraternalistic relative deprivation (although the correlations with the latter two measures were generally weaker for subtle racism), and negatively correlated with intergroup contact. There was also some evidence that subtle and blatant racists had different views on various immigration and deportation policies: blatant racists happily endorsing wholesale forced emigration of all minority groups; subtle racists supporting deportation only of those without immigration papers or of those who had committed crimes.

So far I have only considered modern prejudice towards ethnic groups. However, some have proposed that a similar symbolic form of prejudice is emerging in other intergroup contexts. Benokraitis and Feagin (1986), for example, suggest that women, too, are often the victims of covert forms of discrimination, what they call 'modern sexism'. As just one illustration of what this kind of subtle gender bias might be in operation, consider the results of Shore's (1992) study of candidates at a corporate assessment centre over a five-year period. At this centre white-collar workers from a large petroleum company were the subject of detailed scrutiny involving interviews. At the conclusion of each assessment period the (mainly male) assessors met to pool all this information and provide an overall evaluation of each person's manage-ment potential. On all but one of the 15 objective criteria the women candidates scored better than the men (often significantly so) and yet, in that bottom-line judgement, they were not rated as having any significantly greater management potential. Worse still, several years after the assessment, their job grade was virtually identical to the men's.

With the idea of trying to measure this new kind of gender prejudice we have recently developed a scale of neo-sexism (Tougas et al., in press). The items for this were drawn from some existing modern racism scales (see table 7.2) adapted to the gender domain, and we added some items of our own. We used this scale, a scale of old-fashioned sexism (Rombough and Ventimiglia, 1981), and a measure of men's collective interests in the employment domain to predict the attitudes of male students towards affirmative action programmes for women. Figure 7.2 summarizes the results of one of our studies in the form of a path diagram. Note that whilst old-fashioned and neo-sexism are positively correlated, of the two only the latter reliably predicts attitudes towards affirmative action: the higher the sexism score the less positive the attitudes. Interestingly, and in contrast to some of the research with modern racism reviewed earlier, the collective-interests measure[3] was also an important factor. A follow-up study of male employees in a firm which had recently implemented an affirmative action programme produced essentially the same results (Tougas et al., in press). (See also Glick and Fiske, 1994, and Swim et al., 1995, for related ideas and measures.)

It is possible that current attitudes towards some stigmatized groups may also be construed as modern prejudice. One such group is fat people in the United States, who are the subject of enough social, educational and employment discrimination to have formed their own National Association to Advance Fat Acceptance (Crandall, 1994; *Independent*, 13 June 1994). Crandall (1994) has devised a measure of anti-fat prejudice which he believes is conceptually similar to scales of modern racism. Like the latter, his scale has two correlated components – a measure of anti-fat affect and a measure tapping the tendency to attribute excess weight to a lack of willpower of the fat person. (There is also a third factor, unrelated

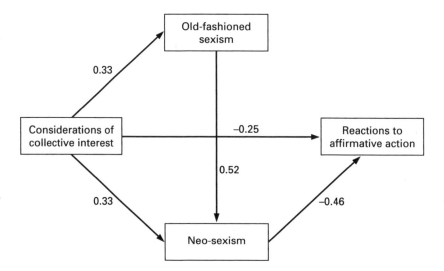

Figure 7.2 Old-fashioned sexism, neo-sexism, and attitudes towards affirmative action programmes for women
Note: The diagram shows path coefficients (which indicate the direction and strength of relationships between variables) derived from a multiple regression analysis including all four variables
Source: Tougas et al. (in press), figure 2

to these two, which taps fear of fatness.) Crandall (1994) also found that the two main sub-scales of his anti fat-measure were correlated with individualistic and conservative value orientations but not at all with the respondent's own obesity, thus apparently mirroring the low personal self-interest–modern-racism correlations noted earlier. It is likely that, as social psychologists widen the scope of their enquiries, similar patterns will emerge in prejudice towards groups such as the elderly, people with Aids, and people with disabilities.

The many variants of the modern prejudice thesis have not escaped criticism. Most of these critiques have focused on modern *racism* but I shall try to generalize their arguments to apply to other new forms of prejudice also (see Bobo, 1988b; Sniderman and Tetlock, 1986). Three issues dominate these debates.

The first is: how distinct are the new forms of prejudice from their old fashioned cousins? Related to this is the question of how subtle are the techniques currently used to measure modern prejudice. Considering this second question first, we are forced to concede that, at least in their surface content, most scales of modern prejudice still seem to be tainted strongly with social desirability – that is, it is usually fairly obvious what the 'socially correct' direction to answer is. As evidence of this, several studies using such scales have reported that the mean sample scores tend to be skewed towards the non-prejudiced end of the scale (Augustinos et al. 1994; Devine et al., 1991; Lepore and Brown, 1994b; Tougas et al., in press; Locke et al., 1994). This somewhat undermines McConahay's (1986) claim that modern racism measures are more subtle and less reactive indicators of prejudice than old-fashioned racism scales, although in his defence he can point to his own experimental evidence which does show exactly that (see p. 221). Potentially more worrying are the consistently high correlations that are repeatedly observed between old-fashioned and modern prejudice. Although theories of modern prejudice predict some association between the two because of their common anti-Black affect component, some have argued that correlations as high as 0.6 between the two measures could well justify treating them as a single construct (Sniderman and Tetlock, 1986). This would be an entirely reasonable position were it not for the fact that the two types of prejudice do seem to have reliably different predictive uses. As we have seen, scales of modern prejudice correlate with attitudes towards such issues as school busing, affirmative action programmes, and conservative political candidates in the way that old-fashioned measures simply do not, or do so much less strongly.

A second issue concerns the interpretability of responses to some items in modern prejudice scales. Focusing particularly on the symbolic racism construct, Sniderman and Tetlock (1986) point out that an item like 'It is wrong to set up quotas to admit Black students to college who don't meet the usual standards' (Kinder and Sears, 1981), to which agreement is taken to indicate symbolic racism, could arguably be used as an indicator of a *non-racist* response. For example, it is plausible to imagine liberal objections to ethnic quotas and affirmative action on the grounds that such measures are patronizing to minority groups and undermine their subsequent academic or professional achievements. Similarly, in Pettigrew and Meerten's (1995) subtle-racism scale there are four items measuring perceived cultural differences (high difference is scored in the racist direction). Yet the position of many ethnic minorities and progressive policy-makers concerned with developing multicultural awareness is precisely to stress the importance of recognizing and respecting intergroup differences as an antidote to the cultural annihilation implied by assimilationist philosophies. It seems to me that these objections have some merit but they apply more to some modern prejudice scales than to others. For instance, it is hard to see how agreement with the four modern racism items in table 7.2, and others proposed by McConahay (1986), could do other than imply something of a prejudiced attitude. Also, as McConahay (1986) has pointed out, while agreement or disagreement with any one particular item could be interpreted equivocally, a *consistent* pattern of (dis)agreement across all the items in the scale is much less open to such ambiguity.

A final question concerns the role of self-interest. A consistent claim of theories of modern prejudice is that self-interest has very little to do with the ways new forms of racism and sexism manifest themselves – for example, in opposition to busing, affirmative action, and the like (McConahay, 1982; Sears, 1988). In response to this claim, critics have argued that 'self-interest', as usually defined by these theorists, only refers to direct *personal* interest – that is, having a child in school, being employed in the organization with an affirmative action programme in place – and hence is too narrowly conceived (Bobo, 1988; Sniderman and Tetlock, 1986). For what is missing from this conception of self-interest is the recognition that, whilst people's own personal position may or may not be at stake by the policy in question, they may still perceive their *group's* interests to be affected by it. Recall from chapter 6 how a consistent finding from the relative-deprivation literature is that *fraternalistic* deprivation is nearly always a much better predictor of intergroup sentiments than egoistic deprivation. The same may be true of modern prejudice, at least in the domains of racism and sexism (Pettigrew and Meertens, 1995; Tougas et al., in press).

Aversive prejudice

Earlier in this chapter I reviewed evidence from a variety of sources which indicated that differential reactions to White and Black people – for example, in offering them help – were most likely when there were no very explicit social norms prescribing appropriate behaviour. In that same section I also noted research which had identified subtle differences in Whites' non-verbal and relatively spontaneous behaviours when the interaction involved Black rather than White participants. It was findings like these which prompted Gaertner and Dovidio (1986) to re-investigate Kovel's (1970) concept of 'aversive racism', a new form of prejudice which they thought might underlie many White (American) people's contemporary behaviour towards members of ethnic minorities.

Like modern racism theorists, Gaertner and Dovidio (1986) believe that overt and blatant prejudice is on the wane. Many White people, they suggest, do genuinely endorse principles of tolerance and ethnic equality and, indeed, may even support progressive public policies. On the other hand, coexisting with these liberal attitudes is some residual anxiety in their dealings with minority group members, an unease stemming from culturally socialized negative images associated with them. It is this anxiety which is thought to colour White people's interactions with Blacks (and other outgroups), betraying itself in certain behavioural indicators of avoidance and coolness. However, this is only likely to happen in those situations where there are ambiguous or conflicting norms because then the aversive reaction may more easily be rationalized as non-prejudiced. Where anti-discrimination norms are more salient then even aversive racists are expected to adhere to them.

Notice the differences between this approach and some of the modern racism theories I considered in the previous section. According to Gaertner and Dovidio (1986), aversive racists may really endorse progressive attitudes on such questions as busing and affirmative action; however, for Sears (1988) and McConahay (1986) these are the linchpin issues for modern racists because of their dissonance with traditional individualistic values. Gaertner and Dovidio (1986) believe that aversive racism reveals itself unconsciously and only in situations with no normative structure. Because of this there are inherent difficulties in measuring it with reactive instruments like a questionnaire. In contrast, modern prejudice theorists suggest that the 'new' form of prejudice is part of a consciously worked out ideology which can be measured with conventional attitude scales. In the aversive racism thesis the negative affect is characterized as fear, discomfort or unease; in the modern racism approach the underlying negative affect is hostility or dislike.

In support of their theory Gaertner and Dovidio (1986) have marshalled a considerable body of evidence. Some of this comes from naturalistic settings in which they have listened to White respondents' reactions to receiving a bogus 'wrong number' telephone call to a garage requesting help with a car breakdown. The ethnicity of the person requesting the help is systematically varied. Discrimination is evident if a 'Black' caller receives a less-helpful response than a 'White' caller. In several studies this is exactly what has been observed (for example, Gaertner, 1973; Gaertner and Bickman, 1971). Notice that in this 'remote victim' situation there are no strong normative guidelines indicating that help should be given. Similar effects have been observed in laboratory studies. In one experiment, Gaertner and Dovidio (1977) created a mock extra-sensory perception experiment in which subjects had to try to receive telepathic messages from a 'sender' (who could be Black or White). Half the subjects believed that they and the 'sender' were the only participants in the situation; the remainder believed there were two other 'receivers' as well. Then, half-way through the experiment, a stack of chairs was heard to fall, with accompanying cries of distress from the 'sender'. Those hearing the emergency 'alone' probably perceived strong norms to intervene and, indeed, a very high proportion of them (about 90 per cent) did so, irrespective of whether the victim was White or Black. On the other hand, as we know from Latane and Darley's (1970) pioneering work on bystander intervention, where others are present social responsibility norms are much less keenly felt. Consistent with this, in the 'together' conditions the level of helping was lower *and* discriminated between the 'White' and 'Black' victim: the latter was half as likely to receive help as the former (see figure 7.3). Moreover, these effects occurred irrespective of subjects' previously measured prejudice levels. Thus, the situational contingencies of norm salience and the victim's ethnicity proved more significant than the subjects' prior disposition to be prejudiced or not.

Frey and Gaertner (1986) manipulated situational norms in a different way. They arranged for the help-seeker to appear to need assistance *either* because of her failure to try hard enough on an easy task (internal locus of need) *or* because of failing on a difficult task despite her best efforts (external locus of need). In addition, the request for help was made either by a third party or by the potential recipient herself. Frey and Gaertner reasoned that in the external locus case, when the request also came from a third party, there the norms for helping would be most unambiguous. Where, however the recipient had brought her situation on herself *and* made the request for help (apparently with no one else observing this), subjects could find reasons *not* to help. So it turned out. In the latter situation the White recipient was given help twice as often as the Black recipient; in the former where *not* to help would have seemed like an obvious slight, the Black recipient actually received marginally more help than the White.

Another way in which normative expectations can vary is through different role relationships: it is 'normal' for a supervisor to assist a

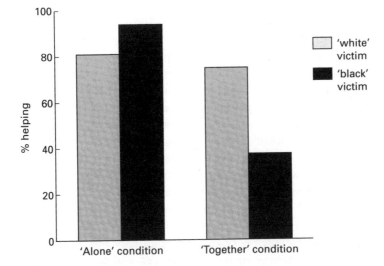

Figure 7.3 Help-giving to 'White' and 'Black' victims as an index of aversive racism
Source: Gaertner and Dovidio (1977), table 1

subordinate in need; somewhat less so the other way around. In two experiments Dovidio and Gaertner (1981, 1983) exploited these role expectations, varying the ethnicity of the recipient in the first, and of gender in the second. In a laboratory task subjects were assigned to work with a confederate who was alleged to be of higher or lower ability than them. In this task, half the subjects acted as 'supervisors', half as 'subordinates'. Just before the task began the confederate 'accidentally' knocked over a container of pencils on to the floor and covertly monitored whether the subject offered assistance. The results of the two studies showed a remarkable convergence. When the confederate was White or male the likelihood of helping was determined mainly by ability (high-ability persons were helped more than the low-ability), and slightly by role (supervisors helped more than subordinates). On the other hand, when the partner was Black or female the only determinant of helping was role: *subordinates* were helped more than supervisors, the confederate's role position comfortably confirming the societal stereotypes for Blacks and women.

To these studies of helping behaviour we can add several other pieces of evidence already presented elsewhere in the book. Earlier in this chapter I described some studies which closely examined non-verbal and paralinguistic behaviours in interethnic interactions. The findings there showed that Whites interacting with Blacks often revealed signs of tension and social distance. Langer et al. (1976) observed something similar with a physically disabled person as the confederate partner. In chapter 4 I reviewed a number of experiments which demonstrated spontaneous cognitive associations between ingroup category labels and positive trait words, and contrasting dissociations with negative stimuli. All in all, a consistent picture emerges of well-intentioned people, apparently endorsing tolerant and progressive attitudes towards minority groups but being unable to rid themselves entirely of unconscious aversive reactions to them, especially in situations where a deliberate adherence to non-discriminatory norms is not called for. With his usual prescience, Allport (1954, p. 311) encapsulated this in a memorable phrase, 'Defeated intellectually, prejudice lingers emotionally.'

The idea that emotions such as anxiety and uncertainty (rather than anger and hostility) often pervade intergroup encounters is buttressed by research which has investigated the antecedents and consequences of contact between members of different groups. Stephan and Stephan (1985) were among the first to draw attention to the role of anxiety in intergroup relations. They speculated that anxiety might be heightened by a lack of contact with (and hence knowledge of) an outgroup and that this, in turn, might lead to greater stereotyping because of the narrowing of attention typically associated with increased arousal. In a correlational study of Hispanic students they found some support for their model since amount of contact with Anglos was, indeed, negatively correlated with their stereotyping of Anglos. However, other studies have identified certain conditions under which contact actually increases anxiety. In two experiments Wilder and Shapiro (1989a, b) showed that a subject anticipating a competitive task with another group showed considerably more anxiety than those expecting to co-operate. This anxiety led to less-favourable intergroup ratings. Islam and Hewstone (1993) studied factors associated with contacts between Hindus and Muslims in Bangladesh. Hindus, the low-status minority group, expressed greater anxiety about their dealings with Muslims than vice versa. More importantly, however, for both groups this anxiety was negatively correlated with the amount and quality of contact (that is, interactions that were pleasant, equal status and co-operative – see chapter 8), but *positively* correlated with measures indexing the extent to which the contact took place on an intergroup level (that is, whether or not the outgroup members were seen as typical of their group). Thus, the more intergroup contact they reported the more anxious they felt. Like Wilder and Shapiro (1989a, b), Islam and Hewstone found that anxiety also was linked to more negative and stereotypical images of the outgroup. Finally, in a study conducted in the Netherlands, Dijker (1987) found that the prospect of meeting Surinamers, Turks, or Moroccans was associated by his Dutch respondents with feelings of anxiety, irritation, and concern.

Integrating modern and aversive prejudice

In this discussion of aversive prejudice I have concentrated on the situational factors likely to allow people to discriminate covertly between ingroup and outgroup members. This is the main direction taken by Gaertner and Dovidio (1986), the principal originators of the concept. Indeed, as noted earlier, they specifically eschew the use of questionnaire instruments designed to distinguish between those high and low in aversive racism. However, it is possible that their situational emphasis can be reconciled with the individual-difference approach favoured by proponents of the modern prejudice models. One hint that this might be so comes from some work by Monteith and her colleagues

(Devine et al., 1991; Monteith, 1993; Monteith et al., 1993). Drawing upon an idea first floated by Allport (1954), these researchers have suggested that what distinguishes high and low (modern) prejudiced people are their reactions to discrepancies between how they think they should and how they think they actually *would* behave. One of the techniques used in their studies is to present people with mini scenarios – for example, a Black or a gay person comes and sits next to them on a bus – and obtain ratings as to how they should and would react. The next step is to elicit their emotional reactions to discrepancies between these two ratings, the most important of which are feelings of guilt, embarrassment, and self-criticism. Monteith and her colleagues showed that what differentiates high and low prejudiced people (as measured by previously administered modern racism or homophobia scales) is their response to these would–should discrepancies: low and moderately prejudiced people feel much more self-blame, or 'compunction' as Allport (1954) called it, than high prejudiced people. As one of Monteith's (1993) subjects put it:

> *When I was younger . . . my brother, who I idolized, used 'fag' as an insulting comment. I picked it up but as I aged and slowly began to assimilate knowledge about homosexuality . . . I began to feel bad about myself. I felt that this was not how I wanted to respond toward minorities.*   (Monteith, 1993, p. 484)

In this conception people's feelings associated with *particular* situationally determined would–should discrepancies might correspond to aversive prejudice; their habitual levels of compunction across *several* such situations would be related more to modern prejudice.

   Further evidence that aversive and modern racism are related has been provided by Kleinpenning and Hagendoorn (1993). They developed questionnaire measures of old-fashioned (biological) racism, ethnocentrism (comprising cultural assimilation of minorities and mild own-nationality bias), symbolic racism, and aversive racism for use with Dutch school children. In addition they administered scales enquiring into their likely behavioural intentions towards minority group members (for example, dating them, avoiding people who tell racist jokes), their attitudes towards affirmative action, and their endorsement of some conventional ethnic stereotypes. Although they found that their various racism measures were all intercorrelated, more careful analysis revealed that they could be ordered in degree of severity. That is, biological racism encapsulated all the other forms of racism; next came symbolic racism which also incorporated ethnocentrism and aversive racism; and aversive racism was the mildest form of the four. Consistent with this rank order, Kleinpenning and Hagendoorn (1993) found that scores on the behavioural intention, affirmative action, and stereotype measures varied systematically across the four types of respondents with 'aversive' racists generally giving the least discriminatory responses and 'biological' racists the most. They conclude that prejudice can be regarded as a cumulative dimension, beginning with the discreet avoidance of ethnic minorities in private contexts (aversive prejudice), running through beliefs in the superiority of one's own group and that ethnic groups have more social and economic benefits than they deserve (modern prejudice), and ending up with the full-blown racist ideology decreeing the genetic inferiority of certain groups and demands for their repatriation or segregation (old-fashioned prejudice).

Summary

1. Surveys of ethnic and gender attitudes and stereotypes reveal a steady decline in prejudice over the past 30 years. However, less reactive unobtrusive behavioural measures indicate that some of this decline may be attributable to changing social desirability norms rather than to internalized non-prejudiced beliefs.
2. Theories of modern prejudice have been proposed to account for the new manifestations of prejudice. These place emphasis on prejudice taking on indirect symbolic forms, in place of the outright intergroup hostility and beliefs in outgroups' inferiority which comprise old-fashioned prejudice. The origins of this modern prejudice are thought to be negative affect coupled with perceived violations (by minority groups) of traditional individualistic values.
3. Other conceptualizations of new prejudice place more emphasis on situational factors which permit dominant group members to avoid close contact with outgroups. This aversive prejudice is thought to stem from intergroup anxiety rather than hostility. It is possible that these different forms of prejudice are related in a hierarchy of increasing severity.

Further Reading

Dovidio, J.F. and Gaertner, S.L. (eds) (1986) *Prejudice, Discrimination and Racism*, chs 1–4. Orlando, Fla: Academic Press.

Notes

1. Augustinos et al. (1994) also report that racism was related to the *speed* with which the stereotype endorsements were made: high racist subjects may have taken longer to associate positive attributes with the outgroup and less time to associate the negative attributes. This differential response time finding should be treated with some caution however. Apparently, about one-fifth of the observations in this analysis were discarded as being 'outliers' (Augustinos et al., 1994, pp. 135–6). Whilst the deletion of some very extreme scores is sometimes justifiable, especially if the sample is small, to lose as much as 20 per cent of the sample does cast some doubt on the robustness of the reported analysis.
2. Although, as the authors admit, it is a moot point whether the optimal solution was really two separate factors or two sub-factors of a single superordinate prejudice construct.
3. This measure is rather akin to fraternalistic relative deprivation since it assesses men's perception that affirmative action programmes put men at a disadvantage relative to women (see chapter 6). Note, however, that it is a measure of collective and not personal interests which may explain why it correlated with attitudes to affirmative action in our study (cf. Jacobson, 1985; Kluegel and Smith, 1983).

Reducing Prejudice

8   Science class

Co-operative equal status contact is an effective way of reducing prejudice.

I began this book with a tribute to Allport's (1954) *The Nature of Prejudice*. As I embark on this final chapter (in 1994), it is the fortieth anniversary of that milestone publication. It is therefore fitting that this chapter should be devoted almost exclusively to Allport's perhaps most enduring contribution to social psychology, the Contact Hypothesis. A recurring theme of Allport's writing, and a theme certainly echoed throughout this book, is the mundanity and pervasiveness of prejudice. Because of our limited cognitive capacities and because of important social motivations inherent in our membership of different groups, the propensity for prejudiced thinking and behaviour is never far away. However, does a recognition of the human potential for prejudice mean that we have to accept its inevitability? Allport himself, and the generations of social psychologists he inspired, believed passionately that it does not. He argued that there are powerful social interventions which will both reduce the intensity of prejudice and counter its worst effects.

I begin the chapter with a detailed examination of the social conditions which research has demonstrated are so important in ensuring that intergroup contact has the positive effects we intend for it. In a second section I focus specifically on contact in educational settings, exploring why some desegregation attempts have not lived up to their promise and what techniques have proved more successful. Finally, I address an enduring issue in work on the Contact Hypothesis: what factors promote – and which inhibit – the generalization of the attitudes generated by the contact experience to other members of the outgroup we have not yet met?

The Contact Hypothesis

One of the most long-lived and successful ideas in the history of social psychology has been the Contact Hypothesis. As might be discerned from its name, its central premise is that the best way to reduce tension and hostility between groups is to bring them into contact with each other in various ways. However, the term 'Contact Hypothesis' is actually somewhat of a misnomer because it implies that mere contact is a sufficient panacea in itself. As Allport (1954) was quick to realize, this is far from being the case. In his discussion of the effects of intergroup contact Allport cited some unpublished data on the relationship between residential proximity between Blacks and Whites in Chicago and anti-Black attitudes amongst White respondents. These data showed a clear correlation between proximity and anti-Black sentiment: the nearer the respondents lived to the Black community the more prejudiced they were. I dare say the same pattern could be replicated in many other cities around the world. In Britain, at least, it is surely no accident that some of the worst incidents of ethnic and religious violence in recent years have occurred in those cities where different groups live literally in the next street to one another: in Brixton, London; in Toxteth, Liverpool; or in the Falls and Shankhill Roads, Belfast.

To these somewhat anecdotal examples we can add the many studies already described elsewhere in this book which testify both to the ease with which intergroup bias can spring up when two groups meet and to the subsequent difficulty of reducing that bias (see chapters 3, 5 and 6). Especially notable are the summer camp studies of Sherif and his colleagues (Sherif, 1966; see chapter 6). Prior to their successful implementation of superordinate goals to reduce the conflict they had created by intergroup competition, the researchers had attempted to attenuate the friction between the groups by arranging for the boys to get together in what should have been enjoyable circumstances. A big feast was organized on one day; a firework display on another. However, these 'mere contacts' did little to ease the hostilities. Indeed, as Sherif (1966, p. 88) noted: 'far from reducing conflict, these situations served as occasions for the rival groups to berate and attack each other'.

So contact alone is not enough. Allport (1954) identified a number of conditions which he believed needed to be satisfied before we could expect it to have its desired effects of reducing prejudice. These have been added to and refined by subsequent commentators (Amir, 1969, 1976; Cook, 1962, 1978; Pettigrew, 1971). Let us examine the four most important of these conditions.

Social and institutional support

The first condition is that there should be a framework of social and institutional support for the measures which are designed to promote greater contact. By this is meant that those in authority, the school headteachers and their staff, the politicians implementing new legislation, and the judges monitoring its administration, should all be unambiguous in their endorsement of the goals of the integration policies. There are at least three reasons why this is important.

The first is that those in authority are usually in a position to administer sanctions (and rewards) for actions which hinder (or promote) the achievement of the desired objectives. Given that businesses, school boards and the like are often receptive to matters which affect their material interests, they can be expected at least to be seen to be following the agreed policies. This, in itself, can often be a useful first step in breaking the vicious cycles of social deprivation and prejudice which many minority groups experience: academic under-achievement and unemployment reinforcing the dominant group's negative stereotypes of them as 'stupid' and 'lazy'; stereotypes which are likely to justify yet further educational and occupational discrimination.

The second benefit, particularly of new anti-discrimination legislation, is that by forcing people to behave in a less-prejudiced manner it may eventually lead them to internalize those behaviours as their own attitudes. Festinger (1957) suggested that most people have a need to bring their beliefs into line with their behaviour to avoid experiencing dissonance. So it may be with prejudice. Being obliged to work alongside a minority-group co-worker, or to go to school with someone of a different religion, may eventually bring about a change of heart in the prejudiced person: 'we work/study together successfully, therefore they cannot be as bad as I thought'. In this regard I am always reminded of car seat-belt legislation which was introduced in Britain and elsewhere in the 1970s to an outcry of opposition from conservative libertarians. And yet, the experience of two decades of *being required* to use seat-belts has made it into such an automatic habit for us that it now feels wrong *not* to fasten a belt as soon as we get into a car.

The third and most important reason for providing institutional support for contact measures is that it helps to create a new social climate in which more tolerant norms can emerge. Thus, the significance of that momentous US Supreme Court decision in 1954, or of the British Race and Sex Discrimination Acts of 1965 and 1975, may not have been that they were in themselves effective in outlawing discrimination. Indeed, many state legislatures and employers did their damnedest to avoid having to implement them for years. But they did have a profound impact on public attitudes so that it became increasingly less acceptable to discriminate openly against minority groups or women openly, and even less so to derogate them in public (see chapter 7).

Research demonstrating the impact of institutional support for integration on the level of prejudice has not been very plentiful, in the main because of the insuperable methodological difficulties involved. When a new piece of legislation is introduced in a country where does one find a comparable control group against which to measure its effects? At a more microscopic level some studies do exist which at least point to the importance of institutional support in creating new norms, even if they do not show this conclusively. For example, two early studies of ethnically integrated housing schemes documented how, in the experimental projects where the integration was taking place, people commented on the social expectations favouring tolerance and intermixing. In contrast, in the segregated areas, Whites made such comments as 'it just isn't done' or 'people would think you're crazy' in response to questions about mixing with Blacks (Deutsch and Collins, 1951; Wilner et al., 1952). Consistent with these different norms, the Whites' intergroup attitudes were markedly more tolerant in the integrated housing projects.

Acquaintance potential

The second condition for successful contact is that it be of sufficient frequency, duration, and closeness to permit the development of meaningful relationships between members of the groups concerned. In Cook's words, it should have 'high acquaintance potential' (Cook, 1978, p. 97). This optimal condition can be contrasted with the infrequent, short and casual quality of some intergroup contact situations. These, it is supposed, will do little to foster more favourable attitudes and may even make them worse. Once again there is a threefold rationale for this condition although there is less agreement amongst contact researchers as to the relative importance of the three reasons.

One reason is that the development of fairly close interpersonal relationships is thought to be positively rewarding. Thus, the argument runs, the positive affect generated by these relationships will 'spill over' to encompass the outgroup as a whole (Cook, 1962). Running alongside this affective response is the acquisition of new and more accurate information about the outgroup. According to some theorists, this will lead to the discovery of many hitherto unknown similarities between the ingroup and the outgroup and hence, according to the similarity-attraction hypothesis (Byrne, 1971; see chapter 3 also), to greater liking for the outgroup (Pettigrew; 1971, Stephan and Stephan, 1984). As we shall see, this second claim is somewhat controversial. The third reason why contacts with high acquaintance potential are important is that they can lay the ground for the disconfirmation of some negative stereotypes of the outgroup. They may do this again by providing new information but it is not assumed that this information necessarily will lead to perceptions of greater intergroup similarity, only to the revision of stereotypical beliefs (Hewstone and Brown, 1986; see chapter 4).

The evidence testifying to the importance of high acquaintance potential is readily available in the literature. The early research on integrated housing projects pointed the way (Deutsch and Collins, 1950; Wilner et al., 1952). These studies found that the relative proximity between Black and White families was an important correlate of positive attitude change. Also, and of relevance here, greater proximity was usually associated with more frequent and more intimate contact between the ethnic groups. Stephan and Rosenfield (1978) confirmed this relationship between closeness of contact and changes in prejudice in a longitudinal study (over two years) of White American elementary school children's attitudes towards Mexican Americans. The biggest single predictor of positive attitude change was the increase in the frequency of interethnic contact (for example, how often they played at each other's houses). Stephan and Rosenfield were also able to demonstrate that it was the contact which caused the attitude change rather than vice versa. This was achieved by means of the cross-lagged correlation technique: contact at time 1 was positively correlated with attitudes at time 2; however, attitudes at time 1 were *not* related to contact at time 2. This asymmetrical pattern is suggestive of a causal relationship in which contact determines attitude. Interestingly, and in line with the 'institutional support' condition discussed earlier, parental opposition to integration was also correlated (negatively) with prejudice reduction, although in the overall regression analysis this effect dwindled to statistical insignificance. Stephan and Stephan (1984) provided further evidence for the information–giving role played by contact. They surveyed Anglo and Chicano high school students' opinions on a number of issues. As well as the usual intergroup attitude measures which overall showed an ethnocentric pattern of bias for both groups, they included measures of frequency and closeness of contact and some items tapping each group's knowledge of the other's cultural values and customs. Correlational path analysis revealed that contact was positively associated with knowledge, and that each was positively associated with more favourable intergroup attitudes (see also Pettigrew, 1994, for further evidence on acquaintanceship from a European survey).

Nevertheless, despite these findings, we should be a little cautious in ascribing too much weight to the role of direct acquaintance in the contact–prejudice-reduction process (Hewstone and Brown, 1986). Some of the reasons for this caution will become apparent later, but for now the findings of Hamilton and Bishop's (1976) longitudinal study of residential integration should give us pause for thought. Hamilton and Bishop interviewed around 200 White residents, some of whom had recently acquired new Black neighbours, the remainder new White neighbours. After one year the former had significantly lower modern racism scores than the latter even though both groups had started out with similar scores (see figure 8.1). This might seem to support a simple acquaintance–prejudice-reduction model were it not for some additional information that Hamilton and Bishop had the foresight to collect. This concerned whether or not the residents ever interacted with their neighbours, whether they knew their names, and a number of other 'acquaintanceship' measures. The interaction measure turned out to be related to modern racism, but in a surprising way. It only had an effect within the first three months of the new residents moving in and the effect was as strong, if not stronger, for those with new White neighbours as it was for those with new Black neighbours: those who interacted had lower racism scores than those who did not (see figure 8.1). At the end of a year this variable had ceased to have an effect and, as Hamilton and Bishop point out, it could in any case hardly explain the final Black–White neighbour difference in racism. The reason for this is that there was rather *less* knowledge of the Black neighbours than of the White. For example, after a month only 11 per cent of the residents knew the last name of their Black neighbours. Hamilton and Bishop suggest that what caused the reductions in racism may have been the disconfirmation of stereotypical expectation provided by the Black neighbours rather than changes mediated by getting to know them. Prior to the arrival of the new neighbours the White residents may have feared that their neighbourhoods would become dirtier and more violent places to live in. The year-long experience when this manifestly did not happen was probably a more potent cause of their attitude change than the minimal amount and rather casual nature of their social interactions with their Black neighbours.

Equal status

The third condition necessary for contact to be successful is that it should take place as far as possible between equal-status participants. The reason for this is simple. Many prejudiced stereotypes of outgroups comprise beliefs about their inferior ability to perform various tasks. If, then, the contact situation involves an unequal-status relationship between the ingroup and outgroup members, with the outgroup person in the subordinate role, the existing stereotypes are likely to be

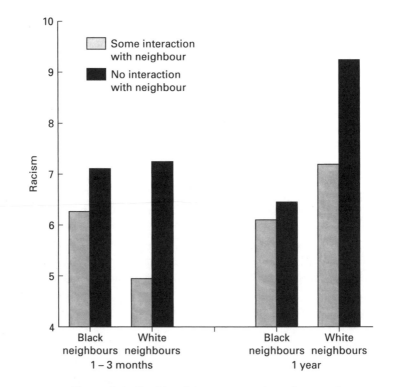

Figure 8.1 Residential contact and modern racism
Note: At 1–3 months the effect of interaction is significant; at year 1 it is not. At 1–3 months there is no effect for ethnicity of neighbour; at 1 year this effect is highly significant.
Source: Hamilton and Bishop (1976), table 4

reinforced rather than weakened. That is one of the reasons why prejudice against Blacks in the Southern States of the US proved so resistant to change. Many Whites had a great deal of contact with Blacks, but always with the latter in subservient positions – as nanny, cook, doorman, and so on. If, on the other hand, it can be arranged that the groups meet on an equal footing – as a peer in the class-room or a co-worker in the factory – then the prejudiced beliefs become hard to sustain in the face of the daily experience of the outgroup people's obvious task competence.

There is a wealth of evidence showing the advantages of equal-status contact for reducing prejudice (Amir, 1976). For example, when Blacks and Whites work together relationships between them are often harmonious (Harding and Hogrefe, 1952; Minard, 1952). Both of these studies are interesting because, although they were conducted in very different settings (a city department store and a coal mine in West Virginia), they both revealed how context-specific contact-induced changes can be. The positive attitudes engendered at work did not seem to generalize beyond the factory gate. One of the miners interviewed by Minard gave a nice illustration of this:

> 'Do you see that bus there? [pointing to the miners' bus which took them to and from the pit]. *The men ride in that bus all mixed up together and pay no attention. A white man sits with a Negro or anyway just however it comes handy. Nobody cares or pays any attention. But the white man will get right off that bus and on the interstate bus and he will not sit near a Negro.'* (Minard, 1952, p. 31)

As we shall see, this issue of generalization is absolutely central to any discussion of the effects of intergroup contact and I shall return to it at some length in a later section.

Experimental evidence has also confirmed the value of equal-status contact. In chapter 6 I described a study of mine which showed that school children anticipating a co-operative encounter with another equal-status school showed less bias and slightly more liking than those expecting to meet a better or worse school (Brown, 1984a). In a series of summer camps, reminiscent of those of Sherif (1966), Clore et al. (1978) found that 8-12-year-old children, split into small ethnically balanced groups for the duration of the camp, showed improved intergroup attitudes on several indices. For instance, choice of partners in various games showed significant ingroup (that is, same ethnicity) preferences at the start of four out of the five camps, but by the end of the camps these preferences were much more evenly balanced between ethnic groups, showing a significant bias in only one camp.

Perhaps the definitive study demonstrating the effect of equal-status contact is that by Blanchard et al. (1975). They arranged for some White American airmen to play a management training game with two confederates, one White, one Black. The perceived competence of these confederates was varied so that they appeared to be similar to, worse than, or better than the subjects. At the conclusion of the game it was announced that the team of three had either done well or badly (better or worse than the average of other teams). The White subjects' attraction for the Black confederate was affected both by his perceived competence and by the team's alleged success (see figure 8.2). When he was seen to be the same or better than the subject he was liked more than when he was thought to be relatively incompetent; and members of successful teams liked their Black team-mates more than members of the unsuccessful teams.[1]

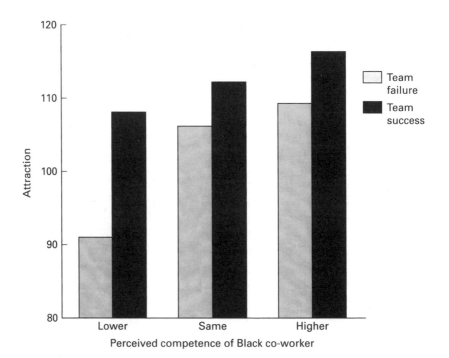

Figure 8.2 The effects of relative status and team success on liking for a Black co-worker
Source: Blanchard et al. (1975), table 1

Co-operation

These studies on equal-status contact all included another element, co-operation, which is the fourth condition which Allport had identified as being necessary for successful prejudice reduction. The rationale for this follows directly from realistic group conflict theory (see chapter 6). In so far as members of different groups are dependent on each other for the achievement of some jointly desired objective, they have instrumental reasons to develop friendlier relationships with each other. This common goal is usually something concrete and small-scale, achievable by a joint task performance. We shall consider several examples of these presently. But superordinate goals can also arise out of larger-scale threats which are experienced by the groups concerned. This was the case in central India in October 1993 which was devastated by a huge earthquake in which 30,000 people were estimated to have died. Faced with a disaster of this scale, the sectarian hatred between Hindus and Muslims was submerged in the common rescue effort. As one youth said, 'It doesn't matter to me whether this house belongs to a Hindu or a Muslim. Whoever it is, they need our help' (*Independent*, 3 October 1993).

Research has unambiguously supported this co-operation condition. From Sherif (1966) onwards, field and laboratory studies alike have demonstrated that intergroup co-operation leads to more friendliness and less ingroup bias than competition (see Brown, 1988). The only qualification we need to note at this stage is that the outcome of the co-operative endeavour needs to be successful to maximize the positive attitude change. As we saw above in that study of Blanchard et al. (1975), the Black colleague was always liked better if the team did well rather than badly, whatever his individual competence. Indeed, Worchel et al. (1977) showed that members of *ad hoc* experimental groups actually liked outgroup members with whom they had been co-operating somewhat less after failure if that failure had been preceded by a history of competition between the groups. What may happen in these cases is that we find it convenient to blame the outgroup member(s) for our collective shortcomings.

By way of summarizing these four additional components of the optimal contact situation let me conclude this section with two studies – one in the laboratory, one in the field – both of which tried to incorporate them into their designs. The first was by Cook (1978) and involved a prolonged series of co-operative activities between some fairly prejudiced White subjects and Black confederates. The activities themselves lasted 20 days and there were unobtrusive follow-up tests several months later. Consistent with the Contact Hypothesis, it was arranged that the task roles assigned to the Black and White participants were of equal status. There were repeated opportunities for them to get to know each other, not only during the co-operative tasks but also in the lunch breaks during which the Black confederates made specific efforts to interact with the real subjects. Social norms favouring egalitarianism and ethnic tolerance were promoted by the use of ethnically mixed supervisory staff and the use of a White confederate expressing pro-integration views. The Whites' attitudes and behaviour towards the Black confederates became uniformly more positive over the duration of the experiment. Some of this positive change was reflected in the post-test measures of their ethnic attitudes. Compared to control subjects who had not participated in the contact intervention, they did show significant decreases in their prejudice scores although these were not consistent on all measures. In subsequent studies Cook (1978) was to confirm this imperfect relationships between attitude change towards the particular people with whom one has had contact and attitudes towards the groups as a whole. I shall return to it again on pp. 259–68.

The second study was conducted in Bangladesh and was a survey of Hindu and Muslim students' attitudes towards one another (Islam and Hewstone, 1993). Included in the questionnaire were questions about the amount of contact with the outgroup (for example, frequency of interaction, number of friends), the quality of contact (for example, equal status or not, superficial or intimate, competitive or co-operative), whether the contact took place on an interpersonal or an intergroup level (for example, perceived typicality of outgroup persons), and the anxiety they felt in interacting with outgroup members. These variables were used to try to predict the overall positivity of their attitude towards the outgroup and how homogeneous (or stereotypical) they perceived it to be. Some of the correlations Islam and Hewstone obtained are presented in figure 8.3 in the form of a path diagram. Notice that both the quantity and quality of contact were directly related to a more positive attitude towards the outgroup. These correlations strongly supported the Contact Hypothesis. They were also negatively related to anxiety, which in turn was negatively correlated with positive inter-group attitudes (as we already noted in chapter 7).[2] Finally, the more intergroup the contact was felt to be the more anxious the respondents felt. This, too, I shall return to later.

Contact in Schools

One November day in 1987 in Enniskillen in the North of Ireland a bomb went off killing 11 people attending an Armistice Day ceremony. Sadly, this event was all too typical an example of the sectarian hatred which has for so long divided that part of the island of Ireland. Much less typical of the same region was another event in Enniskillen some two years later. This was the opening of an integrated primary school for the children of all religions (*Observer*, 5 November 1989). This school is one of a tiny handful of integrated schools in Northern Ireland. Elsewhere in the province the segregation of schools by religion is as complete as it was in the Southern United States prior to that famous 1954 Supreme Court decision which ruled that such segregation was unconstitutional. According to one report, there are just 21 integrated schools in Northern Ireland out of a total of over 1200 (Smith, 1994). What motivated the people of Enniskillen to set up the

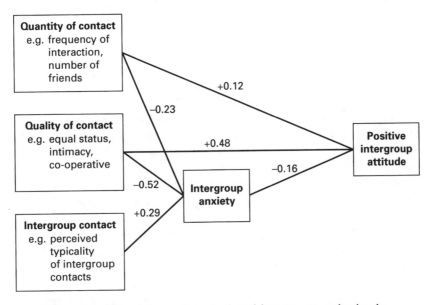

Figure 8.3 Dimensions of contact and intergroup attitudes in Bangladesh

Note: The diagram shows path coefficients (roughly equivalent to correlations) derived from a multiple regression analysis.

Source: Islam and Hewstone (1993), adapted from figure 1

school? According to one of the parents, it was explicitly with the aim of reducing the religious prejudice which pervades every corner of Northern Irish society:

> *We know that an integrated primary school is not a panacea for our problems, but we hope that what we're doing is laying the foundations for a long, slow process.* (John Maxwell, quoted in the *Observer*, 5 November 1989)

How justified is that hope that sending children of different religions (or classes or ethnicity) to the same school will result in more tolerant intergroup attitudes?

The outcomes of school desegregation

Unfortunately, there is precious little evidence from Ireland itself, mainly because of the extreme scarcity of desegregated schools, to provide the basis for a proper evaluation (McWhirter, 1983). However, the past 40 years in the United States have seen an enormous research effort directed at assessing the effects of school desegregation on levels of prejudice and cross-ethnic friendship choices. Reviews of this work have reached rather equivocal conclusions as to whether desegregation has led to a reduction in prejudice. Stephan (1978), for example, was able to locate 18 studies of the effect of desegregation on prejudice. Although many of these were plagued with methodological difficulties, Stephan concluded that about half of them showed that desegregation actually *increased* Whites' prejudice towards Blacks, and only a minority (13 per cent) showed the expected decrease in prejudice. Looking at the effects on Blacks' prejudice towards Whites produced a slightly more encouraging but equally ambiguous picture: about half showed a decrease in prejudice and slightly less than a half showed an increase. A decade or so later, Schofield (1991) reached a similar conclusion that the effects of desegregation on intergroup attitudes were often not demonstrable, and were certainly not always beneficial.

In a moment I shall consider why this might be so and why, too, it should not cause us to feel unduly pessimistic about 40 years of desegregation policies. Before I do so, let me present the findings from two studies which illustrate these conclusions that I have just summarized. The first is by Gerard and Miller (1975). This was a massive longitudinal study (spanning five years) of the effects of desegregating elementary schools in Riverside, California. Much of their research focused on school achievement outcomes and hence is not of immediate concern here. However, they were able to obtain socio-metric data from over 6000 children both before the desegregation programme took effect and then again after. Two indices are of particular interest. One is the proportion of children receiving few (zero to two) friendship choice nominations in any classroom. This gives an indication of how stratified the class is, because in a perfectly destratified classroom there should be an approximately equal distribution of friendship choices – that is, there should be few very popular or unpopular children. When Gerard and Miller examined the percentage of 'unpopular' children before and after desegregation they found that this actually *increased* in the desegregated schools for Mexican-American children. A second index was the number of friendship choices received by minority-group children overall, and specifically from Anglo children, the dominant White group. The latter is a straightforward measure of cross-ethnic friendship. The overall measure showed that Black and Mexican-American children generally lost popularity after desegregation, while the Anglo children's popularity remained un-changed. When just the choices received from Anglo children were considered it was clear that there was little increase in cross-ethnic friendship over the first few years of desegregation. One year post-desegregation the minority-group children received an average of just over one friendship nomination from Anglo children. Three years later this figure was virtually unchanged. Thus, despite the increased contact brought about by integrating the schools in Riverside, there was little immediate measurable effect on cross-ethnic friendships.

A second study, by way of contrast, was conducted in a single school in a city in the north-east of the United States (Schofield, 1979, 1982; Schofield and Sagar, 1977). This school was unusual in that it was created with an explicitly integrationist ideology in mind. Indeed, many of the policies with which it opened (in 1975) were designed with specific reference to Allport's (1954) conditions for successful intergroup contact. For example, a numerical balance between Blacks and Whites was achieved; teachers of different ethnicities were employed; the school authorities and teachers were publicly associated with desegregationalist ideals; attempts were made (not always successfully) to minimize competition in the school; and so on. In this way, the school hoped to avoid some of the problems that had been associated with other desegregation policies – for example, compulsory busing, and so on – which almost certainly were implicated in the Riverside schools studied by Gerard and Miller (1975). Nevertheless, despite the favourable conditions in which this school opened, Schofield's careful observations of the children's behaviour revealed considerable evidence of ethnic segregation in their informal interactions. One measure of this was derived from noting seating patterns in the dining hall. Borrowing a seating aggregation index from Campbell et al. (1966), Schofield and Sagar (1977) showed that Black and White children generally preferred to sit next to (or opposite) a peer of the same ethnicity as them than to someone of different ethnicity.

However, despite this ethnic cleavage there were some positive indications in these seating aggregation data. One came from a comparison between grade 7 children who were taught in hetero-geneous mixed ability classes and grade 8 children who, despite the school's otherwise egalitarian philosophy, were 'streamed' by ability, resulting in disproportionate numbers of Whites in the 'accelerated' track and higher numbers of Blacks in the 'regular' track. Over the four month observation period Schofield and Sagar (1977) observed a significant increase in cross–ethnic seating patterns in grade 7, but no increase at all and, if anything, a *decrease*, in cross-ethnic interaction in grade 8. This provides a good illustration of the importance of maintaining equal-status contact for improving intergroup relations. The second encouraging finding from this research concerned the persist-ence of changes brought about by the school's integrationist policies. Schofield (1979) compared the seating aggregation indices of two cohorts of grade 8 children, separated by one year. The significance for this comparison was that the later cohort (1976–7) had had two years' experience of the integrated school compared with only one year for the 1975–6 cohort. Recall also that in grade 8 the children tended to become ethnically more segregated, perhaps because of the academic streaming that began there. However, despite these adverse conditions, the 1976–7 cohort showed significantly less ethnic aggregation than the 1975–6 cohort, giving some hope that prolonged exposure to favour-able intergroup contact conditions can generate lasting changes in behaviour (see figure 8.4).

At first glance the findings of these studies make rather pessimistic reading for those of us who have always supported the idea of integrated schools. However, there are a number of reasons why they should not cause us to abandon the principle of desegregated education. First and foremost we need to recognize that what happens in schools, even if it is arranged for optimal effect, is only a part of children's experience of intergroup relationships. Thus, however well designed the curriculum and its accompanying pedagogic activity, if children from different groups return daily to a world outside the school gates which is still

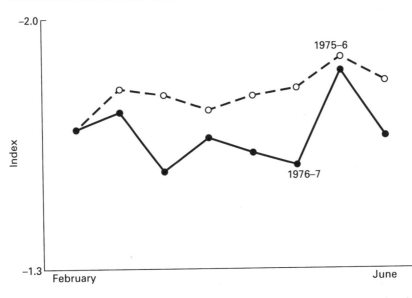

Figure 8.4 Ethnic aggregation in two cohorts of an integrated school
Note: Larger negative values indicate greater ingroup clustering.
Source: Schofield (1979), figure 1

largely segregated and dominated by prejudiced values it would be surprising indeed to find much general change in their intergroup attitudes. Recall those studies I discussed earlier which showed how changed attitudes at the work place did not always survive the transition to other social contexts (Harding and Hogrefe, 1952; Minard, 1952).

Secondly, there are a variety of methodological reasons why studies attempting to evaluate the effects of desegregation may often record little or no change in children's attitudes. Some of these reasons are of a rather technical nature and have to do with the difficulties of measuring attitude change in this domain (see Schofield, 1991, for a more detailed discussion). One other obvious difficulty with some evaluation studies is that they are aiming to detect changes over quite a short time period, perhaps too short for the intended consequences of desegregation to take effect.[3] It would be quite unrealistic to expect a few months' or even a year's experience of integrated schooling to rectify several years of segregation and (perhaps) mutual suspicion. There is also the possibility that some integration programmes may actually militate against producing generalized changes in intergroup attitudes by concentrating too hard on trying to ignore category differences in their activities and teaching materials. As I shall argue in a later section, there is a risk that such programmes will generate positive changes in social relations that are confined only to those outgroup members with whom one has had immediate contact.

A third reason for not becoming too depressed at the apparent outcome of school desegregation policies is the realization that few are actually being implemented in anything approaching the 'ideal' conditions which we identified in the first section. Many school districts in the US only abandoned segregation unwillingly and under the threat of legal sanction. Thus, there was little of the 'institutional support' which Allport (1954) had proposed as being so important for intergroup contact to have its desired effects. Furthermore, the furore created by all the legal controversies surrounding school busing, often an inherent component of desegregation programmes, is hardly the ideal atmosphere in which to introduce a new social policy. Ironically enough, however, it may be that an initial period of controversy need not be all that harmful to long-term intergroup relations. Crain and Mahard (1982) investigated the interethnic attitudes amongst Black students in over 100 school districts in southern states in America. All these school districts had resisted in varying degrees the introduction of desegregation in the 1960s. Crain and Mahard attempted to assess the degree of conflict associated with desegregation by tapping the recollection of community leaders in each school district. Somewhat surprisingly, there was a *positive* correlation between their recall of the degree of conflict over the previous decade and the students' interethnic attitudes: the more conflict there had been, the more positive were the Black students' subsequent attitudes towards Whites. As Coser (1956) and Deutsch (1973) have argued, it may be that some forms of intergroup conflict, provided they can be resolved constructively, are not necessarily detrimental to subsequent intergroup relations.

Other features of the ways in which schools have gone about the business of integration have also often fallen far short of the optimal contact conditions. Typical classroom activities in many schools involve little co-operation between students. Indeed, the reverse may often be the case as students compete with each other for prizes or, more routinely, teachers' attention or approval (Aronson et al., 1978). Furthermore, children from different groups may not interact on an equal-status footing. Some ethnic groups experience social and economic hardships which will put their members at a potential disadvantage in the classroom relative to members of dominant or privileged groups, unless curricula are carefully designed to avoid this. To compound these problems of unequal socio-economic status, teachers themselves may favour streaming even within integrated schools, especially if they themselves are not very supportive of integration in the first place (Epstein, 1985). Such streaming will inevitably be correlated with ethnicity, further reinforcing the existing status inequalities between the groups.

In short, much school desegregation has been introduced in less than ideal circumstances and has seldom incorporated the features necessary for successful intergroup contact. Let us now compare this piecemeal approach to integration with those interventions which have set out to maximize the chances of success by deliberately structuring student activities in ways suggested by the Contact Hypothesis. The most common method of achieving this has been through the use of co-operative learning groups mixed by sex, ethnicity, or other relevant categories.

Co-operative learning groups

There are a number of different ways co-operative learning groups can be used in schools (Aronson et al., 1978; Johnson, 1975, Slavin, 1983). However, from the point of view of the Contact Hypothesis, all these techniques share four essential characteristics. Most crucially of all they organize the learning experience of students so that they are co-operatively interdependent on one another in a small group. This can be achieved by devising learning tasks which are structured in ways that involve a division of labour among the students so that each needs the other for the successful achievement of the group task. Thus, in a project on some particular historical event each student might be given a different facet to research – one, say, to locate some demographic information, another some economic data, another the political situation at the time, and so on. The aim is that they should pool the results of each others' work to form the group report. Alternatively, the interdependence can be created simply by allocating rewards to the group as a whole according to its overall performance. Either way, the key feature is that the students are dependent on each other for the achievement of their goals. A second aspect of co-operative learning activities is that they frequently necessitate a high degree of student–student interaction in contrast to the student–teacher interaction pattern typical in most whole-class teaching methods. This greater amount of social interaction amongst students of different backgrounds is, of course, likely to generate the 'acquaintance potential' thought so important for successful contact. Thirdly, some co-operative learning techniques attempt to achieve equal status amongst the group members. This is achieved either by role differentiation or by emphasizing the importance of each member's contribution to the overall group product (or score on an achievement test). Finally, because co-operative learning is introduced and managed by the teacher it is implicitly receiving institutional support in the eyes of the students. Thus, all the key conditions of the Contact Hypothesis are satisfied.

So much for what co-operative learning techniques have in common. There are also some important differences between the various strategies which have been tried in integration settings. One concerns the presence or absence of competition *between* the co-operative learning groups. Some interventions have explicitly included such an intergroup competitive element with the rationale that such competition will be likely to foster greater cohesiveness and liking *within* the heterogeneous learning groups (DeVries et al., 1978; Slavin, 1983). On the other hand, others have deliberately eschewed all competition on the grounds that with competition there are inevitably losers and that, by and large, failure experiences lead to lower cohesion (Johnson and Johnson, 1975). Another issue has been the importance of co-operative *task* structures as compared to co-operative *reward* structures (Miller and Davidson-Podgorny, 1987). It is possible to have students work together but be rewarded individually, work individually but be jointly rewarded or, as is more usual, to combine the task and reward structures. Finally, techniques vary in the extent to which the teacher assigns the students to particular roles within the group. Some theorists have argued that this is important to ensure roughly equal participation of all students in the learning activity and to counter prior expectations regarding the competence of minority or disadvantaged group members (Aronson et al., 1978; Cohen, 1982). Other models place much less emphasis on task specialization, assuming that it is the nature of the overall reward structure which is the controlling variable (Slavin, 1983).

There is by now a sizeable body of evidence which demonstrates unambiguously the effectiveness of co-operative learning groups for increasing attraction between members of different social categories. Slavin (1983) located 14 studies, all of them conducted in ethnically mixed classroom settings in the United States, which had compared the effects of a co-operative learning programme with 'normal' classroom teaching methods on cross-ethnic friendship. Eleven of these demonstrated a statistically significant advantage to the co-operative group interventions, the remaining three showed no difference. A few years later Miller and Davidson-Podgorny (1987) were able to find a further 11 studies and conducted a meta-analysis on the accumulated data set. The overall effect was highly significant and showed that co-operative learning groups produced reliably higher levels of interethnic attraction than comparable 'control' groups. Using the statistical precision afforded by meta-analysis, Miller and Davidson-Podgorny also found that it was task rather than reward interdependence which had the most effect on liking, and also that assigning specific task roles and ensuring a roughly equal distribution of different ethnicities within the groups both had beneficial effects. A third review, also using meta-analysis, confirmed the overall superiority of co-operative over competitive or individualistic learning methods in promoting cross-ethnic friendship (Johnson et al., 1984). They also showed that exactly the same effects are observed when it is students with learning difficulties that are the group being integrated. Finally, by adding in a large number of laboratory studies Johnson et al. also found that when co-operative learning groups with and without *intergroup* competition are compared, the results showed an advantage of *not* including competition. To give some flavour of the kind of research that has been included in these reviews let me now present the results of three individual studies evaluating the effects of co-operative learning. One was conducted in the area of ethnic relations, the other two were concerned with attitudes toward students with disabilities. The integration of the latter group into mainstream schools is an increasingly common feature of educational policies in many countries.

Slavin (1979) evaluated the effect of introducing a ten-week co-operative learning programme into the English curriculum of two desegregated junior high schools in an American city. Half the class worked together in small ethnically mixed groups on such topics as grammar and punctuation. They were tested regularly and the scores of the team members were pooled to form a team score; the team scores were then announced to the class. The remaining 'control' classes were taught in conventional ways and their test results were returned to them individually. It is important to note that the intervention only took place in the English classes; the remainder of the school curriculum continued as normal. The key outcome measure was simply the proportion of cross-ethnic friends that each student nominated in answer to the question, 'Who are your friends in this class?' Figure 8.5 presents Slavin's (1979) results. Notice that at the start of the intervention both the control and experimental proportions of cross-ethnic friendship choices were about equal. By the end of the intervention this figure had risen slightly in the experimental classes but actually *fallen* in the control classes. Slavin (1979) was able to conduct a follow-up study some nine months later. Although unfortunately there was substantial attrition of data, an endemic problem in such longit-udinal studies, these long-term results were quite remarkable. In the experimental students the level of cross-ethnic friendship remained stable at just under 40 per cent. In the control students, however, it fell still further to under 10 per cent.

Armstrong et al. (1981) showed that the effects of co-operative learning can be extended to change attitudes towards students with disabilities. In an American elementary school some children were randomly selected to participate in a four-week programme involving working in a co-operative learning group with a learning-disabled peer. The children had to work together on group assignments and were praised, as a group, by the teacher for their completion. The remaining children worked on their own and were praised individually for their work. In the co-operative groups there was evidence of a more favourable attitude from the mainstream children towards their disabled peers. On one key attitude dimension ('smart–dumb') the disabled

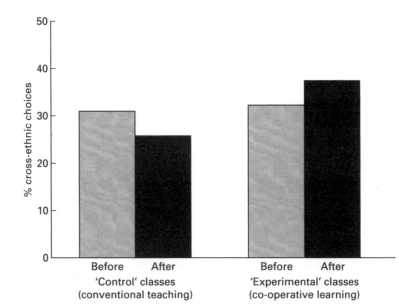

Figure 8.5 The effects of co-operative learning groups on cross-ethnic friendships
Source: Slavin (1979), taken from table 1

children were rated more positively by those with whom they had co-operated than they were by the 'control' children. Interestingly, there was also evidence that both the mainstream and learning-disabled children worked harder in the co-operative groups, as measured by the number of assignments completed (see also Johnson and Johnson, 1981, and Johnson et al., 1979).

Quite recently we were able to confirm these findings in a study involving a school for children with very severe learning disabilities (Maras and Brown, 1994). These were children who, by reason of genetic, congenital, or other accident, had a wide range of physical and cognitive impairments. Some had little or no physical mobility; others had only very limited language skills; most demonstrated some behavioural disturbance. In a pioneering experiment this school was linked to a nearby mainstream primary school in an exchange programme. Each year a number of mainstream children are randomly selected to spend some part of each week working in pairs with the disabled children on some carefully planned co-operative activities. These take place in both schools. We were fortunate enough to be able to administer a series of attitude measures over the first three months of this exchange programme, both to those who participated in the exchanges and to those who did not. Our findings showed clearly the benefits of the programme. On a number of rating dimensions the 'exchange' children showed a progressive decline in how differently they assessed the abilities of disabled and non-disabled children; the 'control' children's perceptions of these groups changed very little over the same period. When we presented some standardized photographs of children with different disabilities – these were children not known to the participants – the exchange students rated them as increasingly more attractive play partners; the 'control' children's rating tended to decline (see figure 8.6). These play preferences were for unknown children and hence showed that the programme was having some generalized effects on the mainstream children's attitudes and was not restricted merely to those disabled children with whom they were interacting.

In sum, therefore, there is ample evidence showing that when school integration takes place in a manner consistent with the tenets of the Contact Hypothesis, particularly if it involves a change in teaching methods to incorporate co-operative learning groups, then improvements in intergroup relationships are very likely to occur. An added bonus of employing more co-operation in the classroom is that academic achievement, of both advantaged and disadvantaged students, will also increase (Johnson et al., 1981; Slavin, 1983). To this optimistic

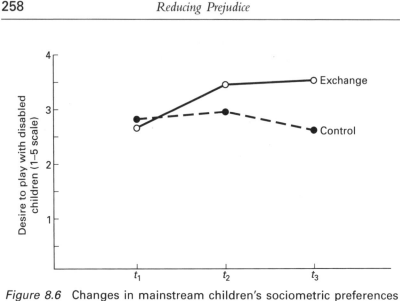

Figure 8.6 Changes in mainstream children's sociometric preferences
in a co-operative exchange programme with children with severe
disabilities
Source: Maras and Brown (1994), table 7

conclusion I would add just one cautionary note. The vast majority of
evaluation studies reporting positive effects of co-operative learning
experiences have measured these effects by observing students' socio-
metric preferences for *known* peers. Those few studies which have
attempted to assess more generalized attitude change have generally
reported null results (for example, DeVries et al., 1979; Weigel et al.,
1975).

There are several factors which could explain this. Interventions
involving co-operative learning programmes often last only a few weeks
and this may simply be too short a time to expect any change in
entrenched attitudes. The interventions also usually form a part,
frequently only a minor part, of the students' school experience.
Typically, they are introduced in just a single academic subject or for just
a few hours each week. Thus, the majority of the students' time is spent
in conventional classroom settings which, as I noted earlier, may be
antithetical to the goals of desegregation. In addition to these two
constraints, a third limiting factor is the extent to which the contact
experience permitted or inhibited the cognitive generalization of the
positive attitudes generated towards the members of the particular co-
operative learning group. This issue has preoccupied researchers into

intergroup contact over the past two decades and it is considered in some detail in the next section.

The Contact Hypothesis Revisited: the Generalization of Attitude Change

INTERVIEWER: Do white kids act differently to blacks now than when they first came?

STACY (black): Yes, they didn't want to be around blacks. I guess they was prejudiced or something, too cute for the blacks. But now they are nice, you know. They are friends with mostly everybody.

INTERVIEWER: Has being in a school like Wexler changed white kids' *ideas* about what blacks are like?

MARTIN (white): It's still the same old stereotype. Parents tell you what to believe, and then you probably believe it . . .

(Schofield, 1982, p. 161)

These comments were recorded in a newly integrated city high school in the United States and they capture quite well the question I want to address in this final section. As we saw in the previous two sections, there is little doubt that, provided the contact between members of different groups fulfils certain criteria, relationships between those group members who actually interact with one another will become friendlier and more tolerant. The teachers and administrators at Wexler High School had gone to some lengths to organize the integration of Black and White students as well as possible and the results, as Stacy (and many others) observed, seemed to have repaid their efforts. On the other hand, Martin's remark - again, apparently not untypical – warns us that despite the increased frequency of interethnic friendships in desegregated schools, more general stereotypes may not change that much. Cook (1978), a pioneer in the promotion of contact theory and research, had earlier identified the problem as follows:

attitude change will result from co-operative interracial contact only when such contact is accompanied by a supplementary influence that promotes the process of generalization from favourable contact with individuals to positive attitudes toward the group from which the individual comes. (Cook, 1978, p. 103; my emphasis)

Three models of intergroup contact

Since Cook wrote that, there have been three new developments of the Contact Hypothesis, all of which address more or less explicitly the issue of generalization (Brewer and Miller, 1984; Gaertner et al., 1993; Hewstone and Brown, 1986). Each of these three approaches has its origins in Social Identity Theory since they all recognize that group memberships get incorporated into people's self-concepts and that these social identifications have important consequences for behaviour (see chapter 6). However, despite this common theoretical base, the three models make different and occasionally conflicting predictions concerning the optimal conditions for facilitating the generalization of the positive effects of contact beyond the contact setting itself.

Brewer and Miller (1984) take as their starting point the phenomena of enhanced intergroup discrimination and stereotyping that are frequently attendant on social categories becoming psychologically salient (see chapters 3, 4 and 6). It follows from this, they argue, that during the contact the boundaries between the groups should be made less rigid, ultimately to be dissolved altogether. In this way the situation should become 'decategorized' and all interactions should take place on an interpersonal level. In this 'personalized' form of contact the participants should be more likely to attend to idiosyncratic information about each individual and be correspondingly less attentive to group-based – that is, stereotypical – information. Repeated interpersonal contact of this kind is thought to result in the disconfirmation of pre-existing (negative) stereotypes of the outgroup which ultimately is

> more likely to generalize to new situations because extended and frequent utilization of alternative informational features in interactions undermines the availability and usefulness of category identity as a basis for future interactions with the same or different individuals. Thus permanent changes occur in both the cognitive and motivational aspects of social interaction with outgroup members.
>
> (Brewer and Miller, 1984, pp. 288–9).

In support of this model Brewer and Miller have carried out a number of studies using a similar paradigm (Bettencourt et al., 1992; Miller et al., 1985). Typically two artificial categories are created (for example, 'overestimators' and 'underestimators'). Then members of these two categories are brought together into co-operative work groups so that both overestimators and underestimators are represented in each group. The subjects are given different instructional sets for the group tasks:

some are encouraged to focus on each other to find out what the 'fellow team members must really be like' (Bettencourt et al., 1992, pp. 305–6); others are told to concentrate particularly on the task at hand. In this way it is hoped to 'personalize' or 'depersonalize' the contact situation respectively. After the task the subjects allocate rewards to the members of their team and also to members of another team unknown to them, portrayed on a short video clip. The key dependent measure in these experiments is the degree of bias in these allocations between over- and underestimators, both for the known team members and the 'strangers' shown on video. A consistent finding has been that those undertaking the task with the 'personalization' instructions show less bias than those who are concentrating much more on the task.

Starting from the same premises as Brewer and Miller (1984), Gaertner et al. (1993) reach a different conclusion. They too are mindful of the biases which seem to be so readily generated by the presence of category divisions. But their solution to this problem is not to try to eliminate the categories; instead they suggest that cognitively or physically redrawing the category boundaries will be a more productive strategy. The aim of this is to subsume the previous ingroup and outgroup into a new superordinate category so that the former outgroupers can be perceived as fellow ingroupers. Thus, rather than attempting to eschew group references altogether, Gaertner et al. hope to harness the power of a common ingroup identity to reduce pre-existing intergroup differentiation. Where Brewer and Miller propose *decategorization*, they advocate *recategorization*.

To test this model Gaertner and his colleagues have conducted a number of experiments in which they have first created two artificial groups and then, by varying the seating arrangements in a subsequent intergroup encounter and by providing different interdependencies between the groups, they manipulated the extent to which the subjects perceived the situation as one in which there were present one single group, two groups, or just separate individuals (Gaertner et al., 1989, 1990, 1993; see chapter 3 where I presented one of these experiments). Typically they find least ingroup bias in the first of these three arrangements and most in the second. Moreover, the participants' cognitive representations of the situation in these terms tend to be correlated with corresponding levels of bias (Gaertner et al., 1990). Nor are their findings confined to the laboratory. In a survey of a multi-ethnic high school in America they found that students' positive attitudes towards other groups were positively correlated with responses to items stressing a superordinate identity (for example, 'Despite the different groups at school, there is frequently the sense that we are all just one group'), but negatively related to items emphasizing the existence of different groups (Gaertner et al., in press).

One way or another, the two models I have considered so far propose the dissolution of the existing group boundaries. Although each has a sound rationale for this, one problem that it creates for both of them is that the process of generalization is made more difficult. Suppose I interact with an outgroup person under either decategorized or recategorized conditions. To the extent that these conditions have been successful in preventing me from perceiving that person as a member of an outgroup (or, indeed, any group at all), then any change in attitudes I experience towards that person cannot easily be extrapolated to other members of his or her group whom I have not yet met. Thus, my more general intergroup attitudes may remain intact, unaffected by the contact situation. It was this consideration which led Hewstone and me to propose a rather different model of intergroup contact (Hewstone and Brown, 1986; Vivian et al., in press). We suggest that rather than attempting to eliminate the existing ingroup–outgroup division there may be some virtue in keeping it at least minimally salient whilst simultaneously optimizing the various Allport (1954) conditions for successful contact. In this way the contact will take place at an intergroup rather than an interpersonal level, between people acting as group representatives rather than unaffiliated individuals (see chapter 1). If this can be successfully arranged then any positive change engendered during contact is likely to transfer readily to other members of the outgroup because one's contact partners are seen as somehow typical of that group (see Rothbart and John, 1985, for a similar argument).

In some ways this seems a somewhat paradoxical strategy. In order to reduce prejudice towards an outgroup we are suggesting that maintaining the psychological salience of the intergroup distinction can be advantageous. Nevertheless, various lines of evidence are beginning to converge to this conclusion. Wilder (1984b) varied how typical a member of a rival college was seen to be during a co-operative encounter. In addition, this outgroup member behaved pleasantly or unpleasantly. Only the pleasant encounter with a 'typical' outgrouper produced significant improvements in the evaluation of the outgroup as a whole. Unpleasant encounters or encounters with an atypical person produced little change in attitude. Using the outgroup category 'former mental patient', Desforges et al. (1991) compared the efficacy of different kinds of co-operative learning situations. Although they did not vary the typicality of the confederate, who was alleged to have had a history of mental illness, in all conditions she was portrayed as a typical former mental patient and this category remained salient during the experiment. As expected, co-operative encounters with this person produced more attitude change towards mental patients as a whole than the minimal-contact control conditions. Studies of stereotype change also indicate that disconfirming information needs to be associated with people who are otherwise typical members of the category concerned if they are not to be sub-typed and treated as exceptions, leaving the general category stereotype unchanged (Johnston and Hewstone, 1992; Weber and Crocker, 1983; see also chapter 4).

In an attempt to test our model directly we have carried out studies in which we could examine the effects of making group membership more or less salient (Vivian et al., 1994). One was an experiment involving a co-operative encounter with someone of a different nationality. Our British subjects arrived at the laboratory and were required to work with a German confederate for a substantial joint reward (if successful). This confederate was depicted as someone who possessed some characteristics which were either stereotypical for how British people viewed Germans or rather atypical. In addition we provided some bogus information about how homogeneous German people were on various attitudinal and personality characteristics. Depending on experimental condition, they were seen as homogeneous or heterogeneous. Our reasoning was that the situation would be seen in the most 'intergroup' terms when typicality was combined with homogeneity, and that there the link between the target person and the group as a whole would be strongest. Conversely, if they met an atypical member of a heterogeneous group the encounter would be more 'interpersonal' and the chances of generalization correspondingly lower. Our primary interest was in our subjects' subsequent perceptions of German people as a whole. These we divided into four groups of traits: positive and negative, and stereotypical or not of Germany (as determined by pre-testing). We found little change on the negative indices but on the positive measures there was a more favourable perception after interaction with a 'typical' rather than an 'atypical' partner, and on one of these measures this was particularly pronounced in the 'homogeneous' conditions (see figure 8.7).

In the Netherlands, using a different method of invoking category salience and a different intergroup context (Dutch–Turk), Van Oudenhoven et al. (1994) have observed similar results. The ethnicity of the Turkish confederate was either kept quite implicit by the experimenter never making reference to it (low salience), or was drawn to people's attention only at the end of the interaction (moderate salience), or was emphasized throughout (high salience). After two hours of working co-operatively with this confederate, the Dutch subjects evaluated both him and Turks in general. The individual confederate ratings did not vary across conditions but the general attitudes towards Turks were reliably more favourable in the two conditions where his ethnicity had been made salient than in the low-salience condition.

We followed up these experiments with a survey conducted in six different European countries (Vivian et al., 1994). One of the sections of the survey questionnaire asked respondents to think of a person from another country with whom they had had some contact. There then followed a series of questions exploring the nature of this contact – how frequent was it, was it competitive or co-operative, how typical of the country did they regard the person, and how salient was nationality in their conversations with this person? The final and crucial question asked how much they would like to live in the country concerned. We took this to be our index of a favourable and generalized intergroup attitude. Consistent with the traditional Contact Hypothesis, more frequent contact of a co-operative nature was positively correlated with

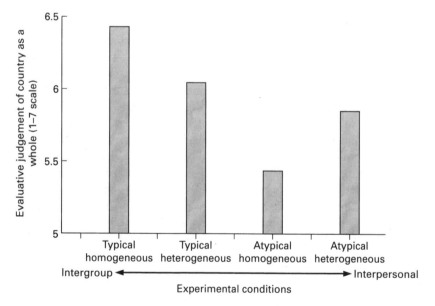

Figure 8.7 Change in a positive national stereotype after intergroup or interpersonal contact
Source: Vivian et al. (1994), table 1

positive attitudes. However, this was especially true if the contact person was seen as typical of the country (again we selected Germany so as to be consistent with the laboratory study) *and* if their respective nationalities featured regularly in their interactions (that is, were salient). As we had predicted, therefore, positive attitudes towards the outgroup as a whole were associated with favourable *intergroup* contact with someone from that outgroup.

Although the Hewstone and Brown model seems to offer a promising way of tackling the generalization problem it is an approach fraught with difficulties. One of these follows directly from the very same argument which provided the rationale for the model in the first place. If intergroup (as opposed to interpersonal) contact permits greater generalization of the attitudes promoted by the encounter then, in principle, both positive *and* negative attitudes can be generalized. Indeed, if the co-operative interaction goes wrong, perhaps in failing to achieve the common goal or because it turns competitive, then structuring the interaction at the intergroup level could well make matters worse. Not only might one's fellow interactant(s) be derogated but there is a risk of reinforcing negative stereotypes of the outgroup precisely because those people are seen as typical of it. This danger is heightened by a second problem which has recently come to light. This is that intergroup encounters may be more anxiety-provoking than interpersonal ones and, as I pointed out in the previous chapter, too much anxiety is usually not conducive to harmonious social relations. As noted earlier, in studying Muslim–Hindu contact in Bangladesh, Islam and Hewstone (1993) found that features indicative of intergroup relationships tended to be correlated with increased anxiety which, in turn, was correlated with less-favourable attitudes towards the outgroups (see figure 8.3).

If this finding is replicated with other populations then it might suggest that the decategorization or recategorization models discussed earlier provide less-hazardous strategies for prejudice reduction, especially since there is some evidence that decategorization is still compatible with attitude generalization (Bettencourt et al., 1992; Miller et al., 1985). However, I fear that even this may be too easy an answer. To begin with, the experiments which have supported the decategorization model have only employed *ad hoc* laboratory groups with probably rather little psychological significance for their members. This may have made it relatively easy for the participants to shed these group identities in the conditions favouring 'personalized' interaction. In real intergroup settings, such as the multi-ethnic schools I discussed earlier, it may not be so easy to distract people's attention from their group memberships. Moreover, in those experiments there was probably more than a vestige of group salience even in the decategorized conditions. For example, in the Bettencourt et al. (1992) experiment, team members wore large badges around their necks for the duration of the study proclaiming their original group affiliations. Likewise the 'strangers' viewed on the video recording. This need to maintain some cognitive link between those with whom one has interacted and the wider outgroup is also recognized by Gaertner et al. (1993). In discussing the generalization question they suggest that there may need to be a trade-off between the salience of the original group identities and the new superordinate group identity which is intended to subsume them. Without this, they concede, interventions designed to reduce prejudice may have only context specific effects.

Assimilation or pluralism

This bring us to the final and perhaps the thorniest issue of all, and one of special relevance to those working in any real multicultural setting. Should intervention programmes, then, draw explicit reference to group differences amongst participants or should they adopt an essentially 'colour-blind' policy, avoiding all reference to group distinctions? As will be clear from the above, this is not a simple matter to resolve. On the one hand, the 'colour-blind' policy seems an obvious one to pursue. It has a sound theoretical basis in the Brewer and Miller (1984) decategorization model and it is completely consistent with the goals of many integration programmes, namely the breaking down of ethnic (national or religious) barriers. What better way to do this than to treat each student (or worker or resident) as an individual without regard to group affiliations?

However, such an apparently progressive approach has its pitfalls. First of all, to ignore group differences can mean that, by default, existing intergroup inequalities persist. The case of desegregated schooling is instructive. As Schofield (1986) has pointed out, given that many schools still practise some form of ability streaming, a 'colour-blind' policy can result in the re-establishment of ethnic desegregation as socially and educationally deprived minority-group students end up in the lower ability streams and the majority group dominates the academically more prestigious streams. It seems to me that to prevent this happening close attention needs to be paid to the ethnic composition of different classes in schools and to the design of curricula which will be consistent with teaching more heterogeneous groups. In occupational settings, too, 'colour-blind' or 'gender-blind' or 'handicap-blind' approaches can easily mean the continued exclusion of disadvantaged groups from the higher echelons of organizations, or, indeed, from the world of work altogether (Blanchard and Crosby, 1989; Glasser, 1988). In fact, there is some evidence from research on affirmative action programmes that a denial of categorical information in connection with performance evaluations can actually result in less-favourable judgements. Ferdman (1989) presented a videotape of a Hispanic manager to some White non-Hispanic managers. In some viewing conditions they received only individuating information about the target person (for example, his hobbies), and in others they learned also about how important his ethnicity was to him and about his involvement with Hispanic organizations, and in others both individuating and categorical information was presented. On a series of measures the latter condition elicited the most favourable evaluations, especially when compared to the individuating information-only conditions.

Secondly, interventions which are not attentive to group differences can quickly lead to an 'assimilationist' policy in which members of minority groups are expected to conform to the norms and values of the dominant group (Berry, 1984). Such an outcome, which implies that minority-group members give up their distinctive social identities, can have deleterious consequences. On the one hand, it can be associated with a greater incidence of health problems in the minority groups (Berry et al., 1987). But, perhaps more seriously from the point of view of the goals of any intervention programme, such a surrendering of linguistic or cultural identity may be strenuously resisted by those minority groups with corresponding negative implications for the final outcome of the programme itself. Viewed from their political perspective, such policies can be seen as attempts by the dominant group to impose an alien social order on less-powerful groups struggling for economic and psychological survival.

An alternative to the 'colour-blind' perspective is what Berry (1984) calls the 'pluralist' strategy. In this approach group diversity is recognized and different value systems are acknowledged. The aim is to develop programmes – whether in schools or in the wider society – which actually capitalize on group differences for the mutual benefit of both majority and minority group members. Thus, to return to the co-operative learning groups discussed in the previous sections: in designing group projects it might be possible to allocate students to sub-tasks which would allow them to contribute something unique to the overall group goal *because of* the knowledge or experience which derives specifically from their religion or ethnicity. There is, at present, precious little research evidence which has examined the effectiveness of such a strategy. However, two laboratory experiments which we have conducted suggest that it may not be completely without merit (Brown and Wade, 1987; Deschamps and Brown, 1983). In these we arranged for two groups to work together for a superordinate goal, either in ways in which their roles were very similar or so that they had distinctive and complementary roles to play. In general, liking for the other groups was higher in the latter conditions. However, such positive effects of distinguishing task roles very clearly may be restricted to co-operative encounters at the intergroup level I am advocating here; when the interaction is more personalized the beneficial effects of clear-cut role assignment may be diminished (Marcus-Newhall et al., 1993).

Of course, such a pluralist approach, based as it is on retaining the salience of some group distinctions, must tread a very delicate path between fostering positive mutual differentiation between groups and avoiding the regression into familiar and destructive patterns of prejudice which so often, as we have seen in the pages of this book, are associated with salient category divisions. Yet, although this path is narrow and its true direction as yet uncertain, it is a journey we must surely attempt if we are serious about doing something to reduce prejudice in today's conflict-ridden world. My rather immodest hope is that this book may serve as something of a guide for others thinking of embarking on it.

Summary

1. A substantial body of research has shown that contact between groups can reduce prejudice provided that it takes place under certain conditions. These are: there should be social and institutional support for the measures designed

to promote the contact; the contact should be of sufficient frequency, duration and closeness to permit the development of meaningful relationships between members of the groups concerned; as far as possible the participants in the contact situation should be of equal status; the contact should involve co-operative activity.

2. A major focus of contact research has been on integrated schools. Some of this research, particularly on the effects of school desegregation in the United States, suggests that integration has not always had the hoped-for effects on ethnic relations. The reason for this is that desegregation has seldom met all the four optimal conditions for successful contact. However, specific intervention programmes, especially those involving co-operative learning groups, have been very successful in increasing attraction between members of different social categories.

3. An abiding problem in research evaluating the Contact Hypothesis has been how to promote the generalization of positive attitudes towards individuals to the group from which those individuals come. Three recent models have attempted to address this issue: one stresses decategorization, another recategorization, and the third the importance of maintaining the salience of the original categorization. Each has empirical support; each is not without its problems. Ultimately, any solutions to the reduction of prejudice must find a way of minimizing the destructive potential of maintaining category divisions whilst permitting groups to retain their distinctive identities.

Further Reading

Hewstone, M. and Brown, R. (1986) *Contact and Conflict in Intergroup Encounters*, chs 1, 4, 10. Oxford: Basil Blackwell.

Miller, N. and Brewer, M.B. (1984) *Groups in Contact: The psychology of desegregation*, chs 1, 2, 5, 8, 9, 13. New York: Academic Press.

Slavin, R.E. (1983) *Cooperative Learning*, chs 2–4. New York: Longman.

Notes

1. Changes in liking for the White confederate were much weaker, non-significant for the 'competence' variable and less reliable (though significant) for the 'team success' variable (Blanchard et al., 1975).
2. Similar relationships were observed for the other main dependent measure, perceived outgroup homogeneity.
3. Evidence is beginning to emerge that the long-term effects of desegregation, even desegregation under sub-optimal conditions, are greater than might have been supposed. For example, it has been found that Black graduates from desegregated high schools tend to find better-paying jobs than those from segregated schools, possibly because of the easier access to wider job information networks that such an integrated background provides (Braddock and McPartland, 1987).

References

Abeles, R.P. (1976) Relative deprivation, rising expectations and black militancy, *Journal of Social Issues, 32,* 119–137.

Aboud, F.E. (1977) Interest in ethnic information: a cross-cultural developmental study. *Canadian Journal of Behavioral Science, 9,* 134–146.

Aboud, F. E. (1980) A test of ethnocentrism with young children. *Canadian Journal of Behavioral Science, 12,* 195–209.

Aboud, F.E. (1984) Social and cognitive based identity constancy. *Journal of Genetic Psychology, 145,* 217–230.

Aboud, F. (1988) *Children and Prejudice.* Oxford: Basil Blackwell.

Abrams, D. (1990) Political identity: relative deprivation, social identity and the case of Scottish Nationalism. *ESRC 16–19 Initiative Occasional Papers.* London: Economic and Social Research Council.

Abrams, D. and Hogg, M. (1988) Comments on the motivational status of self-esteem in social identity and intergroup discrimination. *European Journal of Social Psychology, 18,* 317–334.

Ackerman, N.W. and Jahoda, M. (1950) *Anti-Semitism and Emotional Disorder.* New York: Harper.

Adorno, T.W., Frenkel-Brunswick, E., Levinson, D.J. and Sanford, R.N. (1950) *The Authoritarian Personality.* New York: Harper.

Allen, B.P. (1975) Social distance and admiration reactions of unprejudiced whites. *Journal of Personality, 43,* 709–726.

Allen, V.L. and Wilder, D.A. (1975) Categorization, belief similarity, and group discrimination. *Journal of Personality and Social Psychology, 32,* 971–977.

Allen, V.L. and Wilder, D.A. (1979) Group categorization and attribution of belief similarity. *Small Group Behavior, 10,* 73–80.

Allport, G.W. (1954) *The Nature of Prejudice.* Reading, Mass.: Addison-Wesley.

Allport, G.W. and Kramer, B.B. (1946) Some roots of prejudice. *Journal of Psychology, 22,* 9–39.

Altemeyer, B. (1988) *Enemies of Freedom: Understanding right-wing authoritarianism.* San Francisco: Jossey-Bass.

Amir, Y. (1969) Contact hypothesis in ethnic relations. *Psychological Bulletin, 71,* 319–342.

Amir, Y. (1976) The role of intergroup contact in change of prejudice and ethnic relations. In P.A. Katz (ed.), *Towards the Elimination of Racism*, New York: Pergamon.

Angelou, M. (1969) *I Know Why a Caged Bird Sings*. London: Hutchinson (1988 edition).

Applegryn, A.E. and Nieuwoudt, J.M. (1988) Relative deprivation and the ethnic attitudes of Blacks and Afrikaans-speaking Whites in South Africa. *Journal of Social Psychology, 128*, 311–323.

Armstrong, B., Johnson, D.W. and Balow, B. (1981) Effects of cooperative vs. individualistic learning experiences on interpersonal attraction between learning-disabled and normal-progress elementary school students. *Contemporary Educational Psychology, 6*, 102–109.

Aronson, E., Blaney, N., Stephan, C., Sikes, J. and Snapp, M. (1978) *The Jig-saw Classroom*. London: Sage.

Asch, S.E. (1952) *Social Psychology*. New York: Prentice-Hall.

Asher, S.R. and Allen, V.L. (1969) Racial preference and social comparison processes. *Journal of Social Issues, 25*, 157–166.

Augustinos, M., Ahrens, C. and Innes, M. (1994) Stereotypes and prejudice: the Australian experience. *British Journal of Social Psychology, 33*, 125–141.

Bandura, A. (1977) *Social Learning Theory*. Englewood Cliffs, NJ: Prentice-Hall.

Banks, W.C. (1976) White preference in Blacks: a paradigm in search of a phenomenon. *Psychological Bulletin, 83*, 1179–1186.

Banton, M. (1983) *Racial and Ethnic Competition*. Cambridge: Cambridge University Press.

Bartsch, R.A. and Judd, C.M. (1993) Majority–minority status and perceived ingroup variability revisited. *European Journal of Social Psychology, 23*, 471–483.

Bass, B.M. (1955) Authoritarianism or acquiescence? *Journal of Abnormal and Social Psychology, 51*, 616–623.

Beauvois, C. and Spence, J.T. (1987) Gender, prejudice, and categorization. *Sex Roles, 16*, 89–100.

Benokraitis, N.V. and Feagin, J.R. (1986) *Modern Sexism: Blatant, subtle, and covert discrimination*. Englewood Cliffs, N.J.: Prentice-Hall.

Berkowitz, L. (1962) *Aggression: A social psychological analysis*. New York: McGraw-Hill.

Berndt, T.J. and Heller, K.A. (1986) Gender stereotypes and social inferences: a developmental study. *Journal of Personality and Social Psychology, 50*, 889–898.

Bernstein, M. and Crosby, F. (1980) An empirical examination of relative deprivation theory. *Journal of Experimental Social Psychology, 16*, 442–456.

Berry, J.W. (1984) Cultural relations in plural societies: alternatives to segregation and their sociopsychological implications. In N. Miller and M.B. Brewer (eds) *Groups in Contact: The Psychology of Desegregation*, New York: Academic Press.

Berry, J.W., Kalin, R. and Taylor, D.M. (1977) *Multiculturalism and Ethnic Attitudes in Canada*. Ottawa: Supply and Services Canada.

Berry, J.W., Kim, V., Minde, T. and Mok, D. (1987) Comparative studies of acculturative stress. *International Migration Review, 21*, 491–511.

Bettencourt, B.A., Brewer, M.B., Croak, M.R. and Miller, N. (1992) Cooperation and the reduction of intergroup bias: the role of reward structure and social orientation. *Journal of Experimental Social Psychology, 28*, 301–309.

Biernat, M. (1991) Gender stereotypes and the relationship between masculinity and feminity: a developmental analysis. *Journal of Personality and Social Psychology, 61*, 351–365.

Biernat, M. and Vescio, T.K. (1993) Categorization and stereotyping: effects of group context on memory and social judgement. *Journal of Experimental Social Psychology, 29*, 166–202.

Biernat, M., Manis, M. and Nelson, T.E. (1991) Stereotypes and standards of judgement. *Journal of Personality and Social Psychology, 60*, 485–99.

Biernat, M. and Vescio, T.K. (1994) Still another look at the effects of fit and novelty on the salience of social categories. *Journal of Experimental Social Psychology, 30*, 399–406.

Billig, M. (1976) *Social Psychology and Intergroup Relations*. London: Academic Press.

Billig, M. (1978) *Fascists: A social psychological view of the National Front*. London: Harcourt Brace Jovanovich.

Billig, M. and Cochrane, R. (1979) Values of political extremists and potential extremists: a discriminant analysis. *European Journal of Social Psychology, 9*, 205–222.

Billig, M.G. and Tajfel, H. (1973) Social categorization and similarity in intergroup behaviour. *European Journal of Social Psychology, 3*, 27–52.

Bird, C., Monachesi, E.D. and Burdick, H. (1952) Infiltration and the attitudes of white and negro parents and children. *Journal of Abnormal and Social Psychology, 47*, 688–699.

Blanchard, F.A. and Crosby, F.J. (1989) *Affirmative Action in Perspective*. New York: Springer Verlag.

Blanchard, P.A., Weigel, R.H. and Cook, S.W. (1975) The effect of relative competence of group members upon interpersonal attraction in cooperating interracial groups. *Journal of Personality and Social Psychology, 32*, 519–530.

Block, J. and Block, J. (1950) An investigation of the relationship between intolerance of ambiguity and ethnocentrism. *Journal of Personality, 19*, 303–311.

Bobo, L. (1988a) Attitudes toward the black political movement: trends, meaning, and effects on racial policy preferences. *Social Psychology Quarterly*, *51*, 287–302.

Bobo, L. (1988b) Group conflict, prejudice, and the paradox of contemporary racial attitudes. In P.A. Katz and D.A. Taylor (eds) *Eliminating Racism*, New York: Plenum.

Bourhis, R.Y. and Giles, H. (1977) The language of intergroup distinctiveness. In H. Giles (ed.), *Language, Ethnicity and Intergroup Relations*, London: Academic Press.

Bourhis, R.Y., Giles, H., Leyens, J.P. and Tajfel, H. (1978) Psycholinguistic distinctiveness: language divergence in Belgium. In H. Giles and R. St Clair (eds), *Language and Social Psychology*, Oxford: Basil Blackwell.

Bourhis, R.Y., Sachdev, I. and Gagnon, A. (1994) Intergroup research with the Tajfel matrices: methodological notes. In M.P. Zanna and J.M. Olson (eds), *The Psychology of Prejudice: The Ontario Symposium*, vol. 7. Hillsdale, N.J.: Lawrence Erlbaum.

Braddock, J.H. and McPartland, J.M. (1987) How minorities continue to be excluded from equal employment opportunities: research on labour market and institutional barriers. *Journal of Social Issues*, *43*, 5–39.

Braha, V. and Rutter, D.R. (1980) Friendship choice in a mixed-race primary school. *Educational Studies*, *6*, 217–223.

Branch, C.W. and Newcombe, N. (1980) Racial attitudes of Black pre-schoolers as related to parental civil rights activism. *Merril-Palmer Quarterly*, *26*, 425–428.

Brand, E.S., Ruiz, R.A. and Padilla, A.M. (1974) Ethnic identification and preference: a review. *Psychological Bulletin*, *81*, 860–890.

Branthwaite, A., Doyle, S. and Lightbown, N. (1979) The balance between fairness and discrimination. *European Journal of Social Psychology*, *9*, 149–163.

Breakwell, G.M. (1978) Some effects of marginal social identity. In H. Tajfel (ed.), *Differentiation Between Social Groups*, London: Academic Press.

Breakwell, G.M. (1986) *Coping with Threatened Identities*. London: Methuen.

Breakwell, G.M., Collie, A., Harrison, B. and Propper, C. (1984) Attitudes towards the unemployed: effects of threatened identity. *British Journal of Social Psychology*, *23*, 87–88.

Brewer, M.B. (1979) Ingroup bias in the minimal intergroup situation: a cognitive motivational analysis. *Psychological Bulletin*, *86*, 307–324.

Brewer, M.B. (1986) The role of ethnocentrism in intergroup conflict. In S. Worchel and W. Austin (eds), *The Psychology of Intergroup Relations*, Chicago: Nelson.

Brewer, M.B. (1991) The social self: on being the same and different at the same time. *Personality and Social Psychology Bulletin*, *17*, 475–482.

Brewer, M.B. and Campbell, D.T. (1976) *Ethnocentrism and Intergroup Attitudes: East African evidence*. New York: Sage.

Brewer, M.B. and Miller, N. (1984) Beyond the contact hypothesis: theoretical perspectives on desegregation. In N. Miller and M.B. Brewer (eds), *Groups in Contact: The psychology of desegregation*, New York: Academic Press.

Brewer, M.B., Dutt, V. and Lui, L. (1981) Perceptions of the elderly: stereotypes as prototypes. *Journal of Personality and Social Psychology, 41*, 656–670.

Brewer, M.B., Ho, H.-K., Lee, J.-Y. and Miller, N. (1987) Social identity and social distance among Hong Kong schoolchildren. *Personality and Social Psychology Bulletin, 13*, 156–165.

Brown, Roger (1965) *Social Psychology.* New York: Macmillan.

Brown, R.J. (1984a) The effects of intergroup similarity and cooperative vs. competitive orientation on intergroup discrimination. *British Journal of Social Psychology, 23*, 21–33.

Brown, R.J. (1984b) The role of similarity in intergroup relations. In H. Tajfel (ed.), *The Social Dimension*, vol. 2, Cambridge: Cambridge University Press.

Brown, R.J. (1988) *Group Processes: Dynamics within and between groups.* Oxford: Basil Blackwell.

Brown, R.J. and Abrams, D. (1986) The effects of intergroup similarity and goal interdependence on intergroup attitudes and task performance. *Journal of Experimental Social Psychology, 22*, 78–92.

Brown, R.J. amd Deschamps, J.C. (1980–1) Discrimination entre individus et entre groupes. *Bulletin de psychologie, 34*, 185–195.

Brown, R.J. and Ross, G.R. (1982) The battle for acceptance: an exploration into the dynamics of intergroup behaviour. In H. Tajfel (ed.), *Social Identity and Intergroup Relations*, Cambridge: Cambridge University Press.

Brown, R. and Smith, A. (1989) Perceptions of and by minority groups: the case of women in academia. *European Journal of Social Psychology, 19*, 61–75.

Brown, R.J. and Turner, J.C. (1979) The criss-cross categorization effect in intergroup discrimination. *British Journal of Social & Clinical Psychology, 18*, 371–383.

Brown, R.J. and Turner, J.C. (1981) Interpersonal and intergroup behaviour. In J.C. Turner and H. Giles (eds), *Intergroup Behaviour*, Oxford: Basil Blackwell.

Brown, R.J. and Wade, G.S. (1987) Superordinate goals and intergroup behaviour: the effects of role ambiguity and status on intergroup attitudes and task performance. *European Journal of Social Psychology, 17*, 131–42.

Brown, R. and Wootton-Millward, L. (1993) Perceptions of group homogeneity during group formation and change. *Social Cognition, 11*, 126–149.

Brown, R.J. and Yee, M.D. (1988) Children's social comparisons: effects of interpersonal and intergroup information upon children's self-evaluations. *Final Report to ESRC (UK)*, University of Kent, Canterbury.

Brown, R., Hinkle, S., Ely, P.G., Fox-Cardamone, L., Maras, P. and Taylor, L.A. (1992) Recognising group diversity: individualist–collectivist and autonomous–relational social orientations and their implications for intergroup processes. *British Journal of Social Psychology, 31,* 327–342.

Brown, R.W. (1953) A determinant of the relationship between rigidity and authoritarianism. *Journal of Abnormal and Social Psychology, 48,* 469–476.

Bruner, J.S. (1957) On perceptual readiness. *Psychological Review, 64,* 123–151.

Burnstein, E. and McCrae, A.V. (1962) Some effects of shared threat and prejudice in racially mixed groups. *Journal of Abnormal & Social Psychology, 64,* 257–263.

Byrne, D. (1971) *The Attraction Paradigm.* New York: Academic Press.

Byrne, D. and Wong, T.J. (1962) Racial prejudice, interpersonal attraction and assumed dissimilarity of attitudes. *Journal of Abnormal & Social Psychology, 65,* 246–253.

Cacioppo, J.T., Petty, R.E., Losch, M.E. and Kim, H.S. (1986) Electromyographic activity over facial muscle regions can differentiate the valence and intensity of affective reactions. *Journal of Personality and Social Psychology, 50,* 260–268.

Caddick, B. (1982) Perceived illegitimacy and intergroup relations. In H. Tajfel (ed.), *Social Identity and Intergroup Relations,* Cambridge: Cambridge University Press.

Campbell, D.T. (1956) Enhancement of contrast as a composite habit. *Journal of Abnormal and Social Psychology, 53,* 350–355.

Campbell, D.T. (1958) Common fate, similarity, and other indices of the status of aggregates of persons as social entities. *Behavioural Science, 3,* 14–25.

Campbell, D.T. (1963) Social attitudes and other acquired behavioral dispositions. In S. Koch (ed.), *Psychology: A study of a science,* vol. 6. New York: McGraw-Hill.

Campbell, D.T. (1965) Ethnocentric and other altruistic motives. In D. Levine (ed.), *Nebraska Symposium on Motivation,* Lincoln, Nebr.: University of Nebraska Press.

Campbell, D.T. and McCandless, B.R. (1951) Ethnocentrism, xenophobia, and personality. *Human Relations, 4,* 185–192.

Campbell, D., Kruskal, W. and Wallace, W. (1966) Seating aggregation as an index of attitude. *Sociometry, 29,* 1–15.

Caplan, N. (1970) The new ghetto man: a review of recent empirical studies. *Journal of Social Issues, 26,* 59–73.

Carver, C.L., Glass, D.C. and Katz, I. (1978). Favorable evaluations of blacks and the handicapped: positive prejudice, unconscious denial, or social desirability? *Journal of Applied Social Psychology, 8,* 97–106.

Chapman, L.J. (1967) Illusory correlation in observational report. *Journal of Verbal Learning and Verbal Behaviour, 6,* 151–155.

Chin, M.G. and McClintock, C.G. (1993) The effects of intergroup discrimination and social values on level of self-esteem in the minimal group paradigm. *European Journal of Social Psychology, 23*, 63–75.

Christie, R. (1954) Authoritarianism re-examined. In R. Christie and M. Jahoda (eds) *Studies in the Scope and Method of 'The Authoritarian Personality'*. Glencoe, Ill.: Free Press.

Christie, R. and Cook, P. (1958) A guide to published literature relating to the Authoritarian Personality through 1956. *Journal of Psychology, 45*, 191–199.

Christie, R. and Jahoda, M. (eds) (1954) *Studies in the Scope and Method of 'The Authoritarian Personality'*. New York: Free Press.

Cialdini, R.B., Borden, R.J., Thorne, A., Walker, M.R., Freeman, S. and Sloan, L.R. (1976) Basking in reflected glory: three (football) field studies. *Journal of Personality and Social Psychology, 34*, 366–374.

Clark, A., Hocevar, D. and Dembo, M.H. (1980) The role of cognitive development in children's explanations and preferences for skin color. *Developmental Psychology, 16*, 332–339.

Clark, K.B. and Clark, M.P. (1947) Racial identification and preference in Negro children. In H. Proshansky and B. Seidenberg (eds), *Basic Studies in Social Psychology*, New York: Holt Rinehart and Winston (1955 edition).

Clore, G.L., Bray, R.M., Itkin, S.M. and Murphy, P. (1978) Interracial attitudes and behaviour at a summer camp. *Journal of Personality and Social Psychology, 36*, 107–116.

Cohen, E. (1982) Expectation states and interracial interaction in school settings. *Annual Review of Sociology, 8*, 209–235.

Cohen, J. and Streuning, E.L. (1962) Opinions about mental illness. *Journal of Abnormal and Social Psychology, 64*, 349–360.

Colman, A. and Lambley, P. (1970) Authoritarianism and race attitudes in South Africa. *Journal of Social Psychology, 82*, 161–164.

Cook, S.W. (1962) The systematic analysis of socially significant events. *Journal of Social Issues, 18*, 66–84.

Cook, S.W. (1978) Interpersonal and attitudinal outcomes in cooperating interracial groups. *Journal of Research and Development in Education, 12*, 97–113.

Corenblum, B. and Annis, R.C. (1993) Development of racial identity in minority and majority children: an affect discrepancy model. *Canadian Journal of Behavioural Science, 25*, 499–521.

Coser, L. (1956) *Functions of Social Conflict*. New York: Free Press.

Cowen, E.L., Landes, J. and Schaet, D.E. (1958) The effects of mild frustration on the expression of prejudiced attitudes. *Journal of Abnormal and Social Psychology, 58*, 33–38.

Cox, O.C. (1948) *Caste, Class, and Race: A study in social dynamics*. New York: Monthly Review Press.

Crain, R.L. and Mahard, R.E. (1982) The consequences of controversy accompanying institutional change: the case of school desegregation. *American Sociological Review, 49,* 697–708.

Crandall, C.S. (1994) Prejudice against fat people: ideology and self interest. *Journal of Personality and Social Psychology, 66,* 882–894.

Crano, W.D. and Mellon, P.M. (1978) Causal influence of teachers' expectations on children's academic performance: a cross-lagged panel analysis. *Journal of Educational Psychology, 79,* 39–49.

Crawford, T.J. and Naditch, M. (1970) Relative deprivation, powerlessness and militancy: the psychology of social protest. *Psychiatry, 33,* 208–223.

CRE (1990) *'Sorry it's gone': testing for racial discrimination in the private rented housing sector.* London: Commission for Racial Equality.

CRE (1993) *Race through the 90s.* London: Commission for Racial Equality.

Crosby, F. (1976) A model of egotistical relative deprivation. *Psychological Review, 83,* 85–113.

Crosby, F. (1979) Relative deprivation revisited: a response to Miller, Bolce, and Halligan. *American Political Science Review, 73,* 103–112.

Crosby, F., Bromley, S. and Saxe, L. (1980) Recent unobtrusive studies of Black and White discrimination and prejudice. *Psychological Bulletin, 87,* 546–563.

Daniels, W.W. (1968) *Racial Discrimination in England.* Harmondsworth: Penguin.

Darley, J.M. and Fazio, R.H. (1980) Expectancy confirmation processes arising in the social interaction sequence. *American Psychologist, 35,* 867–881.

Darley, J.M. and Gross, P.H. (1983) A hypothesis-confirming bias in labeling effects. *Journal of Personality and Social Psychology, 44,* 20–33.

Davey, A. (1983) *Learning to be Prejudiced.* London: Edward Arnold.

Davies, J. (1978) Communication. *American Political Science Review, 72,* 1357–1358.

Davies, J. (1979) Comment. *American Political Science Review, 73,* 825–826.

Davies, J.C. (1969) The J-curve of rising and declining satisfactions as a cause of some great revolutions and a contained rebellion. In H.D. Graham and T.R. Gurr (eds), *The History of Violence in America: Historical and comparative perspectives,* New York: Praeger.

Davis, J.A. (1959) A formal interpretation of the theory of relative deprivation. *Sociometry, 22,* 280–296.

Deschamps, J.-C. and Brown, R.J. (1983) Superordinate goals and intergroup conflict. *British Journal of Social Psychology,* 22, 189–195.

Deschamps, J.-C. and Doise, W. (1978) Crossed category memberships in intergroup relations. In H. Tajfel (ed.), *Differentiation between Social Groups,* London: Academic Press.

Desforges, D.M., Lord, C.G., Ramsey, S.L., Mason, J.A., van Leeuwen, M.D., West, S.C. and Lepper, M.R. (1991) Effects of structured cooperative contact on changing negative attitudes towards stigmatized groups. *Journal of Personality and Social Psychology, 60,* 531–544.

Deutsch, M. (1973) *The Resolution of Conflict.* London: Yale University Press.

Deutsch, M. and Collins, M.E. (1951) *Interracial Housing.* Minneapolis: University of Minneapolis Press.

Deutscher, I. (1959) *The Prophet Unarmed: Trotsky 1921–1929.* London: Oxford University Press.

Devine, P. (1989) Stereotypes and prejudice: their automatic and controlled components. *Journal of Personality and Social Psychology, 56,* 5–18.

Devine, P.G. and Sherman, S.J. (1992) Intuitive versus rational judgment and the role of stereotyping in the human condition: Kirk or Spock? *Psychological Inquiry, 3,* 153–159.

Devine, P.G., Monteith, M.J., Zuwerink, J.R. and Elliot, A.J. (1991) Prejudice with and without compunction. *Journal of Personality and Social Psychology, 60,* 817–830.

DeVries, D.L., Edwards, K.J. and Slavin, R.E. (1979) Biracial learning teams and race relations in the classroom: four field experiments on Teams-Games-Tournament. *Journal of Educational Psychology, 70,* 356–362.

Diehl, M. (1988) Social identity and minimal groups: the effects of interpersonal and intergroup attitudinal similarity on intergroup discrimination. *British Journal of Social Psychology, 27,* 289–300.

Diehl, M. (1990) The minimal group paradigm: theoretical explanations and empirical findings. In W. Stroebe and M. Hewstone (eds), *European Review of Social Psychology,* vol. 1, Chichester: John Wiley.

Dijker, A.J.M. (1987) Emotional reactions to ethnic minorities. *European Journal of Social Psychology, 17,* 305–325.

Dion, K. (1973) Dogmatism and intergroup bias. *Representative Research in Social Psychology, 4,* 1–10.

Doise, W. (1976) *L'articulation psychosociologique et les relations entre groupes.* Brussels: de Boeck. Translated as *Groups and Individuals: Explanations in social psychology,* Cambridge: Cambridge University Press, 1978.

Doise, W., Deschamps, J.-C., and Meyer, G. (1978) The accentuation of intra-category similarities. In H. Tajfel (ed.), *Differentiation between Social Groups: Studies in the social psychology of intergroup relations,* London: Academic Press.

Dollard, J., Doob, L.W., Miller, N.E., Mowrer, O.K. and Sears, R.R. (1939) *Frustration and Aggression.* New Haven, Conn.: Yale University Press.

Doty, R.M., Peterson, B.E.A. and Winter, D.G. (1991) Threat and authoritarianism in the United States, 1978–1987. *Journal of Personality and Social Psychology, 61,* 629–640.

Dovidio, J.F. and Fazio, R.H. (1992) New technologies for the direct and indirect assessment of attitudes. In J.M. Tanur (ed.), *Questions about Questions: Inquiries into the cognitive bases of surveys,* New York: Russell Sage.

Dovidio, J.F. and Gaertner, S.L. (1981) The effects of race, status, and ability on helping behavior. *Social Psychology Quarterly, 44*, 192–203.

Dovidio, J.F. and Gaertner, S.L. (1983) The effects of sex, status, and ability on helping behavior. *Journal of Applied Social Psychology, 13*, 191–205.

Dovidio, J.F. and Gaertner, S.L. (eds) (1986) *Prejudice, Discrimination and Racism*, ch. 1. New York: Academic Press.

Dovidio, J.L., Evans, N. and Tyler, R.B. (1986) Racial stereotypes: the contents of their cognitive representations. *Journal of Experimental Social Psychology, 22*, 22–37.

Doyle, A.B., Beaudet, J. and Aboud, F. (1988) Developmental patterns in the flexibility of children's ethnic attitudes. *Journal of Cross Cultural Psychology, 19*, 3–18.

Duckitt, J. (1988) Normative conformity and racial prejudice in South Africa. *Genetic, Social and General Psychology Monographs, 114*, 413–437.

Duncan, B.L. (1976) Differential social perception and attribution of inter-group violence: testing the lower limits of stereotyping of blacks. *Journal of Personality and Social Psychology, 34*, 590–598.

Durkin, K. (1985) *Television, Sex Roles, and Children*. Milton Keynes: Open University Press.

Duveen, G. and Lloyd, B. (1986) The significance of social identities. *British Journal of Social Psychology, 25*, 219–230.

Eagly, A.H. and Steffen, V.J. (1984) Gender stereotypes stem from the distribution of women and men into social roles. *Journal of Personality and Social Psychology, 46*, 735–754.

Eagly, A.H. and Wood, W. (1982) Inferred sex differences in status as a determinant of gender stereotypes about social influence. *Journal of Personality and Social Psychology, 43*, 915–928.

Eagly, A.H., Mladinic, A. and Otto, S. (1991) Are women evaluated more favourably than men? An analysis of attitudes, beliefs and emotions. *Psychology of Women Quarterly, 15*, 203–216.

Easterbrook, J.A. (1959) The effect of emotion on cue utilization and the organization of behavior. *Psychological Review, 66*, 183–201.

Eaves, L.J. and Eysenck, H.J. (1974) Genetics and the development of social attitudes. *Nature, 249*, 288–289.

Eccles, J.S., Jacobs, J.E. and Harold, R.D. (1990) Gender role stereotypes, expectancy effects, and parents' socialization of gender differences. *Journal of Social Issues, 46*, 183–201.

Eccles-Parsons, J., Adler, T. and Kaczala, C. (1982) Socialization of achievement attitudes and beliefs: parental influences. *Child Development, 53*, 310–321.

Eiser, J.R. (1971) Enhancement of contrast in the absolute judgement of attitude statements. *Journal of Personality and Social Psychology, 17*, 1–10.

Eiser, J.R. and Stroebe, W. (1972) *Categorisation and Social Judgement*. London: Academic Press.

Elashoff, J. and Snow, R. (1971) *Pygmalion Reconsidered*. Worthington, Ohio: C.A. Jones.

Ellemers, N., Van Knippenberg, A., de Vries, N. and Wilke, H. (1988) Social identification and permeability of group boundaries. *European Journal of Social Psychology, 18*, 497–513.

Ellemers, N., Wilke, H. and Van Knippenberg, A. (1993) Effects of the legitimacy of low group or individual status as individual and collective status-enhancement strategies. *Journal of Personality and Social Psychology, 64*, 766–778.

Epstein, I.M., Krupat, E. and Obudho, C. (1976) Clean is beautiful: identification and preference as a function of race and cleanliness. *Journal of Social Issues, 32*, 109–118.

Epstein, J.L. (1985) After the bus arrives: resegregation in desegregated schools. *Journal of Social Issues, 41*, 23–43.

Esmail, A. and Everington, S. (1993) Racial discrimination against doctors from ethnic minorities. *British Medical Journal, 306*, 691–692.

Evans-Pritchard, E.E. (1940) *The Nuer*. Oxford: Clarendon Press.

Eysenck, H.J. (1952) *The Scientific Study of Personality*. London: Routledge and Kegan Paul.

Eysenck, H.J. (1954) *The Psychology of Politics*. London: Routledge and Kegan Paul.

Eysenck, H.J. (1956) The psychology of politics: a reply. *Psychological Bulletin, 53*, 177–182.

Eysenck, H.J. (1967) *The Biological Basis of Personality*. Springfield, Ill.: Thomas.

Eysenck, H.J. and Wilson, G.D. (1978) *The Psychological Basis of Ideology*. Lancaster: MTP.

Fagan, J.F. and Singer, L.T. (1979) The role of simple feature differences in infants' recognition of faces. *Infant Behavior and Development, 2*, 39–45.

Ferdman, B.M. (1989) Affirmative action and the challenge of the color-blind perspective. In F.A. Blanchard and F.J. Crosby (eds), *Affirmative Action in Perspective*, New York: Springer Verlag.

Ferraresi, L. (1988) Identità sociale, categorizzazione e pregiudizio. Tesi di Laurea, University of Bologna.

Festinger, L. (1954) A theory of social comparison processes. *Human Relations, 7*, 117–40.

Festinger, L. (1957) *A Theory of Cognitive Dissonance*. Evanston, Ill.: Row, Peterson.

Fiedler, K. (1991) The tricky nature of skewed frequency tables: an information loss account of distinctiveness-based illusory correlations. *Journal of Personality and Social Psychology, 60*, 26–36.

Fiske, S.T. and Taylor, S.E. (1991) *Social Cognition*, 2nd edn. New York: McGraw-Hill.

Forbes, H.D. (1985) *Nationalism, Ethnocentrism, and Personality.* Chicago: University of Chicago Press.

Frable, D.E.S. and Bem, S.L. (1985) If you are gender schematic, all members of the opposite sex look alike. *Journal of Personality and Social Psychology, 49,* 459–468.

Frenkel-Brunswik, E. (1949) Intolerance of ambiguity as an emotional and perceptual personality variable. *Journal of Personality, 18,* 108–143.

Frenkel-Brunswik, E. (1953) Prejudice in the interviews of children: attitudes toward minority groups. *Journal of Genetic Psychology, 82,* 91–136.

Frey, D. and Gaertner, S.L. (1986) Helping and the avoidance of inappropriate interracial behavior: a strategy that can perpetuate a non-prejudiced self-image. *Journal of Personality and Social Psychology, 50,* 1083–1090.

Furnham, A. (1982) Explanations for unemployment in Britain. *European Journal of Social Psychology, 12,* 335–352.

Gaertner, S.L. (1973) Helping behavior and discrimination among liberals and conservatives. *Journal of Personality and Social Psychology, 25,* 335–341.

Gaertner, S.L. and Bickman, L. (1971) Effects of race on the elicitation of helping behavior: the wrong number technique. *Journal of Personality and Social Psychology, 20,* 218–222.

Gaertner, S.L. and Dovidio, J.F. (1977) The subtlety of white racism, arousal and helping behavior. *Journal of Personality and Social Psychology, 35,* 691–707. .

Gaertner, S.L. and Dovidio, J.F. (1986) The aversive form of racism. In J.F. Dovidio and S.L. Gaertner (eds), *Prejudice, Discrimination and Racism,* New York: Academic Press.

Gaertner, S.L. and McLaughlin, J.P. (1983) Racial stereotypes: associations and ascriptions of positive and negative characteristics. *Social Psychology Quarterly, 46,* 23–30.

Gaertner, S.L., Mann, J., Murrell, A. and Dovidio, J.F. (1989) Reducing intergroup bias: the benefits of recategorization. *Journal of Personality and Social Psychology, 57,* 239–249.

Gaertner, S.L., Mann, J., Dovidio, J.F., Murrell, A.J. and Pomere, M. (1990) How does cooperation reduce intergroup bias? *Journal of Personality and Social Psychology, 59,* 692–704.

Gaertner, S., Dovidio, J.F., Anastasio, P.A., Bachevan, B.A. and Rust, M.C. (1993) The common ingroup identity model: recategorization and the reduction of intergroup bias, pp. 1–26 in W. Stroebe and M. Hewstone (eds), *European Review of Social Psychology,* 4. Chichester: John Wiley.

Gaertner, S.L., Rust, M., Dovidio, J.F., Bachman, B. and Anastasio, P. (in press) The contact hypothesis: the role of a common ingroup identity on reducing intergroup bias. *Small Group Research.*

Gerard, H.B. and Miller, N. (1975) *School Desegregation.* New York: Plenum.

Gilbert, D.T. and Hixon, J.G. (1991) The trouble of thinking: activation and application of stereotypic beliefs. *Journal of Personality and Social Psychology,* *60,* 509–517.

Gilbert, G.M. (1951) Stereotype persistence and change among college students. *Journal of Abnormal and Social Psychology, 46,* 245–254.

Giles, H. (ed.) (1977) *Language, Ethnicity and Intergroup Relations.* London: Academic Press.

Giles, H. and Johnson, P. (1981) The role of language in ethnic group relations. In J.C. Turner and H. Giles (eds), *Intergroup Behaviour,* Oxford: Basil Blackwell.

Glasser, I. (1988) Affirmative action and the legacy of racial injustice. In P.A. Katz and D.A. Taylor (eds) *Eliminating Racism,* New York: Plenum.

Glick, P. and Fiske, S.T. (1994) The ambivalent sexism inventory: differentiating hostile and benevolent sexism. Unpublished MS: Lawrence University, Kansas.

Glick, P., Zion, C. and Nelson, C. (1988) What mediates sex discrimination in hiring decisions? *Journal of Personality and Social Psychology, 55,* 178–186.

Gluckman, M. (1956) *Custom and Conflict in Africa.* Oxford: Basil Blackwell.

Goodman, A. and Webb, S. (1994) *For Richer, For Poorer: The changing distribution of income in the United Kingdom 1961–1991.* London: Institute for Fiscal Studies.

Goodman, M.E. (1952) *Race Awareness in Young Children.* New York: Collier Macmillan (1964 edition).

Gosh, E.S.K., Kumar, R. and Tripathi, R.C. (1992) The communal cauldron: relations between Hindus and Muslims in India and their reactions to norm violations. In R. de Ridder and R.C. Tripathi (eds), *Norm Violation and Intergroup Attitudes,* Oxford: Clarendon Press.

Grant, P.R. (1992) Ethnocentrism between groups of unequal power in response to perceived threat to social identity and valued resources. *Canadian Journal of Behavioural Science, 24,* 348–370.

Grant, P.R. (1993) Reactions to intergroup similarity: examination of the similarity-differentiation and the similarity-attraction hypotheses. *Canadian Journal of Behavioural Science, 25,* 28–44.

Grant, P.R. and Brown, R. (in press) From ethnocentrism to collective protest: responses to relative deprivation and threats to social identity. *Social Psychology Quarterly.*

Grant, P.R. and Holmes, J.G. (1981) The integration of implicit personality theory schemes and stereotypic images. *Social Psychology Quarterly, 44,* 107–115.

Guimond, S. and Dubé-Simard, L. (1983) Relative deprivation theory and the Quebec nationalist movement: the cognition–emotion distinction and the personal-group deprivation issue. *Journal of Personality and Social Psychology, 44,* 526–535.

Gurr, T.R. (1970) *Why Men Rebel.* Princeton, NJ: Princeton University Press.

Gurwitz, S.B. and Dodge, K.A. (1977) Effects of confirmations and dis-confirmations on stereotype-based attributions. *Journal of Personality and Social Psychology, 35*, 495–500.

Haeger, G. (1993) Social and temporal comparisons in a European context. Unpubl. MSc. thesis: University of Kent.

Hagendoorn, L. and Henke, R. (1991) The effect of multiple category membership on intergroup evaluations in a North-Indian context: class, caste, and religion. *British Journal of Social Psychology, 30*, 247–260.

Hamilton, D.L. (ed.) (1981) *Cognitive Processes in Stereotyping and Intergroup Behaviour.* New York: Lawrence Erlbaum.

Hamilton, D.L. and Bishop, G.D. (1976) Attitudinal and behavioral effects of initial integration of white suburban neighbourhoods. *Journal of Social Issues, 32*, 47–67.

Hamilton, D.L. and Gifford, R.K. (1976) Illusory correlation in interpersonal perception: a cognitive basis of stereotypic judgements. *Journal of Experimental Social Psychology, 12*, 392–407.

Hamilton, D.L. and Rose, T.L. (1980) Illusory correlation and the maintenance of stereotypic beliefs. *Journal of Personality & Social Psychology, 39*, 832–845.

Hamilton, D.L. and Sherman, S.J. (1989) Illusory correlations: implications for stereotype theory and research. In D. Bar-Tal, C.F. Graumann, A.W. Kruglanski and W. Stroebe (eds), *Stereotypes and Prejudice: Changing conceptions*, New York: Springer.

Hanson, D.J. and Blohm, E.R. (1974) Authoritarianism and attitudes towards mental patients. *International Behavioural Scientist, 6*, 57–60.

Harding, J. and Hogrefe, R. (1952) Attitudes of white department store employees toward Negro co-workers. *Journal of Social Issues, 8*, 18–28.

Harkness, S. and Super, C.M. (1985) The cultural context of gender segregation in children's peer groups. *Child Development, 56*, 219–224.

Harris, M.J., Milich, R., Corbitt, E.M., Hoover, D.W. and Brady, M. (1992) Self-fulfilling effects of stigmatizing information on children's social interactions. *Journal of Personality and Social Psychology, 63*, 41–50.

Haslam, S.A., Turner, J.C., Oakes, P.J. and McGarty, C. (1992) Context-dependent variation in social stereotyping. I: The effects of intergroup relations as mediated by social change and frame of reference. *European Journal of Social Psychology, 22*, 3–20.

Hayden-Thomson, L., Rubin, K.H. and Hymel, S. (1987) Sex preferences in sociometric choices. *Developmental Psychology, 23*, 558–562.

Heaven, P.C.L. (1983) Individual versus intergroup explanations of prejudice among Afrikaners. *Journal of Social Psychology, 121*, 201–210.

Heinmann, W., Pellander, F., Vogelbusch, A. and Wojtek, B. (1981) Meeting a deviant person: subjective norms and affective reactions. *European Journal of Social Psychology, 11*, 1–25.

Hendrick, C., Bixenstine, V.E. and Hawkins, G. (1971) Race vs. belief similarity as determinants of attraction: a search for a fair test. *Journal of Personality and Social Psychology*, *17*, 250–258.

Hendricks, M. and Bootzin, R. (1976) Race and sex as stimuli for negative affect and physical avoidance. *Journal of Social Psychology*, *98*, 111–120.

Hepworth, J.T. and West, S.G. (1988) Lynchings and the economy: a time-series reanalysis of Hoyland and Sears (1940). *Journal of Personality and Social Psychology*, *55*, 239–247.

Hewstone, M. (1989) *Causal Attribution*. Oxford: Basil Blackwell.

Hewstone, M. and Brown, R.J. (1986) Contact is not enough: an intergroup perspective on the contact hypothesis. In M. Hewstone and R. Brown (eds), *Contact and Conflict in Intergroup Encounters*, Oxford: Basil Blackwell.

Hewstone, M. and Ward, C. (1985) Ethnocentrism and causal attribution in Southeast Asia. *Journal of Personality and Social Psychology*, *48*, 614–623.

Hewstone, M., Johnston, L. and Aird, P. (1992) Cognitive models of stereotype change. 2: Perceptions of homogeneous and heterogeneous groups. *European Journal of Social Psychology*, *22*, 235–250.

Hewstone, M., Islam, M.R. and Judd, C.M. (1993) Models of crossed categorization and intergroup relations. *Journal of Personality and Social Psychology*, *64*, 779–793.

Higgins, E.T. (1989) Knowledge accessibility and activation: subjectivity and suffering from unconscious sources. In J.S. Uleman and J.A. Bargh (eds), *Unintended Thought*, New York: Guildford.

Himmelweit, H.T., Oppenheim, A.N. and Vince, P. (1958) *Television and the Child: An empirical study of the effect of television on the young*. Oxford: Oxford University Press.

Hinkle, S. and Brown, R. (1990) Intergroup comparisons and social identity: some links and lacunae, pp. 48–70 in D. Abrams and M. Hogg (eds), *Social Identity Theory: Constructive and critical advances*, Hemel Hempstead: Harvester Wheatsheaf.

Hinkle, S., Brown, R. and Ely, P.G. (1992) Social identity processes: some limitations and limiting conditions. *Revista de Psicologia social, monografico*, 99–111.

Hoge, D.R. and Carroll, J.W. (1973) Religiosity and prejudice in Northern and Southern churches. *Journal of Scientific Study of Religion*, *12*, 181–197.

Hogg, M. and Abrams, D. (1990) Social motivation, self-esteem and social identity, pp. 28–47 in D. Abrams and M. Hogg (eds), *Social Identity Theory: Constructive and critical advances*, Hemel Hempstead: Harvester Wheatsheaf.

Hogg, M.A. and Sunderland, J. (1991) Self-esteem and intergroup discrimination in the minimal group paradigm. *British Journal of Social Psychology*, *30*, 51–62.

Hogg, M.A. and Turner, C. (1987) Intergroup behaviour, self stereotyping and the salience of social categories. *British Journal of Social Psychology, 26,* 325–340.

Horowitz, E.L. (1936) The development of attitude towards the Negro. *Archives of Psychology, 194,* 5–47.

Horowitz, E.L. and Horowitz, R.E. (1938) Development of social attitudes in children. *Sociometry, 1,* 301–338.

Horwitz, M. and Rabbie, J.M. (1982) Individuality and membership in the intergroup system, pp. 241–274 in H. Tajfel (ed.), *Social Identity and Intergroup Relations,* Cambridge: Cambridge University Press.

Hovland, C. and Sears, R.R. (1940) Minor studies in aggression. VI: Correlation of lynchings with economic indices. *Journal of Psychology, 9,* 301–310.

Howard, J.W. and Rothbart, M. (1980) Social categorization and memory for ingroup and outgroup behaviour. *Journal of Personality and Social Psychology, 38,* 301–310.

Hraba, J. and Grant, G. (1970) Black is beautiful: a re-examination of racial preference and identification. *Journal of Personality and Social Psychology, 16,* 398–402.

Hunter, J.A., Stringer, M. and Watson, R.P. (1991) Intergroup violence and intergroup attributions. *British Journal of Social Psychology, 30,* 261–266.

Hyman, H.H. and Sheatsley, P.B. (1954) 'The Authoritarian Personality': a methodological critique. In R. Christie and M. Jahoda (eds), *Studies in the Scope and Method of 'The Authoritarian Personality',* Glencoe, Ill.: Free Press.

Insko, C.A., Nacoste, R.W. and Moe, J.L. (1983) Belief congruence and racial discrimination: review of the evidence and critical evaluation. *European Journal of Social Psychology, 13,* 153–174.

Islam, M.R. and Hewstone, M. (1993) Intergroup attributions and affective consequences in majority and minority groups. *Journal of Personality and Social Psychology, 64,* 936–950.

Islam, M.R. and Hewstone, M. (1993) Dimensions of contact as predictors of intergroup anxiety, perceived outgroup variability and outgroup attitude: an integrative model. *Personality and Social Psychology Bulletin, 19,* 700–710.

Jacklin, C.N. and Maccoby, E.E. (1978) Social behavior at thirty-three months in same-sex and mixed-sex dyads. *Child Development, 49,* 557–569.

Jacobson, C.K. (1985) Resistance to affirmative action: self interest or racism? *Journal of Conflict Resolution, 29,* 306–329.

Jahoda, G. (1963) The development of children's ideas about country and nationality. *British Journal of Educational Psychology, 33,* 47–60.

Jahoda, G., Thomson, S.S. and Bhatt, S. (1972) Ethnic identity and preferences among Asian immigrant children in Glasgow: a replicated study. *European Journal of Social Psychology, 2,* 19–32.

Johnson, D.W. and Johnson, R.T. (1975) *Learning Together and Alone*. Englewood Cliffs, N.J.: Prentice-Hall.

Johnson, D.W., Maruyama, G., Johnson, R., Nelson, D. and Skon, L. (1981) Effects of co-operative, competitive and individualistic goal structures on achievement: a meta-analysis. *Psychological Bulletin, 89*, 47–62.

Johnson, R., Rynders, J., Johnson, D.W., Schmidt, B. and Haider, S. (1979) Interaction between handicapped and nonhandicapped teenagers as a function of situational goal structuring: implications for mainstreaming. *American Educational Research Journal, 16*, 161–167.

Johnson, D.W., Johnson, R.T. and Maruyama, G. (1984) Goal interdependence and interpersonal attraction in heterogeneous classrooms: a meta-analysis. In N. Miller and M.B. Brewer (eds), *Groups in Contact: the psychology of desegregation*, Orlando, Fla.: Academic Press.

Johnston, J. and Ettema, J.S. (1982) *Positive Images: Breaking stereotypes with children's television*. Beverly Hills, Cal.: Sage.

Johnston, L. and Hewstone, M. (1992) Cognitive models of stereotype change. 3: Subtyping and the perceived typicality of disconfirming group members. *Journal of Experimental Social Psychology, 28*, 360–386.

Joly, S., Tougas, F. and Brown, R. (1993) L'effet de la catégorisation croisée sur la discrimination intergroupe en milieu universitaire. Unpubl. MS, Université d'Ottawa.

Jones, E.E., Wood, G.C. and Quattrone, G.A. (1981) Perceived variability of personal characteristics in ingroups and outgroups: the role of knowledge and evaluation. *Journal of Personality and Social Psychology, 7*, 523–528.

Jones, J.M. (1972) *Prejudice and Racism*. Reading, Mass.: Addison-Wesley.

Judd, C.M. and Park, B. (1993) Definition and assessment of accuracy in social stereotypes. *Psychological Review, 100*, 109–128.

Jussim, L. (1989) Teacher expectations: self-fulfilling prophecies, perceptual biases, and accuracy. *Journal of Personality and Social Psychology, 57*, 469–480.

Kahn, W. and Crosby, F. (1985) Change and stasis: discriminating between attitudes and discriminating behaviour. In L. Larwood, B.A. Gutek and A.H. Stromberg (eds), *Women and Work, an Annual Review*, vol. 1, 215–238. Beverly Hills, Cal.: Sage.

Kanter, R.M. (1977) Some effects of proportions on group life: skewed sex ratios and responses to token women. *American Journal of Sociology, 82*, 965–990.

Karlins, M., Coffman, T.L. and Walters, G. (1969) On the fading of social stereotypes: studies in three generations of college students. *Journal of Personality and Social Psychology, 13*, 1–16.

Katz, D. and Braly, K. (1933) Racial stereotypes of one hundred college students. *Journal of Abnormal and Social Psychology, 28*, 280–290.

Katz, P.A. (1983) Developmental foundations of gender and racial attitudes. In

R. Leahy (ed.), *The Child's Construction of Social Inequality*, New York: Academic Press.

Katz, P.A. and Zalk, S.R. (1974) Doll preferences: an index of racial attitudes? *Journal of Educational Psychology, 66,* 663–668.

Kedem, P., Bihu, A. and Cohen, Z. (1987) Dogmatism, ideology, and right-wing radical activity. *Political Psychology, 8,* 35–47.

Kelly, C. (1988) Intergroup differentiation in a political context. *British Journal of Social Psychology, 27,* 314–322.

Kelly, C. (1989) Political identity and perceived intragroup homogeneity. *British Journal of Social Psychology, 28,* 239–250.

Kelman, H.C. (1961) Processes of opinion change. *Public Opinion Quarterly, 25,* 57–78.

Kinder, D.R. and Sears, D.O. (1981) Prejudice and politics: symbolic racism versus racial threats to the good life. *Journal of Personality and Social Psychology, 40,* 414–431.

Klandermans, B. (1984) Mobilization and participation: social psychological expansions of resource mobilization theory. *American Sociological Review, 49,* 583–600.

Kleck, R., Ono, H. and Hastorf, A.H. (1966) The effects of physical deviance upon face to face interaction. *Human Relations, 19,* 425–436.

Kleinpenning, G. and Hagendoorn, L. (1993) Forms of racism and the cumulative dimension of ethnic attitudes. *Social Psychology Quarterly, 56,* 21–36.

Kluegel, J.R. and Smith, E.R. (1982) Whites' beliefs about Blacks' opportunity. *American Sociological Review, 47,* 518–532.

Kluegel, J.R. and Smith, E.R. (1983) Affirmative action attitudes: effects of self-interest, racial affect and stratification on whites' views. *Social Forces, 61,* 797–824.

Kohlberg, L. (1966) A cognitive developmental analysis of children's sex-role concepts and attitudes. In E. Maccoby (ed.), *The Development of Sex Differences*, Stanford, Cal.: Stanford University Press.

Koomen, W. and Fränkel, E.G. (1992) Effects of experienced discrimination and different forms of relative deprivation among Surinamese, a Dutch ethnic minority group. *Journal of Community and Applied Social Psychology, 2,* 63–71.

Kovel, J. (1970) *White Racism: A psychohistory.* London: Allen Lane.

Krueger, J. and Clement, R.W. (1994) Memory-based judgements about multiple categories: a revision and extension of Tajfel's Accentuation Theory. *Journal of Personality and Social Psychology, 67,* 35–47.

Krueger, J. and Rothbart, M. (1988) Use of categorical and individuating information in making inferences about personality. *Journal of Personality and Social Psychology, 55,* 187–195.

La Freniere, P., Strayer, F.F. and Gauthier, R. (1984) The emergence of same-sex affiliative preferences among pre-school peers: a developmental/ ethological perspective. *Child Development,* *55,* 1958–1965.

Lalonde, R.N. and Gardner, R.C. (1989) An intergroup perspective on stereotype organization and processing. *British Journal of Social Psychology,* *28,* 289–303.

Lambert, W.E. and Klineberg, O. (1967) *Children's Views of Foreign Peoples.* New York: Appleton Century Crofts.

Langer, E.J., Fiske, S., Taylor, S.E. and Chanowitz, B. (1976) Stigma, staring, and discomfort: a novel-stimulus hypothesis. *Journal of Experimental Social Psychology,* *12,* 451–463.

Langlois, J.H., Roggman, L.A., Casey, R.J., Ritter, J.M., Rieser-Donner, L.A. and Jenkins, V.Y. (1987) Infant preferences for attractive faces: rudiments of a stereotype. *Developmental Psychology,* *23,* 363–369.

Langlois, J.H., Ritter, J.M., Roggman, L.A. and Vaugh, L.S. (1991) Facial diversity and infant preference for attractive faces. *Developmental Psychology,* *27,* 79–84.

Latane, B. and Darley, J.M. (1970) *The Unresponsive Bystander: Why doen't he help?* New York: Appleton-Crofts.

Lee, R.E. III and Warr, P.B. (1969) The development and standardization of a balanced F-scale. *Journal of General Psychology,* *18,* 109–129.

Lemaine, G. (1966) Inegalité, comparaison et incomparabilité: esquisse d'une théorie de l'originalité sociale. *Bulletin de Psychologie,* *20,* 1–9.

Lemyre, L. and Smith, P.M. (1985) Intergroup discrimination and self esteem in the minimal group paradigm. *Journal of Personality and Social Psychology,* *49,* 660–670.

Lepore, L. and Brown, R. (1994a) Category activation and stereotype accessibility: is prejudice inevitable? Unpublished MS, University of Kent.

Lepore, L. and Brown, R. (1994b) Stereotype accessibility and automatic cognitive processes. Paper presented to the III European Social Cognition Meeting, Vendôme, France.

LeVine, R.A. and Campbell, D.T. (1972) *Ethnocentrism: Theories of conflict, ethnic attitudes and group behaviour.* New York: John Wiley.

Levinson, D.J. and Schermerhorn, R.A. (1951) Emotional-attitudinal effects of an intergroup workshop on its members. *Journal of Psychology,* *31,* 243–256.

Levy, B. and Langer, E. (1994) Aging free from negative stereotypes: successful memory in China and among the American deaf. *Journal of Personality and Social Psychology,* *66,* 989–997.

Leyens, J.-P. and Yzerbyt, V.Y. (1992) The ingroup overexclusion effect: impact of variance and confirmation on stereotypical information search. *European Journal of Social Psychology,* *22,* 549–569.

Leyens, J.-P., Yzerbyt, V.Y. and Schadron, G. (1992) The social judgeability approach to stereotypes. In W. Stroebe and M. Hewstone (eds), *European Review of Social Psychology*, vol. 3. Chichester: John Wiley.

Leyons, J.-P., Yzerbyt, V.Y. and Schadron, G. (1994) *Stereotypes and Social Cognition*, London: Sage.

Linville, P.W., Fischer, F.W. and Salovey, P. (1989) Perceived distributions of characteristics of ingroup and outgroup members: empirical evidence and a computer simulation. *Journal of Personality and Social Psychology, 42,* 193–211.

Lippmann, W. (1922) *Public Opinion*. New York: Harcourt Brace.

Locke, V., Macleod, C. and Walker, I. (1994) Automatic and controlled activation of stereotypes: individual differences associated with prejudice. *British Journal of Social Psychology, 33,* 29–46.

Locksley, A., Borgida, E., Brekke, N. and Hepburn, C. (1980) Sex stereotypes and social judgment. *Journal of Personality and Social Psychology, 39,* 821–831.

Locksley, A., Hepburn, C. and Ortiz, V. (1982) On the effects of social stereotypes on judgments of individuals: a comment on Grant and Holmes' 'The integration of implicit personality theory schemes and stereotypic images'. *Social Psychology Quarterly, 45,* 270–273.

Luhtanen, R. and Crocker, J. (1991) Self-esteem and intergroup comparisons: towards a theory of collective self-esteem. In J. Suls and T.A. Wills (eds), *Social Comparison: Contemporary theory and research*, Hillsdale, NJ: Lawrence Erlbaum.

Maass, A., Salvi, D., Arcuri, L. and Swim, G.R. (1989) Language use in intergroup contexts: the linguistic intergroup bias. *Journal of Personality and Social Psychology, 57,* 981–993.

Maass, A., Corvino, P. and Arcuri, L. (in press) Linguistic intergroup bias and the mass media. *Revue de Psychologie Sociale.*

Maccoby, E.E. (1980) *Social Development*. New York: Harcourt Brace Jovanovich.

Maccoby, E. (1988) Gender as a social category. *Developmental Psychology, 24,* 755–765.

Maccoby, E.E. and Jacklin, C.N. (1974) *The Psychology of Sex Differences*. Stanford, Cal.: Stanford University Press.

Maccoby, E. and Jacklin, C. (1987) Gender segregation in childhood. *Advances in Child Development and Behaviour, 20,* 239–287.

Mackie, D.M. and Hamilton, D.L. (eds) (1993) *Affect, Cognition and Stereotyping: Interactive processes in group perception*. San Diego: Academic Press.

Mackie, D.M., Hamilton, D.L., Schroth, H.H., Carlisle, L.J., Gersho, B.F., Meneses, L.M., Nedler, B.F. and Reichel, L.D. (1989) The effects of induced mood on expectancy-based illusory correlations. *Journal of Experimental Social Psychology, 25,* 524–544.

Mackie, D.M., Allison, S.T., Worth, L.T. and Asuncion, A.G. (1992) The generalization of outcome-biased counter-stereotypic inferences. *Journal of Experimental Social Psychology, 28*, 43–64.

Mackie, D.M., Allison, S.T., Worth, L.T. and Asuncion, A.G. (in press) The impact of outcome biases on counter-stereotypic inferences about groups. *Personality and Social Psychology Bulletin.*

Macrae, C.N. and Shepherd, J.W. (1989) Stereotypes and social judgements. *British Journal of Social Psychology, 28*, 319–325.

Macrae, C.N. and Shepherd, J.W. (1991) Categorical effects on attributional inferences: a response-time analysis. *British Journal of Social Psychology, 30*, 235–245.

Macrae, C.N., Hewstone, M. and Griffiths, R.J. (1993a) Processing load and memory for stereotype-based information. *European Journal of Social Psychology, 23*, 77–87.

Macrae, C.N., Milne, A.B. and Bodenhausen, G.V. (1994a) Stereotypes as energy-saving devices: a peek inside the cognitive toolbox. *Journal of Personality and Social Psychology, 66*, 37–47.

Macrae, C.N., Stangor, C. and Milne, A.B. (1994b) Activating social stereotypes: a functional analysis. *Journal of Experimental Social Psychology, 30*, 370–389.

Major, B., Testa, M. and Bylsma, W.H. (1991) Responses to upward and downward social comparison: the impact of esteem-relevance and perceived control. In J. Suls and T.A. Wills (eds), *Social Comparison: Contemporary theory and research*, Hillsdale, N.J.: Lawrence Erlbaum.

Maras, P.F. (1993) The integration of children with disabilities into the mainstream. Unpubl. PhD thesis, University of Kent.

Maras, P. and Brown, R. (1994) Effects of contact on children's attitudes toward disability: a longitudinal study. Unpubl. MS, University of Kent.

Marcus-Newhall, A., Miller, N., Holtz, R. and Brewer, M.B. (1993) Cross-cutting category membership with role assignment: a means of reducing intergroup bias. *British Journal of Social Psychology, 32*, 125–146.

Martin, J., Brickman, P. and Murray, A. (1984) Moral outrage and pragmatism: explanations for collective action. *Journal of Experimental Social Psychology, 20*, 484–496.

Martin, W., Eaves, L.J., Heath, A.C., Jardine, R., Feingold, L.M. and Eysenck, H.J. (1986) Transmission of social attitudes. *Proceedings of National Academy of Science, 83*, 4364–4368.

Maykovich, M.K. (1975) Correlates of racial prejudice. *Journal of Personality and Social Psychology, 32*, 1014–1020.

McCarthy, J.D. and Zald, M.N. (1977) Resource mobilization and social movements: a partial theory. *American Journal of Sociology, 82*, 1212–1241.

McConahay, J.B. (1982) Self-interest versus racial attitudes as correlates of anti-busing attitudes in Louisville: is it the buses or the blacks? *Journal of Politics*, *44*, 692–720.

McConahay, J.B. (1983) Modern racism and modern discrimination: the effects of race, racial attitudes, and context on simulated hiring decisions. *Personality and Social Psychology Bulletin*, *9*, 551–558.

McConahay, J.B. (1986) Modern racism, ambivalence, and the modern racism scale. In J.F. Dovidio and S.L. Gaertner (eds), *Prejudice, Discrimination, and Racism*, New York: Academic Press.

McConahay, J.B., Hardee, B.B. and Batts, V. (1981) Has racism declined in America? It depends upon who is asking and what is asked. *Journal of Conflict Resolution*, *25*, 563–579.

McFarland, S.G., Agehev, V.S. and Abalakina-Paap, M.A. (1992) Authoritarianism in the former Soviet Union. *Journal of Personality and Social Psychology*, *63*, 1004–1010.

McGarty, C. and Penny, R.E.C. (1988) Categorization, accentuation and social judgement. *British Journal of Social Psychology*, *27*, 147–157.

McGarty, C., Haslam, S.A., Turner, J.C. and Oakes, P.J. (1993) Illusory correlation as accentuation of actual intercategory difference: evidence for the effect with minimal stimulus information. *European Journal of Social Psychology*, *23*, 391–410.

McGuire, W.J., McGuire, C.V., Child, P. and Fujioka, T. (1978) Salience of ethnicity in the spontaneous self-concept as a function of one's ethnic distinctiveness in the social environment. *Journal of Personality & Social Psychology*, *36*, 511–520.

McPhail, C. (1971) Civil disorder participation: a critical examination of recent research. *American Sociological Review*, *36*, 1058–1973.

McWhirter, L. (1983) Contact and conflict: the question of integrated education. *Irish Journal of Psychology*, *6*, 13–27.

Meloen, J.D., Hagendoorn, L., Raaijmakers, Q. and Visser, L. (1988) Authoritarianism and the revival of political racism: reassessments in the Netherlands of the reliability and validity of the concept of authoritarianism by Adorno et al. *Political Psychology*, *9*, 413–429.

Messick, D. and Mackie, D. (1989) Intergroup relations. *Annual Review of Psychology*, *40*, 45–51.

Miles, R. (1982) *Racism and Migrant Labour*. London: Routledge.

Miles, R. (1989) *Racism*. London: Routledge.

Miller, A. and Bolce, L. (1979) Reply to Crosby. *American Political Science Review*, *73*, 818–822.

Miller, A., Bolce, L. and Halligan, M. (1977) The J-curve theory and the Black urban riots: an empirical test of progressive relative deprivation theory. *American Political Science Review*, *71*, 964–982.

Miller, N. and Davidson-Podgorny, F. (1987) Theoretical models of intergroup relations and the use of cooperative teams as an intervention for desegregated settings. In C. Hendrick (ed.), *Group Processes and Intergroup*

Relations: Review of personality and Social psychology, vol. 9, Beverly Hills, CA: Sage.

Miller, N., Brewer, M.B. and Edwards, K. (1985) Cooperative interaction in desegregated settings: a laboratory analogue. *Journal of Social Issues, 41,* 63–79.

Miller, N.E. and Bugelski, R. (1948) Minor studies in aggression: the influence of frustrations imposed by the ingroup on attitudes toward outgroups. *Journal of Psychology, 25,* 437–442.

Milner, D. (1973) Racial identification and preference in Black British children. *European Journal of Social Psychology, 3,* 281–295.

Milner, D. (1983) *Children and Race: Ten years on,* 2nd edn. London: Ward Lock.

Minard, R.D. (1952) Race relationships in the Pocahontas coal field. *Journal of Social Issues, 8,* 29–44.

Mischel, W. (1966) A social learning view of sex differences in behavior. In E.E. Maccoby (ed.), *The Development of Sex Differences,* Stanford, Cal.: Stanford University Press.

Mischel, W. (1970) Sex typing and socialization. In P.H. Mussen (ed.), *Carmichael's Manual of Child Psychology,* vol. 2, New York: John Wiley.

Monteith, M. (1993) Self-regulation of prejudiced responses: implications for progress in prejudice-reduction efforts. *Journal of Personality and Social Psychology, 65,* 469–485.

Monteith, M., Devine, P.G. and Zuwerink, J.R. (1993) Self-directed versus other-directed affect as a consequence of prejudice-related discrepancies. *Journal of Personality and Social Psychology, 64,* 198–210.

Morgan, M. (1982) Television and adolescents' sex-role stereotypes: a longitudinal study. *Journal of Personality and Social Psychology, 43,* 947–955.

Morgan, N. (1988) *The Equality Game: Women in the Federal Public Service (1908–1987).* Ottawa: Canadian Advisory Council on the Status of Women.

Morland, J.K. (1969) Race awareness among American and Hong Kong Chinese children. *American Journal of Sociology, 75,* 360–374.

Mosher, D.L. and Scodel, A. (1960) Relationships between ethnocentrism in children and the ethnocentrism and authoritarian rearing practices of their mothers. *Child Development, 31,* 369–376.

Mullen, B. and Hu, L. (1987) Perceptions of ingroup and outgroup variability: a meta-analytic integration. *Basic and Applied Social Psychology, 10,* 233–252.

Mullen, B., Brown, R. and Smith, C. (1992) Ingroup bias as a function of salience, relevance, and status: an integration. *European Journal of Social Psychology, 22,* 103–122.

Mummendey, A., Simon, B., Dietze, C., Grünert, M., Haeger, G., Kessler, S., Lettgen, S. and Schäferhoff, S. (1992) Categorization is not enough:

intergroup discrimination in negative outcome allocations. *Journal of Experimental Social Psychology, 28,* 125–144.

Myrdal, G. (1944) *An American Dilemma: The negro problem and modern democracy.* New York: Harper and Row.

Nagata, D. and Crosby, F. (1991) Comparisons, justice and the internment of Japanese-Americans. In J. Suls and T.A. Wills (eds), *Social Comparison: Contemporary theory and research,* Hillsdale, NJ: Lawrence Erlbaum.

Nakanishi, D.T. (1988) Seeking convergence in race relations research: Japanese-Americans and the resurrection of the internment. In P.A. Katz and D. Taylor (eds), *Eliminating Racism: Profiles in controversy,* New York: Plenum.

Nelson, T.E., Biernat, M. and Manis, M. (1990) Everyday base rates (sex stereotypes): potent and resilient. *Journal of Personality and Social Psychology, 59,* 664–675.

Neuberg, S.L. and Fiske, S.T. (1987) Motivational influences on impression formation: outcome dependency, accuracy-driven attention, and individuating processes. *Journal of Personality and Social Psychology, 53,* 431–444.

Ng, S.H. and Cram, F. (1988) Intergroup bias by defensive and offensive groups in majority and minority conditions. *Journal of Personality and Social Psychology, 55,* 749–757.

Oakes, P.J. (1994) The effects of fit versus novelty on the salience of social categories: a response to Biernat and Vescio (1993), *Journal of Experimental Social Psychology, 30,* 390–398.

Oakes, P.J., Haslam, A. and Turner, J.C. (1994) *Stereotyping and Social Reality.* Oxford: Blackwell Publishers.

Oakes, P.J. and Turner, J.C. (1980) Social categorization and intergroup behaviour: does minimal intergroup discrimination make social identity more positive? *European Journal of Social Psychology, 10,* 295–302.

Oakes, P.J. and Turner, J.C. (1986) Distinctiveness and the salience of social category membership: is there an automatic perceptual bias towards novelty? *European Journal of Social Psychology, 16,* 325–344.

Orpen, C. (1970) Authoritarianism in an 'authoritarian' culture: the case of Afrikaans-speaking South Africa. *Journal of Social Psychology, 81,* 119–120.

Padgett, V.R. and Jorgenson, D.O. (1982) Superstition and economic threat: Germany 1918–1940. *Personality and Social Psychology Bulletin, 8,* 736–741.

Park, B., Judd, C.M. and Ryan, C.S. (1991) Social categorization and the representation of variability information, pp. 211–245 in W. Stroebe and M. Hewstone (eds), *European Review of Social Psychology,* vol. 2, Chichester: John Wiley.

Pendry, L.F. and Macrae, C.N. (1994) Stereotypes and mental life: the case of the motivated but thwarted tactician. *Journal of Experimental Social Psychology*, *30*, 303–325.

Perdue, C.W., Dovidio, J.F., Gurtman, M.B. and Tyler, R.B. (1990) 'Us' and 'Them': social categorization and the process of intergroup bias. *Journal of Personality and Social Psychology*, *59*, 475–486.

Perlmutter, H.V. (1954) Some characteristics of the xenophilic personality. *Journal of Psychology*, *38*, 291–300.

Perlmutter, H.V. (1956) Correlates of two types of xenophilic orientation. *Journal of Abnormal and Social Psychology*, *52*, 130–135.

Pettigrew, T.F. (1958) Personality and sociocultural factors in intergroup attitudes: a cross-national comparison. *Journal of Conflict Resolution*, *2*, 29–42.

Pettigrew, T.F. (1971) *Racially Separate or Together?* New York: McGraw-Hill.

Pettigrew, T.F. (1979) The ultimate attribution error: extending Allport's cognitive analysis of prejudice. *Personality and Social Psychology Bulletin*, *5*, 461–476.

Pettigrew, T.F. (1985) New patterns of racism: the different worlds of 1984 and 1964. *Rutgers Law Review*, *1*, 673–706.

Pettigrew, T.F. (1994) The deprovincialization hypothesis: generalized intergroup contact effects on prejudice. Unpublished MS, University of Santa Cruz.

Pettigrew, T.F. and Meertens, R.W. (1995) Subtle and blatant prejudice in Western Europe. *European Journal of Social Psychology*, *25*, 57–75.

Pettigrew, T.F., Allport, G.W. and Barnett, E.O. (1958) Binocular resolution and perception of race in South Africa. *British Journal of Psychology*, *49*, 265–278.

Piaget, J. (1954) *The Construction of Reality in the Child.* New York: Basic Books.

Piaget, J. and Weil, A.M. (1951) The development in children of the idea of the homeland and of relations to other countries. *International Social Science Journal*, *3*, 361–378.

Pilger, J. (1989) *A Secret Country.* London: Vantage.

Plomin, R. and Daniels, D. (1987) Why are children in the same family so different from one another? *Behavioural and Brain Sciences*, *10*, 1–15.

Popper, K. (1963) *Conjectures and Refutations: The growth of scientific knowledge.* London: Routledge and Kegan Paul.

Porter, J.D.R. (1971) *Black Child, White Child: The development of racial attitudes.* Cambridge, Mass.: Harvard University Press.

Powlishta, K.K., Serbin, L.A., Doyle, A.-B. and White, D.R. (1994) Gender, ethnic and body type biases: the generality of prejudice in childhood. *Developmental Psychology*, *30*, 526–536.

Quanty, M.B., Keats, J.A. and Harkins, S.G. (1975) Prejudice and criteria for identification of ethnic photographs. *Journal of Personality and Social Psychology*, *32*, 449–454.

Quattrone, G.A. (1986) On the perception of a group's variability. In S. Worchel and W. Austin (eds), *Social Psychology of Intergroup Relations*, Chicago: Nelson.

Rabbie, J.M. and Horwitz, M. (1969) Arousal of ingroup–outgroup bias by a chance win or loss. *Journal of Personality and Social Psychology*, 13, 269–277.

Redpath, R. and Harvey, B. (1992) *Young People's Intentions to Enter Higher Education*. London: HMSO.

Reicher, S.D. (1986) Contact, action and racialization: some British evidence. In M. Hewstone and R.J. Brown (eds), *Groups in Contact and Conflict*, London: Basil Blackwell.

Repetti, R.L. (1984) Determinants of children's sex-stereotyping: parental sex-role traits and television viewing. *Personality and Social Psychology Bulletin*, 10, 457–468.

Rex, J. (1973) *Race, Colonialism and the City*. London: Oxford University Press.

Richardson, S.A. and Green, A. (1971) When is black beautiful? Coloured and white children's reactions to skin colour. *British Journal of Educational Psychology*, 41, 62–69.

Roccas, R. and Schwartz, S.H. (1993) Effects of intergroup similarity on intergroup relations. *European Journal of Social Psychology*, 23, 581–595.

Rojahn, K. and Pettigrew, T.F. (1992) Memory for schema-relevant information: a meta-analytic resolution. *British Journal of Social Psychology*, 31, 81–109.

Rokeach, M. (1948) Generalized mental rigidity as a factor in ethnocentrism. *Journal of Abnormal and Social Psychology*, 43, 259–278.

Rokeach, M. (1956) Political and religious dogmatism: an alternate to the authoritarian personality. *Psychological Monographs*, 70, no. 18 (whole number).

Rokeach, M. (1960) *The Open and Closed Mind*. New York: Basic Books.

Rokeach, M. (1973) *The Nature of Human Values*. New York: Free Press.

Rokeach, M. and Hanley, C. (1956) Eysenck's tender-minded dimension: a critique. *Psychological Bulletin*, 53, 169–176.

Rokeach, M. and Mezei, L. (1966) Race and shared belief as factors in social choice. *Science*, 151, 167–172.

Rokeach, M., Smith, P.W. and Evans, R.I. (1960) Two kinds of prejudice or one? In M. Rokeach, *Open and Closed Mind*, New York: Basic Books.

Rombough, S. and Ventimiglia, J.C. (1981) Sexism: a tri-dimensional phenomenon. *Sex Roles*, 7, 747–755.

Rosch, E. (1978) Principles of categorization. In E. Rosch and B. Lloyd (eds), *Cognition and Categorization*, Hillsdale, N.J.: Lawrence Erlbaum.

Rosenberg, M. and Simmons, R.G. (1972) *Black and White Self-esteem: The urban school child*. Washington, D.C.: American Sociological Association.

Rosenthal, R. (1966) *Experimenter Effects in Behavioral Research.* New York: Appleton.

Rosenthal, R. and Jacobson, L. (1968) *Pygmalion in the Classroom: Teacher expectations and student intellectual development.* New York: Holt, Rinehart, and Winston.

Ross, L.D. (1977) The intuitive psychologist and his shortcomings: distortions in the attribution process. In L. Berkowitz (ed.), *Advances in Experimental Social Psychology,* vol. 10. New York: Academic Press.

Rothbart, M. (1981) Memory processes and social beliefs. In D.L. Hamilton (ed.), *Cognitive Processes in Stereotyping and Intergroup Behavior,* Hillsdale, NJ: Lawrence Erlbaum.

Rothbart, M. and John, O.P. (1985) Social categorization and behavioural episodes: a cognitive analysis of the effects of intergroup contact. *Journal of Social Issues,* 41, 81–104.

Rothbart, M. and Park, B. (1986) On the confirmability and disconfirmability of trait concepts. *Journal of Personality and Social Psychology,* 50, 131–142.

Ruble, D., Boggiano, A., Feldman, N. and Loebl, J. (1980) A developmental analysis of the role of social comparison in self-evaluation. *Developmental Psychology,* 12, 192–197.

Runciman, W.G. (1966) *Relative Deprivation and Social Justice.* London: Routledge and Kegan Paul.

Ryen, A.H. and Kahn, A. (1975) Effects of intergroup orientation on group attitudes and proxemic behaviour. *Journal of Personality and Social Psychology,* 31, 302–310.

Sachdev, I. and Bourhis, R. (1987) Status differentials and intergroup behaviour. *European Journal of Social Psychology,* 17, 277–293.

Sachdev, I. and Bourhis, R.Y. (1991) Power and status differentials in minority and majority group relations. *European Journal of Social Psychology,* 21, 1–24.

Sagar, H.A. and Schofield, J.W. (1980) Racial and behavioural cues in Black and White children's perceptions of ambiguously aggressive acts. *Journal of Personality and Social Psychology,* 39, 590–598.

Sales, S.M. (1972) Economic threat as a determinant of conversion rates to authoritarian and non-authoritarian churches. *Journal of Personality and Social Psychology,* 23, 420–428.

Sales, S.M. (1973) Threat as a factor in authoritarianism: an analysis of archival data. *Journal of Personality and Social Psychology,* 28, 44–57.

Schaller, M. (1991) Social categorization and the formation of group stereotypes: further evidence for biased information processing in the perception of group-behaviour correlations. *European Journal of Social Psychology,* 21, 25–35.

Schaller, M. and Maass, A. (1989) Illusory correlation and social categorization:

toward an integration of motivational and cognitive factors in stereotype formation. *Journal of Personality and Social Psychology*, 56, 709–721.

Schofield, J.W. (1979) The impact of positively structured contact on intergroup behavior: does it last under adverse conditions? *Social Psychology Quarterly*, 42, 280–284.

Schofield, J.W. (1982) *Black and White in School: Trust, tension, or tolerance.* New York: Praeger.

Schofield, J.W. (1986) Black and White contact in desegregated schools. In M.R.C. Hewstone and R.J. Brown (eds), *Contact and Conflict in Intergroup Encounters*, Oxford: Basil Blackwell.

Schofield, J.W. (1991) School desegregation and intergroup relations: a review of the research. In G. Grant (ed.), *Review of Research in Education*, vol. 17, pp. 335–409. Washington, D.C.: American Educational Research Association.

Schofield, J.W. and Sager, H.A. (1977) Peer interaction patterns in an integrated middle school. *Sociometry*, 40, 130–138.

Seago, D.W. (1947) Stereotypes: before Pearl Harbor and after. *Journal of Social Psychology*, 23, 55–63.

Sears, D.O. (1988) Symbolic racism. In P.A. Katz and D.A. Taylor (eds), *Eliminating Racism*, New York: Plenum.

Sears, D.O. and Kinder, D.R. (1971) Racial tensions and voting in Los Angeles. In W.Z. Hirsch (ed.), *Los Angeles: Viability and prospects for metropolitan leadership*, New York: Praeger.

Secord, P.F. and Backman, C.W. (1974) *Social Psychology*, 2nd edition. Tokyo: McGraw-Hill.

Sears, R.R., Maccoby, E.E. and Levin, H. (1957) *Patterns of Child Rearing.* Stanford, Cal.: Stanford University Press.

Serbin, L.A., Tonick, I.J. and Sternglaz, S.H. (1978) Shaping cooperative cross-sex play. *Child Development*, 48, 924–929.

Sherif, M. (1936) *The Psychology of Social Norms.* New York: Harper and Row.

Sherif, M. (1966) *Group Conflict and Co-operation: Their social psychology.* London: Routledge and Kegan Paul.

Sherif, M., White, B.J. and Harvey, O.J. (1955) Status in experimentally produced groups. *American Journal of Sociology*, 60, 370–379.

Sherif, M. and Sherif, C.W. (1953) *Groups in Harmony and Tension: An integration of studies on intergroup relations.* New York: Octagon.

Sherif, M., Harvey, O.J., White, B.J., Hood, W.R. and Sherif, C.W. (1961) *Intergroup Conflict and Co-operation: The robber's cave experiment.* Norman, Okla: University of Oklahoma.

Shils, E.A. (1954) Authoritarianism: 'right' and 'left'. In R. Christie and M. Jahoda (eds), *Studies in the Scope and Method of 'The Authoritarian Personality'.* Glencoe, Ill.: Free Press.

Shore, T.H. (1992) Subtle gender bias in the assessment of managerial potential. *Sex Roles*, *27*, 499–515.

Siegel, A.E. and Siegel, S. (1957) Reference groups, membership groups, and attitude change. *Journal of Abnormal & Social Psychology*, *55*, 360–364.

Sigall, H. and Page, R. (1971) Current stereotypes: a little fading, a little faking. *Journal of Personality and Social Psychology*, *18*, 247–255.

Simon, B. (1992a) The perception of ingroup and outgroup homogeneity: re-introducing the intergroup context, pp. 1–30 in W. Stroebe and M. Hewstone (eds), *European Review of Social Psychology*, vol. 3, Chichester: John Wiley.

Simon, B. (1992b) Intragroup differentiation in terms of ingroup and outgroup attributes. *European Journal of Social Psychology*, *22*, 407–413.

Simon, B. and Brown, R.J. (1987) Perceived intragroup homogeneity in minority–majority contexts. *Journal of Personality and Social Psychology*, *53*, 703–711.

Simon, B., Glässner-Boyerl, B. and Stratenworth, I. (1991) Stereotyping and self stereotyping in a natural intergroup context: the case of heterosexual and homosexual men. *Social Psychology Quarterly*, *54*, 252–266.

Simpson, G.E. and Yinger, J.M. (1985) *Racial and Cultural Minorities: An analysis of prejudice and discrimination*. New York: Harper and Row.

Simpson, G.E. and Yinger, J.M. (1972) *Racial and Cultural Minorities: An analysis of prejudice and discrimination*. New York: Plenum.

Sinha, R.R. and Hassan, M.K. (1975) Some personality correlates of social prejudice. *Journal of Social and Economic Studies*, *3*, 225–231.

Skowronski, J.J., Carlston, D.E. and Isham, J.T. (1993) Implicit versus explicit impression formation: the differing effects of overt labelling and covert priming on memory and impressions. *Journal of Experimental Social Psychology*, *29*, 17–41.

Slaby, R.G. and Frey, K.S. (1975) Development of gender constancy and selective attention to same-sex models. *Child Development*, *46*, 849–856.

Slavin, R.E. (1979) Effects of biracial learning teams on cross-racial friendships. *Journal of Educational Psychology*, *71*, 381–387.

Slavin, R.E. (1983) *Co-operative Learning*. New York: Longman.

Small, M.Y. (1990) *Cognitive Development*. New York: Harcourt Brace Jovanovich.

Smith, A. (1994) Education and the conflict in Northern Ireland. In S. Dunn (ed.), *Facets of the Conflict in Northern Ireland*, London: Macmillan.

Sniderman, P.M. and Tetlock, P.E. (1986) Symbolic racism: problems of motive attribution in political analysis. *Journal of Social Issues*, *42*, 129–150.

Snyder, M. and Swann, W.B. (1978) Hypothesis-testing processes in social interaction. *Journal of Personality and Social Psychology*, *36*, 1202–1212.

Snyder, C.R., Lassegard, M.A. and Ford, C.E. (1986) Distancing after group success and failure: basking in reflected glory and cutting off reflected failure. *Journal of Personality and Social Psychology*, *51*, 382–388.

Snyder, M. (1981) On the self-perpetuating nature of social stereotypes. In D.L. Hamilton (ed.), *Cognitive Processes in Stereotyping and Intergroup Behaviour*, New York: Lawrence Erlbaum.

Snyder, M., Tanke, E.D. and Berscheid, E. (1977) Social perception and interpersonal behavior: on the self-fulfilling nature of social stereotypes. *Journal of Personality and Social Psychology, 35,* 656–666.

Spencer, M.B. (1983) Children's cultural values and parental rearing strategies. *Development Review, 3,* 351–370.

Spilerman, S. (1970) The causes of racial disturbance: a comparison of alternative explanations. *American Sociological Review, 35,* 627–649.

Stagner, R. and Congdon, C.S. (1955) Another failure to demonstrate displacement of aggression. *Journal of Abnormal & Social Psychology, 51,* 695–696.

Stangor, C. (1988) Stereotype accessibility and information processing. *Personality and Social Psychology Bulletin, 14,* 694–708.

Stangor, C. and Ford, T.E. (1992) Accuracy and expectancy-confirming processing orientations and the development of stereotypes and prejudice, pp. 57–89 in W. Stroebe and M. Hewstone (eds) *European Review of Social Psychology,* vol. 3, Chichester: John Wiley.

Stangor, C. and McMillan, D. (1992) Memory for expectancy-congruent and expectancy-incongruent information: a review of the social and social developmental literature. *Psychological Bulletin, 111, 42–61.*

Stangor, C., Lynch, L., Dunn, C. and Glass, B. (1992) Categorization of individuals on the basis of multiple social features. Journal of Personality and Social Psychology, 62, 207–218.

Stein, D.D., Hardyck, J.A. and Smith, M.B. (1965) Race and belief: an open and shut case. *Journal of Personality & Social Psychology, 1,* 281–289.

Steiner, I.D. (1986) Paradigms and groups. In L. Berkowitz (ed.), *Advances in Experimental Social Psychology,* vol. 19. London: Academic Press.

Stephan, W.G. (1977) Cognitive differentiation in intergroup perception. *Sociometry, 40,* 50–58.

Stephan, W.G. (1978) School desegregation: an evaluation of predictions made in Brown vs. Board of Education. *Psychological Bulletin, 85,* 217–238.

Stephan, W.G. and Rosenfield, D. (1978) Effects of desegregation on racial attitudes. *Journal of Personality and Social Psychology, 36,* 795–804.

Stephan, W.G. and Stephan, C.W. (1984) The role of ignorance in intergroup relations. In N. Miller and M.B. Brewer (eds), *Groups in Contact: The Psychology of Desegregation.* New York: Academic Press.

Stephan, W. and Stephan, C.W. (1985) Intergroup anxiety. *Journal of Social Issues, 41,* 157–175.

Stouffer, S.A., Suckman, E., DeVinney, L.C., Star, S.A. and Williams, R.M. (1949) *The American Soldier: Adjustment during army life,* vol. 1. Princeton, N.J.: Princeton University Press.

Stroessner, S.J., Hamilton, D.L. and Mackie, D.M. (1992) Affect and stereotyping: the effect of induced mood on distinctiveness-based illusory correlations. *Journal of Personality and Social Psychology, 62*, 564–576.

Struch, N. and Schwartz, S.H. (1989) Intergroup aggression: its predictors and distinctness from in-group bias. *Journal of Personality and Social Psychology, 56*, 364–373.

Suls, J. and Sanders, G.S. (1982) Self-evaluation through social comparison: a developmental analysis. In L. Wheeler (ed.), *Review of Personality and Social Psychology*, vol. 3. Beverly Hills, Cal.: Sage.

Suls, J. and Wills, T.A. (1991) (eds) *Social Comparison: Contemporary theory and research*. Hillsdale, N.J.: Lawrence Erlbaum.

Sumner, W. (1906) *Folkways*. New York: Ginn.

Sutton, C.D. and Moore, K.K. (1985) Probing opinions: executive women 20 years later. *Harvard Business Review, 63*, 43–66.

Swim, J.K., Aikin, K.J., Hall, W.S. and Hunter, B.A. (1995). Sexism and racism: old-fashioned and modern prejudices. *Journal of Personality and Social Psychology, 68*, 199–214.

Taft, R. (1954) Selective recall and memory distortion of favourable and unfavourable material. *Journal of Abnormal and Social Psychology, 49*, 23–28.

Tajfel, H. (1959) The anchoring effects of value in a scale of judgements. *British Journal of Psychology, 50*, 294–304.

Tajfel, H. (1969a) Cognitive aspects of prejudice. *Journal of Social Issues, 25*, 79–97.

Tajfel, H. (1969b) Social and cultural factors in perception. In G. Lindsey and E. Aronson (eds), *Handbook of Social Psychology*, vol. III, Reading, Mass.: Addison-Wesley.

Tajfel, H. (ed.) (1978) *Differentiation between Social Groups: Studies in the social psychology of intergroup relations*. London: Academic Press.

Tajfel, H. (1981a) *Human Groups and Social Categories*. Cambridge: Cambridge University Press.

Tajfel, H. (1981b) Social stereotypes and social groups. In J. Turner and H. Giles (eds), *Intergroup Behaviour*, Oxford: Basil Blackwell.

Tajfel, H. (1982) Social psychology of intergroup relations. *Annual Review of Psychology, 33*, 1–30.

Tajfel, H. and Turner, J. (1986) The social identity theory of intergroup behaviour, pp. 7–24 in S. Worchel and W.G. Austin (eds) *Psychology of Intergroup Relations*, Chicago: Nelson.

Tajfel, H. and Wilkes, A.L. (1963) Classification and quantitative judgment. *British Journal of Psychology, 54*, 101–114.

Tajfel, H., Flament, C., Billig, M.G. and Bundy, R.P. (1971) Social categorization and intergroup behaviour. *European Journal of Social Psychology, 1*, 149–178.

Tajfel, H., Jahoda, G., Noneth, C., Rim, Y. and Johnson, N. (1972) Devaluation by children of their own national or ethnic group: two case studies. *British Journal of Social and Clinical Psychology, 11*, 235–243.

Taylor, D.M. and Jaggi, V. (1974) Ethnocentrism and causal attribution in a South Indian context. *Journal of Cross-Cultural Psychology, 5*, 162–171.

Taylor, S.E. (1981) A categorization approach to stereotyping. In D.L. Hamilton (ed.) *Cognitive Processes in Stereotyping and Intergroup Behaviour.* N.J.: Lawrence Erlbaum.

Taylor, S.E. and Falcone, H.-T. (1982) Cognitive bases of stereotyping: the relationship between categorization and prejudice. *Personality and Social Psychology Bulletin, 8*, 426–436.

Taylor, S.E., Fiske, S.T., Etcoff, N.L. and Ruderman, A.J. (1978) Categorical and contextual bases of person memory and stereotyping. *Journal of Personality and Social Psychology, 36*, 778–793.

Tetlock, P.E. (1983) Cognitive style and political ideology. *Journal of Personality and Social Psychology, 45*, 118–126.

Tetlock, P.E. (1984) Cognitive style and political belief systems in the British House of Commons. *Journal of Personality and Social Psychology, 46*, 365–375.

Tetlock, P.E., Hannum, K.A. and Micholetti, P.M. (1984) Stability and change in the complexity of senatorial debate: testing the cognitive versus rhetorical style hypothesis. *Journal of Personality and Social Psychology, 46*, 979–990.

Thompson, S.K. (1975) Gender labels and early sex-role development. *Child Development, 46*, 339–347.

Thorndike, R.L. (1968) Review of Rosenthal and Jacobson's 'Pygmalion in the Classroom'. *American Educational Research Journal, 5*, 708–711.

Tougas, F., Brown, R., Beaton, A. and Joly, S. (in press) Neo-sexism: plus ça change, plus c'est pareil. *Personality and Social Psychology Bulletin.*

Triandis, H.C. and Davis, E.F. (1965) Race and belief as shared determinants of behavior intentions. *Journal of Personality and Social Psychology, 2*, 715–725.

Tripathi, R.C. and Srivastava, R. (1981) Relative deprivation and intergroup attitudes. *European Journal of Social Psychology, 11*, 313–318.

Turner, J.C. (1978a) Social categorization and social discrimination in the minimal group paradigm. In H. Tajfel (ed.), *Differentiation Between Social Groups: Studies in the social psychology of intergroup relations,* London: Academic Press.

Turner, J.C. (1978b) Social comparison, similarity and ingroup favouritism. In H. Tajfel (ed.), *Differentiation Between Social Groups: Studies in the social psychology of intergroup relations.* London: Academic Press.

Turner, J.C. (1980) Fairness or discrimination in intergroup behaviour? A reply to Braithwaite, Doyle and Lightbown. *European Journal of Social Psychology, 10*, 131–147.

Turner, J.C. (1981) The experimental social psychology of intergroup behaviour. In J.C. Turner and H. Giles (eds), *Intergroup Behaviour*, Oxford: Basil Blackwell.

Turner, J.C. (1982) Towards a cognitive redefinition of the social group. In H. Tajfel (ed.), *Social Identity and Intergroup Relations*, Cambridge: Cambridge University Press.

Turner, J.C. (1983) Some comments on 'The measurement of social orientations in the minimal group paradigm'. *European Journal of Social Psychology*, *13*, 351–367.

Turner, J.C. and Brown, R.J. (1978) Social status, cognitive alternatives, and intergroup relations. In H. Tajfel (ed.), *Differentiation between Social Groups: Studies in the social psychology of intergroup relations*, London: Academic Press.

Turner, J.C., Hogg, M.A., Oakes, P.J., Reicher, S.D. and Wethrell, M.S. (1987) *Rediscovering the Social Group: A self-categorization theory*. Oxford: Basil Blackwell.

Turner, M.A., Fix, M., Steyk, R.J., Read, V.M., Elmi, H.H.N., Zimmermann, W. and Edwards, J.G. (1991) *Opportunities Denied, Opportunities Diminished: Discrimination in hiring*, Washington, D.C.: The Urban Institute.

UCCA (1990) *Statistical Supplement*. London: Universities Central Council on Admissions.

US Department of Labor (1992) Trends in wage and salary inequality, 1967–1988. *Monthly Labor Review*, *115*, 23–39.

Van Avermaet, E. and McClintock, L.G. (1988) Intergroup fairness and bias in children. *European Journal of Social Psychology*, *18*, 407–427.

Vanbeselaere, N. (1991) The different effects of simple and crossed categorizations: a result of the category differentiation process or differential category salience, pp. 247–278 in W. Stroebe and M. Hewstone (eds) *European Review of Social Psychology*, vol. 2, Chichester: John Wiley.

van den Berghe, P.L. (1967) *Race and Racism*. New York: John Wiley.

Vanman, E.J., Paul, B.Y., Kaplan, D.L. and Miller, N. (1990) Facial electromyography differentiates racial bias in imagined cooperative settings. *Psychophysiology*, *27*, 563.

Vanneman, R.D. and Pettigrew, T.F. (1972) Race and relative deprivation in the urban United States. *Race*, *13*, 461–486.

Van Oudenhoven, J.P., Groenewoud, J.T. and Hewstone, M. (1994) Co-operation, ethnic salience and generalization of interethnic attitudes. Unpubl. MS, University of Nijmegen.

Vaughan, G.M. (1964a) Ethnic awareness in relation to minority group membership. *Journal of Genetic Psychology*, *105*, 119–130.

Vaughan, G., Tajfel, H. and Williams, J.A. (1981) Bias in reward allocation in an intergroup and an interpersonal context. *Social Psychology Quarterly*, *44*, 37–42.

Vaughan, G.M. (1964b) The development of ethnic attitudes in New Zealand school children. *Genetic Psychology Monographs, 70*, 135–175.

Vaughan, G.M. (1978) Social change and intergroup preferences in New Zealand. *European Journal of Social Psychology, 8*, 297–314.

Vaughan, G.M. (1987) A social psychological model of ethnic identity development. In J.S. Phinney and M.J. Rotheram (eds), *Children's Ethnic Socialization*. London: Sage.

Vivian, J., Brown, R.J. and Hewstone, M. (1994) Changing attitudes through intergroup contact: the effects of membership salience. Unpublished MS, University of Kent.

Vivian, J., Hewstone, M. and Brown, R. (in press) Intergroup contact: theoretical and empirical developments. In R. Ben-Ari, R. and Y. Rich, (eds), *Understanding and Enhancing Education for Diverse Students: An international perspective*. Ramat Gan: University of Bar Ilan Press.

Vollebergh, W. (1991) *The Limits of Tolerance*. Utrecht: Rijksuniversitait te Utrecht.

Walker, I. and Mann, L. (1987) Unemployment, relative deprivation and social protest. *Personality and Social Psychology Bulletin, 13*, 275–283.

Walker, I. and Pettigrew, T.F. (1984) Relative deprivation theory: an overview and conceptual critique. *British Journal of Social Psychology, 23*, 301–310.

Walker, W.D., Rowe, R.C. and Quinsey, V.L. (1993) Authoritarianism and sexual aggression. *Journal of Personality and Social Psychology, 65*, 1036–1045.

Wason, P.C. and Johnson-Laird, P.N. (1972) *Psychology of Reasoning*. London: Batsford.

Weber, R. and Crocker, J. (1983) Cognitive processes in the revision of stereotypic beliefs. *Journal of Personality and Social Psychology, 45*, 961–977.

Weigel, R.H., Wiser, P.L. and Cook, S.W. (1975) The impact of comparative learning experiences on cross-ethnic relations and attitudes. *Journal of Social Issues, 31*, 219–244.

Weitz, S. (1972) Attitude, voice and behavior: a repressed affect model of interracial interaction. *Journal of Personality and Social Psychology, 24*, 14–21.

Wetherell, M. (1982) Cross-cultural studies of minimal groups: implications for the social identity theory of intergroup relations. In H. Tajfel (ed.), *Social Identity and Intergroup Relations*, Cambridge: Cambridge University Press.

White, L.A. (1949) *The Science of Culture: A study of man and civilization*. New York: Farrar Strauss.

Wilder, D.A. (1984a) Predictions of belief homogeneity and similarity following social categorization. *British Journal of Social Psychology, 23*, 323–333.

Wilder, D.A. (1984b) Intergroup contact: the typical member and the exception to the rule. *Journal of Experimental Social Psychology*, *20*, 177–194.

Wilder, D.A. and Shapiro, P.N. (1989a) Role of competition-induced anxiety in limiting the beneficial impact of positive behavior by an outgroup member. *Journal of Personality and Social Psychology*, *56*, 60–69.

Wilder, D.A. and Shapiro, P.N. (1989b) Effects of anxiety on impression formation in a group context: an anxiety assimilation hypothesis. *Journal of Experimental Social Psychology*, *25*, 481–499.

Williams, J.E. and Morland, J.K. (1976) *Race, Color, and the Young Child*. Chapel Hill: University of North Carolina Press.

Williams, T.M. (1986) (ed.) *The Impact of Television: A natural experiment in three communities*. New York: Academic Press.

Wilner, D.M., Walkley, R.P. and Cook, S.W. (1952) Residential proximity and intergroup relations in public housing projects. *Journal of Social Issues*, *8*, 45–69.

Wilson, G.D. (1973) *The Psychology of Conservatism*. New York: Academic Press.

Witt, L.A. (1989) Authoritarianism, knowledge of AIDS, and affect towards persons with AIDS: implications for health education. *Journal of Applied Social Psychology*, *19*, 599–607.

Worchel, S., Andreoli, V.A. and Folger, R. (1977) Intergroup co-operation and intergroup attraction: the effect of previous interaction and outcome of combined effort. *Journal of Experimental Social Psychology*, *13*, 131–140.

Worchel, S., Cooper, J. and Goethals, G.R. (1988) *Understanding Social Psychology*, 4th edition. Chicago: Dorsey.

Word, C.O., Zanna, M.P. and Cooper, J. (1974) The non-verbal mediation of self-fulfilling prophecies in interracial interaction. *Journal of Experimental Social Psychology*, *10*, 109–120.

Wright, S.C., Taylor, D.M. and Moghaddam, F.M. (1990) Responding to membership in a disadvantaged group: from acceptance to collective protest. *Journal of Personality and Social Psychology*, *58*, 994–1003.

Wyer, R.S. and Gordon, S.E. (1982) The recall of information about persons and groups. *Journal of Experimental Social Psychology*, *18*, 128–164.

Yee, M.D. and Brown, R.J. (1988) *Children and Social Comparisons*, final Report to the ESRC, University of Kent.

Yee, M.D. and Brown, R.J. (1992) Self evaluations and intergroup attitudes in children aged three to nine. *Child Development*, *63*, 619–629.

Yee, M.D. and Brown, R. (1994) The development of gender differentiation in young children. *British Journal of Social Psychology*, *33*, 183–196.

Yzerbyt, V.Y., Leyens, J.-P., and Bellour, F. (1995) The ingroup overexclusion effect: identity concerns in decisions about group membership. *European Journal of Social Psychology*, *25*, 1–16.

Zalk, S.R. and Katz, P.A. (1978) Gender attitudes in children. *Sex Roles, 4,* 349–357.

Zander, A., Stotland, E. and Wolfe, D. (1960) Unity of group, identification with group, and self-esteem of members. *Journal of Personality, 28,* 463–478.

Zarate, M.A. and Smith, E.R. (1990) Person categorization and stereotyping. *Social Cognition, 8,* 161–185.

Zuckerman, D.M., Singer, D.G. and Singer, J.L. (1980) Children's television viewing, racial and sex-role attitudes. *Journal of Applied Social Psychology, 10,* 281–294.

Subject Index

Author Index